Medievalism in Finland and Russia

New Directions in Medieval Studies

Series Editors
Helen Young (Deakin University, Australia)
Andrew Elliott (University of Lincoln, UK)

This wide-ranging monograph series responds to emerging themes and interdisciplinary research methods in medieval scholarship, including the reception and reworking of the medieval in the post-medieval period. Particular concerns involve cataloguing the rich variety of experience of medieval people and exploring cultural transfer across different periods, places and groups. In doing so, *New Directions in Medieval Studies* seeks to contribute to the future directions and debates of medieval studies.

Published Titles
The Middle Ages in Popular Imagination, Paul Sturtevant
Medieval Literature on Display, Alexandra Sterling-Hellenbrand
Cultures of Compunction in the Medieval World, Graham Williams and Charlotte Steenbrugge (eds.)
The Middle Ages in Modern Culture, Karl Alvestad and Paul Houghton (eds.)
Medievalism in Finland and Russia, Reima Välimäki (ed.)

Upcoming Titles
Constructing Viking History, Thomas Smaberg
Laughter and Awkwardness in Late Medieval England, David Watt
The Cult of Thomas Becket, Paul Webster
Medieval Radicalism, Daniel Wollenberg

Medievalism in Finland and Russia

Twentieth- and Twenty-First-Century Aspects

Edited by
Reima Välimäki

BLOOMSBURY ACADEMIC
LONDON • NEW YORK • OXFORD • NEW DELHI • SYDNEY

BLOOMSBURY ACADEMIC

Bloomsbury Publishing Plc, 50 Bedford Square, London, WC1B 3DP, UK
Bloomsbury Publishing Inc, 1385 Broadway, New York, NY 10018, USA
Bloomsbury Publishing Ireland, 29 Earlsfort Terrace, Dublin 2, D02 AY28, Ireland

BLOOMSBURY, BLOOMSBURY ACADEMIC and the Diana logo are trademarks of Bloomsbury Publishing Plc

First published in Great Britain 2022
Paperback edition first published 2025

Copyright © Reima Välimäki, 2022

Reima Välimäki has asserted their right under the Copyright, Designs and Patents Act, 1988, to be identified as Editor of this work.

Series design by Tjaša Krivec
Cover Image: © Lorado/Getty Images

All rights reserved. No part of this publication may be: i) reproduced or transmitted in any form, electronic or mechanical, including photocopying, recording or by means of any information storage or retrieval system without prior permission in writing from the publishers; or ii) used or reproduced in any way for the training, development or operation of artificial intelligence (AI) technologies, including generative AI technologies. The rights holders expressly reserve this publication from the text and data mining exception as per Article 4(3) of the Digital Single Market Directive (EU) 2019/790.

Bloomsbury Publishing Plc does not have any control over, or responsibility for, any third-party websites referred to or in this book. All internet addresses given in this book were correct at the time of going to press. The author and publisher regret any inconvenience caused if addresses have changed or sites have ceased to exist, but can accept no responsibility for any such changes.

A catalogue record for this book is available from the British Library.

A catalog record for this book is available from the Library of Congress.

ISBN: HB: 978-1-3502-3288-4
PB: 978-1-3502-3289-1
ePDF: 978-1-3502-3290-7
eBook: 978-1-3502-3291-4

Typeset by Deanta Global Publishing Services, Chennai, India

For product safety related questions contact productsafety@bloomsbury.com.

To find out more about our authors and books visit www.bloomsbury.com and sign up for our newsletters.

Contents

List of illustrations	vi
List of contributors	vii
Preface: Medievalism in Finland and Russia and why it matters	x
Acknowledgements	xxiii
Note on bibliography	xxiv
Introduction: Who owns the Middle Ages? Metamedievalism and structural exclusion *Andrew B. R. Elliott*	1
1 The Middle Ages on the 'map of memory' of Russian society *E. A. Rostovtsev*	21
2 'A thousand years of history': References to the past in the addresses to the Federal Assembly by the president of Russia, 2000–19 *Kati Parppei*	39
3 Mapping the pseudohistorical knowledge space in the Russian World Wide Web *Mila Oiva and Anna Ristilä*	57
4 A lens most obscured: Western perceptions of contemporary Russian medievalisms *Evan Wallace*	73
5 Memorializing the Finnish medieval past *Sirpa Aalto and Timo Ylimaunu*	85
6 The missing Finnish runestones *Kendra Willson*	103
7 Masculine online medievalism in twenty-first-century Finland *Heta Aali*	125
8 Particularizing the universal: Medievalist constructions of cultural and religious difference in *Crusader Kings II* *Jere Kyyrö*	137
Appendix 1	153
Appendix 2	156
Appendix 3	158
Appendix 4	159
Appendix 5	160
Notes	161
Bibliography	209
Index	233

List of illustrations

Figures

2.1	The statue of Vladimir the Great in Moscow, unveiled in 2016	50
3.1	The network of Russian medievalist web discussions with pseudohistorical texts	63
5.1	The memorial of Vesainen in Ylikiiminki, 1936	92
5.2	The statue of Vesainen in Ii, 1950	93
6.1	Runic inscription in Höjsål, Vörå	110
7.1	Väinämöinen versus Thor according to a meme in Ylilauta	134
8.1	Screenshot from the cultural map and King Hakon's character window of a game starting in 936, *Crusader Kings II*	142

Maps

5.1	The map of Finland	88

Tables

1.1	Ideological paradigms of Russian history (Appendix 1)	153
1.2	Russian heroes across different source types (Appendix 2)	156
1.3	Rankings of the local objects of historical memory in the analysed Russian sources (1850–1917) (Appendix 3)	158
1.4	Rankings of the local objects of historical memory in the analysed Russian sources (1918–91) (Appendix 4)	159
1.5	Rankings of the local objects of historical memory in the analysed Russian sources (1992–2020) (Appendix 5)	160
1.6	The number of Russian orthodox churches named after medieval figures	32
1.7	The popularity of objects of historical memory in various Russian online sources	33

Contributors

Heta Aali is a researcher at the Department of Cultural History at the University of Turku, Finland. Her research interests focus on medievalism, gender history, history of France and historiography. She has published on French and Finnish medievalism and historiography. Her most recent monograph is *French Royal Women during the Restoration and July Monarchy: Redefining Women and Power* (2021).

Sirpa Aalto works as a chief of research funding at Hanken School of Economics and is also a docent of medieval Scandinavian history at the University of Oulu. Her research interests include the Viking Age, medieval history of Scandinavia and medieval Norse historiography. She has authored, among others, the articles, 'World View' in *The Routledge Companion to the Medieval Icelandic Sagas* (2017), 'Contextualising Jómsvíkinga Saga' (2018), and translated the Jómsvíkinga saga into Finnish (2019).

Andrew B. R. Elliott is an associate professor in Media and Cultural Studies at the University of Lincoln, where he works on the representation of history in film, television and video games. Author of *Remaking the Middle Ages* (on medieval film) and editor of *The Return of the Epic Film* and *Playing with the Past* (on the twenty-first-century epic and historically themed video games, respectively), he has published on a number of aspects relating to historical film, television and video games, from the classical world to the Middle Ages. His recent research focuses on medievalism in online culture, political discourse and films from Tarkovsky to Tavernier. His most recent book is *Medievalism, Politics and Mass Media: Appropriating the Middle Ages in the Twenty-First Century* (2017).

Jere Kyyrö teaches at the University of Turku in the Study of Cultures Programme. His research interests focus on the intersections of religion, media, politics and national identity. His doctoral thesis (2019, published in Finnish) analyses cultural controversies around the central Finnish national symbol, Field Marshall C. G. E. Mannerheim, in Finnish media in the 2000s and 2010s.

Mila Oiva is a cultural historian specializing in Russian and Polish history and a senior research fellow at CUDAN Cultural Data Analytics Lab at

Tallinn University, Estonia. Her research interest focuses on the circulation of knowledge in different technological settings from the nineteenth-century newspapers to the world wide web in the 2010s. Her latest publications include *Digital Readings of History: History Research in the Digital Era* (co-editors Mats Fridlund and Petri Paju, 2020) and *Yves Montand in the USSR: Cultural Diplomacy and Mixed Messages* (co-authors Hannu Salmi and Bruce Johnson, 2021).

Kati Parppei is an adjunct professor in Russian history and a university lecturer at the Department of Geographical and Historical Studies, University of Eastern Finland. Her scholarly interests include historical image studies, political uses of history and borderland issues. Her most recent book is *The Battle of Kulikovo Refought – 'The First National Feat'* (2017).

Anna Ristilä is a doctoral researcher in digital language use in the Doctoral Programme in Languages and Translation Studies (Utuling) at the University of Turku. Her main research interests are digital language modelling and language processing tools, and her upcoming dissertation centres on Finnish parliamentary speeches.

Evgenii Rostovtsev is professor at St Petersburg State University in the Department of Russian history. His research interests focus on the history of education and Russian universities, Russian historiography and historical memory. He is the head of several research projects in these areas, 'History of St Petersburg University in virtual space' and 'Russian history in the mirror of mass historical consciousness (1991–2020)' in particular. His recent publications include 'Capital University of the Russian Empire: Academic Estate, Society and Power' (2017), and 'The Immortal Host of Prince Igor' in *Vestnik of St Petersburg University*, History 65, no. 3 (2020): 883–903.

Reima Välimäki is an adjunct professor (docent) of medieval history at the University of Turku and a postdoctoral researcher at the Turku Institute for Advanced Studies. He is the author of *Heresy in Late Medieval Germany: The Inquisitor Petrus Zwicker and the Waldensians* (2019), and head of the research project 'The Ancient Finnish Kings: A Computational Study of Pseudohistory, Medievalism and History Politics in Contemporary Finland and Russia' (2019–2022). Välimäki's research interests include medieval heresy and inquisition, polemical literature, the Great Western Schism, authorship attribution and stylometry, and political medievalism and pseudohistory in the twenty-first century.

Evan Wallace is a PhD candidate in Texts & Technology (Digital Humanities) at the University of Central Florida. His research interests focus on Russian medievalisms being referenced and employed in contemporary media and politics.

Kendra Willson is a researcher in Nordic languages at the University of Turku. She is interested in the role of language contacts and language politics in the history of the Nordic region. In addition to Finland's relationship to Scandinavian runic culture, she has written extensively on Icelandic personal names. She is co-editor of *Contacts and Networks in the Baltic Sea Region: Austmarr as a Northern Mare nostrum, ca. 500–1500 AD* (2019).

Timo Ylimaunu works as a university lecturer and is a docent of post-medieval archaeology at the University of Oulu. His research interests include historical archaeology in general, dark or difficult heritage and memory studies. His research articles have been published in the *Journal of Social Archaeology*, *Historical Archaeology* and *World Archaeology*. Ylimaunu is an international associate of the Indiana University-Purdue University in Indianapolis, Indiana.

Preface

Medievalism in Finland and Russia and why it matters

In a fictional short story published in 1954 by Hilda Huntuvuori – a Finnish teacher and author of medievalist youth novels – a younger chief and an old, petty king in tenth-century Southwestern Finland discuss the news about Igor Rurikson's failed expedition to Constantinople. The men are happy that very few Finns had joined forces with the Kiovan prince, and the old man advises the younger: 'one must defend one's home shores to the last man but one should not leave to war expeditions – least of all to east.'[1] The moral of the story – that one should neither heed to the calls of Russian rulers nor wage war against the East – came not from medieval history but from recent events. In 1944, Finland had lost the so-called Continuation War against the Soviet Union, a war in which Finland – heartened by the alliance with the Third Reich – had attempted compensation for the losses in the Winter War (1939–40). After the lost war, the late 1940s were under the threat of Soviet occupation, and some Finnish leftists believed that the future was in the Soviet bloc. In the end, Finland did not become a socialist people's republic and Finnish democracy prevailed, but the country and its people had to adapt to a new political reality and increased influence from the Soviet Union.[2]

Finnish medievalism was not untouched by the changing political currents. In the Finnish schoolbooks, popular history books and medievalist fiction of the 1920 and 1930s, one would never have found any reluctance to wage war against the East. On the contrary, war beacons blazed as the ancient Finns stepped forward to fulfil their historical mission as the vanguard of the West. Using the definition of Derek Fewster, the interwar period in Finland was the time of militant medievalism, where the 'other' mirrored the contemporary threat of Bolshevism.[3] As the blatant nationalism went out of favour in the Finnish society, ancient and medieval warlords were also tamed. Some of the most flagrant anti-Russian representations – such as in Aarno Karimo's illustrated series of historical short stories – were censured.[4] Others like Huntuvuori in the quoted passage were self-censored. Even more importantly, medievalism in Finland lost much of its national appeal, although it continued at the local level.⁵

The background and mission of the volume

The example mentioned earlier illustrates the themes in this volume: medievalism in two countries that share a common history and border but in a very asymmetric relationship. It also illustrates some of the challenges of writing about global medievalism to a global audience. Representations of the Middle Ages are a way to process contemporary issues in a society; this is the so-called bread and butter of studies in medievalism. What follows from such a premise is that one must be familiar with the contemporary issues and recent historical developments that have led to them. When writing within our own reference group, we take much of this knowledge for granted, even in academic papers. One hardly must explain to the readers of a Finnish journal of history that Finland lost the Second World War against the Soviet Union. One cannot expect an American or Korean reader to possess that information. To a reader not familiar with the culture in question, even more enigmatic than such crude historical facts are the schemes of interpreting a nation's past. James V. Wertsch calls such structures 'schematic narrative templates'. These are generalized narrative traditions that guide collective remembering. Their peculiarity is that they are largely unconscious of the 'native speakers' of a culture. Likewise, they are also able to guide interpretation in cases where a non-native does not see their relevance. For the Russians, the triumph-over-alien-forces narrative is one of such templates; for the Americans, the quest-for-freedom narrative could occupy a similar position.⁶

In the context of medievalism, which consists of several centuries of engagement with the medieval past, one can see such structures or templates resulting in 'metamedievalism'. In the introductory chapter to this volume, Andrew B. R. Elliott defines the concept of 'metamedievalism' as 'cumulative medievalisms whose repetition make some of the core elements of our ideas about the medieval past seem inevitable and uncontested'. Rather than referring directly to the medieval past or underscoring a point in the present like 'banal medievalism' does,⁷ such medievalisms rely on already existing general ways of understanding and interpreting the Middle Ages. They are thus secondary, building on the often invisible first layer of medievalism. Metamedievalisms, together with the seemingly participatory culture of online discussions, can act as forms of inclusion and exclusion. Elliott's examples of metamedievalism are three cases from the year 2019 within the Western cultural sphere: Brenton Tarrant and the Christchurch shootings, Jacob Rees-Mogg's *The Victorians* and the Block Museum of Chicago's exhibition 'Caravans of Gold'. The rest of the chapters in this volume discuss Finnish and Russian medievalism and metamedievalism, attempting to make visible the sublayer of culture-specific structures and templates serving as background influence.

The need for such an approach became evident as the editing of this volume progressed. The book began as a conference – 'Medievalism between East and West' – organized at the University of Turku in September 2019. At the conference, the focus was placed on contemporary forms of medievalism in Northern and Eastern Europe. Organized by a research project on medievalist pseudohistories in the Finnish and Russian internet sphere,[8] there was an emphasis on online medievalism that is still visible in this volume. As we started to revise the conference papers into book chapters aimed at a more general academic public we realized that an increasingly large amount of context and background was needed. It is impossible to treat the twenty-first-century medievalism – or rather metamedievalism – in Finland and Russia without explaining the first layer of medievalisms, specifically those that have taken form in the previous decades and centuries. Therefore, instead of only concentrating on the twenty-first-century medievalism, many of the chapters trace the underlying discourses, half-forgotten social conflicts, and continuities and breaks in cultural memory from the twentieth to the twenty-first century. It is hoped that the result will make medievalism in Finland and Russia more understandable, especially to readers not previously familiar with the history and culture of these two countries. The very last revisions to this book were made after Russia attacked Ukraine in February 2022. While it was impossible to comment on the ongoing war and the latest developments in the fight over history related to it, we hope that the chapters in this book can illuminate the uses of history, nationalism and cultural memory, all of which are at play in the current crisis, but which also have much longer roots and broader implications.

The focus on Finland and Russia is a result of the conference and the research project behind it. The authors of this volume are convinced, however, that exploring medievalism in these two countries has a broader significance. The importance of Russia in the study of global medievalism is easily justified. Dina Khapaeva and Richard Utz recently emphasized that Russia should be better addressed in studies on medievalism.[9] This volume answers to these calls and addresses several aspects of Russian medievalism, from long-term cultural memory and memory objects to presidential speeches and online pseudohistories.

There is also a need to bridge the gap between Western and Russian research traditions. In a recent essay, Alexander Filyushkin pointed out that medievalism is primarily a part of ethnic nationalism in Russia and Eastern Europe, while medievalism in the West has been primarily studied as a cultural phenomenon and only secondarily as an element in nation-building and romantic nationalism. Filyushkin adds that in comparison to Western Europe, relatively little has been studied on medievalism in Russia; the focus is often placed on objects and historical heroes.[10] In this volume, the chapter by Evgenii Rostovtsev is a valuable contribution to bringing the research traditions closer. In addition to being a comprehensive survey of how the Middle Ages and medieval events and persons have been remembered in Russia, it summarizes the recent Russian academic discussion on cultural memory and narratives about the past, making its arguments accessible to the Anglophone academic audience.

In comparison to Russia, Finland is an even more exotic example of medievalism. A reader may wonder what its significance is on a global scale. The Finnish cases present a rich local medievalist tradition with characteristics both unique and common to Nordic and Western medievalism. In addition, we wish to challenge and diversify academic literature's prevailing image of the shared online medievalism of European and American right-wing populists. In this context, Finland is usually mentioned merely as the birthplace of the Soldiers of Odin.[11] The street patrol, however, is a marginal phenomenon in Finnish medievalism. In Finnish online forums, crusades do not mark a Western Christian victory over the Muslim East, but a Swedish occupation of Finnish lands, and this interpretation is derived from Finnish national romantic historiography.[12] Finnish medievalism reminds of local variation and adaptations of contemporary international medievalism, an essential aspect in advancing the study of global medievalism.

As in Russia, medievalism studies in Finland are not an established field. The nineteenth and early twentieth centuries have been covered best, thanks to the pioneering work of Derek Fewster.[13] More recent medievalism has been investigated only in individual studies.[14] The aim of this volume is thus not only to present Finnish medievalism studies to the international audience, but also to advance the study of medievalism in Finland.

The reader is called to pay attention to a key difference between Finnish and Russian medievalisms: the relationship between the Middle Ages and both the state and leading politicians. In Russia, references to the medieval past appear in presidential speeches and pre-Petrine figures such as St Vladimir and Ivan the Terrible feature in public monuments. The thousand-year history of Russia is alive and well, and the state authorities display interest in its interpretations. In addition to official history politics, there is the rich alternative field of online medievalism. Online discussions in Russian take place not only in Russia but also in Ukraine and Belarussia as well, which adds further complexity to online medievalism. In Finland, on the contrary, medieval history is near-absent in public history discourse. The Finnish cultural memory is directed towards twentieth-century history, particularly the fight against the Soviet Union in the Second World War. This does not mean that the Middle Ages are free of political connotations. The political use of medievalism takes place at the grass-root level: social media, online discussion groups and image boards. There, ethnic nationalistic, anti-immigrant, antifeminist and anti-Swedish rhetoric flourishes, together with systemic conspiracy theories. All of these provide opportunities for political actors willing to tap into this voting base.

The shared history of Finland and Russia

A brief outline of the shared history of Finland and Russia – and how it affected medievalism in these two countries – is in order. This outline is given from the Finnish perspective, because for Finnish history, Russia is sine qua non, but Russian history can be told with very few references to the Finns and Finland.[15] The shared history of what later became Russia and Finland began before the formation of the states, provinces or even ethnicities of those names. At its beginning, the medieval state of Rus' was a multiethnic conglomerate. This especially applied to the Principality of Novgorod, which covered areas inhabited by different Finno-Ugric peoples, and these peoples played an important role in the early state formation. In the eleventh and twelfth centuries, Novgorod started to consolidate its power in the eastern shores of the Baltic Sea, which were inhabited by the Baltic Finns. The Novgorodian chronicles describe mutual raiding with the Finns living in present-day Southern Finland. Around Lake Ladoga, Novgorod had a more stable influence, accompanied with the spread of Eastern Orthodox Christianity. In the thirteenth century, present-day Finland and the Baltic states became a zone where the expansionist interests of the kingdoms of Sweden and Denmark, the Order of the Sword Brothers and the Teutonic Order, and Novgorod clashed. Consequently, the

Baltic Sea region became a border of the Catholic and Orthodox Churches, although this aspect was of less importance for the contemporaries than it was for later generations.[16]

Two events of the period, the Battle of Neva in 1240 and the Treaty of Nöteborg in 1323, illustrate both the interests of medieval rivals and the diverging traditions of historiography and medievalism in Russia and Finland as well as Sweden. In the early thirteenth century, the Swedish kings had established their power in Southwestern Finland and started to make early attempts to control the waterway from the Baltic Sea to Ladoga, thus making incursions into Novgorod's territory. In July 1240, a Swedish force – possibly supported by Finns and Tavastians – embarked on the bank of the river Neva, near present-day St Petersburg. They were defeated by a Novgorodian prince, Alexandr Yaroslavich. As the Danish historian John H. Lind pointed out, there is a disparity in the reception of the battle. In Russian historiography and popular tradition, it has achieved immense proportions. This was the battle that earned Prince Alexandr the epithet 'Nevskii', and thanks to it and the better-known Battle on the Ice in 1242, he became one of the great heroes of Russian history, a defender of Russia against alien forces.[17] This was, however, a later development. According to Mari Isoaho, Prince Alexandr was a controversial figure in contemporary Novgorod, and his victories in 1240 and 1242 started to acquire their symbolic significance in Russian chronicles only in the fifteenth century.[18]

In comparison, the Battle of Neva is an insignificant incident in Swedish and Finnish historiography, which has treated the topic mainly under the discussion of the Swedish crusade to Tavastia and its dating. The traditional dating of the Swedish crusade to Tavastia and consolidation of Swedish power in the Finnish inland is in 1248–49. Consequently, Swedish and Finnish historians have considered it implausible that a large Swedish expedition, joined by Finns and Tavastians, would have taken place in 1240 before the control of Tavastia. Thus, the Battle of Neva has been regarded as a minor raid in the eyes of these historians.[19] Finnish national romantic historians such as Jalmari Jaakkola have attempted to portray the expedition as a Finnish endeavour led by Bishop Thomas (without any basis in the medieval sources).[20] However, there is no national meaning comparable to the Russian narrative attached to the Battle of Neva from the Finnish side, and it is even less significant to the Swedes. The battle is thus an excellent example of the ambiguity and flexibility of the Middle Ages in the formation of national narratives.

The next stage of Russian-Swedish rivalry in the Gulf of Finland took place between 1293 and 1323. The Swedes launched an expedition to Karelian isthmus (the so-called Third Swedish Crusade in Finnish historiography) in 1292/3 and started to build a castle at Vyborg. The Swedish forces now seriously threatened Novgorod's waterways to the Baltic Sea. The Swedish expansion to Neva was blocked by the construction of the fortress Nöteborg-Orekhovets in 1322. A year later in 1323, a peace between the Principality of Novgorod and the Kingdom of Sweden was concluded in the fortress. Later generations have called it the Treaty of Nöteborg; in the Middle Ages, however, it was referred to as a letter between two princes, Prince Yurii of Novgorod and King Magnus Eriksson of Sweden.[21]

The peace was the first to define the eastern border of medieval Sweden and the western border of the Principality of Novgorod in the north. In addition, the copies of the letter were used and disputed in the diplomatic negotiations between Sweden and Moscow in the fifteenth and sixteenth centuries. Therefore, it is no wonder that Sweden, Finland and Russia all have rich historiographical traditions on the Treaty of Nöteborg. The Russian interest has been mainly academic, although there have been occasional national and political connotations, such as in the Soviet historian I. P. Shaskol'skij's statement in 1940 that with the Treaty of Nöteborg, Finland – which the Swedes had invaded from Novgorod – went to the Swedish state.[22] However, unlike the Battle of Neva, the Treaty of Nöteborg has no comparable national significance in Russia.

The situation is completely different in Finland, where the Treaty of Nöteborg – and especially the resulting borderline – has been a celebrated crux of national historiography. Most of the research has concentrated on defining the exact border markers. In the words of Kimmo Katajala: 'so many historians, folklorists, linguists and amateur historians have recorded their opinions on it that the situation has reached almost comical proportions'.[23]

Without going into the details of the debate, one should note three main aspects that have emerged from it, as these have significantly shaped Finnish medievalism and national historiography. First, the Treaty of Nöteborg has been seen to settle Finland as a borderland where the East and West, Byzantium and Rome clashed. Thus, Finland became the vanguard of Western Europe. This is anachronistic and retrospective; neither the Kingdom of Sweden nor the Principality of Novgorod were strong territorial states in the early fourteenth century, and neither had strong ideological missions at the time.[24] Second, Finnish national romantic scholarship has interpreted that the border line followed ancient tribal borders or zones of influence, separating eastern and western Finns. A still popular version of this idea are articles and columns where journalists and other commentators trace the reasons for party support, social-economic differences, and genetic profiles of Eastern and Western Finland to the Nöteborg border line or to the ancient division it is thought to reflect. Jukka Korpela has dubbed this approach as 'Nöteborg-nonsense' (*Pähkinäsaari-huuhaa*), Samu Sarviaho speaks of 'Nöteborg-fundamentalism' and both see little basis in these claims.[25] One should point out that the recent results of population genetics do not support the theory of an ancient population division between Eastern and Western Finland, instead suggesting rather late genetic shifts.[26] Third, the historiography on the Treaty of Nöteborg has largely bypassed the nomadic and semi-nomadic Sámi and Finnic populations who inhabited large areas in the northern Fennoscandian forests during the Middle Ages. When discussing the rivalry between Sweden and Novgorod, their right to exert influence and tax these populations has been taken for granted and naturalized. The same applies to the expansion of a permanent Finnish agricultural settlement that displaced the semi-nomadic Sámi populations. Only recently have scholars stressed how the state formation process marginalized the populations in the peripheries,[27] or that Viking Age and medieval Finland should be seen as a colonial, ethnically contested space.[28]

Both the Battle of Neva in 1240 and the Treaty of Nöteborg in 1323 have gained their ideological significance in the centuries that followed. Their later reception contributed to the image of enemy nations both in Finland and Russia. As stated earlier, for the Finnish historiography the treaty of 1323 signified Finland's status as the borderland between East and West, as well as the Finns' role as the defenders of the West. The Russians, however, did not see the Finns as their enemies. Rather, it was the Swedes – and in even broader terms the Germans – who were seen as enemies. In fact, the Finns – referred to as *sum'* or *iem'* – disappear from the Novgorod sources after 1323, signalling their belonging to the Swedish realm.[29] This aptly demonstrates the asymmetry of the two nations under discussion in this volume; in Finnish medievalist representations, Russians became the archenemy, culminating in the interwar militant medievalism described earlier. For the Russians, the Finns were a part of a broader Western threat, as well as subjects of the Swedish kings.

If the projection of East–West rivalry to the fourteenth century is anachronistic, Finland did become such a borderland from the fifteenth to the sixteenth century onwards, as both Sweden and Moscow became territorial powers.[30] It is unnecessary to repeat the early modern history of Sweden and Russia, but to sum it up: the sixteenth and seventeenth centuries were times of Sweden's expansion, culminating in the Treaty of Stolbovo (1617) where Russia had to cede Kexholm and Ingria to Sweden. This consequently barred Russia's access to the Baltic Sea. In the eighteenth century, it was Russia's turn to advance. Russians occupied Finland twice in the course of the century, and the first occupation in particular (1714–21) was marked by a reign of terror. In the Napoleonic wars, Russia conquered Finland from Sweden, and for the period of 1809–1917 Finland became a Grand Duchy of the Russian Empire. For the most part, Finland kept its Swedish laws and institutions. In addition to this, Swedish remained the language of administration.

The period under Russian rule is essential for the development of Finnish national romanticism and Finnish medievalism. Separated from Sweden and influenced by German romantic nationalism, the Finnish intellectuals began to seek the roots of the nation in ancient and medieval history. The role of *Kalevala* (1835) cannot be overestimated. It was a collection of epic poems effectively envisioned and written by Elias Lönnrot, but in the nineteenth and early twentieth centuries it was generally considered to be a source to the history and culture of the ancient Finns. For most of the nineteenth century, national romanticism and medievalism were expressed in the antiquarian, literary, artistic and historical endeavours of the academic elite. However, from 1890 to 1917, nationalism and medievalism were politicized and reached an increasing share of the population. In this period, the emperor began to withdraw the Grand Duchy's administrative and legal privileges and standardize the legislation with the rest of the Russian Empire. The Finnish nationalists saw this as persecution and 'Russification'. Medievalism was put to serve the national cause, both as a means to circumvent Russian censorship and to invoke the ancient character of the Finnish people's struggle. When Finland achieved independence in 1917, it was generally regarded as a 'second independence', or the fulfilment of Finland's destiny after centuries of Swedish and Russian rule; the first independence was the imagined ancient independence of the Finnish tribes.[31]

One further aspect of Finnish national romanticism and medievalism must be explicated: the language controversy between Swedish-speaking and Finnish-speaking Finns. The roots of Finland's Swedish population are in the medieval migration and colonization of the relatively sparsely populated southern and western coast, as well as in the elite families that hold secular and clerical offices. Finnish was the language of the majority, but its social and cultural status was low. The situation continued in the Grand Duchy of Finland after 1809; the elite spoke Swedish, which was also the language of administration. The early academic nationalism and medievalism were pursuits of this Swedish-speaking elite, and although there was great interest in the 'common' people and the Finnish language, the concept of Finnishness was not language-specific. This started to change with the emancipation of the Finnish language and the

Fennoman political movement. In the 1860–70s, the Fennoman historians – with Yrjö Koskinen (Georg Z. Forsman) at the head of them – started to define nationality based on the Finnish language. The Finnish-speaking common people were defined as the constituting element of the society, nation and its culture. Consequently, the previously self-evident role of Sweden as the source of Christianity, culture and civilization was questioned. Both academic studies and popular representations started to emphasize the above-mentioned period of 'first independence' of the Iron Age Finns before the Swedish rule. The Swedish language was perceived increasingly as a foreign element and the Swedish influence was downplayed.[32] There was a subsequent counter-reaction; representatives of the Swedish movement (Svecomans) regarded the Finnish speakers and Fennomans with racial and cultural superiority. From the 1870s onwards, the Swedish movement also turned to medievalist images to counter Fennoman claims and the Viking heritage began to signify the continuity of Swedish culture in Finland.[33]

The language question of the nineteenth and early twentieth century has a legacy that lives in contemporary Finnish medievalism. Two chapters in this volume address the language politics. First is the question of missing runestones in Finland, explored by Kendra Willson. This is connected to both the Swedish-Finnish quest for the Viking heritage and recently revived Finnish nationalistic attempts to find an ancient Finnish civilization. Heta Aali discusses masculine medievalism in Finnish imageboards and discussion forums where Finno-Ugric heritage – perceived as masculine – is contrasted with the feminine-framed Swedishness.

It is notable that while the Finnish versus Swedish language conflict continues in the online discussions, Russia has not returned after the Cold War as the archenemy. This is somewhat surprising, given that many forms of online medievalism in Finland are openly nationalistic. Some are even far-right. One possible reason may lie in the following: the pseudohistories about the Ancient Finnish Kings have spread in the Finnish right-wing populist counter-media.[34] These sites lean on Russian sources in order to criticize the West; some of the actors are openly pro-Russian.[35] However, one should note that until the 2022 war in Ukraine, Finland tried to avoid open confrontation with Russia in politics and mainstream media, although there was increased attention to and concern over Russian propaganda and hybrid warfare. Unlike many other nations that had been under Soviet rule or influence, the Finns have not considered Russia an existential threat to the Finnish nation and culture after the Cold War, and this seems to reflect in medievalist representations. In 2018 for example, Turku

Museum Centre, Novgorod State United Museum and Turku Medieval Market organized a joint seminar to commemorate the 700th anniversary of Novgorod's attack on Turku in 1318. During the event, a medieval conflict was treated as shared history. Finally, and perhaps most importantly, the struggle against the Soviet Union in the Second World War occupies a central position in the Finnish cultural memory. For those wishing to emphasize Russia as the enemy, there is no longer a need to turn to the medieval past. After Russia attacked Ukraine in February 2022, popular opinion, media and politicians immediately condemned Russia's aggression together with the rest of the West. More than ever after the Second World War, the Finns perceive Russia as an enemy. This will probably reflect on medievalist representations in the future.

Outline of the book

This book contains nine chapters in addition to this preface. Andrew B. R. Elliott's introduction on metamedievalism and structural exclusion has been previously presented. In addition to 'metamedievalism', it provides an important critique of online participatory culture and begs the question of who has the right and opportunity to talk about the Middle Ages. Elliott's chapter is followed by four chapters on Russian medievalism and three chapters on Finnish medievalism. The final chapter of the book discusses representations of religion and culture of the North and East Europe in the popular computer game, *Crusader Kings II*.

Evgenii Rostovtsev opens the chapters on Russian medievalism with his extensive survey of the Middle Ages in the Russian memory culture. Rostovtsev contextualizes the commemoration of medieval heroes and events with the schema of Russian society's historical representations and competing ideals about the future, which he describes as traditionalist/statist and liberal/Western. Kati Parppei continues with her treatment on Russian presidents' speeches in the twenty-first century. Parppei's analysis is broader than mere medievalist references. She traces the use of history and ideas of a long span of the collective past in the public addresses of Russian heads of state. Both chapters treat what might be termed as mainstream medievalism in Russia.

Mila Oiva and Anna Ristilä turn the reader's attention to more marginal yet influential representations of the past within the Russian internet sphere, including pseudohistories about prehistoric or early medieval Slavic empires. These narratives stretch the idea of a great national past well beyond the one thousand years of Russian history presented in the official accounts. Evan

Wallace ends the section on Russian medievalism with his chapter detailing Western perception on Russian medievalism. Wallace proposes that Western inability to discern Russian medievalism is partially due to a language barrier and partially due to unequal access to resources in the online environment. Echoing Elliott's introduction, both these chapters question what is available and dispersed on the internet.

Sirpa Aalto and Timo Ylimaunu discuss medievalist monuments in twentieth-century Finland. The chapter covers blind spots in Finnish studies in medievalism – including statues and memorials, Northern Finland and the postwar era – tracing the decline of national medievalism and its continuation in local forms. Kendra Willson explores another material manifestation of medievalism, or rather, the lack of it: the missing Finnish runestones. Willson demonstrates how both Swedish and Finnish-speaking amateur historians' quest for runestones relates to language politics and local and national identity.

The last two chapters in the book return to the online and digital environments. Heta Aali analyses online discussions about the Ancient Finnish Kings, a pseudohistorical construct of the imagined Iron Age or early medieval Finnish kingdoms. Aali argues that while Finnish discussion in many ways springs from national historiography, its representations of masculinity can be considered yet another expression of 'muscular medievalism' as defined by Amy S. Kaufman. Jere Kyyrö's chapter on *Crusader Kings II* is not based on Finnish or Russian medievalism as such, but it analyses the representations of medieval Finno-Ugric and Slavic peoples in the game. With his background in the study of religions, Kyyrö demonstrates how particularism and universalism is, on one hand, a feature of the game design. On the other hand, it reiterates long-term Western ideas about religion and culture. Some solutions result in contrahistorical continuities, such as projecting names of modern neopagan revivals to the medieval past.

Several chapters in the volume discuss pseudohistory. While some readers might find the term unnecessarily pejorative, we find that it is justified in the cases we analyse. We understand pseudohistory as part of pseudoscience. Pseudoscience is non-science that poses as science. In other words, pseudoscience claims to present scientific truths, but does not follow generally accepted methods and practices. Pseudoscientific representations often disregard the relevant scholarship or handpick convenient results. Pseudoscience claims to provide the most reliable information available, something that officials and academic researchers refuse to reveal.[36] In line with this flirting with conspiracy theories, pseudohistory typically addresses sensational, huge claims that – had they been real – would upturn our views about world history. Its topics are lost continents and peoples, advanced ancient civilizations and, in our case, glorious empires of the national past, hidden by foreign and corrupting forces.[37] None of the narratives we define as pseudohistorical are seriously considered in the scholarship. Rather, they have been refuted time and time again or are simply too imaginary to be addressed within the means of scholarship.

Finally, one should address what is missing from the volume. No edited collection is a comprehensive treatment of its subject, and this work is no exception to that rule. While Aalto and Ylimaunu address Northern Finland in their chapter, there is no treatment of Sámi medievalism or any appropriations of Sámi culture in Finnish medievalism. The same applies to ethnic minorities and their medievalism in Russia. The most notable omission is the absence of medieval fairs, re-enactment and live-action roleplaying that – since the 1990s – have formed an essential part of medievalist revival in both countries. Finland and Russia have flourishing popular and participatory medievalism scenes: medieval re-enactment, historical martial arts and large, established medieval festivals. For example, the Turku Medieval Market – organized since 1996 – is one of the biggest summer events in Finland with 100,000–150,000 visitors. In Russia, many of the major festivals have professional production companies behind them, with all the slick, appealing media content that comes with the territory of such an arrangement. The Russian festivals serve as meeting points for re-enactors and attract huge audiences; the largest of these in Europe are the Times and Epochs in Moscow, with an annual total of 250,000 visitors.[38] The reason for their omission is simple: for the analysis of medieval festivals and re-enactment, an extensive fieldwork would be needed. As this was outside the scope of this volume, it has been left for future scholarship.

Reima Välimäki, University of Turku, Finland

Acknowledgements

This volume is a result of the research project 'The Ancient Finnish Kings: A Computational Study of Pseudohistory, Medievalism and History Politics in Contemporary Finland and Russia', funded by the Emil Aaltonen Foundation and hosted by the University of Turku, School of History, Culture and Arts Studies. In addition, the editing of this volume was made possible by the Turku Institute for Advanced Studies. I wish to thank both of these institutions for their support. The greatest debt of gratitude I owe to my project's brilliant research team: Heta Aali, Marius Aho, Harri Hihnala, Mila Oiva, Teemu Oivo, Anna Ristilä and our external language technology expert, Aleksi Vesanto.

The starting point of this volume was the 'Medievalism between East and West' conference at the University of Turku in September 2019. Heartfelt thanks are in order for all the conference speakers and other participants. The inspiring spirit of the conference created a great impact on the studies published in this work. Just half a year after the conference, the world changed. This volume was written and edited amid the Covid-19 pandemic, with related tragedies, big and small. Regardless, the contributors of the volume produced superb scholarship, and despite some challenges and minor delays, we reached the goal. Thank you.

In Turku, on 18 March 2022

Reima Välimäki

Note on bibliography

The bibliography contains all the research literature and printed sources cited in the chapters of this volume. Online sources are not contained in the bibliography, including individual web pages, discussion forum threads and online news articles. The same applies to individual newspaper articles. The majority of sources are cited only once, and full bibliographical details are provided in the endnote of the first citation.

Introduction

Who owns the Middle Ages? Metamedievalism and structural exclusion

Andrew B. R. Elliott

Introduction

This chapter is conceived as an intervention into what is emerging as an ongoing debate about political medievalism and its relationship with ideology. In these terms, rather than pointing to questions concerning specific misuses or abuses of power, the following argument seeks to zoom out to a meta-level, by asking a broader question about who owns and controls those Middle Ages, and thus under what kinds of circumstances those medievalisms recirculate. The question, then, obviously comes from a cultural studies approach which, following Stuart Hall and the CCCS at Birmingham, ceases to ask what a given discourse is about, but who owns and controls that discourse. As Hall and others observe, though many institutions contribute to hegemony:

> the mass media systems are probably (along with the schools) the critical ones [. . .] They 'connect' the centres of power with the dispersed publics: they mediate the public discourse between the elites and the governed. Thus they become, pivotally, the site and terrain on which the making and shaping of consent is exercised, and, to some degree, contested. They are key institutions in the operation of cultural hegemony.[1]

Accordingly, by examining medievalisms within the context of the broader platform on and through which discourse is established, this chapter seeks to ask what is not being spoken about in these medievalisms. Unlike the other chapters in this volume, my argument here does not focus on Finland or Russia but seeks to explore the mechanisms by and through which the medievalisms explored in other chapters find themselves remediated. In my effort to analyse the broader themes of medievalism, this chapter uses three case studies from 2019 to explore how limits on discourse become enforced and finally, but most importantly, whom are we excluding from those discussions as a result. My chapter is thus intended to form an introduction to the rest of the volume, outlining some of the general trends that the other chapters analyse in particular Finnish and Russian contexts.

Of course, questions of this size and nature cannot be answered within a short chapter, and neither am I necessarily the right person to offer those answers given my own position and relative privilege. Accordingly, the following argument is designed merely as an entry point, reworking my own early thinking about the ways in which the Middle Ages find themselves being used and – more often than not – abused in the service of modern political and ideological agendas.

It begins with what I have elsewhere termed 'banal medievalism', which I suggested might be a way of thinking about medievalism as a sense of generic pastness without specific reference to the past. In this mode, I hypothesized, banal medievalism is:

> reliant not on the past, but on the absence of that past, and derives its persuasive power not from historicity and representation, but from its retransmission across the mass media. Banal medievalism is not intended to conjure up the medieval past, or return us to that period [. . .] but instead it is designed to underscore a point in the present, which thus transports the medieval into our own world.[2]

These kinds of medievalisms often reveal more about the ideological inflections of the user and their chosen media platforms than they do about the historical Middle Ages.

What is overlooked by the term 'banal' is a kind of medievalism which operates on a secondary level and uses individual appropriations as part of a broader understanding of medievalism in its totality and in aggregate. These secondary medievalisms, I will argue, are more likely to be *seemingly* historical, but in fact rely on a more general understanding of the first level to make their point. They are also structural and relational, rather than absolute, which is why they have often been overlooked and dismissed as uninformed, as I will discuss later. Taken as a whole, they can be seen as a product of a participatory culture which allows for a reading on the broader structural level, the level of the participatory and the cumulative, which in turn allows us to explore the ways in which the confluence between political medievalism and participatory culture operates. I will challenge the concept of participatory culture in more detail later but for now, it can be summarized as an aspect of culture in which authority is rendered open to all.

This mode of using the medieval past falls into what might be described as 'metamedievalisms', that is, cumulative medievalisms whose repetition make some of the core elements of our ideas about the medieval past seem inevitable and uncontested. This is not a totally new idea at all. My idea builds on what Amy Kaufman calls 'medievalism doubled back upon itself',[3] and can be found in the work of many other medievalism scholars.[4] In particular, Carolyn Dinshaw's work on the contexts and frameworks of medievalism stand as the canonical discussions of the topic, particularly in her discussions of the affective pleasures of amateur medievalism, as well as the collapsing of temporal frames of an Augustinian *distentio* which marks the '"noncoincidence" of memory, attention, and expectation.'[5]

By extending Kaufman's idea of 'doubling back' into a framework of metamedievalism, and folding them into an amateur's *distentio*, in this chapter I want to show how these metamedievalisms help us to move away from the implications that medievalisms are always attached to some kind of historically responsible referent. Once they are used as metamedievalisms, I suggest, they actually begin to refer back to the medieval past in a doubly refracted way, refining and shaping our experience of the medieval because they have already been freed from the ropes of responsible historicity. However, as playful as such a process might seem, through my discussion of three case studies, I want to show how these same metamedievalisms can also come to form their own exclusions through ideology and invisible structures of exclusion.

My argument in this chapter, then, is that these metamedievalisms are not a marker of any kind of accuracy or authenticity paradigms. Rather, they are a logical extension of an ostensibly democratizing participatory culture, but in fact are constructed within a walled garden whose gates are in reality firmly closed to those already disenfranchised. As Sirpa Aalto and Timo Ylimaunu argue in Chapter 5 with regards to the Linnukka memorial and its reflection of the patriotic ideals of the 1930s, not the medieval world, what initially seems to be a medievalist project quickly becomes revealed to be a presentist one: the question is not about the authority of a given historical discourse but who gets to talk about that discourse. As a metamedievalism, it is the first sign that we are in the presence of a postmodern simulacrum of the medieval, rather than a modern replica of the period.

In this respect, here I offer three similar examples of medievalisms, all taking place in 2019 within a few months of each other and which are reliant on these kinds of metamedievalisms, to suggest that they are the direct result of a broader, participatory narrative about the past. That narrative, I argue, assails traditional definitions of historical authority by opening up a space into which individual ideological refractions can pour. It is the level of the metamedievalism, I suggest, that allows for the kind of pernicious medievalism which is used in support of extremist politics, since they rely on pervasive and tenacious beliefs about the medieval past, based on asymmetrical discourse and structural inequalities masked by the pretence that internet culture is demotic and democratic. Individually, each example provokes the kind of hand-wringing and nail-biting to which those of us engaged in public medievalism are by now accustomed. Cumulatively, however, I want to suggest that they reveal three processes of structural exclusion which undermine the more celebratory tone of participatory culture theorists.

Medievalism and the Christchurch shootings

The first case study demonstrates the sadly familiar use of medievalism to underpin white supremacist ideologies, which in several cases this century has led to fatal attacks.[6] On 15 March 2019, an Australian national launched a devastating attack on Muslims worshipping at their local mosques in Christchurch, New Zealand, murdering forty-nine innocent victims. This attack, I suggest, is relevant to discussions of historical authority for two reasons. The first is the highly public, and publicity-hungry, nature of the attacks. In addition to a barrage of posts on social media before the shooting, the attack on the mosque was videoed and live-streamed across Facebook and YouTube in a shameless and entirely deliberate act of self-promotion. The attack made front-page news across the world and led to the usual publicity guaranteed by an insatiable twenty-four-hour news cycle – publicity which was exactly what this terrorist was hoping to achieve. Such media attention, obviously, would not have been possible without the means of accessing public-facing social media platforms and is thus one indicator of the potentially nefarious power of Web 2.0 and the alleged democratization of the internet.

The second aspect, however, is more specifically related to medievalism. The parallels of the Christchurch terrorist's actions with those of in Norway in 2011 by Anders Behring Breivik are obvious, as are the similarities in modus operandi and targets of violence with other devastating attacks taking place across the United States, Canada, the United Kingdom, France and all over the world.[7] A certain number of details shared by many of these attacks revolve around highly intentional medievalisms. Identical in both cases is the act of naming weapons and ammunition after medieval actors fêted for allegedly resisting or repelling Muslim attacks, such as Tarrant's mishmash of half-remembered Google searches inscribed on his weapons, naming a range of historical figures who – according to the pseudohistory of the 'counterjihad' blogs which he seems to have consulted – had somehow repelled Muslim invasions in one form or another. Both Breivik and Tarrant wrote largely incoherent manifestoes built out of the so-called counterjihad network of aspiring (but bad) historians, like Fjordman, Richard Spencer, Bat Ye'or and Pamela Geller. Both of these documents were designed to defend their actions through a self-congratulatory pseudomartyrdom, which they transmitted through social media immediately prior to their murders to those whom they thought to be their brethren (and in both cases, it was largely a male audience, and both manifestoes are shot through with fervent and insistent misogyny typical of the incel movement).

Both manifestoes share one defining concern about the future, hypothesized as a Great White fear of a so-called 'Great Replacement', by and through which the 'Christian' population of the world would be replaced by 'Muslims', collapsing and erasing Western European culture, thereby inaugurating a new era of forced conversion, sharia law and so on. Echoes of this hypothetical Malthusian caliphate are shared by many among the online world of neo-Nazis, incels and blogs of varying notoriety from Stormfront to Breitbart. The White Extinction theory is in fact one of the worst-kept secrets of the white nationalist playbook, prominently embodied by politicians like Pat Buchanan in his book, *Suicide of a Superpower*, which directly reuses the language of white nationalism and self-avowed neo-Nazis in Tom Metzger's chapter, 'What We Believe as White Racists'.[8]

So the first example of political terrorism highlights the similarities between two terrorists using explicit references to the Middle Ages as a crutch for their racist ideologies, as well as their use of social media to justify their actions and – no less importantly – as a mechanism for self-promotion. The examples foreground the connection between political medievalism and modern self-identity, and the context in which a specific medievalism makes reference to a widely held belief about the Middle Ages – however wrongly. Such flexibility of the medieval past is only made possible, of course, by harnessing an extremely narrow and deliberately partial reading of the past. As I will argue later, the ability to sustain such a reading is entirely dependent on an infrastructure of participatory media in which users can selectively write and rewrite the past so that it fits a narrow and preconceived agenda. In essence, by a process of co-option, the medieval past can mean pretty much whatever we want it to mean, with powerful consequences. I will return to this point in my conclusions.

Jacob Rees-Mogg and the Victorians

My second example follows on from the first, though it is less obvious as a medievalism: in a moment I will suggest that it is a metamedievalism. In essence, it concerns a very basic book written by Jacob Rees-Mogg, a British MP and darling of the so-called 'traditional' conservative right. As is relatively common for right-wing British politicians,[9] in 2019 Rees-Mogg released a new book that aimed to reconcile a fundamentally divided Britain with a soothing balm of white, male, historical revisionism. The work in question, published by Penguin's Random House and entitled *The Victorians*, offered an unabashedly hagiographical rereading of twelve key Victorian men who were, Rees-Mogg asserts, somehow co-founders of the historical present through their embodiment of apparently fundamental virtues of the modern British work ethic. His choice of titans, perhaps unsurprisingly, included Robert Peel and Benjamin Disraeli, selections which implicitly place these gothic statesmen from the nineteenth century as the logical – or at least teleological – inheritors of a specific flavour of neoconservative pragmatism, birthed within a particularly toxic blend of historical essentialism.

As many commentators gleefully reported, Rees-Mogg's book recorded only 734 copies sold. Further, reviewers roundly condemned its turgid prose, schoolboy lack of nuance and in some cases total fabrication or historical error. However, and this is where the imprecise participatory historicism of Rees-Mogg's project begins to make itself keenly felt, *The Victorians* can also be seen as part of the same medievalist impulse which uses the past in support of practically any modern project.

Rees-Mogg's book is not only about the Victorians, but also about who gets to control the historical dimensions of a national debate. The broader issue at stake – related to the tendency for white, male conservative politicians to write biographies of Great White Men – is that the attempts (literally) to rewrite the past connect all of these vague historicisms to the same project. The Victorian foundations of Britain and the whiteness of its medievalisms are part of a vague and general celebration of empire and historical exceptionalism proposed in the context of almost a decade of fervent Brexit paranoia – even *avant la lettre*. As such they form what Rosk calls 'consensus-objects' (see Chapter 1) like Alexander Nevsky, standing in for a dominant and hegemonic premodern history that props up the conservative historical essentialism.

I do not propose to explore this point in great depth since I have discussed it elsewhere.[10] Nevertheless, to summarise, I suggest that Brexit, Victoriana and medievalism go hand in hand through a gradual, sequential, re-establishment of historical ownership which asserts that the British Empire was a natural point of evolution made possible by European superiority throughout the Middle Ages. According to Rees-Mogg's version of history, the achievements of the Victorians arose because they are the inheritors of a medieval legacy in which England (apparently uniquely) invented the idea of a constitution. As Rees-Mogg crows, celebrating Britain's history by 'having the confidence' heroically and altruistically to 'recognis[e] the civilizing effect of their own nation and understand the good fortune of Britain, as a nation blessed by being the first to receive the benefit of a good Constitution and the rule of law. They [i.e. the Victorians] also had the confidence to say that civilization was a good thing and that it is reasonable to export it to other countries to remove such hardships as exist there.'[11]

The logic at work here functions broadly in the same way as Vladimir Putin's references to the Pecheneg and Cuman people in response to the ravages of Covid-19 discussed in Chapters 2 and 4. As Kati Parppei argues, at first these historical references seem baffling, inconsequential or even amusing. However, when reconfigured as part of a broader national narrative, what is revealed is not their referential value but their symbolic value. As part of a national discourse built out of a habitual national past, a historical reference like Putin's becomes not an irrelevant detail, but an invented tradition undergirded by a fervently insistent repetition. The same pattern is observed in Kendra Willson's discussion of runestones: it is not the individual example of fraudulent runestones that convinces the sceptic, but the cumulative effect. It becomes, in Willson's memorable phrase, 'a truth bubbling from the mouth of the folk, pushing off the lid of silence imposed by the scholarly establishment' (Chapter 6, p. 118). It matters little that it is devoid of historicity because the reference becomes more convincing the more it makes reference to other prevalent beliefs and constructs.

With both Rees-Mogg and Putin, then, the baffling references might seem amusingly inconsequential, but it is the coalescence of medieval-seeming narratives which allows the metamedievalism to emerge. The discussion of the Victorian 'white man's burden' to which Rees-Mogg (perhaps unwittingly) alludes in his book[12] has as a precondition the centuries of self-expression and self-determination of a country that forges its own past by being the first to adopt a constitution. His implicit reference to Magna Carta in the talk of a constitution operates as a metamedievalism because it only works in the context of others' remarks that Magna Carta is a constitution and that it forged the Middle Ages and England.[13] As such, the allure of *Our Island Story*, a children's book of fanciful history to which David Cameron once alluded as the history of Britain, begins in the Middle Ages and is crystallized in the zenith of the Victorian Empire. As such, the medieval myth of the nation[14] naturalizes the UK's desire to 'throw off the shackles of EU imperialism' as a logical necessity born out of historical contingency. None of these figures seem to recognize the irony of their vaunting the legacy of imperialism as the self-evident truth justifying the need to reject imperialism – it seems that empire is good only if you are the colonizer.

So what separates the historical flights of fancy of Rees-Mogg from the rigorous scholarship of the genuine historian? Here is a more depressing answer: in the context of metamedievalism and participatory history, not much. The dismal sales of just over 700 copies do perhaps cause a wry and sadistic smirk among real historians and perhaps reassure us that the public is not as easily fooled as we otherwise might think. However, our smiles soon fade when we compare those figures with sales figures from our own works of rigorously researched and, we hope, historically thoughtful, works of scholarship. I say this not to undermine the academy, or to be deliberately controversial, but rather to point out that in terms of public history, there are almost certainly more members of the public reading even something as bad as Rees-Mogg's invention of the Victorians as there are reading a thoughtful analysis of the period, like Helen Kingstone's *Victorian Narratives of the Recent Past*, a book which acknowledges the imprecision and invented historiographies of the Victorian historians themselves.[15]

Rees-Mogg's failure as a historian was not only due to his strained, lopsided and determinedly political reading of the past but also because it was dependent on establishing a credible degree of historical authority which he struggled to achieve. This authority to speak about history, in a powerfully circular argument, is established by signalling an unassailable belonging to the centre of structural privilege enmeshed in the establishment, of which people like Rees-Mogg are clearly the poster boy. Of course, as Reima Välimäki notes in the preface to this volume, and as Parppei and others make clear, behind almost any question of historical authority there is the real question not about the accuracy of the historical claims, but who has the right to speak them. As Parppei suggests in her discussion of the battle over St Vladimir/Volodymyr between Russia and Crimea, in the context of 'semi-mythical' historical figures the question is not to whom the saint belongs, but who gets to stake their claim to ownership the loudest.

The evidence for this suggestion is found in the counter-debate. Labour MP David Lammy, a Black British MP for Tottenham in London, is a good example of how cryptic racism is hidden beneath a veneer of historical revisionism. When, as he did in a series of parliamentary speeches over the course of 2018 and 2019, he rails against British imperialism with more historical facticity than Rees-Mogg's dream of Victorian nobility and benevolence, the public backlash is not a nuanced review of the relative merits of empire, but outright racism through tweets and letters from unnamed sources.[16]

The debate speaks powerfully to the question posed by Gayatri Spivak: can the subaltern speak?[17] The attempt to deny Lammy's right to address history by racist slurs demonstrates a part of the 'epistemic violence' invoked to 'constitute the colonial subject as Other'.[18] The metamedievalism comes into play here not only in the reference to the historical past but also in its implicit invocation of an inherent power differential on who has the right to speak and on whose behalf. It is here that we see that a part of the debate, and the role in which metamedievalism comes most powerfully into play, then, is not in the individual acts of speech and the platforms from which to do so, but the ongoing role of discourse which dominates the context and ability to decode the meaning of a given medievalism. The plausibility or perceived authenticity of the argument surely comes not from history per se but from other instances of medievalism, as well as a structural imbalance that erases voices deemed not to fit into an arbitrarily established hierarchy of knowledge.

To summarize these two positions then, the argument I have made so far is that the structural preconditions of a toxic blend of exclusionary medievalism involve first banal medievalisms (here in the service of a right-wing agenda), and second the historical authority which allows the subject to speak about those medievalisms, which I have suggested lies in the realm of the metamedievalism. That realm of metamedievalism is, in this case, defined by the creation of a broader rhetoric of belonging and historical contingency, whose abundance in the popular domain thus operates as a self-serving guarantor of perceived authenticity. The missing part is a third element that plays into both by situating medievalism as the concern and exclusive property of a white, eurocentric medievalism, bolstered by the same kind of dismissal of the subaltern as embodied by Lammy's racist attacks. Such a project of medievalism thus reveals the faultlines lurking beneath the thin veneer of contemporary civilization, irrupting through the surface seemingly without warning. The white fragility underpinning Lammy's racist attacks resembles the toxicity of the 'manosphere' discussed by Heta Aali in Chapter 7 who illustrates the fragility of the masculinist discourses surrounding the Ancient Finnish Kings, and the sudden ferocity of those who find that false historicity challenged.

Caravans of Gold

This last point is more subtle, but nevertheless more powerful – or perhaps it is more powerful precisely because of its subtlety. My third case study, then, is one that I think gives us a glimpse into the ways in which a participatory culture can reframe global or international medievalisms within a binary model of structural exclusion by comparison and metaphor. It relates to a 2019 exhibition taking place in the Block Museum of Chicago called 'Caravans of Gold'.[19] The exhibition featured a range of medieval exhibits which were carefully curated together to contest the kind of exclusionary, Western-centric, understandings of the Middle Ages as the preserve of a European Christendom, by focusing on medieval Saharan Africa in the pre-1500s and outlining some of the global networks of power, travel and international relations. One exhibit, for instance, showed the appearance of French pottery in a statue from Mali. Another demonstrated the presence of Qingbai porcelain from the Northern Song dynasty in China's south-eastern Jiangxi province, discovered at sites in Mali and dating from the tenth to the twelfth centuries. Others documented stone monuments in Gao, Mali, inscribed in Almería in Spain whence it originated in the early twelfth century.

Kathleen Bickford Berzock, the organizer and lead curator of the exhibit, writes of the explicit intention of the exhibition to 'shift the focal point of the medieval period [away from the European perspective] to the Sahara desert and the communities in the Sahel, a transitional region between the desert and West African Savanna, which grew wealthy and powerful as centers of exchange and production due to trans-Saharan commerce.'[20] In essence, the exhibition counteracted the dominant narrative of historical actants being concentrated in European Christendom, instead showing the highly active, and interactive trade regions in vast networks stretching from Saharan Africa around the world.

Perhaps the most striking exhibit, and the one which caught the attention of news services reporting on the exhibition, relates to Mansā Musā Keita, emperor of Mali in 1339, and the monumental hajj which he undertook to Mecca with his caravans, which is what gave the exhibition its name. The spectacular pilgrimage purportedly marked the ruler's conversion to Islam and the ceremonial pilgrimage he undertook to memorialize his new religion. The exhibition offered glimpses of the pilgrimage route in which caravans distributed loads of gold and lavish gifts along the route, and documented how on his return Musā founded the cultural marvel of Timbuktu.

Equally striking, though for different reasons, is the language used in the coverage of the exhibition. Bloggers and websites were quick to seize upon the rare narrative of West African trade routes and lavish gold and silver archaeological finds which demonstrate the extension of the global networks in and around medieval Africa. Such coverage is in itself interesting, but particularly so during a period in which the term 'caravan' and the concept of mass movements of people across political borders was loaded with political baggage of its own (allegations made by the then President, Donald Trump, claimed that there was a 'caravan of immigrants' making its way to the southern border of the United States). However, the headline of the *Chicago Tribune* is one of the most interesting. Rather than focusing on the centrality of those trade and religious networks, the title of the article devoted to the exhibition relies on the same rhetoric of alterity encountered elsewhere. Focusing on Mansā Musā as the world's richest man, the *Tribune* led with a headline that compared him to contemporary American rich men including Amazon founder Jeff Bezos and Microsoft founder Bill Gates.

If we pause to reflect on this transhistorical comparison, we can see once again the metamedievalism of the global West once again at work here, capitalizing on the othering of Musā both temporally and geopolitically. His success is translated not on its own merits in the past but transposed onto Silicon Valley billionaires amid a fervently neomedievalist rhetoric which can only reduce him to being 'like' the modern American Captains of Industry. Perhaps such a comparison is intended as an innocuous way of framing unimaginable wealth in terms understood by its readers, in the same way as we might say that a dinosaur is like two London buses, or an area is like so many football fields, but the implicit cultural appropriation reveals the specific audience targeted by the comparison and suggests that African archaeological finds can only be important in terms of what they mean to the West.

As soon as the story hit the internet, of course, the media mechanism of user-generated content and automated aggregation began to gather its pace. Picked up by a number of online aggregate websites, the story eventually found its way, complete with the references to Bezos, onto the websites of a number of newspapers around the world. As it happened, *The Week* had already used Musā as part of its list of the richest people of all time in January 2018, so it was unsurprising to find the story picked up by the BBC news website, and then *The*

Sun newspaper, both of whom continued the reference and comparison with Jeff Bezos. Once it hit the right-leaning newspapers, the user-generated comments machine gained traction, leading to some revealing comments left by mainly anonymous users, ranging from the usual fanatical fringe to the conspiracists.

Some, for instance, objected to the rankings on the basis that they did not include King Solomon, who the Bible tells us was the richest man who ever lived. Others made the standard claims about fake news, insisting that any talk of medieval people existing outside Europe, or any kind of African wealth is itself so historically implausible that it must be a part of a giant Cultural-Marxist cover-up campaign. It also introduced an interesting explicit suggestion that we should not 'take seriously some medieval African king', and his fortune would only have been worthwhile if he had come to Europe. The exclusion of anyone alive today is, for George Smith, enough to claim foul play, demonstrating both a pathological jingoism and a failure to grasp the basics of inflation.[21]

The more interesting comments, however, all circle around the second reversal of this kind of eurocentric thinking. Not only is there the inherent orientalism of comparing Musā to Bezos and co, but also thanks to secondary medievalism, this kind of thinking is so entrenched that it seems impossible to imagine that medieval Africa might have such wealth. Following the logic, another range of comments asserts that such wealth must only be measurable by 'magnificent architectural buildings', imagined as only possible using the kind of architecture familiar to the modern world. The absence of modernity is thus indicative of mythological fabrication, and thus medievalism on a secondary level. The world of user-generated content in this third example returns to the question of historical authority to which my title alludes.

Historical authority

It is this final aspect of the medieval past, conducted without historical authority and constructed through metamedievalism, which leads back to my earlier premise about the structural inequalities of participatory medievalism. By exploring these medievalisms as metamedievalisms, all speaking to and drawing on a specific reimagining of the medieval past which is constructed through user-generated content, the individual references to the medieval become more of a challenge to historical authority especially since they draw on each other for their reinforcement. This particular issue of timing and resonance is further explored in the context of Finnish medievalism in Derek Fewster's magnum opus,²² and more specifically in the context of monuments in Chapter 5 of this volume. Sirpa Aalto and Timo Ylimaunu's discussion of the Linnukka memorial and statues of Vesainen are notable, as they expertly demonstrate, not because of an atmosphere of celebration, but precisely the inverse: that celebratory (and thus protoparticipatory) mood was absent, which is what brings about the delay in erecting the monuments. Once an independent Finland returns to its narratives of teleological medievalism (or, as I argue here, metanarratives), then the memorial has a 'particular symbolical value for the Finns as the whole memorial was a reference to the fight against the Russians – and thus against oppression' (Chapter 5, p. 94).

If all of these metamedievalisms are constructed, then it matters most urgently who constructs them. As the title of this chapter suggests: who actually owns the online Middle Ages? My answer uses takes three interrelated questions as a starting point to examine the online networks of medievalism: first, whose heritage is it; second, who grants the power to decide whose heritage it is; third, which processes are in place to 'earn' historical authority to make that decision in the first place? The first of these questions is explored in Stuart Hall's canonical essay, 'Whose Heritage? Unsettling "the heritage," re-imagining the post-nation'.²³ Hall's essay remains an essential text in challenging the extent to which the celebration or commemoration of heritage involves a systemic process of exclusion and cultural forgetting, as well as a powerful structure of entitlement in terms of who gets to decide. Such terms of appropriation and questions of postcolonial power of course also inhere in medievalism itself, and particularly the insistent focus on Western Europe as the focal point of medieval history, as explored by John Ganim in *Medievalism and Orientalism*. At the same time, any question of ownership needs to confront the eurocentrism which often underpins the discipline of medieval studies, from the areas studied to the languages used to do so. This topic is richly mined in Geraldine Heng's landmark work on race in the Middle Ages, which anticipates racial demarcations away from a modernist, presentist concern into the very foundations of premodern nation states. Thus, rather than being a 'myth of race inferiority', invented as an early modern concept 'to rationalize the institution of enslavement of Blacks from Africa',²⁴ race becomes backdated into the Middle Ages as a relational concept, not an absolute.²⁵

Heng's demonstration of the relational elements of racism thus becomes the bedrock on which the third question of digital ownership is constructed. In particular, Heng's argument that 'race is a structural relationship for the articulation and management of human differences, rather than a substantive content'[26] has important implications for the online world. As a structural relationship, rather than a substantive content, Heng's model for race in the premodern expression of difference can be applied surprisingly neatly to the metamedievalisms of the digital sphere, which relies not on a substantive assertion, but a structural and networked relationship. As the examples of Tarrant's weapons, Rees-Mogg's Victorians and Musā's Caravans of Gold all suggest, the reality of the medievalism is constructed on the hidden networks of metamedievalism. Thus the question becomes reframed from one about accuracy or authenticity; instead, we ask who has the right to assert historical authority in these cases?

Web 2.0 and techno-utopianism

The second question which I pose here derives from the first. In such an ostensibly demotic and participatory world, what does the concept of historical authority mean? If medievalisms like the ones discussed earlier emerge and recirculate in powerful, bottom-up, algorithmically dictated filter bubbles,[27] then what is the role of the curator in the new digital realm? Who is able to speak up against the kinds of misappropriations of the past that we have just seen, and how should they do so in the face of such powerful opposition from public ignorance of historical facts and the relentless stream of automated bots? As Evan Wallace argues powerfully in Chapter 4, when Putin makes reference to the Pechenegs and the Polovtsy, the point is not that these references are wrong. 'Had this speech been given before the advent of digital media and Web 2.0', Wallace suggests, 'it is likely that the narrative would have stayed contained and within the "walled garden" of Russian state media.' Instead, however, the copy-and-paste shareability of digital media enables a hyperreal echo well beyond the confines of the state.

Accordingly, it is possible to extend some of those same arguments into the digital sphere, by exploring participatory medievalism as a means of thinking about how the Middle Ages become repackaged for a digital era. In particular, it is important to think about digital medievalism in the context of the often triumphalist techno-utopianism of Web 2.0, as suggested by Tim O'Reilly in 2004.

The premise of participatory or convergence culture, boiled down to its most simple elements, is the gradual (and sometimes not so gradual) erosion of the formerly more rigid lines between the producers of media content and its users.

Often this erosion is historically dated to the advent of the internet, though this is not at all true: Brian Winston has repeatedly and convincingly argued that any media technology, from parchment to Gutenberg, from periodicals to talk radio, and so on, offers a new means of scaling the walls of the informational gatekeepers.[28] Indeed, Henry Jenkins, who most persuasively talks about convergence culture in his book of the same name,[29] was writing about fan communities and oppositional meanings already in his 1992 book, *Textual Poachers*, as a phenomenon that predates by more than a decade the kind of user-generated content outlined earlier.[30]

However, irrespective of precisely when it is historically located, the point about participatory culture is the element, unsurprisingly, of *participation*. The increasing sophistication of media technologies increasingly narrows the distance between the powers of media moguls to manufacture and publish content and that of users who can do the same. Some critics, like Axel Bruns and Joanne Jacobs already fifteen years ago, termed these new active audience members 'prosumers', highly active users who become 'hybrids of producer and user', a concept which 'undermines the distinction between commercial producers and distributors on the one side, and consuming, passive audiences on the other.'[31]

Early adopters of these participatory technologies began to speak glowingly of terms like Web 2.0, which they suggested spoke to a revolution in communication technologies, and which allowed for paradigm-shifting technologies which would democratize the world, bypassing the gatekeepers and allowing anyone to change the world. José Van Dijck for instance, reports on the cyberoptimism of those who suggested that 'this layer of platforms influences human interaction on an individual and community level, as well as on a larger societal level, which the world of online and offline are increasingly interpenetrating.'[32] Again, Bruns and Jacobs speak of this interpenetration as a shift to traditional power structures, allowing anyone to contribute and even shape the global discourse.[33] Clay Shirky even describes this change as a tectonic shift that destroys the barriers and allows for group cohesion to 'get things done'.[34]

In fairness, the data surrounding internet penetration are quite overwhelming, and it is easy to see in them theoretical opportunities for a demotic turn. According to one 2017 study, there were nearly 4 billion estimated internet users, of which 2.789 billion (73.6 per cent) were active social media users with profiles on one of the main social networks. For this study, active meant that they logged into that content at least once a month – those are actually quite stringent rules for inclusion. Of those 2.7 billion, 2.5 billion – a whopping 91 per cent – were able to use a mobile device to do so, meaning that there are 2.5 billion people able to post content to the world armed with a hand-held, portable camera, microphone, GPS, text-editing, word-processing, number-crunching fax machine. In a statistic that is much-vaunted by technology enthusiasts, internet penetration had reached over 50 per cent of the world population to an estimated global coverage of 59 per cent by June 2020. Thus, as Web 2.0 enthusiasts declared, more than one in any two people selected at random is theoretically able to play a part in the world's conversations and contribute to the collective and cumulative knowledge of the world.[35]

The online subaltern

However, much less is said about the missing half of that statistic, and in particular which parts of the globe make up that missing 41 per cent. The obvious point to make, of course, is that if just over one in two has access to an internet-enabled device, it logically follows that just under one in every two has no capacity to do so. In terms of social media, this figure plummets even further. A market penetration of 37 per cent means that fully 63 per cent (almost two in three people) have no access to those social media networks, which are increasingly used as sign-ins to other websites, and therefore are shut out from more than just SNSs. For every connected person posting images to social media accounts and speaking truth to power on platforms like Twitter, there are essentially two others who are shut out of this global, participatory and democratizing project. Of course, such statistics are not surprising; as Curran, Fenton and Freedman observed, 'it is always more likely that social media will replicate and entrench social inequalities rather than liberate them.'[36]

What is surprising is the extent to which the arguments earlier about the power of Web 2.0 omit this crucial exclusion. Even if it is true that power centres are destabilized, that still takes place in a highly centralized power imbalance on a global scale. Only half of the world is actually online, and only about one-third of it is able to participate in discussions taking place on it, and that is not taking into account language of electronic barriers – English remains the most popular language, representing 25.2 per cent of global internet users, with Mandarin Chinese ranked second with 19.3 per cent and Spanish coming third with 7.9 per cent. Yet, if we drill down even further into the statistics on social media usage, even that third is not as vocal as we suggest. A series of studies have sought to explore the precise nature of social media usage, and researchers frequently come up against the shadowy figure of the 'lurker'. The lurker is the term given to the social media user who reads and consumes social media but posts or uploads very little, or nothing, herself. It is difficult to gauge with any certainty – precisely because her presence is measured only by what she uploads – but already in 2006 Nielsen estimated it at 90 per cent, a figure borne out by later studies, offering the 90-9-1 rule: 'that 90% of users are lurkers, 9% contribute from time-to-time, while only 1% are heavy contributors'.[37] Indeed, these figures are confirmed and estimated as perhaps even smaller by other SNSs. On Twitter, for instance, up to 95 per cent are estimated to be lurkers or serial retweeters, leaving an estimated 0.05 per cent of users to attract almost fifty per cent of all attention.[38] For Wikipedia, that drops further: of its 40.5 million registered users, only 133,825 (0.33 per cent) are active contributors, supervised by 1,119 (0.002 per cent) administrators.[39]

So not only is the percentage of actual contributors ironically much closer to traditional, top-down, media broadcasting, but also far fewer of us are as genuinely participatory as we think, creating a new, digital, Potemkin village of the kind to which Evan Wallace refers in Chapter 4. Taking the generous 1 per cent active-user estimate and applying it to the 37 per cent who are online using SNSs suggests that only 0.37 per cent of the world's population is genuinely participating in global discussions, which equates to around 27 million people. For the sake of argument, it is as though all of the writing in the world came from Mozambique alone, or the combined populations of Finland, Sweden, Norway and Denmark. It is certainly impressive to connect 27 million people, but clearly this contribution is not global.

More importantly, following the global user data, it is more likely to be the Scandinavian countries who are contributing more than Mozambique. Hootsuite and WeAreSocial's annual statistics on internet penetration break down internet use by region, as a percentage of the population. Looking at those participation statistics makes it very clear – if ever there was any doubt – that internet usage is the privilege of the Global North. For every North American or Western/Northern European country with 95 per cent penetration, there is a Central Asian, Caribbean or Northern African region with 50 per cent. Moreover, some of the most densely populated areas of the world like Southern Asia record only 42 per cent penetration, and those ranking at the lowest are Western Africa (41 per cent), Eastern Africa (32 per cent) and Middle Africa (12 per cent). The clearly disproportionate uptake of the internet by those in the Global North is hardly surprising but shows where most of those 27 million people are likely to be operating, and so the comments on Mali seen earlier are twice as likely to come from a Euro-American server than one in Mali itself.[40] In that sense, not only are these 'open' networks, in reality, more closed than we think, but they are also networks that are closed within a highly imbalanced systemic and structural inequality.

Conclusion

To return to my three examples, then, it becomes clear that the metamedievalisms are made possible by this very specific infrastructure of the internet. The attention-seeking murders of terrorists like Breivik and Tarrant are possible using the connections to social media channels that privilege white male historical revisionism. Likewise, the online structural inequality is merely a reflection of an offline structural hegemony which is even more dangerous precisely because those who *are* online insist so consistently that it is open to all. The insistence that Web 2.0 breaks down the barriers to publishing, as Rees-Mogg's bad history makes clear, hides the fact that history books are still overwhelmingly written by those handed an upper-middle-class sense of entitlement, often dominated by straight, white, conservative men. Thus history is literally rewritten by those already birthed within the structural privilege, and with the requisite sense of entitlement, to believe themselves worthy to do so. Finally, even when those medievalisms get challenged by a fascinating story like that of Mansā Musā, they can find themselves co-opted or else rewritten into the Global North's measures of success. If they are not appropriated by those narratives, they might otherwise find themselves potentially rejected because they do not align with the narratives written precisely by those like Rees-Mogg, who are unable to imagine a world beyond the coddled bubbles that they occupy.

To counter these powerful structures surrounding metamedievalism, then, we must first recognize the disparity of access. Even the 2018 UN report featuring 51.2 per cent penetration, for instance, fails to condemn the 48 per cent exclusion. Instead, it celebrates that statistic as 'a pointer to the great strides the world is making towards building a more inclusive global information society', according to ITU Secretary-General Houlin Zhao. This is true even though the same report contains the startling statistic that in Africa the penetration statistic plummets to 24 per cent. Like job searches, tenure committees, opera auditions, education, health and so many other areas, the ostensible transparency of the participatory process masks and renders even more invisible the structural biases working against those excluded. Because the playing field is said to be level, the inequalities are unconsciously translated into an individual lack, rather than an endemic and ineluctable consequence of privilege.

So, to finish, I want to return to the question of participatory medievalism by suggesting that we explore not only the medievalisms but also the forums and structures surrounding those metamedievalisms and the ways in which those uses of the medieval past are uttered. Although the participatory nature of online discourse has offered a brave new world of public history, and that is defiantly a good thing, it is also important to remember that the open forums of online discourse nevertheless operate as reflections of offline structural inequalities, which exclude as much as they include. Consequently, the question of historical authority becomes even more urgent in the ostensibly open world of Web 2.0. From white supremacists to terrorist groups to debates over sovereignty and geopolitics, it is perhaps not only on specific medievalisms that we should focus our attention, but also the broader systemic apparatus of metamedievalism.

1

The Middle Ages on the 'map of memory' of Russian society[1]

E. A. Rostovtsev

Introduction

Just as the Middle Ages, understood as a historical era, is represented in the contemporary world in a variety of ways, so has the development of medievalism studies taken a number of different paths.[2] Unlike in the Western world, in Russia, one is unlikely to consider medievalism studies a yet-fully fledged discipline, and most of the activity that would fall under that rubric has been the studies of narratives about the past, that is the history of memory in the most general sense. This particularly applies to the period of 'pre-Petrine' Rus'.[3] Here, it is important to note that the concept of the Middle Ages really came about in its Russian variant at the turn of the nineteenth century. It was driven by the adoption, by Russians, of European history as their own and the construction of the categories of New and Old (pre-Petrine) Russia, to which the concept of the Middle Ages in the Russian sense really refers. These developments preconditioned attempts to find in medieval Russia a series of phenomena that never existed in the true European sense – feudalism and feudal warriors, knights, burghers, city-states and the like.[4]

The construction of social memory about the Middle Ages has been the subject of a large and serious body of scholarship. This corpus of work has been largely concerned with earlier periods in this process, that is to say they study either medieval historical perception itself or representations of the medieval in the early modern period.[5] Multitudinous works by contemporary historians – I. N. Danilevsky, K. Yu. Erusalimsky, P. V. Lukin, A. V. Sirenov, A. S. Usachev, A. I. Filyushkin, B. N. Floria, and many others – paint an extensive picture of how the memory of pre-Mongol and Muscovite Rus' took form.[6] In particular, they show

how a clear chronological narrative of pre-Petrine Rus' cemented itself in the cultural memory and collective historical consciousness between the sixteenth and seventeenth centuries and how, notwithstanding some minor adjustments, this narrative survived unchanged into the modern age.[7]

In this context, the mobilization of the Middle Ages in Russia has been somewhat distinct from other Eastern European countries where medieval events and figures have been used as tools of identity formation and national-myth construction throughout the modern period up to the present day.[8] Nonetheless, the problem of the Middle Ages in Russian historical memory remains interesting in more than one way. First, its methodology opens up various mechanisms of interplay between cultural and communicative memory, and it also offers a unique information base for understanding the development of cultural discourses and widely held understandings of the past. Second, the topic gives insights into the cultural core of a national memory, that is to say into an assembly of cultural objects that structure cultural and societal representations of a national history. Finally, the Russian Middle Ages have been an object of a centuries-long memory politics that has been actively pursued by the state as well as by miscellaneous political forces of different ideological stripes.[9]

The last circumstance is especially important. In the context of disputes about the Russian state policy of memory in modern Russian and Western literature, the problem of *neomedievalism* is widely discussed. Neomedievalism in the Russian case is understood as a phenomenon associated with the exploitation of the Middle Ages as a resource of national political culture, to which the supporters of Russia's 'special way', neo-Eurasians, and other 'statists' attribute 'medieval methods' of organizing social life, in particular the *oprichnina*/protection of the state, as 'primordial' and a positive feature of Russian society, and their opponents in this context directly link the processes of strengthening neomedievalism with the processes of restalinization of Russian society.[10] Such views are justified in the sense that both the conservative elites and the authorities in modern Russia are indeed actively and constantly appealing to the image of strong state leaders of the past, including the medieval one. In this context, while analysing the historical politics of the last twenty years, researchers rightly pay attention to medieval subjects. For example, in the recent book by Mariëlle Wijermars, three case studies out of four are connected with references to the subjects of pre-Petrine Russia (Alexander Nevsky, Ivan the Terrible, The Time of Troubles).[11]

The present inquiry sets itself a number of key questions that relate to the above-mentioned areas: (1) What have been the essential elements in the Russian cultural memory of the Middle Ages as it developed in the modern age?

(2) How are these elements presented in the realm of communicative memory at the beginning of the twenty-first century and in contemporary media? (3) What role do they play in the present-day memory politics of the state and other societal actors? The present study builds on a database of more than thirty source groups dating between 1965 and 2020. All of these source groups were compiled by St Petersburg State University's history department between 2008 and 2020 and relate to the topic of historical memory in Russian society.[12] This chapter presents the results of this research to the Anglophone research community.

Methodology, terminology and the sources of memory

The most pressing historiographical problems concern not so much about the content of representations of past heroes and events as much as trying to understand the mechanisms by which that pantheon of objects came about, the strategies of memory mobilization that have been employed and what the crucial factors in historical politics have been. In large part, this problem concerns uncovering sources of memory development in concrete periods. Existing scholarship has shown the importance of a variety of different sources – religious menologies,[13] etchings,[14] folk monuments,[15] works of monumental art,[16] almanacs,[17] advertisement,[18] anecdotes,[19] computer games[20] and much else. To date, however, it is hard to point to any systematic study that establishes the role and significance of groups of sources in the development of historical memory of the medieval period. An even trickier issue concerns the ways in which the Middle Ages have been mobilized in the contemporary world. While scholarship's decision to look at state politics has been understandable, much remains to be said on a wide variety of social and cultural practices that are linked to the use of medieval images and traditions.[21] Of course, this is not to say that certain topics have not been studied. The publication of documents from the Society for the Rebirth of Fine Arts of Ancient Rus' (Obshchestvo vozrozhdeniia khudozhestvennoi Rusi),[22] which existed at the beginning of the twentieth century, and the study of the practices of the historical re-enactment,[23] both provide good examples. Yet, these types of studies also point to a scattered historiography that is concerned with local and little-integrated problems, methodologies and research horizons.

Overall, therefore, we can say that the results of contemporary memory studies in relation to the Russian Middle Ages have been somewhat contradictory. While cultural memory studies, on the whole, elucidate both the content and development of historical imaginations of the Middle Ages in modern and contemporary society, present-day scholarship desperately needs to develop a research approach for undertaking the substantive archaeology of historical memory as well as the study of the mobilization mechanisms of its constituent memory objects.

Contemporary memory studies apply different approaches and methods for reconstructing a society's map of memory (i.e. the schema of a society's historical representations) of a given period. These are approaches are not always integrated. It goes without saying, we must be aware of the technological limits of the methods that we apply and recognize that in any case, we elaborate only on a model of social memory/collective consciousness that seeks to accurately represent reality.

With this in mind, it is vital we begin by examining our methodology, particularly its terminology which it shares with an array of existing scholarship. First, we distinguish social, cultural and communicative memory. The term 'social' or 'collective memory' draws from the work of Maurice Halbwachs and is used to mean the memory (a system of representations of the past) of a social group at a particular moment in time.[24] In our case, this would mean Russian society/nation in the twentieth and twenty-first centuries. The analysis of a society's cultural memory is a key component of reconstructing national memory, as Jan Assmann has demonstrated.[25] We understand 'cultural memory' to mean a stable system of representations about the past that is fixed/reflected in texts/monuments of culture that have exercised a long-standing influence on a society's collective consciousness. These include works of art, literature, mandatory educational texts, symbols, traditions and acts of commemoration, all of which have conveyed particular information about the past for a long period of time, at least a few generations. Communicative memory reflects the circulation of historical information in social spaces and in the media at a certain point in time, and it is understood to include the totality of discourses and material about the past that the consciousness of an individual in that society perceives (oral traditions, mass media, social media, educational practices and so forth). While cultural memory continuously acts on the formation of communicative memory, today's information environment gives rise to new interpretations of cultural objects as well as new texts and images of key events and figures, which over time become part of society's cultural-memory 'pantheon'.[26]

The question of how systems of historical representations occurring in social (collective) memory are construed is another key consideration. In our opinion, a constructivist approach to historical representations that are connected with particular conceptions of the future is most productive and methodologically workable. At the very least, such an approach is effective for the most important texts, heroes and events of the nineteenth and twentieth centuries – periods where Russian cultural and societal consciousness was characterized by a clash of two ideals of the future, one traditionalist/statist, the other liberal/Western. The first of these ideals viewed the strengthening of the state/*sobornost'*/collectivity/nation as its main priority, and the second – emancipation of the individual and the attainment of civil rights.[27] Certainly, this is a very simplistic and schematic description given that collective consciousness and the political domain saw a clash of wide-ranging ideologies, including various forms of liberalism and westernism (from conservative liberalism, libertarianism, and social liberalism to various types of socialism, from anarchism to Bolshevism). In essence, however, historical interpretations have tended to take one of the two aforementioned base forms.

It is not by accident that scholarship consistently points to an affinity, in terms of their ideologies and character, between autocracy and Soviet totalitarianism,[28] and more recently, Putin's authoritarianism.[29] One further point needs to be made: the traditionalist view of the past and future, characteristic of the state's memory politics in both periods, was firmly repudiated by cultural elites and then suffered permanent rejection in cultural memory and the historiographical tradition. Yet, these main discourses in Russian historiography, which provided the dominant frameworks for interpreting national history, were both formulated by liberal historians at the end of the nineteenth and start of the twentieth centuries. In turn, these discourses became an inalienable part of society and the intelligentsia as they continued to construe history in accordance with theories of the social and political progress of their time.[30]

By the object of historical memory, we understand a construct that refers to any historical phenomenon being evaluated in our sources. Of course, researchers can interpret objects in a manner of ways depending on the available materials and their research goals. 'Fundamental' objects comprise historical eras (pre-Mongol Rus', pre-Petrine Rus', the period of feudalism, the Soviet era, modernity, the nineteenth century, the twentieth century and so on). 'Local' objects – objects linked to a specific place and time – correspond one way or another to eras (fundamental objects). Historical phenomena that have only some approximate temporal or spatial location in historical consciousness may be considered complex local objects. On the Russian map of memory, they are such objects as the Russian intelligentsia, the liberation movement, Cossacks, the Mongol Yoke and the like. Heroes and events are categorized as simple local objects of historical memory, that is to say, objects with a clearly defined location in time and space. In the final analysis, these objects are integral to the construction of more complex objects and for the map of memory on the whole. Across all the sources of historical memory, they are the easiest category for research and analysis.[31]

The discussion so far highlights the importance of having an adequate system for sorting sources relating to historical memory and collective consciousness formation in a given period. It also makes clear that any such work will include a variety of source groups, depending on the period being studied. With this in mind, attempts to sketch out the map of memory of the present day should include sources that have produced historical representations over a long period of time (works of classical literature, paintings and musical culture, sculptures, important journalistic publications, works of political philosophy, historiographical narratives centred on the cultural elite, texts that read as part of a school curriculum, acknowledged cinematic works and others), and texts currently trending in media spaces (such as internet content of various types, including among others: Wikipedia, groups of social networks, journalism and writings on current affairs, political speeches, commentaries by bloggers, historical fiction, cinema, computer games, advertisements, historical anecdotes, TV shows, propaganda by the state and other actors, and much more). It is important to keep in mind that source samples will vary depending on the generation and sphere of Russian society.

This study takes national and social – two of the most important elements of historical consciousness – as base criteria, for it is from their point of view that the main historical ideals of Russia's history have been formulated. Juxtaposing the historical conceptualizations found in literary and socio-political texts allows us to define six main paradigms of history that accord with these two criteria. Furthermore, each of these paradigms in turn can be shown to fall within our two primary discourses, the 'traditionalist' and 'liberal'. These paradigms, as will be made clear, give way to more general groupings on the basis of three main sets of values: (1) national state; (2) social justice; (3) human rights and liberties. Wherever conceptualizations are of a mixed character, one of these elements has been subordinated to the other. These observations, once juxtaposed with the database and the analysis of other source groups, allow us to identify two main discourses for grouping all the isolated paradigms such that they can be used as an analytical tool. All these categories are clarified in Table 1.1 in Appendix 1.

Determining to what extent a particular source group influences historical representations in society is a major challenge. According to a recent societal poll, 40 per cent of respondents stated that they derived historical representations from classical literature.[32] Such statistics should be treated with caution since it is often difficult for people to determine precisely what influences their own ideas. Yet, at the same time, indirect data (see Table 1.2/Appendix 2) shows that narrative sources are dominant sources in the contemporary communicative domain. For instance, classical literature – by which we mean so-called 'normative texts', often used in school instruction – exercises a particularly strong influence and continues to mould our views even after we have forgotten them. Analysis shows that these texts also have a longer shelf life than films, journalistic writings and the like. While cinema, journalism, television and other forms of mass media often affect the episodic component of long-term (historical) memory, texts that have a certain cultural standing tend to have a more lasting impact on language.

In this connection, it is interesting that most of the 'timeless' works of Russian literature (such as A. S. Pushkin, L. N. Tolstoy, I. S. Turgenev and others) depict societies that are full of historical representations belonging to the liberal discourse. To this category also belong a large number of the landmark works of Russian culture in the twentieth century (for example, *Doctor Zhivago* by B. L. Pasternak; *Children of the Arbat* by A. N. Rybakov; *In the First Circle* by A. I. Solzhenitsyn, and many others). Literary classics that belong to the conservative/traditionalist discourse are not as prominent in cultural memory, although it is possible to name a few important ones, such as *Crime and Punishment* by F. M. Dostoevsky, *White Guard* by M. A. Bulgakov, and *Battalions Ask for Fire* by Yu. V. Bondarev.

Over the course of the present study, we have developed a typology for categorizing the objects of historical memory (i.e. persons and events) in relation to what place they occupy in either the liberal or traditionalist models. There are three additional subdivisions that further characterize them: *consensus-objects*, *conflict-objects* and *ambiguous-objects*. Consensus-objects in national memory are objects around and between which there is general agreement. Conflict-objects are those objects that are depicted in direct opposition to the ideological position of the text in which they appear. Ambiguous-objects are objects within texts of a particular ideological position that evoke miscellaneous attitudes.

Some examples will help elucidate this terminology. Consensus-objects in national memory are above all cultural figures like Alexander Pushkin and Leo Tolstoy. They also include political actors from Ancient Rus' (largely seen as a conflict-free period in national memory) such as Alexander Nevsky, Ivan III and others. Alexander Suvorov and Pyotr Stolypin are two later figures that also qualify.

Ivan the Terrible is chronologically the first conflict-object, for he is seen positively in traditionalist (statist-patriotic) discourse and negatively in liberal discourse. The next divisive figure (and at the same time an ambiguous object in national memory) is Stepan Razin, the hero of the peasant war of the seventeenth century. While his actions are positively depicted in liberal-discourse texts, they are seen in multiple ways by traditionalist sources. Ambiguous-objects are not easily tied to one particular conceptualization and within paradigms are assessed in multiple ways. In certain situations, conflict-objects can also be ambiguous-objects.

Finally, it is worth pointing out that historical events are normally closely associated with historical figures. The Christianization of Russia, for example, is linked with Prince Vladimir I (St Vladimir), the Battle of the Neva, the Battle on the Ice with Alexander Nevsky and the Battle of Kulikovo Field with Dmitry Donskoy. This feature is particularly characteristic of pre-Petrine history. Overall, the historical memory of this period is markedly fuller with heroes than it is events.[33]

The Middle Ages as the 'Periphery' of national memory and Ivan the Terrible as the 'Name' of the Russian Middle Ages

Over ten years ago, the TV series *Name of Russia* (2008) – broadcast on the central channel Rossiia-1 – tallied the votes of its viewers regarding who they considered to be the most notable figure in Russian history. The final standings with the total number of votes were as follows: (1) Alexander Nevsky, 524,575; (2) Stolypin, 523,766; (3) Stalin, 519,071; (4) Pushkin, 516,608; (5) Peter I, 448,857; (6) Lenin, 306,520; (7) Dostoevsky, 348,634; (8) Suvorov, 329,028; (9) Mendeleev, 306,520; (10) Ivan the Terrible, 270,570; (11) Catherine II, 152,306; (12) Alexander II, 134,622.[34] At the time, the results of this opinion poll were met by a level of scepticism, in part because a separate poll carried out by the institute, Obshestvennoe Mnenie, the same year had yielded different results, with Alexander Nevsky occupying the fourteenth place, and Peter Stolypin not even appearing in the top twenty.[35] As such, the results seemed fabricated. Indeed, according to the latter study, the 'Name' of Russia should have been Joseph Stalin (but to avoid a scandal he was not declared the winner).

Our own data, shown in Appendix 2 (Table 1.2), ranks Alexander Nevsky among the most popular political persons in Russian national history and demarcates him as a consensus-object. Thus, his TV ranking was thoroughly realistic, even if ultimately it was not arrived at objectively. The majority of the most popular figures featured across source samples are consensus-objects. At the same time, Table 1.2 also shows that the Russian Middle Ages and its pantheon of heroes are located at the periphery of Russian historical memory. Paradoxically, the most popular figure of that time, and the only medieval figure to fall into the list of the most referenced figures in today's collective historical consciousness is Ivan the Terrible, also the first conflict-object in national memory.

This state of affairs is to some degree understandable. At the beginning of the modern period, an assembly of medieval heroes and events cemented itself in society's structure of historical representations and has undergone few substantial changes since. This pantheon, which has dominated historical consciousness in Russian society since the nineteenth century, has been clearly laid out in the work of D. A. Sosnitsky. He gives the ten most important objects of this pantheon as follows (listed chronologically): St Vladimir, Yaroslav the Wise, Prince Igor Svyatoslavich, Alexander Nevsky, the period of Tatar-Mongol rule, Dmitry Donskoy, Ivan the Terrible, the Oprichnina, Boris Godunov, Aleksey Mikhailovich and Stepan Razin.[36]

Overall, the changes that occurred to this pantheon over the course of the last 200 years have been minimal and have largely taken the form of a reshuffling of rankings. The most important development was the emergence and solidification of the concepts of 'Old' and 'New' Russia, according to which pre-Petrine Rus' began to be seen as the prehistory of 'New' Russia. These tendencies continued their development in the Soviet period where we see the newest iteration of the medieval pantheon and pre-Petrine Rus' relegated to the prehistory of prehistory. These developments had a number of positive and negative consequences for the practices of memory mobilization.

The positive consequence was that they led to clear representations of ancient/medieval/pre-Petrine Rus' as a sort of golden age. This was particularly the case for the period predating Mongol rule. All the historical figures of this epoch as well as those belonging to the Muscovite period are well-known in Russian collective consciousness and are objects of positive consensus in Russian historical memory. At the same time, this state of affairs has also made it easy for the politics to exploit these objects: large-scale political and religious occasions are dedicated to them, statues of them are erected, submarines and military awards are named in their honour, their images are printed on banknotes and so on. In other words, these figures have been used to legitimize political regimes across the Russian/Soviet/post-Soviet continuum. A negative implication of their fame has been that the figures of the pantheon have begun to fade and diminish from an actual historical perspective. Indeed, buttressed by the results of societal polls, present-day scholarship on cultural and communicative memory shows that contemporary historical consciousness pays little attention to the pre-Petrine epoch.[37]

Heroes of the Russian Middle Ages and the 'war' over memory

The national memory of the pre-Petrine period has seen little change over the last 170 years. This is shown in part by Table 1.3 in Appendix 3,[38] which gives rankings for objects of memory across various source samples pertaining to the late imperial period (the second half of the nineteenth and start of the twentieth centuries).

The range of objects represented across the various source types is narrow. Table 1.3 also shows that with the exception of monumental sculptures, a category populated exclusively by positive consensus-objects, the other categories feature a conflict-object – Ivan the Terrible – as a high-ranking figure. The dominance of Ivan the Terrible in the pre-Petrine pantheon of heroes continues through to this day. He is both the most referenced figure from the Russian Middle Ages and the dominant topic of research in the field of memory studies both in Russia[39] and abroad.[40] That being said, other personalities, such as Alexander Nevsky,[41] Vladimir the Great,[42] Yaroslav the Wise[43] and Dmitry Donskoy,[44] are still able to command significant, albeit comparatively less attention. This situation is can be explained by the memory politics of the period. The high frequency of pre-Petrine heroes in the media has been largely associated with awards and the naming of churches in their honour. It is also worth remembering that the highest military distinctions in the imperial period were the Order of Saint Alexander Nevsky (1725) and the Order of Saint Vladimir (1782). Monumental sculptures in the pre-revolutionary period were dedicated to either consensus-objects or, at the very least, to personalities who were not controversial within the memory politics of the time. Obviously, Ivan the Terrible did not satisfy either of these conditions (recall, for example, N. M. Karamzin's negative depiction of him).[45]

The Revolution of 1917 brought substantial changes to Russian memory politics. Yet, while it prompted a reappraisal of the heroes of 'New' Russia, the same was not true of the pantheon of figures and events of the pre-Petrine period, which did not undergo significant changes. See Table 1.4 in Appendix 4.

It is probable that the most substantial change was the reappraisal of Stepan Razin, the leader of the great peasant war of the seventeenth century, who in

Soviet memory politics was presented as the main revolutionary of the pre-Petrine period. Although, in fact, this reappraisal was a continuation of a trend of the pre-revolutionary period when Razin was already becoming a more popular figure in literature and journalism, and had already become one in cinema (a medium that catered to the demands of a broader public).[46] In contrast, despite positive appraisals of him in the historiography and the cultural politics of Stalinism from the late 1930s to the early 1950s, Ivan the Terrible remained a divisive figure and no public monuments were built in his honour during the Soviet period. Probably the figure that suffered the greatest loss in standing was that of St Vladimir, who was closely associated with the Christian religion and hence a problematic personality for the atheistic Soviet state. Nonetheless, the official historiography of the period continued, for the most part, to present the actual Christianization of Kievan Rus' as generally positive since it contributed to the development of the Russian state. Accordingly, the regime had no major bones to pick with Vladimir himself – a fact that explains why he remained amid the ranks of the most significant historical figures, despite his overall fall in the rankings. Of all the pre-Petrine figures, it was Alexander Nevsky who was most important for the regime's memory politics because he could be presented as a warrior who had fought against a hostile 'West' intent on destroying the Russian state.

The eventual collapse of totalitarianism at the end of the 1980s and the start of the 1990s brought about a further major reassessment of the recent past. Again, however, the popularity of figures and events from the pre-Petrine period were little impacted by it. See Table 1.5 in Appendix 5.

As Table 1.5 shows, the democratization and modernization of the post-Soviet period did little to change Alexander Nevsky and Ivan the Terrible, two of the most important 'defenders' of pre-Petrine Russia from the West. Ivan the Terrible, in particular, became the central figure in a 'war' over memory over monuments that resulted from the regime's liberalization. This was marked by the appearance of alternative objects, often in the form of a bloodied stake, alongside 'parade' monuments.[47] Sober scholarly assessments interpret this wave of memorials to Ivan of Terrible to reflect the memory politics of Putin's regime, which has sought to promote the image of a powerful sovereign who reconquers lost lands and defends Russia against the West.[48] Stepan Razin was one of the Soviet heroes to fall from grace as a result of this development. An interesting phenomenon is the increasing popularity of Rurik, which can probably be explained by a whole series of state commemorations of the last decades.[49] St Vladimir's rise in popularity has been the inevitable outcome of the newly strengthened role of the Orthodox Church in political and social life. The findings of Table 1.6 are important in this regard as they show St Vladimir in second place according to the number of Orthodox churches that are named after him. The Church also employs other practices aimed to increase the popularity of medieval personalities, above all the dissemination of various forms of visual content. For the sale of icons, Vladimir is also advertised as the patron saint of the Ministry of Internal Affairs. Such associations are likely to increase the market for Vladimir iconography.[50]

The radical transformation of the information sphere over the last twenty years has done little to change the perception of the medieval pantheon in Russian society. This is supported by the analysis of variety of internet sources shown in Table 1.7. These sources include the most popular social media sites in Russia: VKontakte, Instagram and the Russian language Wikipedia (Table 1.7).

These statistics highlight certain differences across various online sites. In our opinion, these differences are not so much the result of distinct user-groups, but of the way in which these sites are structured and operate. Wikipedia allocates considerable space to the foundations of the Muscovite state and this is a probable reason for Ivan III's high ranking (second) on that site. In turn, many references to Saints Peter and Fevronia on VKontakte and Instagram reflect their cultural status as patron saints of lovers (official mass media also promotes their name day as an alternative to Valentine's Day). Content that is associated with these groups and hashtags is not so much interacted with actual historical figures as they are related to public holidays, in this case, a semi-official holiday had begun in 2008 – National day of conjugal love and familial happiness.[51] At the same time, it is important to point out that the host of medieval objects that are represented in these so-called new media, or social networking services, remains fairly traditional in its composition.

Table 1.6 The number of Russian orthodox churches named after medieval figures. Compiled using 'Karta Russkoi Pravoslavnoi Tserki, Beta-Versiia', *Offitsial'nyi Sait Moskovskogo Patriarchata*, accessed 11 august 2017, http://map.patriarhia.ru/?map=59.93093,30.3619,10&t=0.

No.	Patron saint	Number of churches
1.	Alexander Nevsky	281
2.	St Vladimir (Vladimir the Great)	117
3.	Ol'ga of Kiev	46
4.	Dmitry Donskoy	38
5.	Andrey Bogolyubsky	1
6.	Yaroslav the Wise	1

Table 1.7 The popularity of objects of historical memory in various online sources. Statistics taken from E. A. Rostovtsev and D. A. sosnitskii, 'Srednevekovye geroi i sobytiia otechestvennoi istorii v setevykh resursakh', *Istoricheskaia ekspertiza*, no. 1 (2018): 41–58; and Rostovtsev, 'The Immortal Host of Prince Igor', 883–903.

Ranking	Number of entry views on Wikipedia (Russian language, 2015–17)[a]	Popularity according to number of hashtags on VKontakte, 1–7 September 2017[b]	Most referenced object of historical (medieval) memory in among social groups on VKontakte alongside the number of posts that reference them (accessed on 8 September 2017)	Popularity ranking of historical memory objects according to number of hashtags and posts on Instagram (accessed on 8 September 2017)
1.	Ivan the Terrible 3,615,404	St Vladimir 24 (28)	Alexander Nevsky 62,714	St Vladimir 10,816
2.	Ivan III 2,375,008	Dmitry Donskoy 19 (20)	St Vladimir/ the Fair Sun (*krasno sol'nyshko*)/ Prince Vladimir 48,587	Alexander Nevsky 9,368
3.	St Vladimir 2,195,252	Alexander Nevsky 16 (17)	Ivan the Terrible 16,451	SS Peter and Fevronia 9,195
4.	The Christianization of Rus' 2,115,157	Sergiy Radonezhsky 14 (14)	Sergiy Radonezhsky 16,156	Rurik dynasty 8,842
5.	The Battle of Kulikovo Field 2,096,034	SS Peter and Fevronia 10 (10)	Andrei Rublev 14,496	Ivan the Terrible 7,963
6.	Alexander Nevsky 1,729,935	Ivan the Terrible 9 (9)	Dmitry Donskiy 11,023	Boris Godunov 4,374
7.	Rurik 1,413,032	Andrei Rublev 5 (34)	Stepan Razin 8,663	Dmitry Donskoy 3,298
8.	The Battle on the Ice 1,367,238	Stepan Razin 3 (15)	Olga of Kiev 3,297	Yuri Dolgorukiy 2,179
9.	The Time of Troubles 1,311,790	Yaroslav the Wise 2 (3)	SS Peter and Fevronia 2,615	Yaroslav the Wise 2,075
10.	Yaroslav the Wise 1,248,940	The Mongol Yoke 1	Yaroslav the Wise 1,623	Olga of Kiev 1,770

[a] From Wikipedia, accessed 15 August 2017, https://ru.wikipedia.org/wiki/.

[b] The numbers in parentheses denote the total number of entries that include the name of the respective object. Numbers without parenthesis indicate the number of references that are directly dedicated to the respective object.

The state's memory politics is in part responsible for the above state of affairs in so far as it has made use of the same consensus-objects that people learn about in school. From the erection of memorials to medieval heroes to the development of all sorts of computer games – this should all be understood within the framework of this phenomenon.[52] Figures such as Alexander Nevsky and Dmitry Donskoy have for a while been heavily used figures, with a number of warships, military and religious distinctions,[53] in addition to a great number of sites are already named in their honour. However, ongoing competition between Ukraine and Russia has intensified attempts to 'eternalize' as one's own memory of pre-Mongol Russian heroes. Here, in particular, the figures of Vladimir the Great and Yaroslav the Wise – two ancient Russian princes, canonized by the Russian Orthodox Church – are the most used figures in the ongoing fight over history (see also Chapter 2 by Kati Parppei in this volume).

It is worth noting that the cultivation of St Vladimir's image began within the religious tradition of pre-Mongol Rus' – a period that preceded modern notions of the nation and the state. Yet, the foundational features of the myth of St Vladimir have remained unchanged for many centuries. For example, the tradition of venerating his church, which begun in the eleventh century, continues today. The apostolic-like sacrality of Vladimir's image almost certainly explains its centrality to incipient nation-building from the fifteenth to and seventeenth centuries, and to the formation of a Great-Russian identity and an all-Russian myth. However, the secularization of social consciousness and of historical culture and the emergence of the concepts of 'New' and 'Old' Russia in the eighteenth and nineteenth centuries gradually transformed Vladimir into a 'rank-and-file hero', even in the face of attempts by state-led memory politics to break this trend. And while on the whole Vladimir remained a positive consensus-object, this development naturally intensified during the Soviet period. Having said all of this, the 'war' over memory that has unravelled since then in the post-Soviet expanse has led to renewed attempts to make political use out of his figure, likely securing his place among the assemblage of key national heroes in a number of East-European states.

In contrast to Vladimir and other figures of pre-Petrine history, the myth of Yaroslav the Wise had a comparatively later genesis, namely in the nineteenth and early twentieth centuries. On the one hand, this explains his low ranking as an important object of national memory in contemporary Russia as well as his belated entry into the sacred pantheon. On the other hand, this gives us reason to think he, too, will become a long-standing entry, especially when one considers the extent to which his personified values are central to the modern

Weltanschauung (he is seen as the founder of a Russian national ideology and of Russian law; a unifier of Russian lands; and a European ruler). The contest over Yaroslav's legacy and memory, fought between Russian and Ukrainian elites, has and continues to ensure the figure's constant presence in social consciousness.[54]

Overall, the number of sites associated with St Vladimir is greater in Ukraine. This has been in large part due to the funding of projects for renaming places previously honouring now-former communist and Soviet figures. At least thirty-seven localities in Ukraine have street names named after Vladimir. For instance: Prince Vladimir Street in Dnipro (once Dnipropetrovsk) was formerly Plexanov Street; Voroshilov Street in Kherson has become Vladimir the Great Street; in Brovary, a suburb of Kiev, Engels Street has become Prince Vladimir Street; and so on. Although Russia has comparatively few Vladimir landmarks – one village on the outskirts of Moscow has a Vladimir street; in St Petersburg there is a Vladimir square; and in the city of Vladimir there is a Prince Vladimir cemetery – that number is likely to increase. In Ukraine, Vladimir's image appears on banknotes (one hryvnia) as well as on coins (five and ten hryvnia). In Russia, he appears on silver three and five-ruble coins, a more limited circulation. The first of these coins depicts St Vladimir's Cathedral in Kherson; the second shows a part of the Millennium of Russia monument in Veliky Novgorod, which depicts Vladimir as a baptizer. The annexation of Crimea and the Russian propaganda that accompanied it have intensified the memory politics surrounding the figure. Putin, for instance, speaking on the annexation on 4 November 2014, made the following reference to Vladimir in his address to the Federal Assembly: 'It was after all here in Crimea, in ancient Kherson, or Korsun' as the ancient Russian chroniclers called it, that Prince Vladimir accepted Christianity and thereafter baptized Russia.'[55] Exactly two years after making this reference, Putin oversaw the erection of a monumental Vladimir statue alongside the Kremlin. At its consecration, he defined what the medieval figure represented as follows: 'Prince Vladimir will forever be remembered as a gatherer and defender of the Russian lands – a longsighted politician who laid the foundations of a strong, unitary, centralized state that unified into one large family a multitude of equal peoples, languages, cultures and religions.'[56]

The figure Yaroslav the Wise has been no less subject of intense engagement. In 1993, Boris Yeltsin opened a monument to the medieval figure. In 1997 a monument was also erected in Kiev. Interestingly, while the Russian version has the prince holding a model of the Kremlin of the city of Yaroslav in his right hand, the Ukrainian Yaroslav holds the Cathedral of St Sophia in Kiev. In Ukraine in 1995, the Order of Prince Yaroslav the Wise[57] was founded as the highest public award, which it remained until 1998. Meanwhile, in Russia, the provincial Duma of Yaroslav province introduced a law on 23 December 2014 that established among its public holidays a remembrance day for Prince Yaroslav (5 March).[58] A further example of how Ukraine and Russia have competed over Yarsolav's memory is in his depiction on banknotes. Already in 1992, Ukraine had a two-hryvnia note with Yaroslav's image (there was also a two-hryvnia coin with the same depiction). In Russia in 2001, Yaroslav was depicted on the 1000-ruble banknote, the highest-value banknote at the time. Another example is universities. In 1995, Yaroslav's name was given to two universities in Russia and Ukraine at practically the same time – Novgorod State University and the National Law Academy of Ukraine (formerly named after F. E. Dzerzhinksy).[59] This unique rivalry also continues at the church level. In 2004 Yaroslav was entered into the menology of the Ukrainian Orthodox Church (Moscow Patriarchate), and the following year the Russian Orthodox Church gave him his own remembrance day (20 February). In 2008 Yaroslav was canonized as a saintly prince by the Church Council of the Ukrainian Orthodox Church (Kievan Patriarchate). Likewise, on 2–3 February 2016, a decision of the Bishops' Council of the Russian Orthodox Church determined Yaroslav to be a nationally venerated figure.[60] All these examples show how the contest over Yaroslav's memory has inevitably given him a place in the community of saintly figures.[61]

Finally, it is worth noting the appearance of an entirely new object on the Russian map of memory at the turn of the twentieth century, namely Prince Igor's Host as described in the legend, *The Lay of the Host of Igor*. The *Lay* is the most popular cultural artefact from the period of Ancient Rus' and has been used in language instruction in schools in Russia (and Ukraine and Belorussia today) for over 150 years.[62] An obvious feature about the *Lay*, independent of the question of its authorship, is that by the time it was first discovered and introduced into public discourse (in the nineteenth century), the pre-Mongol period had already become, not merely an infinitely far, mythical period, but a heroic age that occupied a consensus-space in Russia's national memory. Furthermore, it appeared right at a time of growing divergence between liberal and more conservative pictures of Russian history, particularly in their respective assessments of the period of 'New' Russia. Under these circumstances the poem became an important unifying cultural artefact, being quickly recognized in both political camps and cementing itself in cultural memory and social consciousness. In the Soviet period, the poem remained in the ranks of essential historical-cultural objects, and it was also instrumentalized in propaganda. The latter trend predetermined ideologically laden historiographical discussions as well as the support of a new generation of sceptically minded thinkers from the liberal-oppositionist *intelligentsia*. Nevertheless, none of these disputes was able to seriously dislodge the poem's place in cultural memory, which was based not so much on propaganda-installed ideology or historiography, but on artistic and literary works as well as educational traditions. In the culture of contemporary East-European states, *The Lay of the Host of Igor* continues to be a widely manipulated object of memory. Even the Donetsk People's Republic did not miss an opportunity to make use of the legend in their own 'war' over memory by establishing a national park which it claimed to have been the location of the legend's events.[63] Another curious, although entirely expected development has been the legend's appearance in the *Hybrid War* poems, in which Igor's legendary host is associated with the military detachments of Igor Strelkov.[64]

Conclusion

A pantheon of medieval figures and events has cemented itself in Russian collective memory as a result of a long historical process. There is no reason to believe that this pantheon will be easily changed. Overall, the size of this pantheon is very narrow and it is unlikely that we will see the addition of new members. As we have shown, fundamental changes in memory politics and collective ideologies over the last several centuries exerted only a minute influence on this assembly of figures and events. At the same time, various social upheavals have diminished the overall relevance and significance of ancient heroes in the collective memory. Already at the beginning of the nineteenth century, pre-Petrine Rus' began to be understood as merely a prehistory to the history of 'New Russia.' And after 1917, this period was further relegated to a kind of preface for a prehistory. In other words, the Soviet period in fact further marginalized 'Ancient Rus'' in Russian historical consciousness. Modern heroes decisively replaced ancient ones in the memory of the national past.

Yet, despite their marginalization in memory, these medieval objects continue to play a substantive role in historical culture and in the politics of history in contemporary Russia. This is because the majority of these figures have solidly established themselves in cultural memory and collective historical consciousness as consensus-objects. 'Golden-age' heroes also continue to prove that they have particular currency in a wide range of cultural and social practices, such as computer games, tourism, advertisement and the memory wars of the post-Soviet domain. In this context, the peculiar character of Russian medievalism seems to be that it addresses types of objects that are extremely rare in the Russian mnemonic continuum, namely positive heroes who are acceptable to all members of society irrespective of political views or ideological preferences. In our opinion, this particular character remains to be explained.

2

'A thousand years of history'
References to the past in the addresses to the Federal Assembly by the president of Russia, 2000–19

Kati Parppei

Introduction

On 8 April 2020, during his meeting with regional heads on combatting the spread of the coronavirus in Russia, President Vladimir Putin announced that 'Our country has suffered through many ordeals: both Pechenegs and Cumans attacked, and Russia got through it all. We will also defeat this coronavirus infection. Together, we can overcome anything.'[1] This comparison of a virus pandemic to the ancient nuisance of Kievan Rus' – peoples from the steppe – aroused amused as well as bemused reactions on social media.[2] However, it is a fine example of how the idea of a national past, a national historical narrative, is used to pepper the contemporary political rhetoric in Russia and to add symbolic value to the message conveyed.[3]

To contextualize the contemporary political rhetoric utilizing references to history, it is essential to begin by briefly examining the formation of the national narrative of the collective past in Russia, since certain layers of meanings can be traced all the way from the Middle Ages to contemporary discourses, as also demonstrated by E. A. Rostovtsev in the previous chapter. They are also reflected in the ideas and images of history as they are presented in Russia today.

Dating back all the way from medieval textual sources, a certain dualistic tone has dominated the representations of Rus'/Russia in relation to other ethnic and religious groups, and later on, other nations.[4] This, of course, is not a unique phenomenon; collective identities in general, including national ones, are formed and formulated in relation to 'other'.[5] In medieval texts, produced in the area of contemporary Russia and preserved from the fourteenth century onwards, the basic juxtaposition exists between Orthodox Christians and Muslims, pagans and other Christians.

During the sixteenth century, this textual trend was further accelerated and combined with ideas of the history of the Muscovite power as a continuum.[6] Also, the ideas of unity and strong central power, expressed in Russian political rhetoric for centuries – and today – can be traced to the text production and consolidation of the Muscovite power structure in the sixteenth century.[7]

These idea(l)s, as applicable to the premodern Russian Empire as they had been in medieval Moscow, were transferred to national history writing during the eighteenth and nineteenth centuries, when the first historians – professional and amateur ones alike – used medieval texts, such as chronicles and tales, as their source material in sketching cohesive narratives of the national past. Thus, for instance, the perceptions of allegedly decisive battles and other events, created in the fifteenth and sixteenth centuries contexts and in accordance with contemporary political interests, were transferred more or less as such to national narrative in formation.[8]

The collectively traumatic occupation by Napoleon's troops of Moscow in 1812 further accelerated the geopolitical and cultural search for 'Russianness' in relation to other nations. Also, new ideas of the 'West' as an entity hostile to the Russian Empire per se began to form. Simultaneously, during the nineteenth century, growing literacy and the emergence of printed popular publications contributed to the distribution of imagery of Russia's past and present among ordinary Russian people.[9]

The ideas based on the medieval texts and further formulated during the nineteenth century found their applications in the twentieth- and twenty-first-century discourses, as well. For instance, in contemporary Russia 'fascists' have acquired a role of an external archenemy of some kind, but beneath the surface, this enemy image has features of all the previous external threats found in the national narrative of Russia.[10]

In general, the usability of history for political purposes is valued highly in Russia. For instance, President Vladimir Putin has stated the importance of history to national coherence numerous times. He has also named 'distortion of history' as one of the major threats in contemporary Russia, and promoted the production of unified history textbooks for schools.[11]

History education in contemporary Russia has taken many forms. For instance, theme parks called 'Russia – My History' (*Rossiia – moia istoriia*) have been established in larger cities around Russia. The project has been carried out by instances such as the Patriarchal Council for Culture and the Foundation for Humanitarian Projects, and supported by, for instance, Gazprom. The parks use multimedia to create colourful representations of the national history all the way from the Middle Ages to the present. These theme parks, one of the main target groups of which are schoolchildren, have been criticized by professional academics for being historically inaccurate and propagandistic by nature.[12] However, they can be seen as some kind of showcase of the collective imagery of history that the contemporary power structure of Russia wants to convey and distribute.

Another showcase is the references to history made by presidents of Russia in their major speeches. This article examines the addresses to the Federal Assembly during 2000–19, the time span covering the presidential tenures of Vladimir Putin (1999–2008, 2012–ongoing) and Dmitrii Medvedev (2008–12). The focus is explicitly on these addresses since their audience and distribution are wider than talks about special issues or to specific audiences, some of which would give more information on, for instance, Putin's ideas about history in general, or other related themes touched upon in this article.[13] The message of these addresses is aimed at the people of Russia as a whole; in addition, they are conveyed to international audiences as well. Also, they give a chance to examine how history is used to treat contemporary political and socio-economical issues, which form the main part of the addresses to the Federal Assembly.

In general, the twenty-first-century presidents of Russia have referred to Russia's past only occasionally in these speeches. The theme has not been touched on in every address, while some deal more with historical issues. However, certain patterns in the references can be found. Most of the references have taken place in several, partly overlapping contexts.

The article categorizes, contextualizes and examines a representative sample of these references according to their assumed function. The first chapter is about the general consolidation of patriotic feelings. The second one examines how historical rhetoric has been used in the context of contemporary threats. The third chapter concentrates on the use of history for justifying certain decisions and acts by the power structure.

The focus of this examination is explicitly on the references to history, especially to medieval history and ideas of a long span of the collective past. The viewpoint is that of a historian examining how the idea of common history shared by all Russians is put into use in the addresses to Federal Assembly – and similarly to a large audience, domestic and abroad – and how the national historical narrative is formulated and referred to by the presidents. For further arguments and understanding of the political rhetoric and its connection to ideas and ideologies of the presidents of Russia, a wide array of literature is available.

Patriotism: 'Cultural traditions and common historic memory'

On 8 July 2000, Vladimir Putin, the newly elected president of Russia, gave a speech to the Federal Assembly. At the beginning of the new millennium, Russia was in a turbulent state, and after pondering upon serious demographic and economic challenges, Putin called for 'common goals', to which he included spiritual and moral ones. In this context he noted:

> The unity of Russia is strengthened by the patriotism inherent in our people, by cultural traditions and the common historic memory. And today in Russian art, in theatre and the cinema, there is a growth of interest in Russian history, in our roots and what is dear to us all. This, without doubt – I, at any rate, am certain of this – is the beginning of new spiritual development.[14]

Patriotism is something Putin emphasized right from the beginning of his presidential career. Along with numerous reforms, he attempted to promote the idea of national belonging.[15] One of his tools was a familiar one, used already in the nineteenth century for the same purpose across Europe: the idea of the common history of the fatherland.[16] It can be said that his view on the past in this sense is quite pragmatic: according to him, history shapes the past as well as determines the future of Russia, and it should be effectively used to inspire people to serve their country.[17]

President Dmitrii Medvedev, in turn, made a connection between patriotism and history in his first address to the Federal Assembly on 5 November 2008. His ideas on history were slightly more on the critical side: 'There is patriotism, along with the most sober and critical look at our country's history and our far from ideal present, belief in Russia that shines through no matter what the circumstances.'[18]

When talking about the importance of the constitution in the context of civil rights, Medvedev expressed an even more disapproving view on certain aspects of Russia's past:

> The cult of the state and the illusory wisdom of the administrative apparatus have prevailed in Russia over many centuries. Individuals with their rights and freedoms, personal interests and problems, have been seen as at best a means

and at worst an obstacle for strengthening the state's might. This view endured throughout many centuries.[19]

In general, references to history in the addresses increase from 2012 onwards, also in the context of patriotic encouragement. In the address of 2012, given by Putin as he had once again been elected to the presidency, history was brought out more than before. The year had been declared the Year of Russian History, and more effective usage of the collective past seems to have been a part of the development of Putin's approach to nationalism and his ideas of Russia's future after his re-election.[20]

In the address, he took a firmer stance on patriotism and defined that being a patriot 'means not only to treat one's national history with love and respect, although, of course, that is very important, but first and foremost to serve one's country and society. As Solzhenitsyn said, patriotism is an organic, natural feeling'.[21] Putin further brought out the long span of history:

> In order to revive national consciousness, we need to link historical eras and get back to understanding the simple truth that Russia did not begin in 1917, or even in 1991, but rather, that we have a common, continuous history spanning over one thousand years, and we must rely on it to find inner strength and purpose in our national development.[22]

The idea of 'linking historical eras' and a 'common, continuous history' implicitly includes the universal national romantic idea of the history of a nation as a continuum, interpreted in hindsight to find causalities and even a purpose.[23] This, according to Putin, is a 'simple truth', which does not need any further arguments or justification.

The rhetorical value of this notion is strong in emphasizing the continuity between the past, present and future of Russia. For instance, in his address on 1 March 2018, Putin talked about 'the thousand-year-long history of our nation' when talking about Russia's ability 'to develop and renew itself, discover new territories, build cities, conquer space and make major discoveries'.[24] The repeated notion of the history of a thousand years in the addresses is thus a good example of 'banal medievalism' as formulated by Andrew B. R. Elliott; 'a sense of generic pastness' rather than any detailed reference to a past event, aimed at emphasizing a certain point in the present.[25] Also, by emphasizing the long history of Russia, the focus could be conveniently shifted from the problematic and awkward Soviet era, difficult to use effectively for political purposes.[26]

In the 2012 address to the Federal Assembly, the collective past of Russia was linked more prominently to military history than in previous addresses.

President Putin praised the revival of historical societies in Russia, and thanked 'the search parties that are restoring the names of heroes for our nation and for their families, honourably interring the remains of soldiers who fell in the Great Patriotic War and caring for war memorials'.[27] Further, he called for a memorial for the soldiers of the First World War, and underlined the importance of the remembrance of the past for the military success of Russia: 'Meanwhile, the morale of our Armed Forces is held up by traditions, by a living connection to history, by the examples of bravery and selflessness of our heroes'.[28]

For dealing with the awkwardness of Soviet times, the 'Great Patriotic War' has offered an especially usable option, and it is the most frequent of the historical events referred to in the addresses. Its importance in the history politics of Russia has grown all through the post-Soviet decades, finding its most prominent and emotional expressions in the celebrations of Victory Day on 9 May.[29] The memory of war, combined with celebrations and activities, offers people a unifying experience with positive connotations of victory and success (albeit also with loss and suffering).

Also, the imagery concerning the war has almost limitless rhetorical possibilities to be utilized for consolidating societal cohesion from above. For instance, President Putin announced in 2005:

> Our people fought against slavery. They fought for the right to live on their own land, to speak their native language and have their own statehood, culture and traditions. They fought for justice and for freedom. They stood up for their right to independent development and they gave our Motherland a future.[30]

In this light, the warnings against 'distortion of history', mentioned earlier, fit in the picture, for they have been mainly aimed at revisionist and competing views on the war and the role of the Soviet Union and its troops in the events, represented, for instance, in Eastern European countries.[31]

Of the other events and issues of the twentieth century, only fleetingly has Putin mentioned 'historical divides that are still alive in people's memory and major challenges Russia had to face over the course of its history'.[32] On 1 December 2016, after the legislative elections, he praised the result and added:

> I am not talking, of course, about any kind of dogmas or a false unity put on for show, and I am certainly not talking about imposing a particular world view. We have already gone through all of this in our history, as you know, and we have no intention of returning to the past.[33]

He also noted that the following year, 2017, marked the centenary of the February and October revolutions and called for 'an objective, honest and deep-reaching analysis of these events'. He reminded his audience that 'we need history's lessons primarily for reconciliation and for strengthening the social, political and civil concord that we have managed to achieve':

> It is unacceptable to drag the grudges, anger and bitterness of the past into our life today, and in pursuit of one's own political and other interests to speculate on tragedies that concerned practically every family in Russia, no matter what side of the barricades our forebears were on. Let us remember that we are a single people, a united people, and we have only one Russia.[34]

Thus, the history of Russia, as the presidents have treated it in their addresses, offers grounds for patriotic feelings and collective pride, but also warning examples of discord and disunity. As we shall see in the next section, the latter has been implicitly presented as a major threat to the overall development of the country.

Unity as protection against threats: 'A unique community of peoples'

The collapse of the Soviet Union was a complicated geopolitical process, resulting in (still ongoing) turbulence and conflicts in the frontier areas of post-Soviet Russia and its neighbours. In the beginning of the new millennium, the persistent tensions in Northern Caucasus were once again escalating. In October 2002, a hostage crisis in a theatre in Moscow took place, ending with the death of at least 170 people. In March 2003, a referendum was held, re-integrating Chechnya back into Russia.

On 16 May (only four days after a suicide bombing claimed the lives of almost sixty and injured some in Znamenskoe in Chechnya), President Vladimir Putin addressed the Federal Assembly in his annual speech. Not surprisingly, one of his themes was contemporary threats: the proliferation of nuclear weapons, and the spread of terrorism, for which he criticized 'certain countries' that 'sometimes use their strong and well-armed national armies to increase their zones of strategic influence rather than fighting these evils we all face'.[35]

What the president suggested as the main strategy for warding off the threat posed by external as well as internal enemies was the traditional one: cherishing and consolidating national unity. For this, history – and invoking the idea of the 'historic fate' of Russia in the spirit of banal medievalism – proved a useful tool:

> [. . .] throughout our history Russia and its people have accomplished and continue to accomplish a truly historical feat, a great work performed in the name of our country's integrity and in the name of bringing it peace and a stable life. Maintaining a state spread over such a vast territory and preserving a unique community of peoples while keeping up a strong presence on the international stage is not just an immense labour, it is also a task that has cost our people untold victims and sacrifice. Such has been Russia's historic fate over these thousand and more years.[36]

Not surprisingly, this alleged essential unity *(edinstvo)* of the peoples of the area governed by Russia/the Soviet Union was a theme that was constantly repeated in the addresses of the following years, as tensions and unrest in Northern Caucasus continued. In the address to the Federal Assembly on 25 April 2005, President Putin noted the following, drawing attention from the media abroad:

> Above all, we should acknowledge that the collapse of the Soviet Union was a major geopolitical disaster of the century. As for the Russian nation, it became a genuine drama. Tens of millions of our co-citizens and compatriots found themselves outside Russian territory. Moreover, the epidemic of disintegration infected Russia itself.[37]

This rhetorically powerful and rare reference to the Soviet Union as an integrated unit, the collapse of which was the starting point of disintegration (as an undesirable, disease-like opposite of unification and unity) was connected to the approaching sixtieth anniversary of the end of the Second World War, in connection with which Putin also reminded about learning from the past:

> It is clear for us that this victory was not achieved through arms alone but was won also through the strong spirit of all the peoples who were united at that time within a single state. Their unity emerged victorious over inhumanity, genocide and the ambitions of one nation to impose its will on others. But the terrible lessons of the past also define imperatives for the present. And Russia, bound to the former Soviet republics – now independent countries – through a common history, and through the Russian language and the great culture that we share, cannot stay away from the common desire for freedom.[38]

During 2006 and 2007, in addition to the persisting problems caused by Caucasian Islamists to the government of Russia, the opposition was becoming more active in the form of a coalition called 'Other Russia', organizing rallies and marches against Putin's administration. Undoubtedly, these developments added to the need to further emphasize the importance of national cohesion and rely on the idea(l) of historical unity as the foundation of Russia's development:

> Having a unique cultural and spiritual identity has never stopped anyone from building a country open to the world. Russia has made a tremendous contribution to the formation of European and world culture. Our country has historically developed as a union of many peoples and cultures, and the idea of a common community, a community in which people of different nationalities and religions live together, has been at the foundation of the Russian people's spiritual outlook for many centuries now.[39]

Along with the idea of unity, the uniqueness of Russian culture and history emerged in the rhetoric of the president. On 5 November 2008, after the Russo-Georgian war for the regions of South Ossetia and Abkhazia had taken place in August, President Dmitrii Medvedev emphasized, 'interethnic peace is one of our key values. Historically we have enjoyed a unique and extraordinarily rich experience of tolerance and mutual respect.' He mentioned the unity of the multiethnic people – and once again, 'a thousand years of history' – in Russia several times during his speech:

> I think it could hardly be otherwise when we are talking about a people with more than a thousand years of history, a people that have developed and brought civilisation to a vast territory, created a unique culture and built up powerful economic and military potential, a people who act on the solid basis of values and ideals that have taken shape over the centuries and stood the test of time.[40]

From references to history in the addresses to the Federal Assembly, the emphasis on this allegedly unique unity is the most prominent one. On 12 December 2012 – as problems in the Caucasus area persisted – Vladimir Putin once again underlined the multiethnicity of Russia right from the beginning:

> We must value the unique experience passed on to us by our forefathers. For centuries, Russia developed as a multi-ethnic nation (from the very beginning), a civilization-state bonded by the Russian people, Russian language and Russian culture native for all of us, uniting us and preventing us from dissolving in this diverse world.[41]

The question of who Russians are and of whom the Russian people is composed of has been a crucial one ever since the 1990s, reflected on the changing and fluctuating meanings of the concepts *russkii* and *rossiiskii/rossianin* (both translated as 'Russian', but the first referring to ethnic Russianness while the second rather to 'civil' belonging).[42] For our viewpoint, it is interesting to note that the often-used persuasive argument is that Russia has 'always' consisted of numerous ethnic and religious groups and that the internal unity, as some kind of a natural state for the nation, is the most important guarantee against any threats.

This notion provides an interesting contrast to the Western European national narratives, mostly based on the idea(l)s of one people and one language.[43] It also differs from national romantic ideas in Russia; even though de facto in the eighteenth and nineteenth centuries, the Russian Empire consisted of multiple cultures and religions, the national narrative in formation was basically about Orthodox Russians and their past – even though the borderline between them and other East Slavic groups such as Ukrainians and Belarusians was not always so clear – as modelled by medieval and premodern history writing.[44]

Rather, the twenty-first-century ideas seem to reflect echoes of the fluctuating policies towards non-Russians in the Soviet Union; despite certain periods of repression, the general tendency was to tolerate and, to some extent, even support the existence of diverse languages and cultures in the area on condition that loyalty to the central power was not compromised.[45] The emphasis on the allegedly unique multiethnic and multicultural nature of Russia also flirts with Eurasianistic ideas, even though in realpolitik and economical thinking a certain distance has been kept from the ideology as a whole.[46]

The seemingly inclusive emphasis on the multiculturality and multiethnicity of the region by the contemporary Russian central administration can also be seen as downplaying the factual diversity of the area. A certain ethnic hierarchy, promoting the inherent primality of ethnic Russianness, has either implicitly or explicitly coexisted with the idea of a historically multiethnic nation.[47]

The years 2014 and 2015 were turbulent ones for Russia in its dealings with its neighbours and beyond: in 2014, the revolution in Ukraine took place, leading to the annexation of Crimea, and in September 2015 Russia had started the military intervention in the Syrian Civil War. In addition, on 24 November, the Turkish Air Force had shot down a Russian military aircraft near the border of Syria and Turkey. The increased tensions in external politics can be seen in the address to the Federal Assembly on 3 December 2015.

President Putin called Russia's 'ethnic and religious accord' the 'historical foundation for our society and the Russian statehood' and continued by announcing that the 'fight against terrorism' has the full support of the Russian people, who firmly believe 'that we must defend our national interests, history, traditions and values'.⁴⁸ Further, he – once again – noted that the international community should have learned from the past lessons:

> The historical parallels in this case are undeniable. Unwillingness to join forces against Nazism in the twentieth century cost us millions of lives in the bloodiest world war in human history. Today we have again come face to face with a destructive and barbarous ideology, and we must not allow these modern-day dark forces to attain their goals.⁴⁹

Therefore, appealing for unity on the basis of history also has an international level in the presidential rhetoric. However, compared to the alleged internal unity of Russia, presented as a unique and almost primordial feature, cooperation with other nations has often failed in history, leaving Russia allegedly alone to defend morality and righteousness – and its own interests, as the next chapter shows.

Justification: 'Invaluable civilizational and even sacral importance for Russia'

One of the most prominent and controversial events in the twenty-first-century Russia has been the annexation of Crimea in the spring of 2014. The event, which President Putin called the 'historical reunification of Crimea and Sevastopol with Russia' in his address to the Federal Assembly on 4 December 2014, was justified by (myt)historical issues:

> It was an event of special significance for the country and the people, because Crimea is where our people live, and the peninsula is of strategic importance for Russia as the spiritual source of the development of a multifaceted but solid Russian nation and a centralised Russian state. It was in Crimea, in the ancient city of Chersonesus or Korsun, as ancient Russian chroniclers called it, that Grand Prince Vladimir was baptised before bringing Christianity to Rus'.⁵⁰

This statement can be said to be the most glaring example of the pragmatic (or, one could say, opportunistic) usage of early history in the presidential speeches during the past two decades. St Vladimir, one of the tenth-century rulers of Kiovan Rus', has become a competed semi-mythical figure in the Ukrainian and Russian national narrative. In both of them – based on the medieval Slavic texts – the prince, who is called St Volodymyr in Ukrainian, is considered a founder figure, who brought the Orthodox Christian faith to the area. By appealing

Figure 2.1 The statue of Vladimir the Great in Moscow, unveiled in 2016. Photo: Kati Parppei.

to Prince Vladimir's baptism in Crimea in the context of the annexation, the president effectively took control of the alleged historical event in favour of Russia.[51]

Besides rhetoric, the contemporary symbolic value of Vladimir the Great has been utilized also in ways that are more concrete and – literally – prominent. For instance, in 2016, on National Unity Day, a statue of St Vladimir was unveiled in Moscow, near the Kremlin (an act that, together with the erection of other statues representing medieval figures, can be interpreted to reflect certain neo-medievalistic tendencies in Russian contemporary state ideology).[52] Vladimir's role, seamlessly connected to Crimea, is prominently brought out in the early history section of 'Russia – My History' theme parks, too.

In his talk of December 2014, Putin also referred to the unification of Eastern Slavs into Russia, implicitly pointing out that Ukraine is voluntarily opting out of this sacred union, the 'unifying force' of which was Christianity, in addition to 'ethnic similarity', a common language and shared cultural features:

> [it] was a powerful spiritual unifying force that helped to involve various tribes and tribal unions of the vast Eastern Slavic world in the creation of a Russian nation and Russian state. It was thanks to this spiritual unity that our forefathers

for the first time and forevermore saw themselves as a united nation. All of this allows us to say that Crimea, the ancient Korsun or Chersonesus, and Sevastopol have invaluable civilizational and even sacral importance for Russia, like the Temple Mount in Jerusalem for the followers of Islam and Judaism. And this is how we will always consider it.[53]

This notion was a stab aimed at Ukraine in the context of the emphasis on unity; contemporary Ukrainians voluntarily opted out of the Orthodox Christian Slavic union. The comparison of Crimea to the Temple Mount of Jerusalem is also a symbolically powerful one, apparently aimed at emphasizing that the annexation was not just justified due to the importance of the place to Russians, but has taken place for good, as Putin emphatically pointed out.

In his address to the Federal Assembly on 3 December 2015, President Putin returned to the issue by noting that 'reunifying' Crimea and Sevastopol to Russia was an important milestone also in relation to Russia's status in the international community of nations (once again, he also brought out the thousand years' history of Russia): 'Russia declared a *voce piena* its status as a strong state with a millennium-long history and great traditions, as a nation consolidated by common values and common goals.'[54]

The rhetoric of justification has taken place also at a more abstract level, in the context of international politics and geopolitics. It refers to history more implicitly than the examples examined earlier. Ever since the Napoleonic wars, a phenomenon I call 'the idea of innocence' has dominated the public discourse on Russia's relationship with other nations, and it has been intertwined with contemporary enemy images and the ideas of Russia under military, economic and moral threat, especially from the 'Western' world.[55]

During the nineteenth century, the idea of Russia as a lonely defender of Christian faith was consolidated, together with the claim that Russia had never wanted or started a war, but only defended its interests when provoked and threatened. Around the same time of the Russo-Turkish War (1877–8), N. A. Danilevskii (1822–85), published his writings on Russia and Europe, asserting that Russia had never been an aggressor in its dealings with its neighbours; rather, the peoples integrated into the empire had greatly benefited from the providence of Russia.[56] Further, according to Danilevskii, the peaceful state had been repeatedly hounded into such positions that defence was the only option:

> And so, the composition of the Russian state, the wars it waged, the goals it pursued, and even more, the frequent favourable circumstances it never utilized: all show that Russia is not an ambitious, aggressive power, and that in

the modern period of its history, it most often sacrificed its own obvious gains, which were legal and just, to European interests, often even considering that its responsibility was to act not as an independent entity (with its own significance and its own justification for all its actions and aspirations) but as a secondary power. So why, I ask, should there be such distrust, injustice, and hatred towards Russia from the governments and public opinion of Europe?[57]

This conception of innocence and righteousness, even victimhood, based on slavophilic doctrines, was firmly integrated into the national narrative of Russia.[58] It is also clearly reflected in the twenty-first-century presidential addresses. For instance, in the address to the Federal Assembly on 12 December 2013, Vladimir Putin noted that:

> We have always been proud of our nation. But we do not claim to be any sort of superpower with a claim to global or regional hegemony; we do not encroach on anyone's interests, impose our patronage onto anyone, or try to teach others how to live their lives. But we will strive to be leaders, defending international law, striving for respect and national sovereignty and peoples' independence and identity. This is absolutely objective and understandable for a state like Russia, with its great history and culture, with many centuries of experience, not so-called tolerance, neutered and barren, but the actual common, natural life of different peoples within the framework of a single state.[59]

The context of this announcement was the president's notion that all kinds of global competition are increasing and Russia has to defend its position, also 'on defending traditional values that have made up the spiritual and moral foundation of civilization in every nation for thousands of years.' Also, he criticized the 'destruction' of those traditional values by many nations: 'Society is now required not only to recognise everyone's right to the freedom of consciousness, political views and privacy, but also to accept without question the equality of good and evil, strange as it seems, concepts that are opposite in meaning.'[60] Moreover, Putin argued, referring to certain countries in the Middle East and North Africa, 'how attempts to push supposedly more progressive development models onto other nations actually resulted in regression, barbarity and extensive bloodshed'.[61]

This viewpoint, which Putin himself admitted to be a conservative one, has been argued to reflect some kind of a change in the rhetoric as well as in the policies of the Russian government from 2012 onwards, as noted earlier. From the viewpoint of references to history, it can be said that a certain turn has taken place in the emphasis: while before 2012, ideas of the collective past were referred to in the context of internal cohesion, since then they have been used more to reflect Russia's relation to other nations, 'Western' ones in particular.[62]

Further, as the tensions grew along with international sanctions aimed at Russia, the 'idea of innocence' was repeated in the speeches. For instance, on 1 June 2016, President Putin mentioned that Russia had encountered pressure from abroad, including 'spreading myths about Russian aggression, propaganda and meddling in others' elections to persecuting our athletes'. Further, he emphasized that:

> We do not want confrontation with anyone. We have no need for it and neither do our partners or the global community. Unlike some of our colleagues abroad, who consider Russia an adversary, we do not seek and never have sought enemies.[63]

In the address on 1 March 2018, Putin spent considerable time presenting Russia's new military equipment. He emphasized that 'I should specifically say that Russia's growing military strength is not a threat to anyone; we have never had any plans to use this potential for offensive, let alone aggressive goals' and pointed out that Russia's military power is a guarantee of world peace.[64]

It has been claimed that President Putin's top priority in Russia's foreign policy is to maintain stability; that is, he seems to be more interested in keeping the international order than radically changing it.[65] The perception of Russia as a historically peace-loving and non-aggressive entity, presented in the addresses – the emphatic expression 'never' underlining his point – fits the picture; Putin presents his case of independent, powerful Russia assertively, but using the old disclaimer to avoid appearing too provocative to the international audience.

Concluding words

In this article, the references to history by the presidents of Russia in the addresses to the Federal Assembly in 2000–19 were examined in the light of the long development of history politics in Russia and utilizing three loose categories: patriotism, threats and justification. Apparently, these categories not just overlap but are firmly intertwined, even though they form slightly different contexts for the use of history.

First, the idea of the collective past – an (imagined) continuum of a thousand years, created in hindsight – has been used to enhance and consolidate the general feeling of belonging; to give a purpose and bring together the ideas of the past, present and future of Russia. This, of course, is a universal phenomenon, not by any means exclusive to Russia, nor is the challenge to include the troublesome and awkward historical periods and events in the national narrative.

The latter issue has been occasionally touched upon in the presidential addresses, but especially President Putin's main history-related message to the audience, peppered with memories of military achievements, has been to respect the history of one's nation and to consider it as a foundation for patriotic feelings. So it can be said that his view on history in the addresses is indeed quite pragmatic and that he sees the idea and imagery of the collective past as one of the tools to add to the cohesion of the people – as has been seen from the nineteenth century onwards.

Cohesion, or unity, is in itself one of the main themes – or even *the* main theme – related to the references to history in the addresses, especially in relation to internal and external threats. The presidents emphatically and repeatedly presented Russia as a historical unit of ethnic and religious diversity and noted that this particular feature is the one on which the strength of the country is based. This, of course, is not surprising considering the internal challenges of twenty-first-century Russia. As noted in the beginning of this chapter, the combination of unity (the exact definition depending on contemporary political and cultural settings) and strong central power has been the core around which representations of the history of Moscow, and later on Russia, have largely been compiled from the fifteenth century onwards, and it has been applicable to numerous political situations at each given time after that.

The third category – justification – was examined here from two viewpoints. The first was the concrete claims concerning history justifying contemporary acts, of which the connecting of Prince Vladimir to the annexation of Crimea is the most obvious example. The other is a more implicit one: the idea of Russia as a nation that has never shown unprovoked aggression towards others but only wants to protect its interests and citizens. This 'idea of innocence' was formulated already during and in the context of the military conflicts of the nineteenth century and since 2012, President Putin has been repeatedly referring to it when talking about international tensions and Russia's response to them. This may be connected to the increased emphasis on Russia as an independent and internally strong actor in the international field.

It can be said that references to history have been one of the rhetorical tools of the twenty-first-century presidents of Russia. In the case of references to early history, they operate on the level of national myth-making and banal medievalism, creating vague, yet emotionally persuasive, images of a thousand years of coherent history. In the addresses, the references have been fully subordinate to contemporary needs. Together with other history-related media aimed at ordinary Russians – such as the school textbooks or 'history parks' – they consolidate the idea(l) of a historical continuum of Russia as an exceptional multiethnic and multireligious nation right from the beginning to the present and, provided the Russians comply with the governance of their leaders and do their part for societal cohesion, to the future.

3

Mapping the pseudohistorical knowledge space in the Russian World Wide Web[1]

Mila Oiva and Anna Ristilä

Introduction

An occasional web surfer, fascinated by the stories of Russian princes of the medieval past, or perhaps desperately searching material for a school essay, may encounter stories of the powerful Aryan-Slavic reigns ruling the whole of Eurasia for thousands of years, whose memory has been forcefully suppressed by malicious conspirators. These pseudohistorical[2] representations, pretending to reveal the 'real truth' about the past, are connected to a variety of knowledge spaces, ranging from neopagan and extremist-Orthodox to UFO-believing contexts, in which the radical historical views are made to appear as natural and understandable. When aiming to understand the potential influence and meaning of any information, analysing the context in which it is located provides a key.[3] As this essay seeks to explain the role of pseudohistory within Russian web contents, understanding the knowledge space of pseudohistory – by which we mean the wider thematic contexts where they are made understandable – can help in assessing their role in the larger history culture. Mapping the knowledge space of pseudohistory is critical because it is a global phenomenon, comparable to other antiscientific epistemological movements affecting our spheres of knowledge and, through that, social and political activities in our societies.

The prior scholarship on Russian pseudohistorical contents created by social media groups has noted that the proponents of these views connect their individual identities with the grand narratives of the glorious past of their nation.[4] In her analysis of the visual representations of the history in the social media and websites of Russian traditionalists adhering to the past of the 'Aryan-Slavic' people, Ksenia Zharchinskaya demonstrates that the reasons for this longing arise from deep disappointment in both the Western soulless and liberal culture and the corrupt post-Soviet society and a desire to feel proud for their ancestors. She also points out that some groups form homogenous knowledge spaces inclining towards radical right-wing ideologies and occasionally ecological thinking.[5]

Simultaneously, concerning the wider discussions on the medieval past, E. A. Rostovtsev and D. A. Sosnitskii show that the Russian state authorities are willing to influence the knowledge space of Russian medieval history with the help of memory politics and that the contents of those web resources that have connections to the state are in line with the messages of the state information policy.[6] The identification of the extremist right-wing connections of pseudohistories together with the state's willingness to take an active part in the discussions on medieval history opens up the question on the larger epistemological contexts of pseudohistories in Russian history culture.

The contemporary Russian historical knowledge space involves different actors ranging from academic scholars and political elites to cultural figures and a variety of small marginal groupings. Like their colleagues in the West, Russian scholars are also concerned about the spreading of misinformation on the web. However, the situation is more complicated in Russia as the state leadership has taken an active role in promoting the kinds of interpretations of history that support its politics. Due to this active state involvement in determining the correct interpretations of history, these discussions become easily politicized, and the stigma of pseudohistory is easily used to mark the opposing political and social views. The discussions concerning what is pseudohistory, how the contemporary media spreads it and how it affects society have given birth to a number of polemic essays among Russian scholars in recent years. These publications thoroughly visit the development of the concepts of 'pseudohistory', 'historical myth' and 'invented archaic' but are only seldom based on a systematic analysis of a representative sample of sources.[7] The political elite's concerns over the population becoming 'infected' by falsified history is also visible on the internet. For example, a website run by the Russian Military-Historical Society – an organization associated with promoting the Russian patriotic interpretations of the past and political uses of history[8] – lists Russian authors distributing false information on Russia's past and explains that the reason for the rise of the pseudohistorical web contents is the ideological vacuum created by the fall of the Soviet Union.[9] Although the central government's role in the public discussions about history is disproportionally large, particularly in the traditional mass media, other actors, such as local authorities and societal, cultural and religious groups, have also actively taken part in forming the public's understanding of history and raising alternative or critical voices into the public sphere.[10] Despite the state's strong involvement, the Russian society also has long roots of disbelief in official information and forming alternative publishing spheres, such as the *samizdat* underground self-publishing culture during the Soviet era. This also means that the contemporary knowledge space concerning Russia's medieval past is not black-and-white and that there is room for different kinds of alternative and radical views to mushroom.

Medieval history was a source of Russian nation-building even before the October Revolution, and Stalin's time saw the glorification of medieval heroes for their defence of the motherland. After the collapse of the Soviet Union, medieval history became an important point of reference regarding the formation and origins of statehood although the Second World War era continues to dominate the history discussion.[11] Since the mid-2010s, the Russian government has also been increasingly using medieval history to support its legitimacy, promote patriotic feelings and discredit the political opposition.[12] Simultaneously, the Russian language segment of the web has grown rich with contents inspired by medieval history, ranging from scholarly research projects, extracts of digitized books, blogs by history enthusiasts, photos and videos from events that enliven history and collections of school essays.

The World Wide Web is a peculiar place of knowledge formation that combines the potential for a wide reach of content distribution with an inclination towards closed knowledge spaces. It has become a platform for forming and disseminating knowledge in a networked fashion, where anyone interested can create and distribute content on the historical past, and the traditional political and academic opinion leaders have limited authority.[13] In Russia, with the shrinking freedom of expression and increasing control of the traditional media outlets, the internet has become the major platform for marginal, alternative and oppositional views.[14] Globally, the web provides an efficient platform for a variety of players, including groups with radical beliefs, to form closed epistemic communities. They can form so-called fringe media ecosystems, which are public or semi-public platforms loosely connected to the mainstream media where false beliefs, rumours, disinformation and fake news spread. Populists, often right-wing groupings, use the fringe media to challenge the mainstream knowledge and to undermine institutional knowledge.[15] Simultaneously, as Andrew B. R. Elliott points out in this volume, the knowledge formation of these groups can be ostensibly democratic but is in effect constructed within closed circles by framing out undesired discussions.[16]

Due to the underlying technological and digital structure together with the using conventions of websites, knowledge formation on the internet is largely carried out collectively by sharing contents via hyperlinks, comment threads, followings, friendships and similar linkages that form a complex relational structure.[17] Hyperlinks are crucial components in this effort by pulling the web pages together and providing exact references for further information. They also define the visibility of the web pages since search engines use the number of hyperlinks – calculating each incoming link as a vote for the 'importance' of the target web page – as a category for defining the rank of the web pages. Furthermore, previous research has recognized that hyperlinks cluster web pages and websites into knowledge communities with like-minded or related content.[18] Thus, the hyperlinks supply information on the centrality and associations of the websites, both providing meaningful contexts for them. Although this approach does not take into account the actual number of web page visitors and references without mentioning the URL or other potential measures of attention or contextualization, it nevertheless offers a useful approach to the analysis by providing an easily traceable connection.

Taking into consideration the findings of the preceding scholarship concerning the formation of homogenous epistemic communities of groups holding pseudohistorical understandings on the web and the varied nature of Russian history culture, this chapter explores the extent and position of pseudohistorical web contents. It studies the position and meaning-making contextualization of pseudohistorical web pages within the network of interconnected hyperlinks of the Russian language medievalist web. The underlying research questions ask how central the selected pseudohistorical web contents are and in what kinds of contexts they appear in the Russian language medievalist web. Using the methods of network analysis and critical close reading, we analyse how the position of web pages within the wider network of web contents explains the potential influence of this phenomenon. We also explore the hyperlinks leading out and into the web pages to reveal the wider context in which the contents should be understood.

As the main sources of this essay, we analyse three web pages with pseudohistorical contents that represent different pseudohistorical theories of the Russian medieval past.[19] This choice allows us to grasp some varieties of this genre. We analyse the selected web pages within the context of over 350,000 Russian language medievalist web pages, forum discussions and blogs with over 1.5 million hyperlinks altogether. All the texts were collected by identifying via the Yandex[20] search engine a subset of seed links discussing topics such as 'the true history of ancient Rus" and 'founders of Rus" and scraping them and all their hyperlinks to the second step.[21]

Pseudocontents in the network of web medievalism

The pseudohistorical web contents are versatile, and the three web pages at the focus of this study have different approaches to the origin of the Russian nation and the nature of Russian medieval history. According to the web page titled 'The Forbidden History of Rus", containing a lengthy extract of a book authored by Vladislav Karabanov, the genetic origin of the people of Rus', and through that the contemporary Russians, descends from the Goths. Their great kingdom was located in the area between the Baltic and Black Seas and from the Elbe River to the Ural Mountains. The author – who has also published online books on history and nations as well as a series of fantasy novels[22] – shows how the old Goth's name of *Hreidhgotar* actually leads to the self-nomination of the Rus' people in the Gothic language, which testifies that the nation of Rus' was actually the Goths. According to the web page, Russians are not genetically Slavic people, and they adopted the Slavic language only in the tenth century due to the tightening trade relations with the Slavs that had newly arrived in the region. The adoption of religion and bureaucracy in Bulgaria further strengthened the position of the Slavic languages. The imported Orthodox Church suppressed the Gothic culture and the invasion of Tatar-Mongols wiped out the remnants of the elite that could still remember the Gothic past.[23]

The second web page, titled 'The Unknown History of Ancient Rus", contains a short written introduction and an embedded YouTube video titled 'How Rus' Turned into Europe'. These sources convey the theory that the Celtic heritage of Great Britain and the whole of Western Europe originates in effect from Scythian tribes who were actually Russians. The similarities in artefacts and words testify to this connection. For example, many English language words, such as the 'Celts', 'Druid' and 'London', purportedly originate from the Russian language.[24] The web page shows how pseudohistorical accounts can borrow elements; shift their focus selectively to cultural, linguistic and genetic ancestry; and recognize similarities where needed. Unlike the first web page, 'Forbidden History', which denies the Slavic origin of Russians and the Russian language as their original language, 'The Unknown History' takes for granted the inseparable connection between the Russian language and the Russian-Scythian nation. By showing this connection, the video demonstrates that the Western European cultures are actually of Russian origin. The hidden truth about the Russian origin of the British culture is the reason for the genetic hostility of the English people against Russians, according to the authors of the video.[25]

The third web page, containing a lengthy text titled 'Another Look at the History of Rus'', implies that Russians are descendants of the Huns, who originate from the area of present-day Russia. However, unlike the two other web pages, 'Another Look' does not focus on proving the connection between the Huns and Russians. The main message of the web page is that the West has been for over a hundred years fighting an information war against the Russian people by brainwashing them with the assistance of the Russian education system. The text gives several examples of historical facts that have been concealed and demonstrates how the Russians have an ancient continuous statehood. It shows that the Russians had state structures well before Rurik, who, according to the more established views of history, was the founder of Russian statehood. According to 'Another Look', the first capital was Slovensk, which ruled a vast territory. It was located at the same place as Novgorod and had already been established by '2409 BCE (in year 3099 after the creation of the World)'.[26] Interestingly, while 'The Forbidden History' emphasizes the antagonism between the Orthodox Church and the paganism of the Goths, 'Another Look' sees Orthodox religiousness as a natural part of Russian heritage and refers to the creation of the world counted with the help of the Bible.[27] Further examples from 'Another Look', such as that Rus' was called 'the Country of Cities' in the old days and that the Russians produced all the weapons used in seventeenth-century Europe, provide proof of a sophisticated civilization mastering high technologies. During the Tatar-Mongol period, the Russians attacked the Tatars constantly and actually controlled the territory and thus were not subordinated to the occupiers, as often told. This demonstrates that Russians have been controlling their vast territory for thousands of years.[28]

Similarly, as the contents of the three analysed web pages differ from each other, they also diverge largely from the academic view of the Russian medieval past as well as in many ways from the interpretations promoted by the Russian state authorities.[29] To analyse the centrality and importance of these contents, we will now zoom out to explore them in the larger hyperlink network of Russian web medievalism, after which we will move on to a more detailed analysis of their hyperlink connections.

Drawing a network of Russian medievalist web contents with their interconnected hyperlinks reveals a 'map' of websites, where the links draw web pages into communities of varying sizes based on the density of interlinking connections (see Figure 3.1).[30] The OpenOrd layout algorithm used pulls the

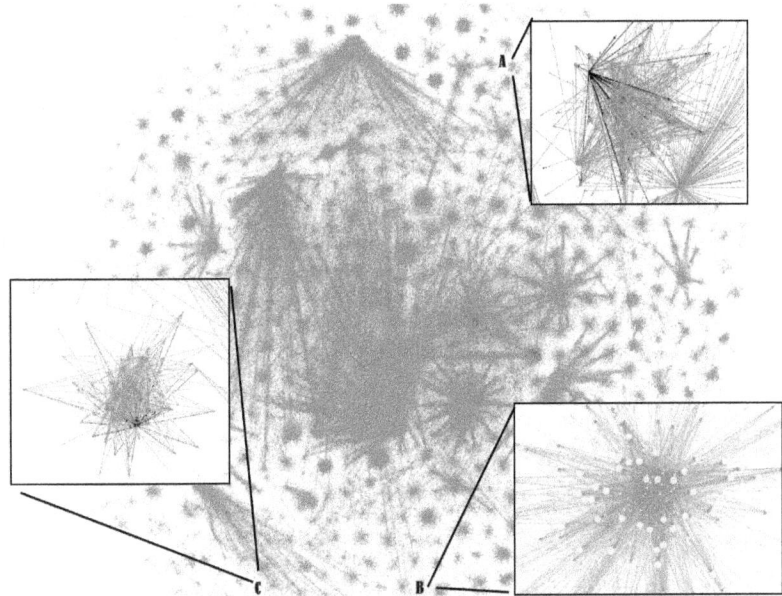

Figure 3.1 The network of Russian medievalist web discussions with pseudohistorical texts of (A) 'The Forbidden History of Rus" (ARI website), (B) 'Another Look at the History of Rus" (White Brotherhood website) and (C) 'The Unknown History of Ancient Rus" (Secret Info website). Each node stands for a web page, and the edges represent the hyperlinks between them. The visualization was made with Gephi 0.9.2. We wish to thank Tillmann Ohm for converting the image into black-and-white.

web pages with more interlinking hyperlinks closer to each other and pushes those with few connections apart.[31] This means that the nodes in the centre have more connections with different parts of the network, while the nodes on the sides have few. Following the idea of the network analysis, where the most important nodes are identified by determining their structural centrality by looking at the number of other nodes connected to them,[32] in the visualization, the size of the nodes (web pages) depends on the number of incoming edges (hyperlinks). Thus, the bigger the node is in the visualization, the more other web pages have linked to that particular web page.[33]

The network shows that the majority of Russian language medievalist content resides on platforms where anyone, regardless of their institutional connections, financial means or technical skills, can provide content. The mutual hyperlinks of the Russian language medievalist web organize the information space following predominantly the domain names and platforms as the main pages and maintenance pages – such as links to the main page, instructions, website policies and so forth – draw the web pages and websites into communities.[34] The main communities (see the sizeable star-like clusters in Figure 3.1) are formed around the popular Russian blog platform LiveInternet (www.liveinternet.ru, over 21 per cent of the whole network), Wikipedia websites (12 and 9 per cent), other encyclopedic websites (such as wikiznanie.ru and wiki-wiki.ru, 5 per cent), Earth Chronicles (http://earth-chronicles.ru/, a news aggregator and discussion forum focusing on esoteric and speculative contents, 6 per cent) and LiveJournal blogs (www.livejournal.com, 4 per cent). The remaining communities are small, mostly separated 'islands' that cover 1.5 per cent or less of the whole network. The large coverage of blogging platforms, such as LiveInternet and LiveJournal, shows that a significant part of the content is provided on platforms that anyone can reach. As discussions on history often use references, different kinds of online encyclopedias provide good links. The presence of the Earth Chronicles news portal hints that at least some of the medievalist discussions are related to the wider genre of speculative web content.

The three web pages at focus – 'The Forbidden History', 'The Unknown History' and 'Another Look' – all reside on the separated 'islands' in the margins of the knowledge space of the Russian medievalist web, isolated, and without any mutual interlinking connections (see A, B and C in Figure 3.1). Their small size also shows that they have very few incoming hyperlinks and therefore are not central in the hyperlink network. Although they share a similarly radical approach to history, they are not connected through mutual hyperlinks directly or through other web pages, for that matter. Thus, it seems that the pseudohistorical discussion on Russian medieval history is scattered and that there is no central website where the majority would refer to.

Hyperlinks to the past and from the future

Although placed in the margins of the Russian language medievalist web, the analysed web pages do have hyperlinks connecting them to their close neighbours in the 'islands' and through them to the themes circulating within the web medievalisms. We will now move on to analyse in detail the immediate outgoing and incoming links of the web pages at focus. The outgoing and incoming hyperlinks have different meanings as the outgoing hyperlinks reveal the context in which the web page creators wanted to place it at the time of creating it, while the links coming from the other web pages measure how the importance and appreciation of the target web page have developed after its creation. In other words, our assumption is that the outgoing and incoming hyperlinks denote different kinds of meaning-making processes and have disparate temporality within the knowledge space.

The outbound hyperlinks of two of the three analysed web pages connect them tightly to the internal worlds of the websites in which they are located. The first web page, 'The Forbidden History', revealing the Gothic genesis of Russian people and showing a critical approach to the role of the Orthodox Church in the history of the Russians, has altogether twenty-nine outgoing hyperlinks (see A in Figure 3.1). Out of these links, twenty-two are internal references pointing to the main site, the Agency of Russian Information (Agentstvo Russkoi Informatsii, ARI) website, where the web page is located, or its Facebook, VKontakte or Twitter profiles. Similarly, 'Another Look', the pro-Orthodox web page disclosing the ongoing Western information war against the Russian people, has altogether 123 outgoing links, of which the great majority points to the other web pages of the main site, the White Brotherhood (Beloe Bratstvo) (see B in Figure 3.1). The rest of the outgoing links on this page refer to WordPress maintenance web pages and web analysis services.[35]

Hyperlinks bear meanings since the web page creators do not create them randomly but rather select their references intentionally. Previous scholarship has identified the following four types of motivations behind hyperlinks: they are used to provide further information; to enhance the web page's online presence and perceptions of the wider level of support for its message; to dismiss opponents as negative links to opposing websites; and, above all, to identity confirmation or reinforcement. Hyperlinks are used as means of concentrating attention on key aspects of the web page's message, and therefore they reveal the communicating intents of the web page creators and how they shape the representation of the world.[36] In this light, the inward-looking hyperlinking of the two web pages has reasons and connotations.

The contracted linking of the two web pages reveals a website design that pulls the individual pages of the website into a coherent whole with the help of built-in hyperlinking. A large number of internal linkages of the web pages arises from the banners containing links to the other web pages published on the website and buttons for sharing the content on social media. Extensive internal linking can be motivated by an attempt to enhance the visibility of the website in search engines. In effect, many of the hyperlinks reflect the situation at the time of scraping the website, and by the time of publishing this essay, some of the links have been replaced by other, more topical URLs within the website. These outgoing hyperlinks point steadily to the website they are located on, but the exact websites they refer to change over time. Thus, the context of the contents fluctuates within the website, but nevertheless, the majority of the links point to the website in question. In addition, it needs to be noted that not all links are equally meaningful as some stand quietly at the end of the website, while others are trumpeted with big headings.[37] The links located on the banner are crucial in creating a larger understanding of the contents since even if the visitors would not follow the links, they nevertheless glimpse them briefly and through that grasp the context in which the contents should be understood.

The intended meaning-making context of 'The Forbidden History', suggesting that Russians originate from the Goths, is the ARI website, which is an online 'news agency' reporting on contemporary events and historical topics from a Russian national perspective. In addition to contents on Russian medieval history, the website provides topical news with an emphasis on conspiracies and scandalous themes in the Second World War history and present-day international politics, military and digital technologies. It resembles similar yellow-press-like popular views that the web provides globally. Interestingly, alongside contents discussing Russian medieval history and the origin of nations, very few contents tackle contemporary Russia as the focus is more on international contemporary themes. ARI is a relatively mainstream website as it attracts a comparably large number of approximately 100,000 visitors within a two-month period.[38] A noteworthy detail, to which we will return later, is that the name of the website, the Agency of Russian (*russkoi*) Information, indicates that the information on the website is provided from the ethnically Russian and not the multiethnic civic Russian perspective. Also, the few outgoing links of 'The Forbidden History' web page that refer outside the ARI website contain the social media profiles of individuals posting Russian patriotic content.[39] Thus, the outgoing hyperlink context of the web page suggests that questions of the origin of Russians should be understood within the present-day chaotic international situation full of conspiracies, where the revealed truth about Russians' ethnic roots may represent a safe haven.

The outbound hyperlinks of 'Another Look' uncover a more marginal world view. The web page is located in a website titled the White Brotherhood. It contains a mixture of Orthodox-flavoured mysticism disclosing connections of the crucifix and horoscopes, prophesies of the forthcoming new Russian tsar or a war that will start in the near future. In addition, the authors of the website have produced a number of contents on the history and traditions of ancient Rus' and Western attacks on Russia. Alongside the Orthodoxy-inspired contents, the website also has contents that point to more esoteric interpretations. The logo of the website contains the so-called Slavic swastika, which is often used in the

Russian neopagan Rodnoverie contents to stimulate religious emotions.[40] The website also provides links for monitoring solar activity and flares, magnetic storms and global weather forecasts as well as volcanic and seismic activity.[41] The slogan of the website – 'New Teachings come from Russia, Russia will be pure, will be White Brotherhood in Russia'[42] – emphasizes that the aim of the website is to deliver spiritual and historical teachings, leading to an enlightened and purified Russia. The website does not explicitly say who maintains it, but the name of the website points to extremist-Orthodox brotherhoods or groupings, parting from the mainstream Russian Orthodox Church by their fundamentalist views. Some of these groupings live in isolated communities and worship, for example, Ivan the Terrible and his strong but violent leadership.[43]

Although in English the word 'white' bears strong racial connotations, in the Russian context the word also has several other meanings. For example, in the Orthodox context, white refers to a dedication to spiritual life without monastery commitment. Some scholars have suggested that the 'whiteness' of the area of present-day Belarus would have signified the areas inhabited by the Slavic people who were free from the Tatar-Mongol rule,[44] which obviously can be interpreted in racial terms and as demarcating cultural and religious differences. It seems that the White Brotherhood is a relatively marginal community as it attracts the interest of a significantly smaller group than, for example, the ARI website analysed earlier.[45] Overall, 'Another Look', by providing examples of a continuous Western information war against the Russian people, lays foundations for a spiritual awakening backed by Orthodox and Russian national traditions. Here, the ethnically interpreted roots provide the basis for a bright future. In this context, the past not only explains the present but also reaches to the future as well.

Despite the evident differences in the worldviews and the lack of interconnecting hyperlinks of 'The Forbidden History' and 'Another Look', the web pages share thematic commonalities that transcend the simple contestation of academic mainstream history. One of the major uniting features is their focus on one ethnicity – the Russians. They both focus on the origins of the ethnic Russians (*russkij*) instead of the citizens of the multiethnic Russian Federation (*rossijskij*).[46] The contents of the websites, resembling protochronist representations of history inherent to fascist movements,[47] imply that nations are unchanging entities that have their own consciousness, and subconsciousness, and that remain the same for centuries or even millennia. According to this view, if a nation's historical self-understanding is based on lies, the nation cannot reach its full potential, and it remains in a subordinated position in the hierarchy of nations. In this way, the past of a nation predetermines its present and future. If a nation does not have a 'great' history, it cannot have a bright future, either. That is why revealing the ultimate truth is highly important. The world view also contains an assumption that the nations are unequal – that some are greater than others – and that nations in a way compete with each other. If one nation is great, it means that other nations are not so, and they may be subordinated to it. The 'greatness' of a nation is measured in military battles, the size of the area it rules, the possession of high-level technological knowledge and superior moral status. The primacy and unchanged nature of the Russian nation in the medieval past does not correspond with the academic evidence nor with the state-led interpretation of Russian history that usually emphasizes the civic history of the multiethnic state where the strong state and unity of the national groups lay foundations for prosperity.[48]

Although an ethnonationalistic approach drives the pseudohistorical contents to the margins, the simultaneous appeals to the historical grand narrative of a Western attack on Russia connect them to the more widespread and tightly rooted historical understandings. For example, the ways the White Brotherhood website represents the West as an enemy and the urges for the restoration of national pride align with the official history politics of Russia in many ways. The history exhibition 'My History: Riurikids', opened by President Putin and Patriarch Kirill in Moscow in 2014, stated that Ivan the Terrible fell victim to 'the first information war in the European press', referring to the contemporary portrayal of events in Ukraine by Western media.[49] Along the same lines, 'Another Look' portrays Ivan the Terrible as an active modernizer of Russia, whose benevolent leadership has been overshadowed in the schoolbooks by Western anti-Russian propaganda portraying him as a murderous tyrant.[50] The increasing sentiment of the West as an enemy and the need to restore the national pride intensified in the context of the Ukrainian crisis launched in 2014, during which scholars also reported a turning towards an ethnonationalist interpretation of Russian national identity by the state leadership.[51] Interestingly, all the analysed web pages were created between 2013 and 2015,[52] and it is possible that the wider cultural context of that time affected the worldviews represented in them.

The established historical schemes of Russian historical understanding, such as being a victim of a Western attack, provide means for the pseudohistorical contents to appeal to wider audiences. The established historical schemes, that is, the grand narratives concerning the role of the nation in world history, create cultural constraints for memory production and reception and shape cultural frames of memory dynamics. Schemes, such as being under aggression, resistance, sacrifice, victory, defeat and survival, are an important but often unnoticeable part of the uses of history, and they are present to some extent in all historical interpretations, including the academic ones.[53] In the context of false representations of history, as discussed by Andrew B. R. Elliot in this volume, the usage of this kind of metamedievalism, building upon earlier representations, allows the incorporation of one's own ideological preferences into the historical narratives and into the widely accepted historical schemes.[54] The idea of Russia being under Western attack is deeply rooted in the Russian historical schemes and has long continuities from wars with the Polish-Lithuanian Commonwealth, the Napoleonic wars and the Soviet juxtaposition with the West. Referring to the powerful historical schemata helps both the state officials and the advocates of pseudohistory to gain leverage for their claims.

Moving forward in our analysis of the outgoing hyperlinks to the last of the three web pages at focus, 'The Unknown History' discussing the Celtic-Russian origins of Europe reveals a more outward reaching hyperlinking strategy. The web page's altogether seventy-three outgoing links contain links to both the Secret Info (Tainoe Info) website, where the page is located, as well as to a variety of other websites and VKontakte groups. The Secret Info website is dedicated to a variety of esoteric themes, ranging from the technological miracles of Vedic India and revealing the real truths about the fall of the Soviet Union and Marilyn Monroe's death to the latest news of space exploration. The contents are categorized under the rubrics of the Universe, mysteries, myths, science, prophesies, the past, religions and sects, secrets and civilization.[55] The overarching theme of the website emphasized by its title, Secret Info, uniting the wide catering of a variety of topics, is that it reveals information that is not widely known.

Interestingly, the great number of outgoing hyperlinks pointing outside the Secret Info website reveals a more clearly defined knowledge space. 'The Unknown History' links to web pages that are dedicated to Russian patriotism, the Aryan-Slavic oral heritage, anti-Zionism, the original Vedic religion of the Slavs, Russian traditional medicine, the well-being of explicitly heterosexual relations, design inspired by Russian traditions and books containing higher wisdom.[56] Previous scholarship has pointed out that partisan or extremist websites often use hyperlinks to strengthen and reflect ideological alliances and to create a sense of a great number of people behind the represented worldviews.[57] Often, online networking behaviour is influenced by reciprocity, which allows the deliberate distribution of ideas at a broader scale.[58] Thus, like-minded people behind the interlinked websites can form powerful mini-universes, where pseudohistorical contents can thrive. Although the themes of the identified websites and VKontakte groups vary greatly, they form a larger network of mutually interconnected hyperlinks and individuals maintaining the groups. The common denominator of this knowledge space is the focus on a patriarchal, family-centred, healthy lifestyle together with the study and maintenance of the 'real truths' and 'Aryan-Slavic' teachings that come close to the groups analysed by Zharchinskaya.[59] The intensive linking between the different websites creates a wider knowledge space that is varied enough to attract different kinds of people but simultaneously provides answers that support this more generic world view. In this context, the 'real truth' about the Russian roots of Western Europe is a secret that is revealed only to the select individuals interested in higher wisdom, and all this is backed with an emphasis on Russian traditionalist and conservative views with an anti-Semitic flavour.

To conclude our hyperlink analysis, we will now turn to study the incoming hyperlinks. While the outgoing hyperlinks mark the intended context of the web page demarcated by the web page creators, the incoming links show how other web authors have viewed the importance and the wider context of the web page after its creation. The analysed websites have attracted very few – if any – incoming links. This demonstrates that they have remained at the margins of the larger medievalist Russian language web. 'Another Look' attracted only two hyperlinks. Both links were created with the help of similar kinds of banner links providing suggestions of other similar content to the readers as discussed earlier. Thus, the incoming links tie the contents more tightly to the existing network, while the incoming links from outside would have signalled a wider interest from outside.

The incoming links connect the web page more tightly to the genre of conspiracy theories. The incoming links come from web pages titled 'The "Great" Jewish Revolution of 1917' and 'Petr I – Not a Real Tsar'. Both of these texts were published on the White Brotherhood website around the same time as 'Another Look' in November 2015.[60] These links emphasize the importance of the context of conspiracies of foreigners – be it Western Europeans who replaced the real tsar with another person or Jews plotting the revolution – for the great misery of the Russian people. In effect, the theme of conspiracy against the Russian people is common to all the analysed web pages and actually to pseudohistorical contents overall.

Conclusion

As this chapter has demonstrated, the analysed pseudohistorical contents are marginal within the Russian language medievalist web, with outbound hyperlinks connecting them either only to the immediate context of the website or to the close-by epistemic community. Within the approximately five years of their existence, the analysed web pages have not attracted attention from outside their immediate circles. The analysed pseudohistorical web pages do not form a coherent single community separated from the other websites but merely reside within the other like-minded websites. The pseudohistorical discussions are connected to diverse knowledge spaces varying from Aryan-Slavic or neopaganism and through esoteric and speculative to patriotic and political contexts. For some, the evident enemy is the undefined 'West', while others also blame Russian scholars and the education system for concealing the truth.

Despite the perceived marginality, the analysed contents affiliate with the more generic contemporary cultural and political discussions and historical schemata explaining the Russians' history and identity. Although the pseudohistorical knowledge is not formed in dialogue with scholarly knowledge but within relatively closed knowledge spaces, it does not mean that they would not be in dialogue with other, more generic cultural features surrounding them, such as the schemata of being under attack by the West. By aligning with the generic national historical narratives, the pseudohistorical contents make themselves more understandable and acceptable to their audiences at the same time as they strengthen the narratives by repeating them. Simultaneously, although the pseudohistorical narratives are exclusively interested in the past and destiny of the Russian people, they also use transnational schemes, such as conspiracy theories or an understanding of the importance of a 'great national past' for the future of a nation. These themes transcend the national borders and seem to be shared by pseudohistorians worldwide.

The obvious, pressing question is how seriously we should take the pseudohistorical content spreading on the web. Although this study is not able to give an exhaustive answer, it seems that pseudohistorical contents are relatively marginal, but that in the right social conditions – when they succeed in aligning with pressing contemporary social and political questions – they may increase in popularity and have an effect on the offline world. If the academic representations of history fail to provide answers that satisfy the epistemic needs of the population, there may be room for more radical views.

4

A lens most obscured

Western perceptions of contemporary Russian medievalisms

Evan Wallace

Introduction

On 8 April 2020, Russian President Vladimir Putin addressed the Russian people via digital telecast to update them on the government's response to the ongoing Covid-19 outbreak. In his speech, Putin utilized a historical frame of reference from a millennium ago to compare the Covid-19 pandemic with the armed conflicts Kievan Rus' had against the Pechenegs and Polovtsy (or Cumans). These were Turkic semi-nomadic peoples who had caused much strife in the tenth and eleventh centuries. 'Everything passes, and this will pass', exclaimed Putin in his speech. His oration continued; 'our country has endured serious trials many times: the *Pechenegs tormented it, and so did the Polovtsy* [emphasis by the author]. Russia has dealt with everything, and we will defeat this corona virus infection.'[1] The narrative Putin framed was stripped and devoid of any historical context. In addition, the referenced period represents a history that is shared between multiple Slavic cultures. While the modern Russian state can trace its roots to Kievan Rus' so too can other contemporary Slavic nations. Putin's narrative failed to recognize this shared heritage and turned a blind eye to contemporary debates over predominate historical narratives and in doing so appropriated the period to parse his rhetorical allegory, a common theme in Russian historical rhetoric.[2]

Had this speech been given before the advent of digital media and Web 2.0 it is likely that the narrative would have stayed contained and within the 'walled garden' of Russian state media.[3] But in the digital age, Putin's rhetoric was immediately published by various media outlets online. These articles were distributed, shared and discussed outside of the confines of traditional Russian media. The effect that was rendered was a collection of news articles introduced by Russian and recirculated by Western media outlets. This bricolage enabled the transportation of Putin's narrative to Western areas of the web where participants were devoid of nearly any notion of Russia's past, language and its contemporary utilization of pseudohistorical narratives in political rhetoric. With no ability to vet the authenticity of this content Western users of digital media who engaged this assemblage of sources seemingly both passively and actively increased its distribution of Putin's rhetoric. The hyper pace of circulation and distribution on the internet creates a motif effect wherein media consumers are unable to discern truth from falsehoods.

What seems apparent is that most media consumers outside of Russia often fail to detect these nuances and seemingly act in a complicit fashion by engaging in such content. The purpose of this chapter is to examine the methods and modes of distribution of Russian alternative news. After examining this we will turn our attention to a case study, a very well-documented pseudohistorical event in Russia's fabric of contemporary metamedievalisms, which was presented in a popular Western TV show, to see if fans discussing the series were able to determine these alternative constructs.

Putin's rhetorical appeal to his country was built upon emotional columns. If Russians were able to overcome the Pecheneg and Polovtsy invaders almost a millennium ago certainly contemporary Russians would be able to overcome this new external crisis that had invaded Russia.[4] This historical allegory fits Andrew B. R. Elliott's formulation of 'banal medievalisms' which lack any true historical context and rather '[rely] not on the past, but on the absence of that past, and [derive] [. . .] persuasive power not from historicity and representation, but from its retransmission across the mass media'.[5] After Putin's speech the allegory spread like wildfire online and extended well past the confines of Russian media and into Western media. Of additional interest is that Russian state media disseminated information to shore up Putin's rhetoric and produce a bricolage that was spread online. The day after his speech *Russia Beyond*, a Russian state media outlet, released an article that shored up his claims by offering a brief narrative of the Kievan Rus' struggle with the Pechenegs and Polovtsy.[6] The website, which is aimed at an English-speaking audience, follows a similar rhetoric formation and links the historical events directly to contemporary Russia. Furthermore, the article makes no mention of the aforementioned history wars surrounding contemporary attribution of Kievan Rus' history to any single country.[7] Of particular interest is a heading and subsequent link situated at the end of the article which states 'click here to learn why Kyiv (Kiev) is called the "mother of all *Russian* cities"'. Users who stumble upon such an article with no prior knowledge of medieval Russian history are susceptible to follow such a lead-in link and formulate a Russocentric understanding of the Kievan narrative.

Putin's speech and Russian state media articles which framed his rhetoric additionally adhere to Elliott's model of banality as they both '[force] the medieval world into direct contact with the present', as well as 'pass unnoticed as references to the past and are usually accepted as innocuous or atemporal references to a phenomenon understood by all'.[8] It would appear here that these historical references were digested as innocuous and the bricolage narrative was echoed and redistributed by Western media outlets with no additional analysis.[9] The medieval allegory was thus transported wholesale to Western digital media economies. In doing so these media outlets failed to detect the partial and selective historical narrative context and instead assisted to propagate the narrative to Western observers which afforded additional 'spreadability' of the narrative by enfranchising a new audience.[10]

New modes of distribution

The reproduction of narratives such as these by Western media are not new, nor are they phenomenological. This was not the first or last time that reporters fail to detect fragmentation and falsehoods in Russian media narratives before recirculating them. Rather, what is exhibited here is a mode and practice of dissemination that has existed in Russia for centuries. For students of Russian history, the notion of the Potemkin Village may come to mind. The term refers to the actions of the eighteenth-century Russian statesman Grigory Potemkin who, in 1787, while preparing for the arrival of the Russian Empress Catherine II, Emperor Joseph II of Austria and the Polish King Stanislaw Poniatowski in the newly acquired southern lands (Novorossiya) presented grandiose villages by '[staging] décor which passed at a distance for real buildings and communities'.[11]

A similar effect can be discerned here. As Western media outlets relay wires from Russian state-affiliated media without vetting content they replicate the Potemkin narrative as I have labelled it. From the Western perspective, these sources which have been relayed offer validity in lieu of Western trust in Russian state-affiliated media, which in this case present an easy to believe narrative: the Russian president making an emotionally and historical enfranchised appeal to his citizens using valid history that is presumed recognized and accepted as fact by the target audience (Russian citizens). From this distance, Western observers with no actual context on cultural and political constructs produce a Potemkin narrative, the digital equivalent of a pleasant village observed from afar: nothing amiss or incomplete. In the digital age where circulation, access, and authority rank supreme that digestion and recirculation of these narratives grant additional validity to Russian state media structures in the post-Soviet space where Russians traditionally struggle to spread media within Western confines.

In their article Starbird and others speak to the 'echo-system' model that they evinced when examining Russian and Iranian news media circulation around the Syrian Civil Defence League in 2014. These models of echoing content from one media source to another also produce a similar bricolage as examined by Elliott in his banal medievalisms argument. The researchers noticed that Russian and Iranian news sources had aligned their views with their respective government's positions around the geopolitical landscape surrounding the conflict.[12] The fact that Russian state media used their own media structures to exert their opinion on the Syrian Civil War should not be alerting, as 'Russia initially supported the Assad government with material and financial assistance', and 'later committed troops [to] target Syrian opposition forces and IS (Islamic State) militants'.[13] What the researchers revealed is that in-between the nodes of various media outlets existed 'shadow media outlets', which engaged in 'criticism of mainstream media and scepticism or outright rejection of [mainstream media] narratives'.[14] These structures of these media narratives are similar to the 'banalities' of Putin's allegory in that they provide a base set of sources which demonstrate that seemingly multiple media outlets are providing a similar narrative and offer legitimacy in numbers, also through seemingly critical voices. Any user from a Western audience attempting to vet content presented by Russian state media will undoubtedly face this obstacle.

In the digital age, medieval history has found a new platform for the circulation of history as well as a location for new medievalisms to manifest. Twinned with the affordances of digital media, however, are a set of new problems between access and authority. This bell resonates louder from the cupola belfries in Russia, 'a society in which the Internet is not technically filtered, but where the leading traditional media are tightly controlled by the political elite'.[15] These Russian state media outlets do act as a source of authority, the content they produce is consumed and redistributed. Metzger and Flanagin aptly state that individuals rely 'on traditional information intermediaries such as experts, opinion leaders and information arbiters to help guide their credibility decisions'.[16] As individuals seek (or often do not seek) to vet information it must be considered 'that digital media [has] provided access to an unprecedented amount of information available for public consumption' and that the bar for entry to disseminating information has been lowered as 'networked communication technologies lowered the cost of information production and dissemination'.[17] The state of the publicly available corpus of information on Russian medieval history has, however, in recent years succumbed to the prevailing economic model of paywalls on the internet.

Access and authority

Users looking for academically produced content will face a brick wall when attempting to access records of authority. What is left in the free and publicly accessible content realm must always be examined through a critical lens for both attribution and authority. Access and authority are now held taut between the real force that governs content on the internet, capitalism. Clearly, access to information derived from authority-based structures (i.e. academia) is determined by economic terms. The institutional milieu of sources on the internet leverages the Western audience of observers into consuming sources that are free, open and easy to digest. Knowledge coming from academic structures rarely displays these features. The economic systems now imbued in content consumption models therefore predispose Western observers to witness Potemkin narratives with little-to-no recourse. Luckily, there are some exceptions, such as the open magazine *Public Medievalist*, run by volunteer scholars.[18]

Additional considerations however must also be applied to communities that engage medievalisms around various platforms such as videogames, TV shows and movies. As conversations around these platforms occur online, any inclusion or discussion of Potemkin narratives in these fan and participant-based communities can result in increased conversation around such narratives. The effect that is rendered is a boon to the bricolage of sources around any given Potemkin narrative as the community participants spread articles by sharing, retweeting, and engaging conversations of articles they have read 'because they have a stake in circulation'.[19] Discussions in fan communities offer a near infinite source of material and thus ensure 'spreadable' content, which ensures that a Potemkin narrative can continue to be distributed and gain increased visibility.[20]

Unintentional coherence: *Vikings* and Oleg the wise

Recently in the TV show *Vikings,* a historical actor from the pagan period of Kievan Rus' was brought onto the screen. Oleg the Wise of Novgorod, a Varangian pagan prince who ruled 879–912 CE was presented onscreen in season six by Danila Kozlovsky.[21] An example of fan-based conversations around medievalism presented in this show can be found on Reddit, a popular social forum. Redditors on the subreddit /r/vikingstv engage in historical discussions around all the characters presented in the show as means of deriving understanding and extending show lore. The show breaks from history in presenting Oleg as a Christian to advance the plotline, while the *Primary Chronicle* reports that Oleg and his followers 'were but pagans'. Furthermore, Oleg in the *Chronicle* is shown to not have taken control of Kiev until 882 CE when he 'set himself up as prince in Kiev and declared that it should be the [mother city]'.[22]

In attempting to discern what was authentic in the show as the main characters made their way from Novgorod to Kiev in the sixth season, commentators on this forum were presented with both a slanted and lacklustre corpus of publicly accessible information on the period.[23] Having attempted to data mine the subreddit, I was unable to find a single user that was able to discern the biggest gaffe that was written into the season by show director Michael Hirst. In episode two of season six, Oleg the Wise and Ivar (one of the series' showrunners) are shown flying over the city in a hot air balloon. Unbeknownst to the viewers (as well as potentially the writers?) the narrative that Russians invented the hot air balloon first is a part of the now-infamous *New Chronology* written by a former faculty member of the Russian Academy of Sciences, Anatoly Fomenko.[24]

Fomenko's works are widespread on multiple platforms of media. In Russia his works have 'outsold [. . .] conventional historians many times over'. Actors from Russian state media have been shown to utilize his alternative chronologies in reporting as well,[25] despite the fact that the website istrf.ru, representing the official history teaching in Russia, lists Fomenko among pseudohistorians.[26] Fomenko's interpretations have worked their way into many facets of Russian culture including a large following by the alt-right movement. In a way, Fomenko's *New Chronology* forms a layer of online metamedievalism, one that is not easily perceivable to Western audiences. What is not clear is if the show authors sourced the idea from one of Fomenko's works. It does appear, however, that the authors did not understand the contemporary political attachments with the narrative. The balloon narrative is rhetorized in an anti-Western fashion, as Fomenko claims that a Russian clergyman devised the invention well 'before the Montgolfier brothers'.²⁷ Fomenko's utilization of this claim is not the first instance of this narrative appearing within Russian society, it is over a century old at this point. What is clear is that Fomenko's chronology does not appear within a networked assemblage of information about the period publicly available (i.e. related Wikipedia articles) to Western, non-Russian speaking users. As users attempt to vet and verify content, they are rendered unable to bring analysis to this narrative, or even be cognizant of its existence. Most of the information about Fomenko online is displayed in Russian. His English Wikipedia page and the page on the *New Chronology* do not present any information on this small nuance from his narrative.²⁸ Although in Russian online space, Fomenko is seen utilizing and employing the balloon narrative, individuals who do not read Russian are left unable to unpack this narrative.

However, in Russian websites, there is a clear path to determining the falsehoods of this narrative and finding its origins. The myth can be traced back to a notebook produced by A. I. Sulakadzev that reports:

> [I]n 1731 in Ryazan, under the governor of clerks, the *nerechtite* (scribe) Kryakutnoy made furvin like a big ball, blew out a foul and smelly smoke, made a loop from it, sat in it, and the evil spirits lifted it above the birch, and after hitting him on the bell tower, but he clung to the rope than they call, and Kryakutnoy remained alive, he was kicked out of the city, he went to Moscow and they wanted to bury him alive in the ground, or burn him.²⁹

Sulakadzev later reports that in lieu of being burned for witchcraft, Kryakutnoy accepted monastic vows at the Solovetsky Monastery. The original corpus of the text is inaccessible, but in 1958 the Department of Old Russian Literature in the Institute of Russian Language and Literature produced proceedings that called the document into question, stating that Sulakadzev was writing to 'surprise [contemporaries] with a sensational covering', and 'did not act in this direction unselfishly, and offered his forgeries to gullible people'.³⁰ In examining sources around this pseudohistorical narrative, I run across multiple mentions of an event in 2007 where the Governor of Ryazan Oblast, Georgy Shpak named Kryakutnoy as a 'world pioneer of aeronautics'.³¹ Despite this reported event in 2007, it does appear that most in the Russian internet space who have written on the subject recognize this as a historical forgery. However, this is of little help for users who do not read Russian. It is safe to assume the trail goes cold after this, as most of the citations presented on these pages reference articles in Russian which would be unconsumable for most audience members. Metzger and Flanagin speak to the ability to vet content and how users are often suspicious of Wikipedia articles, but in this case, most Western readers are left with no tools to verify the information.[32] Users approaching the narrative from this perspective are left to take the narrative at face value.

In examining conversations around the Reddit community 'vikingstv', it is clear that users did call into question the narrative but only in a way that was critical to the plotline progression of the series. One user comments on the feasibility of Ivar being able to go on the balloon flight with Oleg as he is portrayed in the series as disabled:

> It is far fetched though, considering he can't walk without his braces. He can't even really stand without them. For him to walk out in the middle of a battle, crutch in one hand and sword in the other without sustaining any injury is very unrealistic, and it's not the first time they've done this in the series, or even this season alone. Remember when he sat up in that birds nest with igor? How did he get up there? And how did he get down? *If ivar has fragile bones how did he not break anything when he and oleg landed the hot airballoon?* Or when he climbed the side of the mountain? It's very frustrating to watch a show break its own rules especially when it involves representation of disabled characters. His physicality has limits that the show ignores, and it also has consequences that are ignored as well.[33]

In examining the various comments around this episode, it is clear that users are obviously more concerned with show continuity and cannon as opposed to validating or critiquing the variant of this Russian pseudohistorical narrative that wound up being featured in the show. Of particular interest is the lacking user-based analysis around the entire Kievan plotline in season six when compared to more common Western historical themes (for example Anglo-Saxon Vikings) in earlier seasons of the show. In earlier seasons of the show, such discussions around the historical provenance made frequent appearances on the subreddit, often dominating discussions around individual episodes that were pinned (placed in a visibly prominent location) by moderators. An example of this comes from the work of one user who spent an extensive amount of time tracing the genealogical lineage between Queen Elizabeth II and Vikings who made an appearance in the TV show.[34] In contrast, the pseudohistorical and implausible early medieval balloon ride is not a grievance for Reddit users, probably because the narrative is set in the exoticized and strange Kievan Rus'. Rather than attempting to vet the narrative as users in this community had previously done with more familiar (Western) historical narratives, users seem to parse the content but not question it.

As long as this fan-based discussion content remains accessible there exists a possibility for the Potemkin narrative to continue to spread. Jenkins suggests that fan-based communities can 'prolong audience engagement', and that these discussions allow users 'to dig deeper into stories that matter to them'.[35] Each individual discussion around season six of *Vikings*, and in particular the balloon narrative provides another node within the assemblage and another potential point for another user to find the narrative and draw ahistorical conclusions or concepts from it.

In season six of *Vikings* there are multiple medievalisms presented to viewers for entertainment purposes. While there was no intention by the show's creators to infuse falsehoods (or fake news) that are attached to ethnocentric nationalisms into the narrative, viewers are left with incomplete and uninformed medievalisms that were generated to progress the plot line of the series. It is doubtful that any connections between the balloon narrative and state media narratives have been made, but nevertheless a parallel narrative to Fomenko and Sulakadzev's pseudohistorical claim has been distributed to a Western audience. Unintentionally the show has infused into its content Russian pseudohistorical narratives that are used by contemporary actors such as Anatoly Fomenko to exert Slavic racial superiority over Westerners. Audiences observing this show consume it for entertainment value, and it is unlikely that connections to contemporary political themes will be made by viewers. However, what does exist in Western media based on this case study is an artefact on Reddit, news articles and other platforms of social media that mention such an occurrence. The potential for a user down the road to draw themes from this certainly exists.

Returning to the Russian state media context, equitable access to records imbued with authority (i.e. academic papers and scholarly monographs) presents additional frustrations when attempting to vet publicly posted content. Since I have established that the Russian government utilizes medievalisms within their false news megaphone, we must consider where the Russian 'firehose of falsehood' of propaganda model sits in the gradient of publicly accessible content to premium, paywall content. Paul and Matthews from the RAND Corporation discuss this subject and lay out four 'distinctive features of the contemporary model for Russian propaganda'. The propaganda is generally (a) high-volume and multichannel, (b) rapid, continuous and repetitive, (c) lacks commitment to objective reality and (d) lacks commitment to consistency.[36]

Of these listed features all of them lend themselves to efficient distribution in publicly accessible content. Freely accessible content is more 'spreadable', or easier to share according to Jenkins and others, meaning that the likelihood of Russian propaganda being circulated is higher than academic articles that sit behind paywalls and may be tweeted out by their author once or twice. Paul and Matthews continue to state that 'in addition to acknowledged Russian sources like RT (Russia Today), there are dozens of proxy news sites presenting Russian propaganda, but with their affiliation with Russia disguised or downplayed'.[37] As free content is more accessible, it is more frequently distributed on social media as opposed to content subject to a charge.[38] Henkel and Mattson in their article about source credibility further corroborate that these free articles, when taken at a glance, build contexts of truth around environmental considerations such as website appearance and domain names. The effect that is produced is that often legitimate-looking websites are 'being taken as being true, with little or no knowledge as to where [the information] came from'.[39] What is clear is that authority imbued records are requisite for source verification when it comes to authenticating medievalisms presented by Russian state media.

The internet has become more dynamic, and the ability for users to publish their own content has lowered the bar to entry for publication. This in turn increases the size of the corpus of medievalisms present online. An increase of medievalisms online made by amateurs may potentially obfuscate material that is verified or change its ranking on search engines as content is often ranked by popularity. Also, as fan communities around various medieval-infused media continue to expand online, there exists another layer of users that act as armchair historians who are attempting to discern the historical accuracy of the content they consume. These enthusiast historians spend significant time attempting to vet and corroborate historical analysis.

However, they are often unable to access content from structures of authority (academic publications) and are left attempting to discern fact from fiction in an ecosystem where, in our case, Russian propaganda and pseudohistorical medievalism run amok. The decline of accurate information in public spaces around the history of Kievan Rus' is further exacerbated by the fact that the field of study is dwindling as an academic area of inquiry since the fall of the USSR. Many universities around the States have rescinded funding, reduced staff and removed resources from these Russian, Eastern European and Eurasian research centres. With this is an authority-based perspective medieval Russia is becoming increasingly inaccessible to Western audiences. As there are reduced faculty members employed in these lines of research the ability for researchers to be cognizant of this medievalism and put this information forward in public spaces also declines. Market forces have thus acted upon both the internet and the academy and have undoubtedly decreased public access to authority records.

Where we are left today is with an understanding that users who set out to research or contextualize medievalisms online face a phenomenological experience. A user who has access to a university student account has a much higher chance of verifying content compared to someone who does not have the same access. Additionally, these latter users are more prone to run into content propagated from Russian state media since this content is spread in free and easily accessible forms. This is not to say that internet users cannot get this content without passing through paywalls, the task just becomes increasingly more difficult when compared to users who have better access to academic journals. What may be discerned from this is the potential for interdisciplinary scholars to move into these specialized areas of research to help fill the void and offer a response from the academy in the age of the internet.

5

Memorializing the Finnish medieval past

Sirpa Aalto and Timo Ylimaunu

A successful celebration was held here yesterday. [. . .] 'People must live even during the hard times', said the speaker, 'they need to gather together, sing together and draw strength from the memories of history.'[1]

(*Uusimaa* 96, 21.8.1899, Transl. by T. Ylimaunu)

Memories of the past, historical narratives were presented and, above all, experienced in 'a successful celebration' in the medieval town of Porvoo in mid-August 1899. The entire celebration programme focused on the Finnish past as part of the Kingdom of Sweden, although Finland had already been part of the Russian Empire for almost 100 years. The reason why celebration organizers did not want to present the historical events of the Autonomous Grand Duchy of Finland was most likely that Tsar Nicholas II had started the so-called Russification process in Finland half a year before. The Tsar had cancelled the autonomous rights of Finland in the so-called February Manifesto. The common history with the Empire of Russia was too politically sensitive to touch upon in 1899, so it was safest to stick to events before the annexation.

Remembrance of the Middle Ages as part of the Finnish national history has concentrated mostly on the period before the Second World War. In the Finnish memory culture (*Erinnerungskultur*) the Civil War[2] (1918), Winter War (1939–40) and Continuation War (1941–44) have been central, and several memorials have been established to commemorate these historical events. Yet, there are some memorials that recall events, places or prominent persons from the Middle Ages in the Finnish past. How these memorials reflect not only the nation's political history but the memory culture on the national and local level has not been analysed. Therefore, in this chapter we will concentrate on the memorials that represent Finland's medieval past. We will compare especially memorials located in (Northern) Ostrobothnia with those located elsewhere in Finland.

The reason for this is that in the historiography of Ostrobothnia, the Middle Ages (here broadly understood to extend up to the end of the sixteenth century) has not been regarded as a decisive period for the area because it is not very prominently present in medieval written sources. The history of Ostrobothnia – as it is presented in local histories – first and foremost concentrates on the Early Modern and Modern periods including such phenomena as tar trade, sawmills and ship building. Therefore, a comparison between these northern, peripheral memorials with those erected in the southern part of Finland, where cities founded in the Middle Ages are located, offers a new viewpoint. When were the memorials in Ostrobothnia erected and what do they convey from that time period? What medieval events or which characters were remembered and why? What people were behind these projects? All in all, do these memorials reflect Finnish medievalism or something else? Is there a connection to today's medievalism?

Medievalism in the Finnish context has been investigated but it has not covered statues or memorials.[3] The end of the nineteenth century and the beginning of the twentieth century was the golden age for romanticism in the arts in Finland, especially the period from 1890 to 1918.[4] Painters were inspired especially by Finnish nature, the *Kalevala* and common people. Also, historical (or even pseudohistorical) characters or events were painted. As Derek Fewster has pointed out, in the Finnish context medievalism was first and most directed to the 'ancient past', that is to the period before annexation to Sweden. Interpretations of this Finnish protohistory were important for the continued creation of national consciousness.[5]

Memory, memorials, collective identity

Memorials and memory markers are mnemonic traces of past events, and they may be unveiled as long as tens of years or even centuries after actual events. Thus, their fundamental purpose is to remind us of the past events, commemorate events and people who participated in them. Therefore, memorials produce and reproduce meanings of the past in the present.[6] Memorials may have different kinds of meanings and temporal levels; they materialize political changes of the surrounding society.[7] They may represent and tell of the official, top-down narratives of the national past, but at the same time they may narrate unofficial histories of political or any other social organization. Or, memorials may illustrate historical myths or mis-histories, which means that they narrate events in the past that never took place, or which happened in another historical context.[8] Memorials are understood to cover more than just monuments.[9] They include many kinds of cultural products that are part of our construction of heritage. Memorials are manifestations of collective memory, and they are an integral part of memory culture, which on its part shapes collective identity. Therefore, it is crucial to realize what kinds of elements the collective memory includes. The community raises certain culturally relevant points to remember, which are considered to be unchangeable and which supposedly reveal the unity and distinctive features of the named group.[10]

In our chapter, we will use memorials as a meaning of a material marker to commemorate or as a material reminder of past events or a historical person. Our starting point for examining the memory of the Middle Ages in the Finnish context is to understand memory as a collective understanding of the past. Pierre Nora has written how it became more and more important to memorize the past in the nineteenth century. This is in connection with the rise of nationalism and shaping of modern societies. In a similar fashion, Nora speaks about memory places as *lieux de mémoires*.[11] However, in the context of this chapter, we are not confining the research to places, but to other aspects of memory.

When investigating memorials through the lens of medievalism, we try to capture the reason why something medieval was worth remembering. According to Andrew B. R. Elliott, there are three phases when a historical event or character is removed from its original context and reused in another: first, there is (1) historical expropriation, then (2) intercultural transmission and after that (3) ideological modification.[12] Is there a connection between historical expropriation and medievalism? Elliott defines the connection of historical expropriation and medievalism as 'the predominant mode of medievalism, the mode through which and in which medieval objects and concepts are invoked in the post-medieval period'. Elliott's definition can be applied to memorials in which medieval concepts are presented in the post-medieval era and reflect contemporary values, mentality and political ideology (Map 5.1).

The Finnish medieval towns and their material past lies in the southwestern and southern coast of the country. However, we wanted to approach the topic from a northern perspective, because Ostrobothnia – or Northern Finland in general – is mainly outside the scope of Finnish medieval overviews and, as mentioned, the local histories of this area do not recognize the Middle Ages as a prominent period. Yet the area had its own medieval history: it was inhabited,

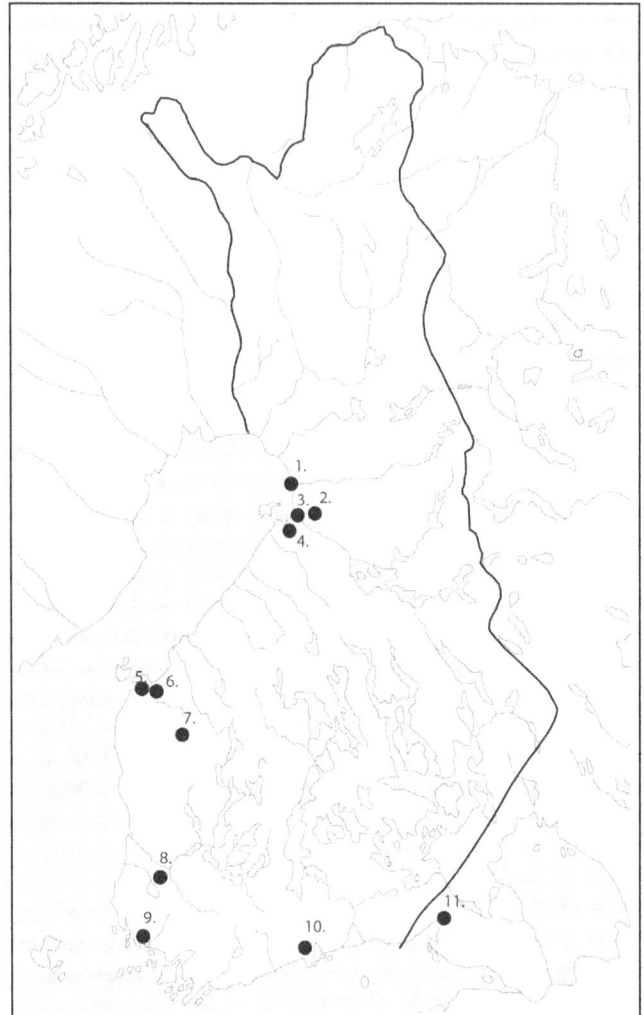

Map 5.1 The map of Finland. The map shows the place names mentioned in the Chapter. 1. Ii, 2. Ylikiiminki, 3. Oulu, 4. Liminka, 5. Vaasa, 6. Vähäkyrö, 7. Ilmajoki, 8. Köyliö, 9. Naantali, 10. Porvoo, 11. Viipuri. Source: Timo Ylimaunu.

in the first place, by the indigenous Sámi people, but also people originally from Southern Finland and Karelia. It had medieval parishes since the early fourteenth century and a fortification in the present-day city of Oulu, established approximately at the end of the fourteenth century.[13]

Finnish towns and municipalities have a list of their memorials available on the internet. We compared the lists and have chosen the following cases: Ilmajoki, Vähäkyrö, Vaasa, Liminka, Ylikiiminki and Ii in Ostrobothnia all have memorials dedicated to some aspect of the Middle Ages. We will concentrate on memorials in Ostrobothnia which are dedicated to historical characters and battles. As a comparison, the following towns from Southern Finland were chosen: Porvoo and Naantali which represent medieval towns, and Köyliö, which is a small locality in Southwestern Finland, but which has unusually many memorials related to the Finnish medieval past. As mentioned, we define the Middle Ages in the (northern) Finnish context very broadly so that it extends to the sixteenth century. This is justified, as the way of life, world view and living conditions did not change remarkably from the Middle Ages to the sixteenth century in Finland, and in the context of Northern Finland the century can be seen as a transition from the Middle Ages to the Early Modern period.[14] We examine the memorials in the chosen case towns and municipalities and investigate their backgrounds, for instance, in local newspapers. We contextualize the time of establishment of the memorial in order to ponder what they convey from the contemporary period and whether they could be interpreted to present medievalism.

Medieval sites and the Club War remembered in Ostrobothnia

The first memorial of the medieval past in Ostrobothnia, a gothic cross, was unveiled in the present-day town of Vaasa in 1894. The cross was erected on the site of a medieval fortress, which was built during the fourteenth century.[15] The State Archaeological Commission had made a suggestion to erect a memorial at the site of the medieval Korsholma fortress.[16] The head of the Archaeological Commission, J. R. Aspelin, stressed in his unveiling speech the Nordic and the Western European cultural and religious legacies in the Finnish past, although the country was at that time an autonomous part of the Russian Empire.[17] Two other memorials dedicated to the Middle Ages have been erected close to Vaasa. One was erected in Mustasaari to commemorate the past of the medieval Mussori village (1957) and the other to commemorate the medieval past of Sundom village (1977). The memorials were erected by the initiative of the local administration or local historical societies, and the congregation of Mustasaari funded part of the expenses for the Mussori village memorial.[18]

While memorials in the Vaasa district are dedicated to medieval sites, memorials in southern Ostrobothnia draw upon the memory of the Club War (1596–7), a Finnish peasant uprising, which is commemorated in Vähäkyrö and Ilmajoki. The reason for this must have been that the war began there and locals were heavily involved in it. A memorial was established in Ilmajoki to commemorate Jaakko Ilkka, a peasant warlord and a leader of the peasant uprising in the Club War (1924).[19] The next year, another memorial to commemorate the Club War was unveiled in Ilmajoki; this time to remember the Santavuori battle where some hundreds of men from the Club War were slaughtered.[20] Both memorials were erected by the initiative of local people and societies. The Jaakko Ilkka memorial was a tetragonal, castle-like structure with a tower in each corner made of grey granite cobblestone. E. Björkenheim, the head of the memorial committee, said in his unveiling speech: 'Now, when we see this statue, we see a symbol of that freedom fight, which men of the Club War started, and which continued and led to a victory by the generations of centuries, to the fight that created independent Finland.' The rector of the University of Turku, Professor Artturi H. Virkkunen, also emphasized the memory of Ilkka and his men and their 'endeavour for freedom' in his speech.[21] Another memorial dedicated to the Club War was unveiled in Vähäkyrö as late as 1996. This epitomizes how the event still holds symbolic importance for the local community's heritage.[22]

The Club War was thus interpreted in the newly independent Finland as an ancient part of the Finnish freedom fight. This was, of course, the interpretation of the winning side of the brutal and bloody Finnish Civil War (1918) in the 1920s and 1930s.[23] President Lauri Relander, who took part in the celebration of unveiling of the Club War memorial in Ilmajoki in 1925, compared the Club War with the devastating Civil War.[24] He understood how broken the contemporary Finnish nation was because of the terror during and after the Civil War. He stressed the importance of unity and efforts to unify the nation beside the memorial of the medieval period of violence. The Club War was presented in the memorials as a prelude to Finnish independence or was compared with the Civil War itself.

Medieval memorials as expressions of militaristic patriotism

Three memorials dedicated to the same era as the Club War period can be found in the neighbouring municipalities of the City of Oulu, the administrative centre in Northern Ostrobothnia. First, the Linnukka memorial which was erected by the initiative of locals in Liminka in 1934. This memorial, a castle wall or tower made of grey granite cobblestones, was unveiled to restore the memory of the battle at Linnukka Hill in 1592, when the local people of Liminka tried to defend their homes against the Russian troops during the so-called Old Hate (1570–95). In the main speeches at the unveiling of the memorial, this battle was seen as and compared to a preliminary fight for the country's independence. The Governor of the Province of Oulu, E. Y. Pehkonen, addressed in his speech that when the past generations were fighting against the Russians, they were laying the cornerstones for the freedom of the country and were defending Western civilization. He and another speaker, local farmer J. Poutala, stressed that local people should keep the memorial in shape, clean and sacred.[25] Hence, the memorial reflects the patriotic ideas of the 1930s projected back in time, but also the importance of the place of memory for the locals. Linnukka Hill and the memorial had a symbolic importance among the local society as part of their heritage.[26]

Even if the patriotism of the 1930s has passed, local pride in the past is strong. A memorial for Hannu Krankka, a leader of Liminka farmers in the Club War, and who was later appointed as the local bailiff, was unveiled in Liminka as late as in 2005. This local hero's name can also be found elsewhere: the local school was named after Hannu Krankka and a local restaurant uses his name.[27] Originally, the memorial was supposed to have been erected at the same time as the Linnukka memorial in 1934. The *Uusi Aura* newspaper wrote in 1934 that the Hannu Krankka memorial committee had been appointed in Liminka, and the committee had a plan that the memorial would have been erected on Linnukka Hill.[28] However, for some reason the original plans were not realized, but the memorial was unveiled in 2005.

Another local 'hero' was Pekka (or Juho) Vesainen who was a peasant warlord in Northern Ostrobothnia and who fought against the Russians in the late sixteenth century during the Old Hate, a period when the Kingdom of Sweden and the emerging Russian Empire struggled over who would govern present-day Northern Finland.[29] Two memorials were erected to commemorate Vesainen: the first memorial was erected by the initiative of local farmers' associations in Ylikiiminki (now part of Oulu) in 1936.[30] The memorial made by Oskari Jauhiainen is peculiar: it consists of granite cobblestones that form the face of a man. The features of the memorial are reminiscent of something ancient, maybe of the Kalevalaic world. It radiates masculinity in the spirit of romanticism, or perhaps Karelianism, which is the Finnish romantic style inspired by Karelia where the national Kalevalaic poetry was recorded. The materials, shape of the head and headgear of the memorial refer strongly to early-twentieth-century styles in architecture and inspiration from the Kalevala figures portrayed by artists of the era. The defence-minded and patriotic feelings were brought forward in the unveiling speeches in Ylikiiminki in 1936. The memorial was supposed to be understood as a symbol of the spirit of forefathers, freedom, love, patriotism, strength and power (Figures 5.1 and 5.2).[31]

The second memorial dedicated to Vesainen was planned to be erected by a local memorial committee in Ii in 1940, but the wartime delayed its unveiling.[32] The memorial in Ii was finally unveiled in 1950,[33] but the pedestal had been erected already in 1941. Engraved on the front side of the pedestal is 'Vesainen' and on the back side '1941'. On one side there used to be the text: 'People of Ii and their leader Vesainen chased foes away from their homesteads in the 1500s' and on the opposite side there was the text: 'The men of Ii followed their ancestral path and rose up in 1918 and 1939–40 with other Finns to repel the assault of the enemy and to protect their religion, homes and their native country's freedom.'[34] However, today there is only the text 'Vesainen' left on the pedestal; all others have been erased.

The Vesainen memorial in Ii was made by sculptor Kalervo Kallio. It represents a typical masculine statue of its time. Vesainen is standing with his legs wide apart looking towards the east and has grabbed his sword, which is

Figure 5.1 The memorial of Vesainen in Ylikiiminki, 1936. Photo: Timo Ylimaunu.

Figure 5.2 The statue of Vesainen in Ii, 1950. Photo: Timo Ylimaunu.

still in its scabbard. Compared to the unveiling speeches in Ylikiiminki in 1936, the tone of the speeches in Ii almost fifteen years later was different. All patriotic and masculine references were absent in the *Uusi Suomi* newspaper report on the unveiling of the Vesainen memorial in Ii in 1950, which probably reflects the postwar mentality and careful choice of words due to the fear of the reactions of the USSR.[35] The original text was erased and thus, the memorial is left without an explanation. The original text mentioned previously combined the late-medieval local hero and his acts with wars against Russia in 1918 (although this was a Civil War, not a war against Russia) and against the Soviet Union in 1939–40. However, for an occasional visitor to Ii the memorial of Vesainen remains a mystery because the commemorative texts are no longer there.

The remembered past is different than the historical or archaeological past.[36] When memorials were raised for Vesainen, it did not really matter that exact information about his person and deeds were missing. Contemporary local patriotism was projected back in time to his person which can be called historical expropriation. As Koselleck has argued 'more than anything else, memorials permanently testify to transitoriness', and meanings and representations of the memorials change in time.[37] Vesainen's importance thus changed in time: first he symbolized local patriotism, but he turned into a mere local hero from the past with no excessive nationalistic and patriotic emphasis after the Second World War. It could be argued that today Vesainen has fallen into oblivion. His character is no more used to boost local identity or patriotism. In fact, this would be questionable considering that today it is also recognized that he and his troops were guilty of terrorizing people in the Russian territory.

So far this chapter has dealt with Ostrobothnian memorials to medieval characters and events, but one memorial could be added as a comparison to the memorials of Vesainen and Hannu Krankka: the memorial of Torgils Knutsson in Viborg, now part of Russia. Torgils Knutsson was the founder of the Viborg Castle at the end of the thirteenth century. To honour him, a memorial was raised in 1908 made by sculptor Ville Vallgren. The memorial was revealed during a period when the first Russification period was over and the second was only about to begin. Therefore, it had a particular symbolical value for the Finns as the whole memorial was a reference to the fight against the Russians – thus against oppression. The memorial of Torgils Knutsson presents the same kind of patriotism as those of Vesainen and Hannu Krankka. Although the memorials of Vesainen and Hannu Krankka were raised after Finland had become independent, they continue to express the patriotic ideas of the time, against the threat of occupation and thus oppression. This includes that the statues are dedicated to men which emphasizes warfare, defence of home and patriotism also on the local level. Symbolism of these memorials is obvious: the memorial of Vesainen in Ii is facing towards the east and holding his hand on his scabbard, and the warlike character of Torgils Knutsson is standing boldly, holding his shield in his left hand and holding a sword in his right hand.

The memorials in Liminka, Ii and Ylikiiminki were not erected because the characters Hannu Krankka or Vesainen or the battle at Linnukka Hill would have been considered medieval, although they were erected between 1918 and 1945, which Fewster calls the phase of militant medievalism in Finnish history.[38] Narratives already from the seventeenth century present Finns as fighters who cleared forests and transformed them into arable fields.[39] These meanings were reproduced again some hundred years later during the 1920s and 1930s, when the nationalistic iconography used these same ideas in memorials emphasizing a certain pioneer spirit combined with a will to fight for one's country. Finnish nationalism was reproduced through the imagined militarism of the past in the contemporary present; the meaning of Finnishness was partly the same as the imagined masculine ancient Finnish 'national' state.[40] Thus, memorials offered an aesthetic way to produce and reproduce past narratives.[41]

The date of the erection of the Linnukka memorial (1934) and statues of Vesainen (1936 and 1941, even if the latter was postponed to 1950) are indeed indicative of the contemporary atmosphere of nationalism and patriotism in Finland. They have been left somewhat in the shadow of memorials dedicated to different wars in the twentieth century, but as such they stand as embodiments and mnemonic traces of local aspirations to remember local, mythical heroes. They form the link to national history, although this link may not be apparent to today's audience which may not necessarily be so well educated in the matters of local history.

Memorials in the south of Finland: Porvoo, Naantali, Köyliö

In the Middle Ages, Ostrobothnia was more or less a borderland and peripheral area compared to the southwestern and southern coasts of Finland. Therefore, it is not surprising that medieval towns and sites in this area memorialize the medieval period in their own ways. Porvoo boasts its history of being the second oldest town in Finland. Originally, the town was thought to have received its privileges in 1346, but later investigations have revealed that the most probable date for this was around 1387. Surprisingly, Porvoo has no memorial dedicated to its medieval past. In the 1940s there was an attempt to raise a memorial for King Magnus Eriksson, who was supposed to have granted the city its privileges, but the city council turned down the suggestion because the memorial would have been too expensive.[42] However, the king is memorized in the townscape as a street name.

It could be claimed that the Old Town of Porvoo itself is a memorial. There are no medieval buildings left except parts of the Old Cathedral which are dated to the fifteenth century, but the town plan in the Old Town is still the same as it used to be in the Middle Ages. The riverside of Porvoo, including the Old Town, has been nominated as one of the national city parks in Finland. The Old Town as a heritagescape may not be associated with the Middle Ages by an occasional tourist if they are not aware of the history of the city. Although the city may be more associated with post-medieval events in Finnish history (such as the Diet of Porvoo in 1809) and culture (national poet J. L. Runeberg who lived there), the city cherishes its old history also by using the medieval coat of arms (letter C standing for *castellum*, in memory of the old fortress in the city).

Even though Porvoo lacks visible memorials, its medieval history has not been forgotten by its inhabitants, at least over a century ago. As the cited newspaper report at the beginning of this chapter showed, in 1899 some residents of Porvoo, mainly members of the educated upper class, decided to organize a historical play in order to collect money for the newly founded local museum. The play was organized on 20 August 1899 by the hill where a medieval wooden fortress had once stood. The occasion was extraordinary for a small town: 4,000 spectators came to see the play, some of them all the way from Helsinki. The play was reported by local newspapers, *Borgåbladet* for Swedish speakers and *Uusimaa* for Finnish speakers.[43]

The play itself is an echo of the medievalism of its time in Finland. The 'actors' of the play were captured by a local photographer, John Granlund.[44] Costumes were partly loaned from the opera in St Petersburg, and artist Albert Edelfelt, himself living in Porvoo, had designed some of them. Commemoration of medieval events was in this case part of a longer historical play, but they served as a reminder of the long history of the city. At the same time, the play was organized during a politically sensitive time and together with other parts of the programme (for instance speeches and singing), offered a way to express nationalistic feelings.

Today the small town of Naantali in Finland Proper makes use of its medieval heritage, namely the Brigittine convent, which no longer exists. The Brigittine convent has its memorial (1931) in the churchyard of the Naantali medieval church. Beside the church lies also a memorial for the friar Jöns Budde (1921) and a memorial of the Brigittine nun (1993). In addition, the medieval Bishop Magnus Tavast has a memorial marker (1933) in the town. Amos Anderson (1878–1961), a famous patron of the Finnish arts, was financing memorials for Jöns Budde and Bishop Magnus. Anderson was a wealthy businessman and interested in the medieval period and history of Naantali, and he personally financed or participated in the financing of medieval memorials also outside of Naantali.[45] The memorials in Naantali thus emphatically concentrate on the ecclesiastical history.

Köyliö, a small rural centre in Finland Proper, is famous for being the place where a Finnish peasant named Lalli allegedly murdered Bishop Henry, the first bishop of Finland, around 1155 CE. There is no historical evidence of this event, but the legend of St Erik written much later and folksongs give their versions of what happened.[46] Memorials unveiled in Köyliö are from the postwar period: a memorial stone for St Henry (1955), a relief in the memory of pilgrimages dedicated to St Henry (1976), a memorial plaque for St Henry's road (1979), a memorial stone for Lalli's homestead (1979), and Lalli's memorial (1989). As in the case of Naantali, where Amos Anderson was active in financing the memorials, also in Köyliö, the memorials have been an initiative of one local man and artist, Väinö Nummisto (1912–87). He became interested in the legend of Lalli and began to promote erecting of memorials. Nummisto was also active in creating anew the medieval pilgrimage route related to St Henry that had connected Köyliö and other medieval parishes in the area.[47]

The memorials erected in Köyliö can be seen in the same context as those erected for medieval bishops in other small rural centres in the southwestern part of Finland. They reflect local interest in history. What is common for the memorials in Naantali and Köyliö is that they have had symbolic heritage significance to the local community as realms of local memory.[48] However, the time of erection of the memorials shows how contemporary atmosphere and political climate affect who is remembered and how. The erection of memorials in Köyliö in the 1970s and 1980s took place during a time when the Soviet Union influenced Finnish politics,[49] and memorializing the past with official memorials had to be in line with the current political view, that is it was not supposed to raise anger in the USSR. Curiously enough, the Middle Ages, which was glorified in the 1920s and 1930s, and even used as a tool of patriotism, turned out to be unpolitical enough in the postwar period, when the commemorated persons such as St Henry and Lalli were not emphatically hostile to the eastern neighbour but important characters for local history.

To conclude, medieval memorials in Naantali and Köyliö were either financed or initiated by one, local individual. Memorials in Naantali convey Anderson's personal interest in the Middle Ages but also the contemporary, prewar nationalistic ideas that can be interpreted to present medievalism of its own time and which were projected back in time by commemorating important characters. Porvoo, with its medieval history but without a memorial dedicated to the Middle Ages, remains a case of its own. It seems that the city has managed to brand the Old Town as a heritagescape which includes both the medieval and Early Modern periods and there is or has been no need for a specifically medieval memorial. When comparing these memorials in the southern and southwestern parts of Finland with those of Northern Ostrobothnia, it can be argued that they were more often dedicated to ecclesiastical history than those in Ostrobothnia which focus on military history.

Discussion

As the case of these memorials in small towns and rural centres shows, the Finnish memory culture related to the Middle Ages is distinctively local, not national. There are no great national monuments dedicated to the Middle Ages if we exclude the medieval castles and cathedrals, which in themselves may be seen as part of a national landscape and thus national history. The local aspect is not surprising because in a similar manner the memory of such important events as the Civil War was first and foremost constructed at the local level. Thus, the perspective of Finnish history rose from the local level so that people could identify themselves as participants in national history through local events and figures.[50] Also, local individuals have been crucial when initiating memorial projects or even in financing them.

Remembering the past is an ongoing, active process throughout nation states and societies that tells narratives about people or events that need to be commemorated. States and societies use material culture, such as memorials, to tell about these important narratives of the past.[51] Memorials of Vesainen and the Club War heroes are mnemonic traces of these narratives and memories of the mythical, heroic, reimagined medieval past in the then-contemporary present. In this sense, reproduction of 'the ancient past' and 'Kalevalaic heroes' in the form of memorials stands as metamedievalism that Elliott brings up in the opening chapter of this book. The memorials repeat the national narrative of the newly born republic of Finland on a local level: in this narrative the Finnish peasant has always been prepared to fight against occupation and oppression, usually from the east. It is notable that this narrative emphasizes the masculine (military history) and thus disregards other aspects of the past. The narrative does not leave space for other kinds of interpretations, because its purpose was to produce a coherent past for a homogenous nation. The people who erected the memorials did not in the first place want to remember the period in question, but the memorials were harnessed to boost national identity.

Nonetheless, the material culture is not necessarily honest in revealing its narratives of the past.[52] These narratives and memories may be propagandistic ones, which have been engraved into shapes of the memorials. Therefore, the memorials were and are still a medium that conveys narratives of the past and versions of the past that have been chosen to be presented to the public.[53] Interestingly, memorializing the medieval characters or battles have very different interpretations depending on the time when they were erected. Before the Second World War, remembering medieval characters such as Vesainen was a patriotic act, whereas in postwar Finland this changed into a safe way to express the national past and patriotic feelings as long as the commemorated persons were not emphatically represented as too patriotic or hostile to the USSR. In postwar Finland the medieval church and its figures were a safe way to express national pride. On the other hand, memorials of St Henry in Köyliö suggest that Finns wanted to express their connectedness to Western Europe in a subtle way during the Finlandization period. Also, memorials of Lalli could be interpreted to be a modest way (meaning that memorials were not overtly pompous) of paying respect to the character of a Finnish 'fighter' that was glorified earlier in prewar patriotic memorials.

Stuart Hall has pointed out that the new independent nation states use their mythical past and founding tales in the process of building up the foundations of the nation state. This process needed ideas and narratives of the pure and original nation, as well as narratives that included tales of victories, battles and losses, and in many cases they included stereotyped gender roles.[54] In the Finnish national narrative, men were presented as active fighters and women were the ones who mourned the dead.[55] Memorials, too, are gendered. If we exclude the statue of a nun in Naantali, the memorials related to the Middle Ages are dedicated to men, battles and some historical sites. In some cases, this is indicative of militant medievalism, but it also reveals how official memory culture concentrates on the masculine.[56]

Same nationalistic ideas were reflected symbolically in the granite cobblestones of Ostrobothnian memorials. The granite was considered to be a typical Finnish building material and it got this status as a nationalistic building material during the period of the Oppression (1899–1917); it was considered to symbolize traits of Finnishness.[57] Memorials that were made of granite symbolized 'the ancient, mythical Finn with his granite rock-hard will' from the mist of the past. This 'rock-hard will' was considered as a synonym to the patriotic will to defend the country in the prewar period. Several memorials, for example, Vesainen in Ylikiiminki, the Linnukka battle in Liminka and Jaakko Ilkka in Ilmajoki, were all built of granite cobblestones to imitate medieval castles and stone churches, but also national-romantic-style buildings. The raising of medieval memorials in Ostrobothnia did not take place during the golden age of emerging 'national' Finnish culture in the 1890s,[58] but the examples given in this chapter show that they were unveiled either before the Winter War or in the postwar period.

In the strict sense, many of the Ostrobothnian memorials represent prewar patriotic imagined scenes of the local pasts and heroes. Thus, they hardly convey medievalism, per se, but are expressions of local patriotism, even metamedievalism in that sense that the memorials draw 'on a specific reimagining of the medieval past' as Elliott puts it in the opening chapter of this book. They were not erected because the locals would have felt that the Middle Ages was an important period in the local history. Through these memorials, these mythical northern figures and events had become 'our past and our forefathers' for the locals. As Alvestad has pointed out when investigating medievalism in the Norwegian context, specific sites can function as anchors and authenticate medievalism by creating a link between the now and then.[59] The memorial sites in Ostrobothnia anchor medievalism – or, maybe even metamedievalism as said – on a local level. In the unveiling speeches, patriotism was a virtue that was added into memorials during the 1920s and 1930s.[60] Another aspect of the memorials emerges through the unveiling speeches: the memorial sites should be considered as holy sites on an emotional level.[61] These sites 'formed a circle', which enclosed the past, present and future generations.[62] Hence, these patriotic and emotional meanings were spoken out loud and clear in the unveiling speeches manifesting the fear of the otherness, and, especially, fear of the East and Russians.

According to Jens Brockmeier social experiences and remembering 'open up a symbolic space of meaning that binds individuals to each other' and societies use 'actions, narratives, images' to transmit experiences and the knowledge of the past in the present to the generations to come.[63] Memory and remembering are in continuous interaction with the outside world, with other humans and with the material culture. However, the material culture changes in time and different things remind us of different events; slowly by slowly, the process will efface the previous things from the collective memory into the mist of the past.[64] Therefore, remembering is connected to forgetting because individuals or societies cannot remember everything.[65] Buchli and Lucas have argued that acts of erasing material culture can be understood as attempts to erase memory, suggesting that 'what is *not* there, what is *absent*' causes forgetfulness (italics in original).[66] Today, the pedestal of Vesainen in Ii has only one text 'Vesainen'. Other texts, which were marked on the pedestal in 1941, had been erased between 1941 and 1950 when the statue was unveiled. Thus, it seems obvious that the erasing of texts from the Vesainen memorial in Ii took place in the postwar period when other Finnish memorials were altered by political guidance.

The erasure itself tells about the contemporary political climate, whereas the erased text was a manifestation of the patriotic feelings before the Second World War, which cleverly combined the 'ancient times' to contemporary struggles. Now that the original text is erased, one layer of memorizing has been stripped from the memorial. The memorial falls thus to the category of metamedievalism.[67]

Memorials were and still are arenas for political discussion and their alteration indicates political changes in the surrounding society;[68] older nationalistic narratives of the past had to be forgotten in a new political situation. Today, the medieval memorials in Ostrobothnia face another kind of eclipse. They do not attract tourists en masse, nor are they especially remembered by the locals. It could be argued that the memorials now stand on the edge of forgetting – forgetting the heroes and battles of the past, because the communities cannot remember everything. However, this does not mean that the Middle Ages itself would have lost its attractiveness to the audience. On the contrary, medieval fairs are popular and some Finnish cities such as Turku and Naantali make use of their medieval history when attracting tourists or branding themselves. Yet this interest in the medieval or premedieval in Finland is rather weak compared, for instance, to Norway, where plays inspired by the Middle Ages have been produced after the Second World War and the starting point for writing the plays was very long ethnic-national interest.[69] Nonetheless, there has been general interest in the Finnish 'mythical past' before the annexation to Sweden, which could be seen as an expression of medievalism, but this is taking place outside the official arena in the fora of the internet. This interest is shadowed by pseudohistories which fabricate a past that is not based on research, but imagination.[70] So far, this interest has not produced memorials.

It is clear that medieval history and characters no longer stand in the centre of the official Finnish identity building and cultural memory. Aleida Assmann divides memory in several categories, for example, political and cultural memory. Both of these memory types are transgenerational, and especially political memory uses material symbols to produce new experiences and memories in the present for future generations. The political memory functions from the top to down. In this sense it is partly ideologically loaded, and therefore its one objective is to create social and political identities.[71] Hence, the experiences and memories, which memorials were intended to evoke, will determine our understanding of the past.[72] Finnish medieval memorials have changed over time and they remind us of different things; different temporalities fade different pasts in the contemporary presents and expose other kinds of pasts for the present and future. Our understanding of the past is in constant change. This is what Brockmeier calls devaluations of traditions, which leads to forgetting and change in memory works; there are no stable and lasting political or cultural memories.[73] Therefore, the concept of medievalism in Finnish memorials can be seen as a process that changes; what was considered important about 100 years ago is now to be forgotten or understood differently.

Concluding remarks

The overall number of memorials dedicated to the Middle Ages in Finland is not great. Compared to the fact that every municipality has in practice memorials to commemorate either the Civil War or Second World War victims, the memory of the Finnish medieval period remains marginal in the collective memory of the Finns. Reasons for this can be found in the way the narrative of Finnish history has been created. This narrative has concentrated on the struggle for independence and maintaining it. The painful memory of wars has been memorized and reworked in the official memory so that today there is place for different interpretations. In general, the Middle Ages does not really present substantial material for the Finnish national narrative. Medievalism – although it appears in Finnish paintings and literature to some extent – was not harnessed in memorials on the official, national level because remembrance of wars was overwhelming in the memory culture in the twentieth century.

The memorials in Ostrobothnia examined in this article can be interpreted to be expressions of metamedievalism today. During the times of the erection of memorials, the local 'heroes' were understood as part of the national and especially local history and they were considered to be role models presenting patriotism in the guise of militaristic medievalism. However, the framework of the Middle Ages has disappeared and the contemporary audience interprets the memorials from their own perspectives. Even if these local heroes are still remembered in naming places (such as a local school or street names), the reason is not the admiration of the medieval period but 'local tradition', which itself may be obscure for local people today. Thus, it is well grounded to say that the memorials of the local heroes are a living example of metamedievalism and also a good example of forgetting.

All in all, in the Finnish context those memorials related to the medieval period and erected before the Second World War convey local patriotism and they connect the local community to national history. Memory culture changed so that the medieval memorials erected after the Second World War may be explained as safe ways to remember the distant past during the time of Finlandization. Memorials, such as those erected to ecclesiastical characters, can be interpreted to show how Finns were linked to the Western civilization via Christianization and annexation to Sweden. Remembering 'ancient' characters or events could not raise the anger of the eastern neighbour. Today, the memorials dedicated to medieval characters and battles in Ostrobothnia are about to be forgotten. In this sense, we see how memory culture changes and how it is reflected in medieval memorials.

6

The missing Finnish runestones

Kendra Willson

Introduction: Few runes in Finland

While few runic inscriptions dating from the Viking Age or Middle Ages have been found in Finland, there is a persistent vernacular belief that there were more. Rumours of lost runestones and attempts to argue that runes have been used in Finland more than seen in the archaeological record have occurred in marginal and alternative histories at least since the early twentieth century. Discussion of runes in Finland has been connected to language politics for at least as long. Swedish speakers have looked to runes for proof of an early Scandinavian presence. There has also been speculation that runes were used to write Finnish (somewhat analogous to the question of 'Slavonic runes' in nineteenth-century Poland), which is tied to notions of a lost Finnish civilization. In this, contemporary pseudohistorical discourses continue a century-long tradition. The present chapter traces some highlights of this discussion, showing persistent and recurring features, as well as ways in which old themes adapt to changing social and political environments.

The total number of known runic inscriptions is close to 7,000, of which roughly half come from Sweden. Of around 3,000 known runestones, a significant majority (c. 1,700–2,500) are found in the area of modern-day Sweden and date from the late Viking Age. Despite geographical proximity to the regions of central Sweden richest in runestones, Finland has only a handful of runic inscriptions and just one runestone fragment generally agreed to stem from the Viking Age (the Hitis stone, discovered in 1997[1]). The few Viking Age finds are on small objects thought to be imported. A few late-medieval inscriptions on everyday objects have been found in Turku[2] and the use of runic calendar sticks spread from Sweden around the Reformation.[3] The inscriptions from Finland are in

Germanic languages or Latin; no runic inscription has to date been established as being in a Finnic or Sámi language.[4]

Many people have thought that if there were Scandinavian speakers in Finnish territory during the Viking Age, there would have been runic inscriptions, although conspicuous runic monuments are not found in all areas visited or settled by Norsemen during that era. Apart from Scandinavia, runestones are found primarily in the British Isles, with a few scattered further afield from Greenland (where the finds are mainly medieval) to Berezan' (Ukraine). Inscriptions on portable objects and runic graffiti show a larger geographical and temporal spread. It has been suggested that the Scandinavian 'runestone boom' from the late tenth to the twelfth century was connected to changes in social and political structures surrounding the transition to Christianity.[5]

The lack of runes has been part of the discussion of the age of the Swedish settlement in Finland at least since the start of Finnish independence at the end of the First World War. The question of when the Swedes came to Finland is the subject of much popular lore.[6] Scholarly discussion on the topic dates from the language conflict of the nineteenth century and has been politicized from the start.[7] The current majority view is that the migration that produced the modern Swedish-speaking communities began in the twelfth and thirteenth centuries with Christianization and the integration of Finland into the Swedish kingdom. While there were almost certainly speakers of Germanic languages in the territory of modern-day Finland at earlier times, there may not have been continuity in language transmission.[8] However, there are many open questions. Arguments for and against an earlier or continuous Scandinavian presence have been proposed at various times by representatives of different disciplines.[9]

Some both pro- and anti-Swedish contingents seem to feel that the legitimacy of Swedish speakers as part of the Finnish cultural landscape is tied to the age of Scandinavian settlement in Finland. Some hostile to the continued status of Swedish as a national language view Swedish speakers as late interlopers connected with colonial rule, although this presents a distorted view of history. Some Swedish speakers in turn go to lengths to demonstrate a Scandinavian presence from early on.

Heikki Ojansuu's study of place names, in an appendix 'Ruotsalaisten ikä Suomessa'[10] [On the age of the Swedish settlement in Finland], mentions the lack of runestones in Finland as evidence for the late arrival of Swedish speakers:

> Tätä tulosta ruotsalaisten iästä Suomessa tukevat muutamat muutkin tosiasiat, ennen kaikkea se, ettei Suomen melko laajoilta ruotsalaisalueilta ole löydetty

ainoatakaan *riimukiveä*,[11] vaikka niitä Ruotsissa on yhteensä n. 2,000.[12] [This conclusion about the age of the Swedish settlement in Finland [that it postdates the Christianization of Scandinavia around 1000 AD] is corroborated by a few other facts, in particular, the fact that in the fairly extensive Swedish-speaking area in Finland, not a single *runestone* has been found, although in Sweden there are a total of around 2000.]

Ojansuu is responding to inter alia Ralf Saxén,[13] who argued that there were many old Scandinavian place names in Finland. T. E. Karsten,[14] who throughout his career promoted the idea of a Germanic homeland in Finland,[15] replies to an earlier piece by Ojansuu by pointing out that in Scandinavia such monuments appear mainly in cultural centres. Arnold Nordling responds to Ojansuu at length in his piece 'Varför tyckas inga runinskrifter ha utförts i Finland?'[16] [Why are no runic inscriptions thought to have been produced in Finland?]. Nordling stresses that a lack of runic inscriptions does not prove a lack of Scandinavian speakers, noting examples of places where Scandinavians were certainly present but no early runic artefacts are preserved: for instance, runes are only known from Dalarna in modern times and no Viking Age runic inscriptions are known from Åland.[17]

Heikki Oja presents some possible reasons for the dearth of runic inscriptions in Finland.[18] The area of present-day Finland was sparsely populated during the Viking Age and relatively poor. The main directions of contacts from Finland were south and east (as seen in the numismatic record[19]). Finland was not a primary area of interest for Viking trade or raiding, more a waystation on the route to Novgorod and Byzantium. By the time Finland entered the Swedish cultural sphere around the twelfth century, the use of runes in Sweden was on the decline.

In discourses that cover the gamut from scholarly to popular to pseudoscientific, with much grey area, various creative strategies have been invoked to suggest that there was more use of runes in Finland than the archaeological record has so far revealed. Some have tried to suggest that there were runic monuments that have disappeared. Matts Dreijer collects legends of vanished runestones in Åland as a way of enhancing its centrality to Viking Age Sweden.[20] There are also marginal theories that imagine an earlier use of runes to write Finnish or related languages. These may be based on some semblance of linguistic or graphematic arguments.[21] Jukka Nieminen speculates on an early use of runes in Finland as part of his vision of an ancient Finnish kingdom that flourished before the arrival of the Swedes during the Baltic Crusades. Nieminen does not engage in linguistic analysis, but collects stories of lost runestones in order to cast doubt on the official archaeological data and narrative.[22]

Carving modern inscriptions – whether intended as forgeries or not – may also be a way of performing the history one intuitively feels is right. Finland has a few rune carvings in stone that are generally thought to date from the nineteenth and twentieth centuries. Some of these are in Swedish, some in Old Norse, likely reflecting book learning. Gunnar Hård, writing in the context of the controversy surrounding the runestones in Vörå, imagines *fin de siècle* Swedish speakers carving runestones as a way of claiming territory:

> Det fanns en period kring förra sekelskiftet, då finlandssvenskarna befann sig i en starkt defensiv ställning. Både förrysknings- och förfinskningssträvandena kändes som ett hot mot den finlandssvenska identiteten. Under en tid, då vikingaskeppet var en vanlig svenskhetssymbol, hade det, enligt min uppfattning, varit fullt möjligt att någon svenskhetskämpe och folkbildare hade 'skapat' några runstenar för att markera svenskarnas hemortsrätt i Finland. Inte heller ett studentskämt föreföll mig uteslutet, när den första runraden upptäcktes.[23] [There was a period around the turn of the last century when the Finland Swedes found themselves in a very defensive position. Both Russification and Fennicization efforts were perceived as a threat to Finland–Swedish identity. During a time when the Viking ship was a common symbol for Swedishness, it would, according to my understanding, have been entirely possible that some champion of Swedishness and popular educator would have 'created' some runestones in order to mark the rightful presence of the Swedes in Finland. Nor did a student prank strike me as out of the question when I heard about the first runic sequence.]

As scientific dating of scratches on rock is in general impossible, the age of an inscription must be inferred from linguistic and stylistic features and similar heuristics, involving the location and some surmises from the qualities of the scratches regarding the tools used in carving them and the degree of weathering. These criteria are subtle and different specialists bring different expertise, which can lead to conflicting statements. Notably in the case of the Vörå inscriptions, during the decade or so starting from the first discovery in 1978, such uncertainties generated a heated debate in which both sides accused the other of political agendas connected with promoting or suppressing an early Swedish presence in Ostrobothnia. A general breakdown in trust between the Ostrobothnian locals and the academic establishment ensued (as discussed further on).

As J. P. Taavitsainen points out, modern inscriptions are not necessarily forgeries, but can be viewed as part of a memorial epigraphic culture and as expressions of antiquarian interest.[24] They are, however, clearly tied to an interest in the Scandinavian past and a desire to connect to it on a personal and performative level. There are modern inscriptions that do not pretend to be old. A carving in Sauvo (Sw. Sagu), in modern Swedish, spells out the date **ottonde : juli : anno : nittonnhundra : ok : tjugotwo** [eighth of July year nineteen hundred and twenty-two].[25] In 2017, my student Sakari Helvamo carved a runestone as a course project. The inscription is in the younger futhark in Old Norse and inspired by the story of Sigurd the dragon-slayer and the iconography of Viking Age runestones. Although the language reflects knowledge of Old Norse grammar and principles of runic orthography, the inscription is carved using modern tools, and stylistically it would not be mistaken for a Viking Age artefact. However, carvers cannot control the later reception of their work when it is left in the landscape. A runic inscription carved by graduate students at the University of Minnesota was reported by media as a case of 'academic fraud' when it was discovered some years later.[26]

The discourse surrounding the Vörå runestones and about Finnish runestones more generally shows many parallels to discussion of runestones in North America, which are almost certainly modern. The most famous example is the Kensington runestone in Minnesota. David M. Krueger discusses the position of the Kensington stone in relation to Scandinavian–American foundation myths.[27] Scandinavian-Americans project continuity between Viking expansion and nineteenth-century immigration. The Kensington runestone as purported evidence of a pre-Columbian presence of Europeans (and specifically Norse) in exactly an area later settled by Swedes seems to mark their presence there as manifest destiny. Carving the runestone and accepting it as authentic are ways of staking a claim to the landscape. A similar impulse has been expressed in other forms, for example in Reider Thorbjorn Sherwin's unscientific hypothesis of Norse 'influence' on Algonquin languages.[28] The racialized connotations of Viking heritage assume different forms at different times, connecting to prevailing discourses. In the twenty-first century many white nationalist groups use symbols such as runes connected with early Norse culture, often the same ones as were exploited by Nazis or related early- to mid-twentieth-century movements.[29] 'Vínland', the name used for North America in Old Norse sources, has come to symbolize an imagined white utopia in North America[30] and is used to obscure Indigenous contributions to shaping Newfoundland.[31]

While runestones are primarily associated with Scandinavian ancestry, there are also other imaginative/alternative histories expressed through runes. For instance, Lithuanian-American Joseph Pashka developed a system for using runes to write the reconstructed Baltic language Sudovian, which then was enacted in a cave in Arizona.[32] Like Finnic speakers, Baltic speakers were relatively near Scandinavian areas during the Viking Age and in some degree of contact with them.

Further on, I discuss proposals that runes were once used to write Finnish. These find parallels in the question of 'Slavonic runes'. At least since the nineteenth century there have been various suggestions that Slavs may have written with runes.[33] While there are allusions to Slavic writing before the invention of Cyrillic, no such texts have survived and it is not known what system was used. The idea of Slavonic runes was mainstream scholarship in the nineteenth century, but abruptly disappeared from scholarly discussion following the First World War, Poland's restored independence and a changed relationship to things German(ic).[34] The idea survives in alternative circles. Tomasz Kosiński views the idea that Slavic peoples were illiterate before the Cyrillic alphabet as 'wierutną bzdurą' [egregious nonsense] and asserts that repression of knowledge of Slavic runes is 'tematem tabu i dogmatem stworzonym na potrzeby propagandy historycznej w czasach zaborów, utrwalonym przez komunizm, a ostatnio także przez zwolenników pangermańskiej polityki europejskiej' [a taboo theme and a dogma created for the needs of historical propaganda in the time of partitions, solidified by Communism and recently also by supporters of pan-Germanic European politics].[35] Winicjusz Kossakowski fancifully interprets some Scandinavian runic inscriptions as poems in Old Polish.[36] Poland's relationship to the Viking world shows some parallels to Finland's: it was part of the Scandinavian sphere of influence during the Viking Age, and there is both historical and archaeological evidence for contacts and a Norse presence on the Polish coast. However, the dominant language in modern times is not Scandinavian and the official national historical narrative does not feature Vikings. The degree of Scandinavian influence on the formation of the Polish state has been a matter of both scholarly and popular debate and speculation. The number of runic inscriptions found in Poland is similar to that found in Finland, and Władysław Duczko argues that the Viking Age inscriptions provide incontrovertible evidence for Scandinavian settlement in Poland.[37] Some modern inscriptions have been carved since the nineteenth century, including both 'forgeries' and ones that do not claim to be old.[38]

Authority crisis in Vörå

The discovery of several runic inscriptions in Vörå (Fi. Vöyri) in Ostrobothnia starting in 1978 prompted intense debate over their authenticity and age. This led to an authority crisis: different experts pronounced them old versus modern with confidence. Discussion broke down. The discussion was closely tied to local Finland–Swedish identity. The idea of long continuity in Swedish settlement has a strong tradition in Ostrobothnia,[39] and the locals were exhilarated to see 'proof' of an early Scandinavian presence in the area during the Viking Age. When the evidence was questioned they suspected a conspiracy to suppress the region's Swedish history, as well as perceiving the scepticism as an attack on the personal integrity of the finders, their ancestors and the community as a whole. Dimensions of the conflict included town versus gown, rural versus urban, Ostrobothnia versus Helsinki, Sweden versus Finland and Swedish versus Finnish-speaking Finns. The debate itself has become a subject of tradition.[40]

The first of the Vörå inscriptions, in Höjsål, is said to have been discovered by the farmer Hugo Berg in midsummer 1978. At that time no runestones were known from Finland, and the only established Viking Age runic find was the Tuukkala brooch (found in 1886).[41] The excitement was crushed when Swedish runologist Sven B. F. Jansson pronounced the inscription modern, likely from the turn of the twentieth century. A second and then a third discovery in 1982 continued the intrigue. According to the accounts in Ralf Norrman's book,[42] on 18 August 1982, while on a walk with Uno and Anna Forss in the Härtull wetland on the island of Båtholmen, Erik Svens caught sight of a **t**-rune on a mossy rock, and when the three cleared away the moss an inscription emerged. A third inscription, from Pethskiften near the Båtholmen site, was said to have been found by Uno Forss that November but was only reported to authorities the following year (Figure 6.1).

A majority of Swedish runologists and Finnish archaeologists concurred with the view that the inscriptions were modern, while several philologists from Swedish-speaking Finland defended their antiquity. The most vocal runologist advocating for an early date was the Swede Evert Salberger, who became a hero to the locals. The inherent difficulty or impossibility of dating inscriptions in stone, confusing and contradictory pronouncements by different experts, and a perfunctory treatment on the part of the runological establishment contributed to a breakdown of trust between academics and the locals. The local community interpreted the questioning of the inscriptions' age both as a personal attack on the finders (accusing them of forgery) and as part of a systematic attempt to suppress evidence of an early Swedish presence in Ostrobothnia.

In conjunction with the controversy, the local 'fria forskare' [free researchers] founded an 'alternative' archaeological organization with conferences and publications that emphasized the rich local record. Investigation of the stones

Figure 6.1 Runic inscription in Höjsål, Vörå. Photo: Mårten Huldén 1980. Archive of Cultural Sciences Cultura, Åbo Akademi University, Cultura KIVÅ B52766. Reproduced with the permission of Archive of Cultural Sciences Cultura.

was hindered by deep mistrust and an apparent feedback loop between reports and findings: the contents of a reported grave find near the Båtholmen site appeared to have been placed there recently.[43] After an archaeological report suggested that the inscription must have been carved with an awl of hard steel, an iron object stated to be an awl was reported to have been found near the site.[44] The 'planting' of remains and artefacts seems to show contempt for the archaeological establishment and a very strong desire to make the findings true on the part of the locals. There were accusations of forgery and libel, with threats of lawsuits. The case became so heated that many scholars did not want to be involved. Uno Forss continued to report further runestone finds up through 1998, but later ones did not receive systematic investigation; he declined to reveal the location of one runestone he claimed to have found. In 1998 Erik Svens sent a letter to the Board of Antiquities claiming that his initial report on the Båtholmen find in 1982 had been misleading – Uno Forss had noticed the runes earlier and arranged for Svens to 'discover' them.[45]

I do not feel qualified to judge the age of the Vörå inscriptions. I consider it plausible that there was settlement in the area during the Viking Age (despite the older hypothesis, stemming from Aarne Europaeus,[46] that southwestern Ostrobothnia was unpopulated at that time) and Scandinavian influences would not be surprising. Certainly an old runestone is more likely to be found in Ostrobothnia than in Minnesota. Nonetheless, I concur with the majority of runologists that at least most of the inscriptions are probably modern. The combination of letter forms and linguistic forms from different periods is suspect. Stylistically they differ from known Viking Age runestones. Joakim Donner argued that the grooves in the Härtull inscription appeared to be made with a harder metal tool than was available before modern times and to show little sign of weathering.[47] However, unambiguous dating of such an inscription is nearly impossible. It would be worth returning to the investigation with fresh eyes now that some decades have passed and – hopefully – tempers calmed.

The intensity of the debate, played out not least in narrative forms – competing first-person accounts of discoveries; reconstructed lives of the carvers and persons mentioned in the inscriptions; even stories about the controversy – shows a desire to take control over the history of the finds and site. Norrman's book[48] expressly sets out to define a normative, authoritative view of the finds and early discussion. Swedish speakers in rural Ostrobothnia felt marginalized both relative to the Helsinki-centred, majority Finnish-speaking academic establishment and to Sweden. A lack of transparency in argument, suspicions of tampering with data and a few key contentious personalities created a situation in which statements about the inscriptions were automatically interpreted as reflecting what is now called identity politics rather than sincere scholarship.

Matts Dreijer, Sund and Birka

If Finland's position in relation to Scandinavia is fraught, Åland's is doubly so. When it became an autonomous region of Finland after the First World War and Finnish independence, there was a strong movement for reunification with Sweden. The importance of history for shaping identity in autonomous Åland during the twentieth century is reflected in the large number of employees at Ålands folkminnesförbund [Åland Heritage Society] (up to 60 full-time employees plus some temporary ones) relative to a small population (around 28,000 in 2020).[49]

The lack of Viking Age runestones in Åland is particularly mysterious, given that the islands appear to have been closely connected to trade routes from central Sweden during the early Viking Age. Probably it is connected to the mystery of late Viking Age Åland. Archaeological finds show a nearly complete gap starting in the late tenth century and lasting for nearly a century. Onomastic evidence suggests that the current place names are from the twelfth century and later. Hence there was a disruption that led to a discontinuity in settlement patterns and place names.[50] This may have been complete depopulation or at least a radical decline in population, occurring just at the time of the 'runestone boom' in Scandinavia. Ella Kivikoski mentions the lack of runestones as corroborative evidence for such depopulation.[51] However, there is a recent proposal that rather than a discontinuity in settlement, there was forced colonization from Sweden in the thirteenth century that imposed more feudal settlement structures along with new place names.[52]

The only runic inscriptions known from Åland are an inscription on the top edges of the arms of a cross found in the church in Sund and a larger copy of the same inscription on the cliff face nearby Kastelholm. The range of letters represented in the inscription is limited, making it difficult to date the inscription by letter forms, and it is disputed whether the symbols on the cross are even runes. Most of the carvings consist of vertical lines that could be decorative or 'rune-like symbols'. Their location on the top edges of arms of the cross is unusual. Most likely the cross stems from the late Middle Ages (around the fourteenth century); the Kastelholm carving may be an early modern copy.[53]

The Sund inscription became the focal point and inspiration for an elaborate alternative history promoted by a person in an official person of authority. Matts Dreijer (1901–98) was born on the Estonian island of Ruhnu (Sw. Runö, historically a place of Estonian–Swedish settlement), but moved to Åland in 1907. After participating in the Finnish Civil War he completed a degree at Högre svenska handelsläroverket (Hanken, the Swedish business school) in Helsinki in 1924. Dreijer completed an undergraduate degree (*kandidat*) at the University of Helsinki in 1930 with the intention to become a teacher. He supplemented this with a degree in archaeology in 1933 and participated in some digs in Finland and Sweden. In 1929 he was hired by Ålands centralandelslag [Åland central cooperative] and returned to Åland, where he served in various positions in business and government. When the position of provincial archaeologist for Åland was created, the person who had been expected to assume the role failed to complete his studies in time, so Dreijer became provincial archaeologist and remained in this position until his retirement in 1970.[54] He was secretary of Ålands folkminnesförbund [Åland heritage association] from 1934 to 1970. Dreijer was an influential personality in Åland's cultural and intellectual life over several decades.

Dreijer is known for his theory placing the Viking Age emporium of Birka in Åland, rather than on the island of Björkö in Lake Mälaren, where an extensive town has been excavated. The cornerstone of his theory was the Sund cross. Dreijer interpreted the inscription on the cross as a memorial to the missionary archbishop Unni. According to Adam of Bremen, Unni died in Birka in 936; his body was buried there, but his head sent to Bremen.[55] In this way Dreijer established a more central role for Åland, emphasizing a Scandinavian (not Finnish) history for the islands. Dreijer first presented this idea in 1950,[56] and pursued and developed it through the following decades, largely in articles in the journal *Åländsk odling*.[57]

While the Lund runologist Ivar Lindquist seemed convinced of Dreijer's theory,[58] it found few other supporters outside Åland. Dreijer seems to have been regarded by the mainland Finnish and international scholarly community as eccentric. However, his personal charisma made him influential in Åland, and his vision of Åland's past contributed to shaping Ålandic identity in the twentieth century.

The vanished runestones of Kökar

In addition to insisting on an early date and specific historical context for the Sund inscription, Dreijer wrote (earlier) about inscriptions that were only speculated to have existed. Dreijer's article 'De försvunna runstenarna från Kökar' [The vanished runestones from Kökar] begins with early modern recordings of legends. In a text from 1667, Gabriel Olai Hamnodius reports on a local tradition that the bog Karlby Oppsjö contained two runestones. A magician (*runkarl*) is supposed to have carved the runes in order to restrain a bog troll, who is supposed to remain powerless as long as the carvings remain visible. According to Hamnodius, the locals no longer believed such nonsense.[59]

In pursuit of these runestones, Dreijer visited the site and searched the swamp for runestones without success.

> Vid letningen undersöktes släta ytor på alla större stenar söder om Oppsjön och belägna ca. 3–8 meter över sjöns yta. For undanröjande av laven användes en stålborste. Men, såsom väntat var, kunde inga spår av ristningen upptäckas.[60] [In the search were inspected flat surfaces on all larger stones south of Oppsjön and located 3–8 meters above sea level. A steel brush was used to clear out lichen. But, as expected, no signs of the inscription could be discovered.]

Dreijer also collected folklore from local residents, looking for persistence of beliefs about the runes. The stories he records are also migratory legend types that do not show marked similarities to the early modern recordings, but he finds connections – for example, that the troll had become a mermaid: 'Den forntida grymma trollet hade förändrats till en sjöjungfru'[61] [The ancient cruel troll had changed into a mermaid], who kept cows in the sea and occasionally provided milk for people on land. Another possible descendant of the magician is a man in a long black coat and a tall hat who mysteriously vanishes.[62]

Although Dreijer recognized that the story about the troll was a legend, he nonetheless believed that the Karlby stone had existed: 'För det första bär pastor Hamnodius' uppteckning sanningens prägel och för det andra har Karlby legat vid Östervägen, där framdragande runkunnigt folk av en eller annan anledning kunnat hugga in skriften.'[63] [First, pastor Hamnodius' note has the ring of truth; and second, Karlby was located along the eastern route, where people with runic knowledge passing through could have carved the inscription for one reason or another.]

He suggests that the harbour Thyckiekærl mentioned in the thirteenth-century 'Danish itinerary' in the *Liber census Daniae* by King Valdemar II refers to Karlby, rather than, as commonly thought, Hamnö, the main port in Kökar in the late fifteenth century.[64] He mentions other runic inscriptions scattered widely along the eastern route, including the runestone from Berezan' at the mouth of the Dniepr (now in Ukraine) and the runic carving on the Piraeus lion from Athens (moved to Venice in 1687).[65]

Dreijer also reports on other legends concerning supposed runestones in Åland:

> En runristing i Svartsmara [. . .] hölls i stor helg av gammalt folk i byn. Det berättades också att ett vikingaskepp gått i kvav vid berget och att dess spanter, som voro av ek, hade stuckit upp ur marken och synts ända tills de blevo övertäckta vid dikets grävning.[66] [A runic inscription in Svartsmara [. . .] was regarded with much reverence by older people in the village. It was also told that a Viking ship had sunk by the rock and that its ribs, which were of oak, had stuck up through the earth and remained visible until they were covered up when the ditch was dug.]

He investigated this site as well and found the grooves to be natural weathering, despite his guide's conviction to the contrary:

> Jag besökte platsen på 1920-talet med en gammal gumma som vägvisare [. . .] Gumman var fast övertygad om att det var en runristing. Jag konstaterade att så ej var fallet. 'Ristningen' bestod av en rad vertikala, ca. 1 dm. höga, parallella ojämnheter i berget, påminnande om en böjd runrad utan kantband.[67] [I visited the place in the 1920s with an old lady as a guide. [. . .] The old lady was firmly convinced that it was a runic inscription. I determined that this was not the case.

the 'inscription' consisted of a row of vertical, ca. 1 dm tall parallel unevennesses in the rock, reminiscent of a bent rune row without a border.]

Even though the specific stories may not check out, he nonetheless seems to consider them aggregately to support the idea that there were runestones in Åland. The Svartsmara legend directly connects them to Vikings. Many of the narratives involve supernatural elements – magic and otherworld beings. While Dreijer does not seem to endorse the truth of these aspects, and admits that the specific runestones either cannot be found or appear to reflect natural weathering, he nonetheless wants to maintain the basic thesis that there were at one point runestones in Åland. Legends generally operate in the territory of the uncanny, testing the limits of what we find plausible. The existence of such stories indicates some vernacular tradition concerning runes among Åland residents. This seems to be tied to a view of Åland's past and Ålandic identity that emphasizes it as part of the Viking and Scandinavian worlds.

Jukka Nieminen: Runes as the writing of the ancient Finnish kingdom

Dreijer used the real and imagined runestones of Åland to strengthen a Swedish/Scandinavian identity. The same tactic of suggesting that there were once more runestones that have disappeared has also been employed more recently by advocates for a Finnish-speaking golden age who regard Swedish speakers with suspicion.

Jukka Nieminen (b. 1967) is a non-fiction writer and amateur historian, former editor of the alternative journal *Ultra*, and blogger. *Vaiettu muinaisuus*[68] [Silenced past] is one of several works in which Nieminen presents a view of a glorious Finnish past, part of a series that began with *Muinaissuomalaisten kadonnut kuningaskunta*[69] [The vanished kingdom of the ancient Finns]. Nieminen promotes a theory of an ancient Finnish civilization, evidence of which is concealed by the scholarly establishment, which he views as being controlled by a Swedish-speaking or pro-Swedish elite. Nieminen states that his approach to the past is closer to anthropology than archaeology.[70] His works have been praised by alternative knowledge organizations but are generally regarded by the scholarly community as conspiracy theories and pseudoscience.[71] His publications are representatives of the same narrative about the secret history of the Ancient Finnish Kings that also manifests in Ylilauta and Hommaforum discussion forums, analysed by Heta Aali in Chapter 7.

Towards the end of *Vaiettu muinaisuus*, Nieminen states that an advanced civilization such as he imagines would have needed to have a system of writing. He suggests, as a general surmise without concrete evidence, that runes might have been used for this purpose.

> Mikäli kirjoitustaitoa ei ole ollut, on melko varmaa, että silloin ei ole ollut hallinnollista byrokratiaakaan, ja sen myötä järjestäytynyttä yhteisöä. Keskiöön nousee tässä kohtaa nykykirjoitusta edeltänyt riimukirjoitus. Myönnän että tässä kohtaa joudun ottamaan asiaan salaliittoteoriamaisen kannan, jonka mukaan riimukirjoituksen todistaminen on osoitus tietystä sivistystasosta, ja tätä sivistystasoa on pyritty tieten peittelemään ja vähättelemään. Tai näin ainakin luulen.[72] [If there was no literacy, it is almost certain that there was no administrative bureaucracy or society organized through it. At this point runic writing, which preceded modern writing, rises to the fore. I confess that at this point I am forced to adopt a conspiracy theory-like attitude to the matter, according to which knowledge of runic writing is an indication of a certain level of civilization, and there has been a deliberate attempt to conceal or downplay this level of civilization. Or at least I think so.]

He proceeds to assemble a hodgepodge of anecdotes suggesting that the existence of runic inscriptions in Finland has been systematically suppressed by the National Board of Antiquities in their desire to conceal evidence of the ancient civilization. While Nieminen in *Vaiettu muinaisuus* views the official line of the National Board of Antiquities as being dominated by pro-Swedish forces, the self-proclaimed 'fria forskare' [free researchers] in Ostrobothnia surrounding the Vörå runes saw the establishment as trying to suppress any signs of an early Swedish presence. Nieminen admits that he has not actually contacted the Board of Antiquities, but nonetheless expresses suspicion that they would not give an honest response.

> Museoviraston kokoelmista en tiedä mitään, ja se onkin näinä vuosina ollut yllättävän haluton esittelemään mitään korkeakulttuurisempaa löydöstä, mutta mielellään ulkopuoliselle esittelee kylläkin primitiivisiä kirveenpalasia. Kirjoitustaidossa, tai sen todistamisessa, on aina jotakin vaarallista. Onko minulla sitten jokin erityinen syy epäillä tiettyjen löydösten pimittelystä. [. . .] Enpä ole kysynyt minäkään paljonko on säilynyt riimukirjoitusta.[73] [I do not know anything about the collections of the National Board of Antiquities, and it has over the years been surprisingly reluctant to present any high cultural finds, but is happy to show outsiders fragments of primitive axes. In literacy and proof of it there is always something dangerous. Might I thus have a particular reason to suspect the concealment of certain finds. [. . .] Nor have I asked how many runic inscriptions are preserved there.]

Rather, he describes his method as collecting rumours from unnamed sources regarding runestones that have been found and then lost again. It is unclear to what extent these narratives reflect genuine oral tradition versus having been invented by Nieminen. Their diversity and in many cases only oblique connection to his main point give an impression that he probably heard or read them somewhere.

> Satunnaisia juoruja ja epämääräisiä huhuja olen kyllä kerännyt, ja joiden todenperään en osa ottaa mitään tarkempaa kantaa. Huhu kertoo että jostain Turun liepeiltä löytyi riimukirjoitettu tuohenpalanen, ja joka on lojunut ratkaisemattomana jonkun tutkijan pöytälaatikossa jo vuositolkulla.[74] [I have, however, collected random gossip and vague rumours, but I do not make a claim about their basis in fact. A rumour says that somewhere near Turku was found a piece of birchbark with runic writing, which has lain unsolved in some researcher's desk drawer for years.]

It is possible that the eventual basis for this rumour is the one birchbark letter found in Turku, which has been dated to the fourteenth century and from the one legible word seems to be in Latin language and script.[75]

In Nieminen's stories, the runestones may be concealed or lost again, or destroyed in the finding process.

> Toinen juoru kertoo, että isäntä löysi peltonsa vierestä ihka aidon riimukiven, ja peitti tämän irtokivillä rajamerkiksi. Koska kylässä ei ollut mitään kansanperinteellistä seuraa, katsoi kyläkunnan hirviseura asiakseen ottaa asiasta selvää, viedä isännälle pullo koskenkorvaa, ja kysyä kiven sijaintia. Isäntä vain otti ja kuoli ennen tätä, ja siellä se riimukivi vielä jossakin on. Toinen isäntä ajoi traktorinrenkaalla kallion päältä, ja sammaleet kun pöllysivät, ne paljastivat alta kokonaisen riimukallion. Isäntä vain kohautti olkaansa, jatkoi matkaansa mutta sentään muisti mainita asiasta kirkonkylän baarissa, josta se moninaisten juorumyllyjen välityksellä on tullut omiinkin korviini. Näitä tarinoita riittää.[76] [Another piece of gossip tells that a farmer found next to his field a genuine runestone and covered it with loose rocks as a border marker. Since there was no ethnographic society in the village, the moose-hunting association took it on to find the truth in the matter, take the farmer a bottle of Koskenkorva and ask the location of the stone. But the farmer just went and died before this, and the runestone is still there somewhere. Another farmer drove his tractor wheel onto rock, and when the moss flew up it revealed underneath a whole runic rock face. The farmer just shrugged his shoulders and continued on his way, but did remember to mention the matter in the village bar, from which, by way of many gossip mills, it reached my own ears. There are plenty of such stories.]

Some of these narratives feature the purported supernatural properties of the stones. Nieminen mentions a supposed healing stone; in this case there is a photograph.[77] I have not been able to trace the source, but the object depicted could be a medieval grave monument (or, of course, a modern emulation). Some vertical and diagonal lines that might be rune-like symbols are visible in the picture. He interprets part of the inscription as Fi. *tauti* 'illness'. This word is a Germanic or Scandinavian loanword, connected to Norse *dauði* 'death'.[78] The simplified orthography of the younger futhark obscures such details as the voiced initial stop (one reason Michelangelo Naddeo connects runes with Finnish[79]). In connection with the anecdote about the healing stone, Nieminen quotes charms connected to the *kipukivi* 'painstone'. It is not clear whether these charms are closely linked to the particular stone pictured or part of a general repertoire of healing charms. Like Dreijer, Nieminen does not focus either on endorsing or dismissing the supernatural aspects of the stories; the purpose is to raise the possibility of such stones having existed. The motif of a healing stone is attested in Finland–Swedish folklore from Ostrobothnia, though in this recording there is no mention of an inscription.[80]

The sequence of different anecdotes, presented in a conversational, free-associative style as in a storytelling session, in Nieminen's account seems intended to give the effect of an overwhelming body of evidence, a truth bubbling from the mouth of the folk pushing off the lid of silence imposed by the scholarly establishment. The cumulative effect of several pages of such anecdotes is to raise doubt in the reader's mind and suggest the plausibility of such things happening – even if an individual story may not be verified, surely these rumours come from somewhere, no smoke without fire. Although migratory legends are typically localized with specific place names and connections to landscapes and persons familiar to the teller and audience in order to increase their believability, some of the anecdotes Nieminen presents lack such details that would facilitate fact-checking.

It is a persistent feature of Nieminen's style that he anticipates readers' possible dismissal or suspicion of his views. In the introduction to the book he sets out his approach:

Sanotaan sitä vaikkapa vaihtoehtohistoriaksi. Sanalla on huono kaiku, se kuulostaa kuin tässä luotaisiin jotakin fantasia- tai pseudohistoriaa, joka ei nojaa mihinkään konkreettiseen, tai että se koostuu aineistosta jota vakavamielinen lukija ei vilkaisekaan niiden alkeellisuutensa vuoksi. Sellainen ei suinkaan ollut tarkoitus.[81] [Let's call it alternative history. The word has a bad echo; it sounds as if I were here creating some fantasy or pseudohistory that does not rest on anything concrete, or that it consists of evidence that a serious reader would not even glance at because of its rudimentary nature. This is not at all the intention.]

He is aware that he is operating at the edge of plausibility. Thematizing the fact that he expects doubt gives the impression of a self-aware narrator who is putting his reputation on the line by reporting things that seem unbelievable but which he nonetheless thinks are or may be true. The style draws heavily on practices of the traditional genre of the legend, which negotiates the boundaries of believability.

In addition to legends about lost runestones, Nieminen reports on other putative or marginal connections between Finland and runes, including ownership marks, message sticks, and runic calendar sticks used in modern times,[82] as well as Ove Berg's use of Finnish to aid in interpretation of runic inscriptions.[83] These other connections are mentioned in various writings by other types of authors.

Other purported runic finds

Curious as to whether Nieminen's rumours of runic finds could be connected to historical news reports, I made a search of the digital newspaper archive of the Finnish National Library for the words *riimukivi* 'runestone' and *riimukirjoitus* 'runic inscription'. The one story about a putative runestone in Finland I found was a report on a find from Pyhtää in July 1926, reprinted in similar versions in numerous different periodicals, containing the sentence 'Wielä ei ole saatu selwille, onko kysysmyksessä riimukirjoituskiwi, waiko muu löytö menneiltä ajoilta'[84] [It has not yet been clarified whether this is a runestone or another find from past times]. I have not found mentions of this artefact after the initial report. Nieminen's collection of rumoured finds does not mention Pyhtää specifically.[85] It is possible that there have been similar reports at other times that are not included in the digital archive.

Such amateur find reports continue. In May 2019 I received an email from someone who thought he had found a runestone in the Turku archipelago. The fact that people are ready to interpret unusual scratches in rock as runes shows that there is a shared belief that the presence of runestones in Finland would be plausible.

The Finnish word *riimu* is first attested in the meaning of 'runic letter' in Christfrid Ganander's dictionary, dating from 1787.⁸⁶ It has more general meanings 'stroke, scratch, carved decoration on a piece of wood; crack, infusion'. A homonym refers to a horse's bridle. This ambiguity, in addition to people's readiness to classify unknown marks in relation to known writing systems, has contributed to some rumours of runestones. Jussi Virratvuori reports on one from Sulkava in Eastern Finland, far from the coast or from any traditional Swedish-speaking area:

> Riimukirjoitusta Sulkavan Kommerniemen kylässä. 'Riimu' tarkoitti eräissä suomalaismurteissa raaputusta tai viiltoa ja nykytiedon mukaan suomea ei ole kirjoitettu riimuilla. Siksi tämän alunperin germaanisen kirjoitustavan löytyminen Etelä-Savosta herättää monia ja avoimeksi [*sic*] jääviä kysymyksiä.⁸⁷ [A runic inscription in the village of Kommerniemi in Sulkava. In certain Finnish dialects the word 'riimu' [rune] means 'scratch' or 'slash'; according to current knowledge, Finnish was not written with runes. Thus finding this originally Germanic way of writing in southern Savo raised many questions that remained open.]

I have not managed to find further information about this find or its subsequent investigation.

Ownership marks (Fi. *puumerkki*, Sw. *bomärke*) have been in use in Finland for centuries. According to lore, many ownership marks are based on runes, although it is difficult either to prove or disprove this claim.⁸⁸ The literature on ownership marks, as in heraldry, tends to be written by amateur enthusiasts and there is not an established scholarly tradition. Finland–Swedish writings about ownership marks tend to stress the connection to runes. Göran Dahl, in his work on ownership marks from Åland, views them as akin to but older than runes.⁸⁹ Georg W. Wallgren emphasizes their Germanic heritage. He states that they spread through Swedish populations to others in Finland and Estonia, while Finno-Ugric cultures do not have such a tradition.⁹⁰ By contrast, Elsa Aaltonen, writing in Finnish, regards ownership marks as ancient Finno-Ugric heritage.⁹¹ However, the linguistic correlation is not absolute – Paavo O. Ekko, who also writes in Finnish, views runes as a source for many ownership marks.⁹² Nieminen briefly mentions Ekko: 'Rovasti Paavo Ekko tutki Kokemäenlaakson talonpoikien puumerkkejä, jotka hän osoitti kiistattomasti riimumerkeiksi'⁹³ [Provost Paavo Ekko studied the ownership marks of farmers in Kokemäenlaakso, which he showed indisputably to be runic characters].

Runes used to write Finnish?

As mentioned earlier, no runic inscription has to date been established as being in a Finnic or Sámi language. Such interpretations have occasionally been proposed by serious scholars, but have generally been regarded with scepticism by the runological community. While I do not deem it impossible that names or words from those languages might occasionally have been written in runes, the specific proposals in the scholarly literature are at best uncertain and at worst anachronistic.[94]

There are also amateur writings that connect runes with Finnish. Michelangelo Naddeo's argument that runes were originally developed for writing Finnish is based on idiosyncratic theories of language change and the development of writing systems. In the simplified system of the Younger Futhark, in which the same symbol was used for several phonemes of Common Scandinavian, he sees parallels to the phonemic inventory of Finnish, which for example lacks voiced stops.[95] Naddeo uses his own terminology, contrasting 'Flavia' (Northern European/Finno-Ugric) with 'Steppico' (Indo-European) languages and cultures. He suggests that the Northern/Uralic 'Flavii' taught runic writing to the southern/Indo-European 'Steppici'.[96]

Ove Berg observes similarities among words in runic inscriptions, modern Swedish including dialects and Finnish and pieces together interpretations of various runic inscriptions.[97] He recognizes that many of the Finnish words are Germanic or Scandinavian loanwords but assumes influence in both directions.[98] Berg discusses various sequences from runic inscriptions and their possible meanings, drawing on Old Norse, Swedish dialects and Finnish. Older meanings may be preserved in loanwords and dialects that are not seen in standard languages. The discursive and conversational style of the book makes it difficult to ascertain the main points, but as far as I can tell he does not seem to make strong claims regarding specific etymologies or to suggest that runestones are in fact written in Finnish. This seems, however, somewhat to get lost in the reception of the book. While Berg's book seems mainly to have been ignored by runologists, it receives a favourable mention from the ethnologist Timo Leisiö of the University of Tampere: 'Ruotsissa ei nähdä suomen osuutta maan muinaiseen historiaan, vaikka se aivan helposti löytyy, jos osaa suomen kieltä.'[99] [In Sweden people do not see the role of Finnish in the ancient history of their country, although it is easily found, if one knows the Finnish language.]. In the same interview, Leisiö claims to have interpreted a Gotlandic inscription as containing the Finnish word *suoja* 'protection' and a depiction of the Finnish folk instrument *kantele*. Nieminen cites Berg approvingly:

> Erikseen kannattaa mainita ruotsalaistutkija Ove Bergin kirja 'Runsvenska svenska finska' jossa hän toteaa käytetyn riimukielen nojaavan etymologisesti suomenkieleen. Kun riimukivessä lukee vaikkapa 'Eski rsti runa pasi' se voidaan tulkita suomenkielen avulla sanoiksi 'Eskil rustasi runopaasin'.[100] [It is worth mentioning separately Ove Berg's book 'Runic Swedish, Swedish, Finnish', in which he shows the language used in runes to be based etymologically on the Finnish language. When a runestone reads, for instance, eskil rsti runa pasi [Eskil carved a rune **pasi**], it can be interpreted with the help of the Finnish language, as the words 'Eskil prepared a poem slab'.]

The runic text here appears to be constructed or invented. No such inscription appears in Samnordisk runtextdatabas; a web search turns up only references to Nieminen. I am not sure what Norse word is indicated by *pasi*. All the words in the Finnish sentence are regarded as Germanic loanwords.[101]

There may be other examples of claims growing in the retelling. The writer Valter Juvelius presents an interpretation of a runic inscription from Aarhus as a poem in a version of Old Estonian.[102] In context this appears to be a methodological object lesson, showing how easy it is to come up with interpretations that are implausible in the cultural context if the search space for languages is unconstrained. However, in a 1926 newspaper report, Juvelius is said to have interpreted the Rök runestone as being in a Finnic language and runic writing in general as Finnic.[103]

Conclusion

A persistent idea that runes 'must' have been used in Finland to a greater extent than known archaeological finds show manifests in different ways in popular, scholarly and pseudoscientific discourse in Finland. Although this discourse is somewhat polarized along language–political lines, similar strategies are employed by both pro- and anti-Swedish writers. There is a tendency to connect the use of runes to a grand past, whether it is imagined as Scandinavian or Finno-Ugric.

Contemporary alternative histories draw on traditions and cite old sources. Pseudohistorical discourses are connected to others. As Sirpa Aalto and Harri Hihnala note, they refer variously to medieval texts, premodern nationalist histories and older scholarship, often selectively and taken out of context, or interpreted with misunderstandings.[104] The different written manifestations over the course of a century indicate that the idea of a Finnish runic tradition has persisted orally and adapted to changing social circumstances and different perspectives. Grandiose narratives would probably not draw as many adherents if the ideas were not already in circulation.

The fact that similar strategies can be used by both pro- and anti-Swedish writers shows the strength and versatility of oral tradition. While runes and especially runestones are canonical symbols of the Scandinavian past, there is also a tradition of connecting obscure writing systems to different languages, which can reflect cryptographic enthusiasm as well as linguistic patriotism. Speculation about the early use of runes to write Finnish relates to this discourse, as well as to widespread theories of substrates and lost civilizations created by the ancestors of groups whose languages are now more marginal.

7

Masculine online medievalism in twenty-first-century Finland

Heta Aali

Introduction

This chapter examines the way masculinities are constructed in online discussions about the Finnish Middle Ages. I will focus on online discussions about Ancient Finnish Kings, which constitute a particular branch of twenty-first-century Finnish medievalism. The theory of the Ancient Finnish Kings appears to appeal especially to male internet users, and this chapter will examine how this fascination manifests itself, what kind of – both contemporary and historical – masculinities are promoted in the discussions and how the construction of masculinities in these discussions is linked to a wider association between masculinity and medievalism. Even though the concept of medievalism and masculinity has been studied before, this is the first time Finnish medievalism, and especially the theory of the Ancient Finnish Kings, is analysed in the international framework of masculinity studies. This chapter will utilize both Finnish and international research on masculinity to contextualize the topic.

The theory of the Ancient Finnish Kings, rather than being one coherent theory circulating on the internet, is a mass of tangled and competing narrative variations. However, they all share the idea of the existence of powerful kingdoms in medieval Finland prior to the Swedish influence in the thirteenth century. According to the supporters of the theory, the medieval Finnish kings would have been known all around Scandinavia, and they would have even been the ancestors of Norwegian and Swedish kings. Yet, once Southwest Finland was annexed to the Kingdom of Sweden in the thirteenth century, the Swedish authorities and their supporters destroyed all the information about the ancient Finnish kingdoms so that the Finnish (-speaking Finns) would stay subordinate and not know about their glorious past. In the discussion forums, as I will show throughout this chapter, the Swedish, the Swedish-speaking minority in Finland and the small Swedish People's Party of Finland are accused of intentionally covering up the 'truth' about the existence of the Ancient Finnish Kings. Even though Finnish historians have refuted the theory already in the eighteenth century, and several times after that, a large number of contemporary online users continue to promote the existence of the Ancient Finnish Kings and to believe in a conspiracy led by the Swedish authorities and their supporters.[1]

The theory of the Ancient Finnish Kings has a long history of its own going back to sixteenth- and seventeenth-century Swedish historiography in which historians such as Johannes Messenius constructed full royal dynasties of medieval 'Finnish kings'. His writings were translated to Finnish and are still referred to in many online discussions about the Ancient Finnish Kings.[2] The theory and its key elements, notably suspicion and open hatred towards the Swedish and Swedish-speaking Finns, have been brought up multiple times since the eighteenth century. As is visible in the twenty-first-century online discussions, the theory is also related to the *Kalevala* folklore, which is sometimes considered to derive from 'authentic' Finnish prehistory. The compilation of *Kalevala* in the nineteenth century was part of the Finnish nation-building process, and especially the late-nineteenth-century and early-twentieth-century national romantic ideas and artwork depicting this Finnish prehistory are still popular in the discussion forums. The theories of Ancient Finnish Kings are not only medievalism in themselves but cumulative medievalism in the sense that they are based on theories that have been piling up since the seventeenth century. The Swedish and Swedish-speaking minority in Finland are seen as the enemy in the theories about the Ancient Finnish Kings even though Sweden lost Finland, the kingdom's eastern part, to Russia in 1809, after which Finland became an autonomous grand duchy. Finland became independent from Russia only at the end of the First World War in 1917. Thus, Finland has not been a part of the Swedish realm for over 200 years, but the Swedish are still perceived as an enemy. The anti-Swedish sentiments and rhetoric in the online discussions hark back to the polemics of the so-called language controversy at the beginning of the twentieth century. In the heated atmosphere debating the status of the Swedish language in the newly independent Finland, both language groups demeaned one another. However, even this controversy subsided in the postwar era.[3]

The discussions about the Ancient Finnish Kings construct representations of Finnish masculinities in relation to both history and women but also in relation to (a perception of) Swedish masculinity. I will analyse how anonymous users construct both ideal medieval masculinity and modern Finnish masculinity. On a theoretical level, I will draw from international and Finnish studies on contemporary masculinity and especially on the construction of masculinity in online communities. Another theoretical dimension is the study of medievalism and particularly the study of masculine medievalism. I shall start by presenting the online discussion forums analysed in the chapter and the theoretical background and concept of the manosphere as applied to studying the Finnish online discussions. The analysis focuses on the following two themes: Finnish kings and swords, and Swedishness and sexuality.

The (conspiracy) theory of the Ancient Finnish Kings is topical for several reasons.[4] First, the internet has provided a new platform for spreading ideas rapidly in various forums, and theories such as the Ancient Finnish Kings can now reach new audiences. As this chapter demonstrates, the discussions related to Ancient Finnish Kings draw extensively from global trends of medievalism such as the use of memes. Second, discussions about national history, no matter on what platform, have nearly always been politicized and are rarely 'only' about history. This is also true in modern-day discussion forums since the history constructed in the discussions is more about what history should have been than what it actually was. Third, and most importantly for the chapter, nearly all users discussing and especially promoting the theory are men. Men almost exclusively populate the online forums with discussions about the Ancient Finnish Kings, and it is difficult to find women who would have written about or discussed the theories even before the internet age.[5]

The theory is gendered in the sense that its supporters are mostly men (or can be identified as such) and because the theory, and the discussions about the theory, depict almost exclusively men, as I will show. On sites where individuals can use pseudonyms, nearly all the names are non-feminine. It is probable, though, that women participating in these discussions might use male pseudonyms so as to not stand out. This shows the exclusive nature of these discussions – even though everyone can join the discussion in the open threads, only certain profiles are accepted among the commentators. The internet culture related to Ancient Finnish Kings appears deeply discriminatory as men control the popular discourse. As we will see, these men often wish to 'take back' the discourse on the Finnish Middle Ages from the Swedish, who have allegedly controlled the discourse for centuries.

The online discussions on the Ancient Finnish Kings on two Finnish online sites, Hommaforum and Ylilauta, construct the core of the analysis.

Hommaforum has by far the longest thread on the topic, starting in 2013 and continuing until 2019.[6] The thread, according to the site, has been read 141,735 times. Ylilauta, which is an imageboard website similar to 4chan, has provided more than 40 threads on the Finnish Middle Ages from 2019 to 2020, with the longest threads having over 900 messages. One of the latest analysed threads on the topic was created on 11 May 2020, and it had more than 800 comments by the end of May.[7] In addition to these two sites, I will examine a number of sites and blogs linked to these forums. Most of the links refer to textual sites, but there are increasingly more YouTube videos where the Ancient Finnish Kings are discussed.[8] Even though most discussions are in Finnish, there are also a number of links to English sites connected to the theme.[9] Most material from social media, such as Facebook and Twitter, is excluded from the article since these forums are not similarly as openly accessible as the online discussion forums that require no registration from readers.

Studying masculinity: The manosphere

The pseudohistorical theories about the Ancient Finnish Kings are a prime example of the way the male has been and continues to be the historical norm due to previous, centuries-old historiographical traditions that have always centred on the male and marginalized the female. Most contemporary online users discuss 'Finns', 'Swedes', 'Jews' and 'Swedish-speaking Finns', but what they actually are referring to in most cases are the males in these groups. The women are the exception, and history's gender is still dominantly male. In addition, nearly all the images posted in the threads represent men (or sexualized women).[10] Nearly all the discussions are specifically about kings and not generally about rulers or monarchs.[11] Two of the oldest (from late 1990s and early 2000s), and in a sense most original versions of the theory currently circulating online, do not profess the type of deeply rooted racism, anti-Semitism or even toxic masculinity[12] as many of the most recent threads do. These older versions, however, adhere to the bygone school of (pseudo)historiography in which history consists only of men. Women are simply nowhere to be found.[13]

There is a lot of recent research on the online masculinities that I am employing to analyse the discussions about the Ancient Finnish Kings. The concept of the manosphere is especially useful in analysing the recent discussion forums. The manosphere is usually defined as 'a complex, fragmentary online ecology' that has movements varying 'from self-help communities' to 'websites offering advice on seduction' or even promoting downright 'antifeminist ideologies'.[14] The concept of the Red Pill, as an analogy from the film *The Matrix* (1999), is equally central to the 'politics of the manosphere'. It signifies becoming enlightened to life's ugly truths and alleges to open men's eyes to feminism's brainwashing.[15] The discussions on the Ancient Finnish Kings are not, as such, part of the manosphere since their purpose does not lie in opposing feminism or in offering self-help for men. Yet, many of them share similar features with the politics of the manosphere, and this feature separates them from the earlier versions of the theory circulating online in the late 1990s and early 2000s. Particularly Ylilauta can be approached from the point of view of the manosphere, as, for example, Finnish researcher Eliisa Vainikka has done in her article (2019) about the hatred of women found on Ylilauta relationship discussion boards. She found many similarities between the conservative and misogynist discourses in Ylilauta and the international alt-right and manosphere.[16]

The Red Pill ideology is adjusted to the Finnish context in Ylilauta in a way that by taking the pill, one can realize how much the Swedish and Swedish-speaking minority in Finland have 'distorted' the history of medieval Finland.[17] This refers directly to the question of who owns the discourse on the Finnish Middle Ages. We find here what Finnish researcher Matias Nurminen calls the ideological 'cross-pollination' between the manosphere and, for example, the alt-right, on which these discussions draw heavily.[18] Many neomasculine writers, as Nurminen calls certain prolific authors in the manosphere, broadly use satire and feel entitled to say anything without consequences, claiming the problem to be in the interpretation.[19] This is also typical of the discussions about the Ancient Finnish Kings. Many of them balance between seriousness and satire and do not refrain from comments fuelled by hatred, sexism, racism, anti-Semitism and homophobia. What generally defines the Finnish discussions is pessimism and mutual discouragement, and the tone of the discussions is in many cases extremely negative. This is equally typical of many incel communities.[20]

Moreover, many of the discussions about the Ancient Finnish Kings and the manosphere share the idea of a white man as a victim. In the manosphere, constituted mostly of (privileged) heterosexual white males, white men are presented and identified as victims of feminism and often profess xeno-, homo- and transphobia. The white men perceive themselves as marginalized.[21] According to a Finnish study on racism on the popular discussion forum Suomi24 ('Finland24'), most users of the service are middle-aged men, and they tend to represent themselves as the victims of, for example, racism on the part of the Swedish-speaking population (a minority comprising 5.3 per cent of the population) and immigrants.²² Similarly, the white, Finnish-speaking male is perceived as the victim of the Swedish, women, the EU, Jews or the academic community in the discussions about the Ancient Finnish Kings. For example, in one thread related to the Finnish Iron Age, there is a meme of a man defined as 'green-left' (viher-vasemmisto), which (originally demeaningly) refers to the Finnish political parties of the Green League and the Left Alliance. The man of the 'green-left' yells slogans such as 'We have a #dream, and it is the white heterosexual men in oven!'²³ A commentator in another thread about the genetic history of Finns argues that the 'real euripid Aryan' Finns have been robbed of their history and identity.²⁴

Moreover, in a long thread about the Ancient Finnish Kings, another commentator claims that Finland is the last hope of the 'white north' because the Swedish and Norwegians have started to 'cuckold' Black men the same way as the Swedish-speaking Finns are doing.²⁵ The comment implies that the white Finnish-speaking heterosexual man is the only hope left in Northern Europe since the women are cheating on their men with Black immigrant men, and the Swedish or Norwegian men are too weak to prevent it. 'Cuckold' (or in Finnish 'aisuri') refers to the manosphere's simplistic use of evolutionary biological concepts and means 'a weak man whose girlfriend cheats on him, usually with black men'.²⁶ This type of misogynist and racist discussion is typical to Ylilauta and seems to have appeared in the threads about Finnish Middle Ages over the last years.²⁷ These kinds of references are absent from the Hommaforum discussion thread. When the most recent (from 2019 to 2020) Ylilauta discussion threads are compared to two other prolific Finnish sites promoting the theory of the Ancient Finnish Kings, Sinikivi and Finnsanity, it is obvious the latter two do not share similar hateful speech. However, they share an extreme distrust of academic research, a view of Finnish-speaking Finns as victims of the Swedish-speaking population and a strong nationalist tendency.²⁸

A concept that applies to many discussion forums related to the theory of the Ancient Finnish Kings is 'muscular medievalism', created by Amy S. Kaufman. She explains: 'Muscular medievalism imagines the past as a man's world in which masculinity was powerful, impenetrable, and uniquely privileged.'²⁹ Muscular medievalism draws from popular culture, such as *Game of Thrones* and other similar phenomena, and similarly to the fantasy version of the Middle Ages created by ISIS, they 'emphasize the superiority of men and trade in women as rewards for brutality'.³⁰ The concept defines well the representations of the Finnish (pre-Swedish) Middle Ages created in the online forums, where heroic and worthy Finnish warriors and kings proud of their heritage and respected by other kings and warriors populated the Finnish kingdoms. Moreover, this was a time before the arrival of Christianity, which is strongly associated with the Swedish and seen as another oppressor. 'Purity', another concept by Kaufman, defines perfectly these constructions of the Finnish Middle Ages. It refers to an image of an unspoiled past that, in the Finnish case, neither the Swedish, Christianity, feminism, immigration nor anything similar had spoiled. The idea of racial purity holds an important place in many discussions about the Ancient Finnish Kings – the medieval kingdom not tarnished by any non-Finnish elements. Christianity is an element that sets apart the American purity described by Kaufman and the Finnish vision of purity since in the first one the unspoiled past includes a monolithic Christian past, but in the Finnish version purity refers to the time before Christianity arrived in Finland.[31] The desire for purity also manifests itself in the immense interest in genetic studies that are hugely popular in all forums where the Ancient Finnish Kings are discussed.[32]

The idea of a pure, masculine Middle Ages is not a new concept in Finland, either. The interwar period witnessed an emergence of medievalist and military imagery with features similar to those of many of the twenty-first-century online discussions. For example, in a popular historical novel about the Finnish Middle Ages, a medieval Finnish man was contrasted with a Swedish man who was, among other things, depicted as vain and feminine. Aarno Karimo's series of historical short stories (1929–32), reprinted three times, presented Finnish men akin to unspoiled nature, whereas the Swedish men represented the dangerous and tarnished modernization. Women had practically no role in this national narrative.[33] The same features can be found from the period's academic historiography as well. For example, professor of Finnish history at the University of Helsinki Jalmari Jaakkola (1885–1964) reconstructed visions of a heroic past set in the Iron Age where the unspoiled Finnish culture welled up from the surrounding nature and the people themselves. The men were pictured as natural leaders, and brave men desired only to die honourably in a battle.[34] The interwar period featured 'militant medievalism', as historian Derek Fewster has described, when, for example, weapons of ancient warfare and ideas of wise tribal leaders were popular in many ways.[35] The twenty-first-century masculine militantism related to the Middle Ages recycles the same features as were used in the 1920s and 1930s even if, probably, most online users are not fully aware of the reused nature of the imagery.

Finnish kings and swords

The union between medievalism and masculinity in the form of muscular medievalism is conspicuous both globally and regionally. Matias Nurminen, for example, has studied the now paused but earlier prominent manosphere blog and website Return of Kings, whose name draws from the hugely popular J. R. R. Tolkien's *The Lord of the Rings* books and movies. One of the main characters in the third movie, *The Return of the King*, is Aragorn, who represents an ideal hero with his sword Andúril.[36] The fixation on the importance of swords in masculine medievalist fantasies is an important feature in the discussions about the Ancient Finnish Kings. This is especially the case of the so-called 'Ulfberht swords'. These specific swords from the Viking Age have been found in Finland (among many other countries) and have the inscription ULFBERHT on the blade.

According to many online commentators, the number of medieval swords found in Finland *must* prove *something*. Since there are very few findings about the Vikings raids in Finland, many conclude that it must be because the Finns were such fierce warriors that even the Vikings did not dare to challenge them.[37] The swords *must* prove that Finland had a glorious past including mighty warriors because why else would there be swords? Many commentators refer to an 'official truth' of the Finnish Middle Ages according to which there was nothing in Finland before the arrival of the Swedish in the twelfth or thirteenth centuries. This 'official truth', a straw man, does not exist anywhere else besides in the discussion forums in which the number of found medieval swords is considered as evidence against this 'official truth'. According to one commentator: 'I was told in school that Finns were literally shitasses who collected berries and could hardly speak. That somebody finds a sword with gold and different kind of symbols related to Finnish mythology [. . .] is a big deal to me and means that Finnish culture was very settled thing before the Swedish and Christians.'[38] The commentator did not specify, however, what the 'Finnish mythology' or 'Finnish culture' signifies. The commentator had added a link to a library site and a description of a sword (not Ulfberht), but the description makes no mention of symbols related to 'Finnish mythology' or 'Finnish culture'.[39]

The Ylilauta users circulate a screenshot from a Wikipedia article about ring-swords in which two sentences are highlighted: 'for kings and high nobility' and 'fourteen of those in Finland'.[40] These sentences are underlined as evidence that Finnish men truly were noble and possessed valuable swords, as if Wikipedia was the ultimate authority on the matter. Another reason why swords are discussed so actively in the forums is a recent archaeological thesis (in English)[41] and a popular book (in Finnish) published about medieval swords in Finland by Mikko Moilanen. Moilanen is one of the rare academic scholars accepted by many online users because he not only studies medieval swords but also makes them, being a blacksmith.[42] According to Moilanen, there are indeed more Ulfberht blades found in Scandinavia than in other parts of Europe, and their quality was probably valued here. He speculates that the marks, or writing on the blade, interested the illiterate people who possibly considered them to be magical.[43] Unsurprisingly, Moilanen draws no connection between the Ulfberht blades and Finnish kingship.

Particularly in the Ylilauta, the users are very keen to share a map of the distribution of Ulfberht blades in Europe. The map has been circulating in Ylilauta since at least 2014.[44] The map shows that there are far more blades found from Scandinavia (Norway, Sweden and Finland) than from the area of the Frankish realm, where the Ulfberht blades mostly originate. The map contains no information as to who created it and where it was made. This, however, does not seem to bother any of the users in the forums because it is simple and clear. In fact, the map comes from a 2008 article by archaeologist Anne Stalsberg, 'The Vlfberht sword blades reevaluated', in which she argues that the number of Ulfberht blades found does not correlate directly to their original number since far more blades have been found from 'pagan' Europe – that is, Scandinavia – than from the area of Frankish realm. One major reason is that in 'pagan' Europe, the blades were used as grave goods unlike in the Christian Frankish realm. Furthermore, it is actually Norway where most of the blades have been found.[45] Most of the users, both in Ylilauta and in other forums, claim to want to find out the 'truth' about the Finnish Middle Ages. Their quest for truth does not seem to include peer-reviewed articles on the topic even when they are quite easily and openly accessible online.[46] This observation supports the conclusions by Andrew B. R. Elliott (Introduction) and Evan Wallace (Chapter 4) that online discussions and information circulating there are only ostensibly open and in fact regulated by metamedievalisms defining the limits of legitimate speech and credible arguments.

Swedishness and sexuality

Particularly in Ylilauta, the contempt towards Sweden and the Swedish, which is at the core of the theories about the Ancient Finnish Kings, is visible in the way the masculinity of Swedish men is challenged. The masculinity of Swedish men is questioned both verbally and visually, and most commonly the Swedish men (and Swedish-speaking Finnish men) are presented as gay, which in Ylilauta seems to be the ultimate insult. On one hand, the threads make fun of Finnish men, but on the other hand, the commentators make fun of everyone else, and the white Finnish man is presented as a victim.[47] Strong racial slurs are common in the threads where the Swedish men are presented as too weak to resist African men who steal 'their' women.[48] In a thread entitled 'Why the Vikings avoided Finland', commentators have shared an image of a 1902 illustration of Thor dressed as the goddess Freyja in order to depict him, and Swedish that worshipped him, as a transvestite and effeminate.[49]

In the same thread, there is an image comparing 'The Virgin Thor' and 'The Chad Väinämöinen' (Figure 7.1). The image draws from the incel imagery of 'Chad' referring to an 'alpha male', in which the Väinämöinen character from the *Kalevala* is associated with the Finns, and the Thor character is associated with the Swedish. Furthermore, Väinämöinen is described as trying to get a 'smoking Stacy', which refers to a hyperfeminine and unattainable woman in incel imagery. The texts in the image not only refer to popular culture such as J. R. R. Tolkien but also present Väinämöinen as immortal and more intelligent and masculine than the effeminate Thor.[50] Internationally, the Norse gods are popular among the alt- and far-right, starting from the Nazi era, but in Finnish discussions the Norse gods are not always idolized even if Ylilauta, and Hommaforum to a lesser extent (and many other blogs and sites promoting the theory of the Ancient Finnish Kings), allow right-wing, racist and sexist opinions to blossom. The Finnish right-wing sphere is not uniform, so it is not surprising to also find groups who draw from the Norse mythology (such as the Soldiers of Odin).[51]

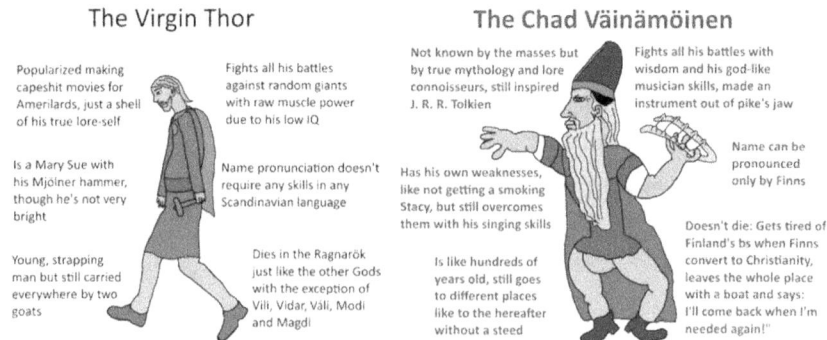

Figure 7.1 Väinämöinen versus Thor according to a meme in Ylilauta. Origin and author unknown.

The image juxtaposes the Finnish *Kalevala* and Norse mythology as in many threads the Finnish (medieval, mythological) past is associated with nineteenth-century romantic notions of the past as seen, for example, in certain paintings. Images of paintings such as Pekka Halonen's *Vainolaista vastaan* ('Against persecutor', 1896) are shared in the threads as they are depicted to portray ancient Finnish heroes. Such depictions not only discuss mythological or historical masculinities but contemporary masculinity as well. In another thread, there is an image of a Swedish man drinking from a large bottle, and the text on the bottle says: 'Grade A Semen (cultural enriched) imported from Somalia'.[52] The image presents the Swedish men as subordinate to Somali men and aims to imply that Sweden has been taken over by immigrants, whereas the Finnish man would protect Finland from such fate. The same themes are repeated over and over again visually and verbally – the Swedish subjugated the Finns and destroyed their history, but now the Swedish (and especially the Swedish men) have been subjugated by the immigrants and the Left.

Women are mostly brought up as sexual objects – either a Swedish man or an immigrant gets the women, or a Finnish man shows who the real man is by having sex with a Swedish woman.[53] This depiction of a woman as a passive and a man as an active agent is associated with the ideal of chivalry, which is very dear to the international right-wing medievalism. The chivalric ideals depend on weak women to make the men heroes.[54] In the same sense, the fantasies about the Ancient Finnish Kings evoke ideas of Finnish medieval men as warrior-aristocrats, and not as peasants, the same way as most Vikings are commonly in popular culture visualized as warriors and not as farmers or merchants. However, the discussion threads are not unanimous, and not all commentators promote the views of Swedish men as less masculine – there are also counterarguments against the theory of the Ancient Finnish Kings, racism, misogyny and anti-Semitism. However, the masculinity most often promoted in the discussions is extremely narrow and violent, toxic in many ways. It is simultaneously performative and imagined as running in the genes – the Finnish-speaking men are depicted differently to the Swedish-speaking men.

Conclusion

The Ancient Finnish Kings fascinate the men in the discussion forums because the commentators desire a past where there were medieval heroes and kings in Finland, as if such a past would make themselves heroes and saviours. As

Lauryn Mayer has argued, 'medievalism provides dispossessed men with fantasies of community and self-sufficiency [...] by rendering women relatively invisible and powerless [...] and reassuring a male audience of its inherent superiority.'[55] In many ways, Finland is pictured as currently in danger (from foreigners, immigrants, Swedish influence, feminism, etc.), and the men want to see themselves as the heroes who can save (the imaginary mono-cultural) Finland. Even though many believers of the theories are ridiculed in the forums, they find there like-minded people with whom they can fetishize swords and other masculine objects and picture themselves fitting into the narrow idea of warrior masculinity.

8

Particularizing the universal
Medievalist constructions of cultural and religious difference in *Crusader Kings II*

Jere Kyyrö

Introduction

This chapter analyses the representations of culture and religion in *Crusader Kings II*, a digital game developed by the Swedish developer Paradox Development Studio and published by Paradox Interactive. The main focus is on the ways in which the game system (including the game rules, graphical representation and naming of game concepts) works to produce an effect and a feel of particular cultures and religions in a medieval setting, and how digital games should be approached as cultural products. Special attention is paid to representations of Northern Europe. My argument is that through a process of 'particularization', which is at some points superficial, apparently different cultures and religions are represented as fundamentally similar. This type of particularization not only results from the programming paradigm the game engine builds on, but especially from the cultural presuppositions and metamedievalist conceptions held by the game designers, which lead to quite different areas and populations being moulded to follow similar paths of development. These presuppositions and conceptions include the projection of modern national states – along with other contrafactual or modern reconstructed entities, such as a medieval 'Kingdom of Finland' or neopagan groups – on the past, as well as the so-called world religions paradigm. As part of the contemporary popular cultural medieval imaginary, the game provides a platform for imagining the origins of the present religio-cultural situation, alternative historical developments and religious and cultural change in general.[1]

Crusader Kings II is a grand strategy game set in medieval Europe, North Africa and the Middle East. Downloaded by more than two million players,[2] the game has various add-ons, and its sequel, *Crusader Kings III*, was released in September 2020. The game is thus an example of a successful medievalist popular cultural product. The add-ons have expanded the original release's game map to include parts of Central, South, South-East and East Asia. It is, according to Adam Chapham, an open-ontological game, which does not tie the player to strict historical narratives, but nevertheless uses framing goals and particular events that encourage the player to adapt his/her ludonarrative (i.e. the actual narrative unfolding through the gameplay) towards real historical events, simultaneously allowing the enactment of contrafactual ludonarratives.[3]

As A. Martin Wainwright points out, *Crusader Kings II* is more individual-centred than most state-oriented games in the grand strategy genre.[4] This is in line, however, with the dynastic and non-nationalist nature of medieval power structures.[5] After all, the objective in the game is to keep the player's dynasty alive and in power, as the player controls one character at a time and, ultimately, a dynastic continuum of characters. Otherwise, the player is free to choose his/her objectives, but for example the selected players' ruled territory (his/her demesne), social organization, player's character's culture and religion set the limits for the objectives in the near future.[6] When the player's character dies, the player then moves on to control the character next in line of succession, inheriting his/her predecessor's properties and holdings according to the laws currently in effect. Keeping the dynasty alive and in power requires planned marriages and intrigue against one's rivals, ruler and/or vassals.

The duality of the state and character orientations is well demonstrated in the following. In addition to a mosaic-like game map, which is divided into provinces that consist of holdings and assemble as duchies, kingdoms and empires, there are characters that comprise the courts of rulers and have various personal traits. Each holding, province, duchy, kingdom and empire has a character as their ruler. The laws in effect and the level of technology define how many holdings one character may effectively hold. In the game, there may be independent vassal kings/queens, dukes/duchesses and counts/countesses. Barons, bishops and mayors, who rule a sub-province holding, cannot be independent; emperors/empresses are always independent, unless they are consorts. Both the provinces and characters each have one religion and one culture (e.g. ethnolinguistic groups such as Anglo-Saxon, Berber or Magyar) that may change during the course of the game through specific game events.[7] Additionally, the game features several inheritance systems (e.g. agnatic or cognatic, gavelkind or primogeniture) that can be changed under certain conditions and accord to the player's culture and religion.

The player may choose from several historical starting dates,[8] but the overall time period is 769–1454. The original version of the game, which was released for Windows on 14 February 2012, had the player start in the year 1066, and characters other than Christian could not be played. Since 2012, fifteen downloadable content packs (DLCs) have been released, which have expanded the playable cultures, religions, territory and time period.[9] For example, *Monks and Mystics* (released in March 2017) adds playability of religious characters, and the *Holy Fury* content pack (released in November 2018) allows the player to design pagan religions. However, these two packages are not my focus at this time. Additionally, the core game rules, as well as the division of the game map into provinces, have changed somewhat in the various versions of the game. This chapter is based on observations made during the writer's playing experience, mostly with v.3.3.3 but also earlier versions, including the content packs *The Sword of Islam* (2012), *Legacy of Rome* (2012), *The Old Gods* (2013) and *Charlemagne* (2014). Additionally, game script files that define certain game mechanics, as well as Crusader Kings II Wiki, which is a knowledge repository maintained by the players and modders of the game and contains descriptions of most of the game mechanics, have been consulted for additional information.

Digital games and representations of cultures and religions

In games research, various approaches may be taken. Perhaps the most relevant distinction is between the ludic and narrative approaches. The researcher may focus on actual gameplay, game worlds and game systems, but also on aesthetics.[10] In regard to historical games, how the unfolding of history is presented is relevant.

Crusader Kings II does not rely on preset historical events, but on so-called triggered events that take place when certain conditions are met. The game narrative unfolds through an interplay of various factors and rules. In this kind of setting, the game rules and variables that structure the unfolding of the game are just as relevant from the point of view of the study of representations as the textual or visual elements of the game.[11] Jeremiah McCall calls this kind of approach, which focuses on 'how the systems and processes of the past functioned', 'conceptual simulation'. He writes: '*Crusader Kings II* does not show how medieval barons lived but tells about the political fragmentation of medieval Europe.'[12] This unfolding of a narrative through actual gameplay – which is conditioned by the game's rules system – is captured very well by Chapham's concept of ludonarrative mentioned earlier.[13] When analysing digital games in terms of historical representations, singular historical facts should not be the focus. Instead, the analysis should concern the mechanics that control the unfolding of the game.[14]

Studies on cultural representation have often focused on specific oppositions between dominant and dominated cultural groups – such as between the Orient and Occident[15] – or, more generally, the West and the Rest.[16] Often in discourses about others, the modern Western cultures have been set as the model against which the other cultures have been evaluated. Representations of cultures and cultural differences also function as means of imagining an 'us' separated from the other.

Along similar lines, within the study of religion, the understandings of religion in general and representations of particular religions have been critiqued on the basis of their Western-centrism: more than often than not, the prototype of religion has been Protestant Christianity.[17] More recently, the discussion has focused on the so-called world religions paradigm, prevalent in both academic and more popular discourses, where the 'big five' (Christianity, Buddhism, Hinduism, Islam and Judaism), sometimes with a few additions, comprise the prototypical model of religion. Typically, this approach emphasizes religions as '-isms', coherent systems with sacred texts, dogmas, places of worship and so on, thus making forms of folk religion or indigenous religions into special cases of religion.[18] What is common to these conceptions is that they focus on interaction between the universal and particular forms of culture or religion, and how often the dominant Western culture or religion takes the place of the universal, thus making the non-dominant, non-Western forms unusual examples and objects of exoticism.

While these discussions have emphasized the cultural–geographical dimension of difference, in this case the temporal dimension is also relevant. The trope of 'medieval' has several functions in contemporary media culture: similarly to the discourse of cultural difference, it functions as a repository of meanings, which may be utilized, for example, in imagining a nation's past glory or as a slur for contemporary practices deemed non-modern.[19] *Crusader Kings II* provides representations of exotic medieval cultures, such as pagan Germans, Fenno-Ugrians and Slavs.

In *Crusader Kings II*, the interplay between the universal and particular is manifest on many levels, including the game's concepts and rules, as well as pictorial and textual representations of places, characters and events. *Crusader Kings II*'s game engine is programmed in object-oriented C++ language.[20] Typical of object-oriented languages is that they employ abstract classes whose attributes or variables are inherited by the child classes, and these classes are blueprints for the actual objects.[21] While it may be argued that the duality of particularism and universalism is a feature of game design inherent to the object-oriented programming paradigm and the thinking related to it, it is nevertheless important to analyse *how* this particularization – that is, creating actual instances of culture and religion based on a common class – is made, as the choices in this regard are by no means limited.[22]

Particularizing cultures and cultural change

As the game's title suggests, it is a sequel to *Crusader Kings*, which was released in 2004. Jason Pitruzzello writes:

> Although the vast majority of strategy-oriented video games depict culture in the Middle Ages in monolithic and unchanging terms, *Crusader Kings* depicts culture as mutable. Members of the ruling class or the people they rule can change culturally, mimicking to some extent the kinds of cultural change found in England and elsewhere in the period. As digital medievalism, *Crusader Kings* models cultural change in the Middle Ages rather than merely assigning cultural labels to people and geographical areas of Europe at specific chronological dates. The game attempts to avoid anachronism through historically based systems of gameplay, rather than through rote inclusion of historical facts.[23]

The same thing may be said about the sequel, *Crusader Kings II*, although I would like to point out that there is still a relative degree of 'merely' assigning culture and monolithicism of culture. In the game, the universal models of culture and religion are particularized in various ways, as I will demonstrate.

The main view in *Crusader Kings II* opens up as a world map, which is divided into county-sized province-tiles (see Figure 8.1). The player can toggle between several map modes, which distinguish the provinces with borders and display by colours the different levels of economic development, dynasties, political entities and opinions towards the player, as well as different cultures and religions, to name a few. Each province has one culture and one religion, both of which may change over the course of the game. Likewise, each character has one of each, not two or more.[24] Religion and culture are inherited from one's parents (usually

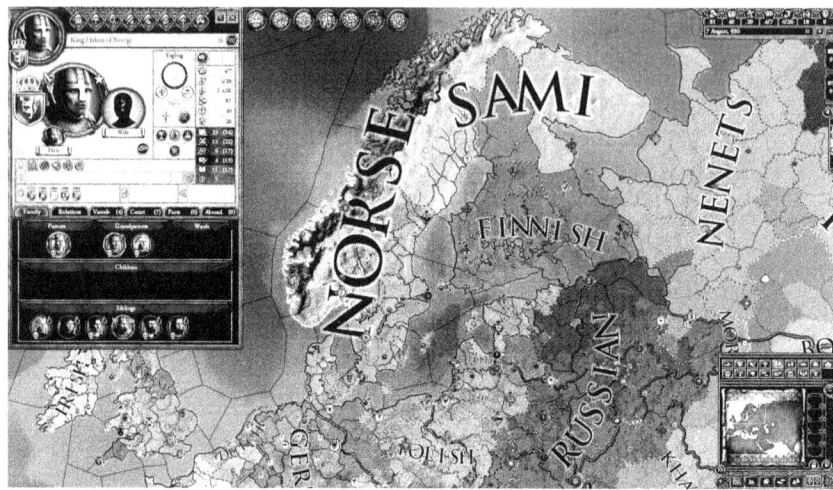

Figure 8.1 Screenshot from the cultural map and King Hakon's character window of a game starting in 936, *Crusader Kings II*, © Paradox Interactive, 2012. Contrast added for clarity.

their father) or taught to a child by a tutor, or they may be changed – actively or passively – through special events. In a sense, religious and cultural change are always 'total'; there are no in-betweens or hybrids. Especially interesting are situations where a new culture begins to emerge. For example, English culture starts to appear in provinces – as triggered events, discussed previously – 'if a Norman ruler owns an Anglo-Saxon province after 1100', or for Frankish culture switching to 'French, the province owner must have either Frankish culture or any culture from the Latin group'.[25] These preset conditions that do not allow imaginary new cultures – that would emerge on the basis of, say, Arabic and Pictish or Finnish and Russian culture – are a way of guaranteeing that the game's history maintains some semblance with the historical narrative we know. In other words, they retain historical particularity.

One important aspect of the game is its moddability (as in 'modding', from 'modification').[26] The game is based on the Paradox Development Studio's Clausewitz engine, which employs plain text scripts that are readable and can be modified by any user with a basic text editor. These include the descriptions of cultures and religions. The specifications on culture are stored in a certain file ('00_cultures'), which includes the names of the cultural groups, particular cultures and some specific information. Thus, it would be fairly easy for a modder to change some basic rules of the game. For example, the file defines the graphic features of the North Germanic group. Its subgroup, Norse, has its own graphical and colour specifications, lists of male and female names, and information on the display of titles and suffixes and prefixes used with dynasty names and patronyms. An interesting feature is that some personal names have variants in different languages. Thus, in Finnish culture, Erkki is an analogue for Erik, Auni doubles for Agnes and so on. The names of the dynasties are listed in another file ('00_dynasties'). Some dynasties, such as the Persian Kârawân, have only the culture defined, while others have religion and other specific aspects (e.g. their own colour) defined as well. New dynasty names are created during the game by adding a place name and a culture-specific suffix or prefix. Thus, a Swedish dynasty created in the game when a non-noble character is granted a holding could be, for example, 'af Åland'. However, for many cultures, such as Finnish or Russian, only an English 'of' prefix is used for newly created dynasties. The particularization of cultures and cultural groups is thus made with rather few variables, if we look at the level of the game's script. Similarly, the provinces have alternative names, which change according to their ruler's culture: Lapland's alternative names for Finnish and Sámi rulers are 'Lappi' and 'Sápmi', and 'Finland' may also be 'Finnland' or 'Suomi'.

The graphics variables affect the portraits of the characters (e.g. Figure 8.1). These include headgear, clothing and hairstyles. Interestingly, the facial features of the characters are not based on their cultural characteristics. In the game files, each character has an 11-letter string of letters called 'DNA', which is inherited from one's parents and does not change during the character's life. This string defines the facial features of the characters, as well as the colour of their skin and hair.[27] The hereditary characteristics of the characters in the historical game starts are set, but again, when the game unfolds, the genetics of the characters in future generations are not bounded by culture but depend on the choices made by human and non-human players. The selection of facial features, clothing and hairstyles can be expanded by culture-specific portrait and clothing packs that have been published independently or as part of larger DLCs. Similarly, several unit and councillor packs have added to the visual particularity of the cultural groups in the game.[28]

Focusing on the representation of Northern Europe in the game, the main cultural groups are North Germanic, Finno-Ugric and East Slavic. Early in the game, the North Germanic group is represented only by the Norse culture, which may develop into Danish, Norwegian and Swedish variations. Conversely, the East Slavic group is represented in the game at first by Ilmenian, Severian and Volhynian cultures, which may develop into the Russian culture. All the cultures in the Fenno-Ugric group (i.e. Finnish, Sámi, Estonian, Komi, Khanty, Nenets,

Mordvin and Meschera) are present early in the game. These cultural mechanics drive the in-game development towards a specific kind of state formation. For example, the player is able to create a contrafactual Russian Empire, supported by a shared Russian culture before the Mongol conquest, if the character rules all the required kingdoms and is him/herself a Russian.

At the beginning of the different paths of play (with given start dates; see note 9), there are several historical characters and dynasties to choose from. Several character portraits even include links to respective Wikipedia pages. Nevertheless, sometimes blanks have been filled with imagination. In the historical start of the Viking Era, the contrafactual Finnish chiefdoms and high chiefdoms[29] are ruled by dynasties with names that refer to Finnish tribes: for example, the high chief of Karelia is Tuure Karjalainen and the chief of Häme (Tavastia) is Mielus Hämäläinen. These surnames are also popular modern Finnish surnames. Similar logic can be found in the names of the East Slavic tribal dynasties – Seversky and Volynsky – in an earlier historical game start of 769. Other more or less common contemporary Finnish surnames, such as Itkonen, Korhonen, Virtanen, Lononen and Kemiläinen, are also present. Although the history of the Itkonen family can be traced to the 1600s,[30] for example, such dynasty names are products of the historical imagination. As such, they produce a certain type of historical particularity, which allows the roots of modern Finland to be projected to the Early Middle Ages.

An additional feature that conditions the unfolding of the game is the concept of de jure holdings. Each province is part of a de jure duchy, which is part of a de jure kingdom, while each kingdom is part of an empire. A player who holds a title has a claim to all the minor de jure holdings of the title. Possessing a claim to foreign territory means that the character may legitimately declare war and attempt to conquer the claim. Additionally, if a de jure title does not exist de facto (not a term used within the game), a player with enough minor holdings of a specific title can create it. The existence of the de jure titles creates a kind of 'conditioned teleology' or, using Chapham's terminology,[31] frames the player's goals: by conquering or inheriting certain provinces, the player may create a kingdom, thus supporting a more stable realm and increased ability to expand even further.

In the game, there are indeed several non-historical de jure titles, such as the Kingdom of Finland and the Empire of Scandinavia. The existence of these titles directs the gameplay towards contrafactual ludonarratives. In most cases, the function of the de jure titles is to increase the possibility for the ludonarrative to unfold towards an actual, predetermined post-medieval state – such as the

Russian Empire or the Kingdom of Finland. For the creation of some titles, there are special requirements for the ruler's culture and religion. For example, to usurp or to create the Kingdom of Sweden, the ruler him/herself must be Swedish, and the creator of the Kingdom of Finland must belong to the North Germanic or Finno-Ugric culture group.[32] Many of the Iberian kingdoms require that the founder is a Christian, thus tying these kingdoms to the historical narrative of Reconquista.[33]

These rules connect the ludonarratives to certain cultures. Contrary to these predetermined or conditionally teleological mechanics, however, there are also mechanics that make constructing and maintaining non-predefined realms easier. The de jure ownerships may change over time. If an empire, kingdom or duchy controls a lower-level title for a certain amount of time – usually 100 years – without interruptions, the latter will become a de jure part of the former.

Representing religions

Crusader Kings II features several religions and religious groups. The contents of one religion resemble those of other religions. Their structure and function within the game are similar, and the differences appear mainly on the surface: for example, pilgrimage made by Christian characters to various places is named differently depending on the religion; called *Hajj* for Muslims, it may be made to Mecca. The images of some events are also different. Similarly, while playing a character of an Eastern religion group, *piety* is called *karma*.

In general, the game operates on the basis of division into three social domains: the nobility, the merchant class and the religious class. These are represented by the holding types: the barony, the city and the bishopric. This basic model also works in the Islamic and Eastern worlds, but with different names. Additionally, the prefeudal world is represented by tribal holdings, where there is no difference between baronies and cities. In this mode, a province may include only one tribal holding, alongside a religious holding. A tribal player may adopt feudalism when certain conditions are met, which causes the existing tribal holding to transform into one or more baronies and/or cities. In *The Republic* DLC, the player may also play as a merchant republic, which is ruled by the merchant class and has a distinct system of inheritance. The religious states are generally not playable.

Each character in the game may have three types of capital: *gold*, which can be used to build different buildings in the holdings, to hire mercenaries and to give as a gift to another character; *prestige*, which affects a character's relations with her/his noble vassals and is especially important for pagan rulers, who may use it to raise a tribal army; and *piety*, which affects a character's relations with religious vassals and the head of the religion. Different amounts of these forms of capital are required for certain actions, such as creating a kingdom or performing a religious ritual. These types of capital are accumulated at different rates by different character traits (cynical, zealous) through actions (e.g. declaring a holy war) and events. The three types of capital are also connected to the three types of social domains and holdings – the towns, castles and churches.

Each religion also has a religious authority factor, which is affected by several other factors, and several holy sites, which are bishoprics in a certain province. Additionally, the more holy sites of a religion are controlled by rulers of the particular religion, becoming more important as the religion's authority is increased. Another significant factor is warfare: lost or won holy wars also affect religious authority. If a religion's moral authority is low, it may lead to heresy and revolts breaking out.

Some religions have religious heads: Catholics have the pope, the Orthodox Church the ecumenical patriarch, and the Sunni and the Shia their own caliphs. Some of the Christian heresies (e.g. the Fraticelli, Monothelites, Iconoclasts, Paulicians) have heads, while some (Cathars, Waldensians, Lollards, Messalians, Bogomolites) do not. Pagan religions do not have religious heads, but dating from the *Holy Fury* expansion pack, when a pagan religion is reformed, the ruler making the reform becomes the head of the reformed religion.[34] Reforming a pagan religion thus makes it more similar to Christianity and Islam. For reformed pagans, as well as Muslim rulers, it is possible to be simultaneously a king or emperor and a religious head; this is not possible for Christians. This has several bonuses, including, for example, the ability to declare a jihad or its counterpart, a Great Holy War.

Religion and culture both affect diplomacy, a game concept that concerns intercharacter relations, and a ruler's ability to govern areas: having a religiously and culturally homogenous realm or demesne is easier to rule, and counties or vassals with the same religion and culture as the rulers are less likely to revolt.

A player may change the religion of a character or province by using a religious advisor to convert them. The characters and provinces of a specific religious group (e.g. Orthodox and Catholic, both being Christian) get along with each other better than with others (e.g. Romuva and Suomenusko, both pagan groups). The same goes with the cultures and culture groups of counties and characters: for example, Finno-Ugric Estonians and Finns are more apt to cooperate together than with Saxons, who belong to the Germanic group. Both religions and cultures may have affinities. Characters are not able to have multiple or syncretistic religious identities, or pay their respects to many religions. Thus, different religions are containers with contents, as seen in the organizational structures of the churches or religion-related activities (e.g. pilgrimage) that increase the player's piety.

In *Crusader Kings II*, the influence of a so-called world religion paradigm[35] is evident. Conversion to a religion is always total: except for the *Monks and Mystics* DLC, the character can only have one religion, and there are no hybrid religious identities. However, the personal characteristic of 'sympathy towards religion X', which may be gained after conversion, is a way of modelling hybrid religiosity within the given framework by making the person more accepting towards characters of his/her former religion. This kind of conception of religious identity as exclusive and confessional seems to be based on a Judeo-Christian prototype.

The religions are divided into groups (Christian, Israelite, Islam, Pagan, Mazdan, Eastern) that share some qualities. Pagan religions allow more open declaration for war, but on the other hand, they are more prone to attacks from other religions. Additionally, pagan religious rulers may not upgrade their tribal holdings to feudal ones, or adopt feudalism, unless they reform their religion or convert to a non-pagan religion. Pagan reformation makes the religion more organized and similar in structure to Catholicism or Sunnism. One of the perks of reforming a religion is that it allows the player to declare a Great Holy War, which is similar to a Catholic crusade or Muslim jihad, as it allows conquering larger areas than most other forms of war. The religions in the pagan group represent an earlier evolutionary stage of religion, which goes hand in hand with the tribal social structure that may develop into a feudal one.

Another special case of religions is represented by heresies. It is possible for non-pagan religions to have heresies that can take over the whole religion (e.g. under certain conditions, iconoclasm may become the Orthodox mainstream). The Eastern religions, which are playable in the *Rajas of India* expansion (2014), are an interesting case: they are an organized religion, but they do not have heresies. Instead they have branches, such as Mahayana and Theravada within Buddhism. The rulers may also change their religion at will once during their life – for example, from Hinduism to Buddhism – which is not possible for characters of non-Eastern religions. The pagan religions do not have heresies, but if they reform, the older version (e.g. Old Romuva) will become a heresy of the Reformed Romuva, again demonstrating the development model of religions from paganism to full-fledged religions.

In the case of the representation of North European forms of paganism, an interesting feature is the naming of these religions. The Norse and Slavic religions are co-terminous with the cultural groups, and then there are the Romuva and Suomenusko, which correspond to areas inhabited by Balts and Fenno-Ugrians. While researchers tend to group the various folk religions of the real-world cultures along with the cultural groups, the names Romuva and Suomenusko unambiguously refer to the contemporary revival or reconstructionalist movements of ethnic pagan traditions. The term 'Suomenusko' (a translation of 'Finnish belief') has been used by Finnish Pagan reconstructionalist groups – such as Taivaannaula (who do not consider themselves as pagan), Karhun kansa and Pakanaverkko – to refer to Baltic Finnish rather than general Fenno-Ugric ethnic religious traditions. As a neologism, the term is connected to the organization and discourses of the Finnish alternative spiritual field.[36] However, the name has fallen out of favour, and for example the Taivaannaula organization has since 2017 renounced the use of the term because of its nationalist connotations and exclusivity towards Karelian customs.[37] Romuva is the name for a modern revivalist movement with its roots in early 1930s Lithuania, which gained officially recognized status in 1992.[38] Thus, it is rather striking that the Slavic and Germanic pagan religions are referred to by the names of the cultural groups – not, for example, by the terms Rodnovere or Ásatrú.[39]

This disparity was also noted by the user Merkatz on the forum of the Steam gaming community, sparking a discussion with multiple replies.[40] Discussions like these are good examples of how players who critique historical games are taking part in a public historical discourse.[41] One possible explanation for this naming practice may be that the Slavic and Germanic neopaganisms and related contestations were more familiar to the game designers than those related to the Baltic or Baltic Finnish. In these two cases, the game system builds contrafactual historical continuity between modern religiosities, analogically with the situation, where the Kingdom of Finland and the Empire of Scandinavia exist de jure.

Religion is a key component in warfare, and warfare is a significant element in the game. Religion affects who may attack whom, and religious differences bring about new types of casus belli. Pagans may conquer small areas even from realms with rulers who have the same religion. Christians may declare holy wars on pagans and Muslims, but not other Christians, except if they are heretics. Conquering areas is much more difficult in a situation where there is a lack of religious differences. Wainwright writes that *Crusader Kings II* and another medievalist strategy game, *Medieval II: Total War*, 'do not have to speculate on, for instance, whether one religion is more pacifist than another in order to model the diplomatic obstacles present between religiously dissimilar factions'. Although there are different mechanics involved with how to launch a crusade or jihad, the most important function of religious differences is, as Wainwright notes, the ability to forge alliances and arrange royal marriages.[42]

Overall, the dynamics of the game emphasize the cultural and religious homogeneity of a realm: the more diverse the realm is, the more difficult it is to control. This, along with anachronistic de jure holdings that fill the gaps of historical narrative, points in the direction of representations of medieval states and ethnicities produced by eighteenth- and early-nineteenth-century historiography and philology, which promoted romantic nationalist conceptions by creating visions of ethnic nations.[43] *Crusader Kings II* adds another link to these medievalist representations, which are prevalent in modern popular culture.

Nevertheless, if a player is to create a large empire, diversity cannot be avoided. While a character with suitable traits and good advisors may be able to assimilate the realm by converting, this may lead to further schisms. On the other hand, the game's technology system has a progressive tolerance factor, which lessens the tensions between cultures and religions. Additionally, adopting a non-pagan religion or reforming a pagan religion allows adoption of feudalism or a republic, which opens up more possibilities for economic and legal development, and, accordingly, integration and expansion of the realm.

Conclusion

Crusader Kings II is an example of an ambitious attempt to model culture and religion, reflect their changes on individual and socio-geographical levels, and demonstrate their effect on politics. The cultural and religious choices and settings affect the gaming experience through audio-visual elements, text (including the names of game concepts), narrative and game mechanics. The representation of culture and religion in *Crusader Kings II* employs a strategy that I have called 'particularization'. By particularizing a common model of culture and religion, the game system produces an experience of specific cultures and religions. In this sense, I argue that a fruitful approach is to look at how this particularization is made. While the practices between different cultures are mostly similar, on the surface level they are particularized. In fact, the process of particularization of religion and cultures works on two levels in *Crusader Kings II*.

First, there are particularities that affect the gameplay via game rules; second, there is the more superficial level, which includes the iconography and other visual representations, colours, graphic user interface (GUI) design, audio-visual cues and naming. The naming takes place in relation to the whole range of game concepts, such as the holding types and ruler titles. Additionally, the possible names of characters depend on their cultural and religious background, just as the names of realms change according to their rulers' culture. There are neither hybrid cultural forms nor syncretic religions, but new cultures do emerge from older cultures under preset strict conditions, constructing a conditional teleology that channels the development of the ludonarrative in certain directions. These strategies of particularization provide ways of producing a feel of cultural and religious difference while simultaneously guaranteeing that the unfolding ludonarratives retain sufficient resemblance to known history.

When we look at the representation of north-east European regions in the game, with their Baltic, Finno-Ugric and Eastern Slavic cultures that have gone through different developments than those of the Western European areas, it is evident that the game system produces contrafactual ludonarratives, such as the (pre-Mongol conquest) Russian Empire or the medieval Kingdom of Finland. The game's rules system is not well suited for representations of such historical situations where the territorial state does not (yet) exist.

Interestingly, there are more differences between religions, namely, between organized and pagan religions. The pagan religions may become organized and gain several benefits by reforming. The main effects of this reformation are that it allows transformation of the society from tribal to feudal, and the waging of more extensive wars against realms of different religions. Thus, the organized religions (i.e. different forms of Christianity and Islam) represent the prototypical – or universal – religions into which pagan religions can develop, which is typical of the world religions paradigm. This religious development is connected to other forms of development as well. While the particularization itself is built into the core of the object-oriented language paradigm, the ways this particularization is done reflects the culturally shared meaning systems. After all, programming is conceptualization. The ways in which the various cultures, religions and states are programmed and scripted reflect cultural and religion-related models and prototypical thinking. For example, the game engine's bias towards religiously and culturally homogeneous states is a product of both the programming paradigm and widely shared, culturally constructed metaconceptions about culture and religion.

Finally, I would like to address the issue of how *Crusader Kings II* may be situated in the context of struggles over the meanings of culture, religion and history. Andrew B. R. Elliott points out that the medieval may act as a repository of meanings which may be employed to various ends. Both jihadists and counter-jihadists employ the trope of the medieval and project the roots of the conflict between civilizations to medieval times.[44] At first sight, it is clear that *Crusader Kings II* focuses on warfare, and merely the mention of 'crusades' in the title hints towards those medievalisms that project the idea of 'clashes of cultures' – namely, the West versus Islam – onto the medieval past. Some of the game mechanics even project the roots of modern states to medieval times. The religious and culture-related dynamics of *Crusader Kings II* allow imagining of the medieval roots of present times in various ways.

This is not the whole story, however. The game contains a plethora of historical, religious and cultural concepts and practices, as well as geographical locations. While their occurrence in the game may not be always accurate, playing the game may inspire one to learn more about them. Furthermore, the conceptual simulation of systems and processes of the past may have pedagogical value, and various representations in the games may spark discussions about interpretations of the past.[45] As a medievalist cultural product, *Crusader Kings II* can be played and enjoyed by Islamophobes as well as radical Muslims, those who dream of a greater past for his/her nation, those interested in learning about historical processes and various cultures in medieval times, and those who simply find entertainment value in a medieval setting.

Appendix 1

For Chapter 1: The Middle Ages on the 'map of memory' of Russian society, by E. A. Rostovtsev

Table 1.1 Ideological paradigms of Russian history

Paradigm	Criteria:			Unifying discourse
	National	Social	Value orientation	
Radical-National (Statist-Patriotic)	Russia follows a special path; the special character of the Russian people; the positive nature of a strong, national, authoritarian government; Russia is surrounded by enemies; there is a world-wide conspiracy against Russia.	The social order is to be subordinated to the interests of the nation (state).	Russia's path is directed towards the greatness of the state (that means national greatness); everything is to be sacrificed to this end, including social and civil rights.	**Traditionalist discourse:** Historical development leads to the strengthening of the collective (the nation/the state/the workers/humanity/and so forth); the flourishing of the collective constitutes the meaning of the life of the individual.

(*Continued*)

Table 1.1 (Continued)

Paradigm	Criteria: National	Social	Value orientation	Unifying discourse
National-Social (Unitary-Social)	Russia follows a special path; the special character of the Russian people; the positive nature of a strong, national, authoritarian government; Russia is surrounded by enemies; there is a world-wide conspiracy against Russia.	In the interests of the nation (state); social welfare for the people.	Russia's goal is to achieve greatness for the state and the nation. These are only achievable by means of strong state power that protects the rights of the masses.	Traditionalist discource (same as above).
Radical-Social (Communist)	The interests of the nation (the state) should be subordinated to the social interests of the working people.	Social oppression of the people; the common people live in dire conditions; a positive assessment of social revolution and social transformation.	Russia's path is towards socialism (social equality); this is to be achieved at any cost (even national sovereignty and liberal ideals).	Traditionalist discource (same as above).
Radical-Liberal	Interests of the nation (the state) should be subordinated to the interests of citizens and the protection of their rights.	Russia's development along a European model is appropriate and imperative; the emancipation of the individual, and the protection of rights and liberties.	Russia is a part of Europe and should develop along the Western model. The protection of the rights of citizens is the end goal of its historical development, and all state interests are to be subordinated to achieving it.	Liberal discourse: Historical development leads to the expansion of the rights and freedoms of the individual.

National-Liberal	Russia follows a special path; the special character of the Russian people; the positive nature of a strong, national, government.	Russia's development along European lines is appropriate and imperative; the emancipation of the individual, and the protection of rights and liberties.	The goal of Russia (and of any developed country) is to build a society in which the rights of the citizen are protected. Only the wisdom of the nation and the state will allow Russia to achieve this goal.	Liberal discourse (same as above).
Social-Liberal	The interests of the nation (the state) should be subordinated to the social and civic interests of the people.	Russia's development along a European model is appropriate and imperative; the emancipation of the individual, and the protection of the rights and liberties; social oppression / the common people live in dire conditions; the lawlike character of socialist revolutions and transformations.	The goal of Russia (and of any developed country) is to build a society in which the rights of the citizen and social justice are guaranteed. Social policies aimed at resolving social problems are the only means towards this goal.	Liberal discourse (same as above).

Appendix 2

For Chapter 1: The Middle Ages on the 'map of memory' of Russian society, by E. A. Rostovtsev

Table 1.2 shows the popularity of various historical figures across a variety of source types: narrative sources; historiography; historical anecdotes; Wikipedia; societal opinion polls and the aforementioned series, *Name of Russia*. The results of the narrative sources are based on the analysis of a series of literary and journalistic literary samples from the Soviet and post-Soviet periods that were carried out by the project, 'Structural Conflicts in the Historical Consciousness of Russians as a Potential Danger to National Security' (2008–9); statistics on anecdotes, Wikipedia entries, and two of the aforementioned societal polls were compiled by the author in previous publications.[1]

Table 1.2 Russian heroes across different source types. The figures written in cursive are those designated by this study as consensus-objects; bold cursive refers to objects around which there is a positive consensus. (This has not been done for the wikipedia and historical-anecdotes columns.) Medieval/pre-Petrine objects are highlighted in gray.

Ranking	Narrative sources (1965–2008)	Historiography (up until 2011)	Anecdotes (2018)	Wikipedia entries (Russian language, 2020)	Russia-wide societal poll (2008)	Societal poll of 18–19 year-olds, open choice (chemistry students)	Societal poll of 18–19 year-olds (2020), asked to pick from suggested figures, (history students)	Project 'The Name of Russia' (2008)
1.	1–3. Peter I	Lenin	Putin	Putin	Peter I	Peter I	1–3 Lenin	1–4 *Alexander Nevsky*
2.	1–3. *Pushkin*	*Pushkin*	Lenin	Pushkin	Lenin	Stalin	1–3 Peter I	1–4. *Stolypin*
3.	1–3. Stalin	*Leo Tolstoy*	Yeltsin	Catherine II	Stalin	Lenin	1–3 Stalin	1–4. Stalin
4.	Lenin	Stalin	Stalin	Stalin	Catherine II	*Ivan the Terrible*	4 *Catherine II*	1–4. *Pushkin*

#								
5.	Ivan the Terrible	Peter I	Brezhnev	Peter I	*Suvorov*	Catherine II	5–6 Ivan the Terrible	Peter I
6.	Catherine II	Catherine II	Gorbachev	Lenin	*Lomonosov*	Mendeleev	5–6 *Alexander II*	Lenin
7.	*Leo Tolstoy*	Gorky	Khrushchev	Nicholas II	Pushkin	*Lomonosov*	*Pushkin*	*Dostoevsky*
8.	*Nicholas II*	Alexander I	Mendeleev	Ivan the Terrible	Mendeleev	Nicholas II	*Ivan III*	*Suvorov*
9.	Pugachev	*Suvorov*	Dostoevsky	Brezhnev	Alexander II	*Pushkin*	St Vladimir	*Mendeleev*
10.	Trotsky	Ivan the Terrible	Ivan the Terrible	Lomonosov	Catherine I	*Suvorov*	Gorbachev	Ivan the Terrible
11.	11–13. *Alexander Nevsky*	Nicholas II	Peter I	Gorbachev	*Kutuzsov*	Putin	12–13 *Nicholas II*	Catherine II
12.	11–13. Khrushchev	Trotsky	Gagarin	Dostoevsky	Nicholas II	*Kutuzov*	12–13 *Alexander Nevsky*	Alexander II
13.	11–13. Alexander I	Nicholas I	Kutuzov	Yeltsin	Ivan the Terrible	*Alexander Nevsky*	Rurik	
14.	14–17. Suvorov	Alexander II	Leo Tolstoy	Khrushchev	*Alexander Nevsky*	Yeltsin	Zhukov	
15.	14–17. Paul I	*Stolypin*	Suvorov	Alexander II	Pugachev	*Gagarin*	15–16 *Leo Tolstoy*	
16.	14–17. Nicholas I	Kutuzov	Andropov	Alexander I	*Minin and Pozharsky*	Gorbachev	15–16 *Yaroslav the Wise*	
17.	14–17. Alexander II	*Alexander Nevsky*	Pushkin	Alexander Nevsky	*Leo Tolstoy*	Alexander II	17–18 Minin and Pozharsky	
18.	Alexander III	*Pseudo-Dmitry I*	Lomonosov	Nicholas I	Yuri Dolgorukiy	Stolypin	17–18 *Dmitry Donskoy*	

Appendix 3

For Chapter 1: The Middle Ages on the 'map of memory' of Russian society, by E. A. Rostovtsev

Table 1.3 Rankings of the local objects of historical memory in the analysed Russian sources (1850–1917). The figures in parenthesis indicate the rankings of the local object in this source type (marked when objects share several positions in the rating). In the case of monumental sculpture, parentheses indicate rankings for monuments erected between 1850 and 1917; the figures in square brackets indicate rankings for the number of monuments before that date. See Sosnitskii, 'Istoricheskaia Pamiat' o dopetrovskoi rusi', 62–3; Rostovtsev, 'The Immortal Host of Prince Igor', 883–903.

Ranking	Fiction	Social and political literature	Periodicals	Cinema	Monumental sculpture
1.	Ivan the Terrible	Ivan the Terrible	St Vladimir	Ivan the Terrible	St Vladimir (1–5) [1–2]
2.	St Vladimir	[2–7] Tatar-Mongol Yoke	Ivan the Terrible	[2–10] Boris Godunov	Olga of Kiev (1–5) [3–7]
3.	Dmitry Donskoy	[2–7] St Vladimir	[3–4] Boris Godunov	[2–10] Pseudo-Dmitry I	Dmitry Donskoy (1–5) [3–7]
4.	Tatar-Mongol Yoke	[2–7] Land (Zemskie) councils	[3–4] Alexander Nevsky	[2–10] Maliuta Skuratov	Ermak (1–5) [1–2]
5.	[5–10] Oprichnina	[2–7] Ivan Kalita	Aleksey Mikhailovich	[2–10] Smuta ('Time of Troubles)	Bogdan Khmelnitsky (1–5) [3–7]
6.	[5–10] Prince Igor the Old	[2–7] Ivan III	[6–9] Igor Novgorod-Seversky	[2–10] Minin and Pozharsky	Baptism of Rus' (6–10) [8–10]
7.	[5–10] Yaroslav the Wise	[2–7] Raskol	[6–9] Ermak	[2–10] St Vladimir	Alexander Nevsky (6–10) [8–10]
8.	[5–10] A. M. Kurbsky	[8–10] Stepan Razin	[6–9] Rurik	[2–10] Stepan Razin	Ivan Fedorov (6–10) [8–10]
9.	[5–10] Sviatoslav	[8–10] Alexander Nevsky	[6–9] Nikon	[2–10] Dmitry Donskoy	Minin and Pozharsky (6–10) [3–7]
10.	[5–10] V. Shuisky	[8–10] Dmitry Donskoy	Ivan III	[2–10] Ermak Timofeevich	Ivan Susanin (6–10) [8–10]

Appendix 4

For Chapter 1: The Middle Ages on the 'map of memory' of Russian society, by E. A. Rostovtsev

Table 1.4 Rankings of the local objects of historical memory in the analysed Russian sources (1918–91). The figures in parentheses indicate the rankings of objects in their respective source type (marked when objects share several positions). See Sosnitskii, 'Istoricheskaia pamiat' o dopetrovskoi Rusi', 113–15; Rostovtsev, 'The Immortal Host of Prince Igor', 883–903.

Ranking	Fiction	Social and political literature	Periodicals	Cinema	Monumental sculpture
1.	Stepan Razin	Ivan the Terrible	[1–3] Igor Novgorod-Seversky	[1–3] Ivan the Terrible	Alexander Nevsky
2.	Ivan the Terrible	[2–4] Alexander Nevsky	[1–3] Stepan Razin	[1–3] Vasily Buslaev	Andrey Rublev
3.	Ilia Muromets (Ilia of Murom)	[2–4] Smuta (Time of Troubles)	[1–3] Ivan the Terrible	[1–3] Oprichnina	[3–7] Stepan Razin
4.	[4–7] Pseudo-Dmitry I	[2–4] Stepan Razin	[4–6] Ivan Susanin	[4–10] Igor Novgorod-Seversky	[3–7] Oleg Veshchy (the Prophet)
5.	[4–7] Nikon	[5–10] Pseudo-Dmitry I	[4–6] Boris Godunov	[4–10] Alexander Nevsky	[3–7] Prince Igor the Old
6.	[4–7] St Vladimir	[5–10] Aleksey Mikhailovich	[4–6] Fedor Ioannovich	[4–10] Tatar-Mongol Yoke	[3–7] Yuri Dolgorukiy
7.	[4–7] Schism	[5–10] Minin and Pozharsky	[7–9] Vladimir Monomakh	[4–10] Battle on the Ice	[3–7] Dmitry Donskoy
8.	[8–10] Aleksey Mikhailovich	[5–10] Baptism of Rus'	[7–9] Alexander Nevsky	[4–10] Maliuta Skuratov	
9.	[8–10] Igor Novgorod-Seversky	[5–10] Tatar-Mongol Yoke	[7–9] Ivan III	[4–10] Oprichnina	
10.	[8–10] Yaroslav the Wise	[5–10] Oprichnina	Baptism of Rus'	[4–10] Andrey Kurbsky	

Appendix 5

For Chapter 1: The Middle Ages on the 'map of memory' of Russian society, by E. A. Rostovtsev

Table 1.5 Ranking of the local objects of historical memory in the analysed Russian sources (1992–2020). The figures in parentheses indicate the rankings of objects in their respective source type (marked when objects share several positions). See Sosnitskii, 'Istoricheskaia pamiat' o dopetrovskoi Rusi', 159–60; Materials of the project 'Russian history in the mirror of mass historical consciousness (1991–2020); headed by E. A. Rostovtsev, https://historymap.spbu.ru/.

Ranking	Fiction (1992–2010)	Social and political literature (1992–2010)	Monumental sculpture (1992–2016)	Sociological polls (2020) (popularity of heroes %)
1.	Ivan the Terrible	Tatar-Mongol Yoke	[1] Alexander Nevsky	Ivan the Terrible (68)
2.	Oprichnina	[2–3] Alexander Nevsky	[2] St Vladimir	Rurik (33)
3.	[3–10] Battle of Kulikovo	[2–3] Sergiy Radonezhsky	[3–4] Olga of Kiev	Alexander Nevsky (27)
4.	[3–10] Time of Troubles	[4–10] Igor Novgorod-Seversky	[3–4] Dmitry Donskoy	St Vladimir (21)
5.	[3–10] Rurik	[4–10] Evpaty Kolovrat	[5] Yuri Dolgorukiy	Yaroslav the Wise (20)
6.	[3–10] Ivan III	[4–10] Epiphanius the Wise	[6] Mikhail Aleksandrovich Tverskoy (of Tver)	Ivan III (18)
7.	[3–10] Igor Novgorod-Seversky	[4–10] Joseph Volotsky	[7–10] Sviatoslav	Vladimir Monomakh (17)
8.	[3–10] Alexander Nevsky	[4–10] Ivan the Terrible	[7–10] Yaroslav the Wise	[8–9] Dmitry Donskoy (12)
9.	[3–10] Boris Godunov	[4–10] Time of Troubles	[7–10] Daniel Moskovsky	[8–9] Boris Godunov (12)
10.	[3–10] Pseudo-Dmitry	[4–10] Aleksey Mikhailovich	[7–10] Ivan the Terrible	Minin and Pozharsky (10)

Notes

Preface

1. Hilda Huntuvuori, *Erämaan nuotiolta Turun linnaan: kuvauksia keskiajalta* (Helsinki: Valistus, 1954), 23: 'Kotirantoja on puolustettava viimeiseen asti, mutta sotaretkille ei pidä lähteä, ei ainakaan itään.'
2. For an English overview on the post-war development in Finland, see Osmo Jussila, Seppo Hentilä, and Jukka Nevakivi, *From Grand Duchy to Modern State: A Political History of Finland since 1809* (London: Hurst, 1999), 217–56.
3. Derek Fewster, *Visions of Past Glory: Nationalism and the Construction of Early Finnish History* (Helsinki: Finnish Literature Society, 2006), 24, 320–30.
4. Ilona Pikkanen, 'The Dangers of "Too Easy a Life". Aarno Karimo's Historical Vignettes and the Post-Civil War Nation', in *Novels, Histories, Novel Nations: Historical Fiction and Cultural Memory in Finland and Estonia*, ed. Linda Kaljundi, Eneken Laanes and Ilona Pikkanen, Studia Fennica Historica (Helsinki: Finnish Literature Society, 2015), 159.
5. See Aalto and Ylimaunu in this volume.
6. James V. Wertsch, *Voices of Collective Remembering* (Cambridge: Cambridge University Press, 2002), 62, 93–94.
7. On 'banal medievalism' see Andrew B. R. Elliott, *Medievalism, Politics and Mass Media: Appropriating the Middle Ages in the Twenty-First Century*, Medievalism 10 (Woodbridge, Suffolk: D. S. Brewer, 2017), 19–23.
8. 'The Ancient Finnish Kings: a computational study of pseudohistory, medievalism and history politics in contemporary Finland and Russia', 2019–21, University of Turku, funded by Emil Aaltonen Foundation, PI Reima Välimäki.
9. Dina Khapaeva, 'Neomedievalism as a Future Society: The Case of Russia', *The Year's Work in Medievalism* 32 (2017); Richard Utz, 'Medievalism is a Global Phenomenon: Including Russia', *The Year's Work in Medievalism* 32 (2017).
10. Alexander Filyushkin, '"To Remember Pskov": How the Medieval Republic was Stamped on the National Memory', *Jahrbücher für Geschichte Osteuropas* 66, no. 4 (2018): 559–60.
11. Andrew B. R. Elliott, 'Internet Medievalism and the White Middle Ages', *History Compass* 16, no 3 (2018): e12441; Amy S. Kaufman and Paul B. Sturtevant, *The*

Devil's Historians: How Modern Extremists Abuse the Medieval Past (Toronto: University of Toronto Press, 2020), 88.

12 See Aali in this volume.

13 Fewster, *Visions of Past Glory*; Derek Fewster, '"Braves Step out of the Night of the Barrows": Regenerating the Heritage of Early Medieval Finland', in *The Uses of the Middle Ages in Modern European States History: Nationhood and the Search for Origins*, ed. R. J. W. Evans and Guy P. Marchal (London: Palgrave Macmillan, 2011), 31–51; see also Pikkanen, 'The Dangers of "Too Easy a Life"'; and Reima Välimäki, '"Uusi Turku tupineen". Hilda Huntuvuoren (1887–1968) historialliset romaanit ja kuva varhaiskeskiajan Turusta', in *Turun tuomiokirkon suojissa: pohjoinen hiippakuntakeskus keskiajan ja uuden ajan alun Euroopassa*, ed. Marika Räsänen, Reima Välimäki and Marjo Kaartinen, Historia mirabilis 8 (Turku: Turun historiallinen yhdistys, 2012), 215–40.

14 See e.g. Leena Valkeapää, 'Historiakulttuurinen keskiaika: tiedon ja mielikuvituksen liitto', in *Ilmaisun murroksia vuosituhannen vaihteen suomalaisessa kulttuurissa*, ed. Yrjö Heinonen, Leena Kirstinä, and Urpo Kovala (Helsinki: Suomalaisen Kirjallisuuden Seura, 2005), 245–62; Leena Valkeapää, 'Käyttökelpoinen keskiaika: historiakulttuuria nykypäivän Ulvilassa ja Raumalla', *Alue ja ympäristö* 35, no. 2 (2006): 79–91; Eva Ahl-Waris, *Historiebruk kring Nådendal och den kommemorativa anatomin av klostrets minnesplats* (Vadstena: Societas Sanctae Birgittae, 2010); Heidi Henriikka Mäkelä, 'The Desired Darkness of the Ancient: Kalevala-Metric Poetry, Medievalism, and Cultural Memory in the Books Niemi and Viiden meren kansa', *Mirator* 21, no. 1 (2021): 24–49.

15 E.g. Paul Dukes briefly mentions the Finns among the people who expressed grievances in the revolution of 1905, but fails to explain how the Grand Duchy of Finland became part of Russia in the Napoleonic Wars, see Paul Dukes, *A History of Russia: Medieval, Modern, Contemporary*, 2nd edn (Basingstoke: Macmillan, 1990), 190.

16 On the early state formation process in the region, see Jukka Korpela, *The World of Ladoga: Society, Trade, Transformation and State Building in the Eastern Fennoscandian Boreal Forest Zone c. 1000 - 1555*, Nordische Geschichte 7 (Berlin: Lit, 2008); see also Jukka Korpela, 'Finland's Eastern Border after the Treaty of Nöteborg: An Ecclesiastical, Political or Cultural Border?', *Journal of Baltic Studies* 33, no. 4 (2002): 384; a recent re-evaluation of the Baltic Crusades is Anti Selart, *Livonia, Rus' and the Baltic Crusades in the Thirteenth Century* (Leiden; Boston: Brill, 2015). Like Korpela, Selart questions the existence of a constitutive religious conflict at the time and regards it as projection of later centuries.

17 John H. Lind, 'Early Russian-Swedish Rivalry: The Battle on the Neva in 1240 and Birger Magnussons' Second Crusade to Tavastia', *Scandinavian Journal of History* 16, no. 4 (1991): 269–70; On Alexander Nevsky's reception, Frithjof Benjamin Schenk,

Aleksandr Nevskij: Heiliger, Fürst, Nationalheld: eine Erinnerungsfigur im russischen kulturellen Gedächtnis (1263-2000) (Köln: Böhlau, 2004) and Mari Isoaho, *The Image of Aleksandr Nevskiy in Medieval Russia: Warrior and Saint* Leiden; Boston: Brill, 2006). See also Rostovtsev in this volume.

18 Isoaho, *The Image of Aleksandr Nevskiy*, 169-70, 188-93.
19 Lind gives a thorough English overview of the debate till 1991, by which point the main arguments had been proposed, see Lind, 'Early Russian-Swedish Rivalry', 283-93; recently, see also Jens E. Olesen, 'The Swedish Expeditions ("Crusades") Towards Finland Reconsidered', in *Church and Belief in the Middle Ages: Popes, Saints, and Crusaders*, ed. Kirsi Salonen and Sari Katajala-Peltomaa (Amsterdam: Amsterdam University Press, 2016), 251-68.
20 Jalmari Jaakkola, *Suomen varhaiskeskiaika*, Suomen historia 3 (Porvoo; Helsinki: WSOY, 1938), 279-92.
21 Lind, 'Early Russian-Swedish Rivalry', 278; Kimmo Katajala, 'Drawing Borders or Dividing Lands?: The Peace Treaty of 1323 between Sweden and Novgorod in a European Context', *Scandinavian Journal of History* 37, no. 1 (2012): 24; in addition, see Korpela, 'Finland's Eastern Border after the Treaty of Nöteborg.'
22 There is an extensive overview of early Russian and Soviet historiography in John H. Lind, 'Nødeborgsfreden i Russisk Forskning', in *Nöteborgsfreden och Finlands medeltida östgräns*, Jarl Gallén and John H. Lind, vol. 2 (Helsingfors: Svenska litteratursällskapet i Finland, 1991), 250-82, see the reference to Shaskol'skij at p. 267; Samu Sarviaho has recently treated the historiography of the Treaty of Nöteborg in his PhD dissertation, see Samu Sarviaho, 'Ikuinen rauha: vuoden 1323 Pähkinäsaaren rauha suomalaisessa historiantutkimuksessa ja historiakulttuurissa 1800-ja 1900-luvuilla' (PhD diss., Oulun yliopisto, Oulu, 2017). See the note 21 above for English overviews.
23 Katajala, 'Drawing Borders or Dividing Lands?', 37.
24 Korpela, 'Finland's Eastern Border after the Treaty of Nöteborg', 384.
25 Jukka Korpela, 'Keskiaikainen itäraja läpi itäisen Fennoskandian metsävyöhykkeen - mikä se on!', *Historiallinen Aikakauskirja* 104, no. 4 (2006): 454-5; Sarviaho, 'Ikuinen rauha', 20-1, 451-60.
26 Sanni Översti et al., 'Human Mitochondrial DNA Lineages in Iron-Age Fennoscandia Suggest Incipient Admixture and Eastern Introduction of Farming-Related Maternal Ancestry', *Scientific Reports* 9, no. 1 (2019): 1-14.
27 Korpela, *The World of Ladoga*.
28 Sirpa Aalto and Veli-Pekka Lehtola, 'The Sami Representations Reflecting the Multi-Ethnic North of the Saga Literature', *Journal of Northern Studies* 11, no. 2 (2017): 7-30; Sami Lakomäki, Sirpa Aalto, and Ritva Kylli, 'Näkymättömissä ja kuulumattomissa? Saamelaiset ja koloniaaliset arkistot', *Historiallinen Aikakauskirja* 118, no. 4 (2020): 438-50.

29 Jukka Korpela, '"The Russian Threat against Finland" in the Western Sources before the Peace of Noteborg (1323)', *Scandinavian Journal of History* 22, no. 3 (1997): 387.
30 Korpela, '"The Russian Threat against Finland"' 387–91.
31 Fewster, *Visions of Past Glory*, 92–310.
32 Pekka Ahtiainen and Jukka Tervonen, *Menneisyyden tutkijat ja metodien vartijat: matka suomalaiseen historiankirjoitukseen* (Helsinki: Suomen historiallinen seura, 1996), 42–6; Fewster, *Visions of Past Glory*, 120–7, 155–8.
33 Fewster, *Visions of Past Glory*, 29, 177–8.
34 Reima Välimäki, Olli Seuri, and Anna Ristilä, 'Pseudohistoriaa Suomen muinaisista kuningaskunnista – Ongelmallisen tiedon kierto laitaoikeiston mediaekosysteemissä', *niin & näin* 1 (2021): 118–35; Reima Välimäki and Heta Aali. 'The Ancient Finnish Kings and Their Swedish Archenemy: Nationalism, Conspiracy Theories, and Alt-Right Memes in Finnish Online Medievalism', *Studies in Medievalism* 31 (2022): 55–78.
35 Elina Noppari and Ilmari Hiltunen, 'Populistinen vastamedia eliittejä haastamassa', in *Media & populismi: Työkaluja kriittiseen journalismiin*, ed. Mari K. Niemi and Topi Houni (Tampere: Vastapaino, 2018), 248–51.
36 Douglas Allchin, 'Pseudohistory and Pseudoscience', *Science & Education* 13, no. 3 (2004): 179–95; Sven Ove Hansson, 'Defining Pseudoscience and Science', in *Philosophy of Pseudoscience: Reconsidering the Demarcation Problem*, ed. Massimo Pigliucci and Maarten Boudry (Chicago: University of Chicago Press, 2013), 61–77; Sven Ove Hansson, 'Science and Pseudo-Science', in *The Stanford Encyclopedia of Philosophy*, ed. Edward N. Zalta, (Metaphysics Research Lab, Stanford University, 2017), available online: https://plato.stanford.edu/archives/sum2017/entries/pseudo-science/ (accessed 20 June 2021).
37 Cf. Ronald H. Fritze, *Invented Knowledge: False History, Fake Science and Pseudo-Religions* (Chicago: Chicago University Press, 2009), 16; Garrett G. Fagan, 'Diagnosing Pseudoarchaeology', in *Archaeological Fantasies: How Pseudoarchaeology Misrepresents the Past and Misleads the Public*, ed. Garrett G. Fagan (London; New York: Routledge, 2006), 34.
38 Bradley Gorski, 'The Battle for (Pre-)Modernity: Medieval Festivals in Contemporary Russia', *The Russian Review* 78 (2016): 547–68.

Introduction

1 Ann Gray et al., ed., *CCCS Selected Working Papers* (London and New York: Routledge, 2007), 382.
2 Andrew B. R. Elliott, *Medievalism, Politics and Mass Media: Appropriating the Middle Ages in the Twenty-First Century* (Woodbridge, Suffolk: D. S. Brewer, 2017), 26.

3 Amy S. Kaufman, 'Medieval Unmoored', *Studies in Medievalism: Defining Neomedievalism(s)* 19 (2010): 4.
4 Daniel T. Kline, 'Participatory Medievalism, Role-Playing, and Digital Gaming', in *The Cambridge Companion to Medievalism*, ed. Louise D'Arcens (Cambridge: Cambridge University Press, 2016), 75–88; *International Medievalism and Popular Culture*, ed. Louise D'Arcens and Andrew Lynch (Amherst, NY: Cambria Press, 2014); John M. Ganim, *Medievalism and Orientalism: Three Essays on Literature, Architecture and Cultural Identity* (London: Palgrave Macmillan, 2008); David W. Marshall, 'Neomedievalism, Identification, and the Haze of Medievalisms', *Studies in Medievalism: Defining Neomedievalism(s) II* 20 (2011): 21–34; Laurie A. Finke and Martin B. Shichtman, eds., *Medieval Texts & Contemporary Readers* (Ithaca; London: Cornell University Press, 1987).
5 Carolyn Dinshaw, *How Soon Is Now?: Medieval Texts, Amateur Readers, and the Queerness of Time* (Durham, NC: Duke University Press, 2012), 15ff.
6 See, for instance, Daniel Wollenberg, *Medieval Imagery in Today's Politics* (Kalamazoo: Arc Humanities Press, 2018); Daniel Wollenberg, 'The New Knighthood: Terrorism and the Medieval', *Postmedieval: A Journal of Medieval Cultural Studies* 5, no. 1 (2014): 21–33; Chris Berzins and Patrick Cullen, 'Terrorism and Neo-medievalism', *Civil Wars* 6, no. 2 (2003): 8–32; Amy S. Kaufman, 'Dark Revivals: Medievalism and ISIS', *The Public Medievalist*, 16 October 2014, available online: http://www.publicmedievalist.com/dark-revivals-medievalism-isis/ (accessed 27 October 2014); Amy Kaufman, 'Muscular Medievalism', *This Year's Work in Medievalism* 31 (2016): 56–66; Mike Horswell and Akil N. Awan, eds., *The Crusades in the Modern World: Engaging the Crusades*, vol. 2 (London: Routledge, 2019).
7 Wollenberg, 'The New Knighthood'; Wollenberg, *Medieval Imagery in Today's Politics*; Daniel Wollenberg, 'Defending the West: Cultural Racism and Pan-Europeanism on the Far-Right', *Postmedieval: A Journal of Medieval Cultural Studies* 5, no. 3 (2014): 308–19.
8 Erich Goode and D. Angus Vail, *Extreme Deviance* (Thousand Oaks, CA: Pine Forge Press, 2008), 127; Jeffrey Kaplan, *Encyclopedia of White Power: A Sourcebook on the Radical Racist Right* (Lanham, MD: Rowman & Littlefield, 2000), 539.
9 Indeed, Rees-Mogg's father, William, was an aspiring historian and economist. At the time of writing, a number of serving Conservative MPs have written historically-inclined books, including Boris Johnson (Winston Churchill, and an abandoned book on Ancient Greece), Jesse Norman (biographies of Edmund Burke and Adam Smith, Kwasi Karteng) (the British Empire and its modern effects) and Chris Skidmore (Edward VI, the Tudors, and Richard III).
10 Andrew B. R. Elliott, 'Medievalism, Brexit, and the Myth of Nations', *Studies in Medievalism* 29 (2020): 31–8. An extensive study of the links between Brexit and

performative citizenship can be found in Chiara Bonacchi, Mark Altaweel, and Marta Krzyzanska, 'The Heritage of Brexit: Roles of the Past in the Construction of Political Identities through Social Media', *Journal of Social Archaeology* 18, no. 2 (2018): 174–92.

11 Jacob Rees-Mogg, *The Victorians: Twelve Titans Who Forged Britain* (London: Random House, 2019), 4–5.
12 Rees-Mogg, *The Victorians*, 3, 6, 7–8.
13 Robert Hazell and James Melton, ed., *Magna Carta and Its Modern Legacy* (Cambridge: Cambridge University Press, 2015), Chapters 1, 2 and 4 in particular.
14 Patrick J. Geary, *The Myth of Nations: The Medieval Origins of Europe* (Princeton, NJ: Princeton University Press, 2002).
15 Helen Kingstone, *Victorian Narratives of the Recent Past: Memory, History, Fiction* (London: Palgrave Macmillan, 2017).
16 It is immensely difficult to attempt to capture the scope and toxicity of ongoing racist threats and campaigns, and even more so in a footnote. Suffice to say, then, that reporting on these threats has been ongoing since at least 2016, featuring a terrifying range of hinted or overt racist threats and insults. See, for instance, Lisa O'Carroll, 'David Lammy Receives Death Threat after EU Referendum Result', *The Guardian*, 4 July 2016, section Politics, available online: https://www.theguardian.com/politics/2016/jul/04/david-lammy-receives-death-threat-after-eu-referendum-result; Lucy Manning and Phillip Kemp, 'MPs Describe Threats, Abuse and Safety Fears', *BBC News*, 6 August 2019, section UK Politics, available online: https://www.bbc.com/news/uk-politics-49247808; or Robert Shrimsley, 'David Lammy: "The British Aren't Interested in Revolution"', *Financial Times*, 6 March 2020, available online: https://www.ft.com/content/a65d55b0-5bf9-11ea-b0ab-339c2307bcd4 (all accessed 9 June 2020).
17 Gayatri Chakravorty Spivak, 'Can the Subaltern Speak?', in *Marxism and the Interpretation of Culture*, ed. Cary Nelson and Lawrence Grossberg (Urbana: University of Illinois Press, 1988), 66–111.
18 Spivak, 'Can the Subaltern Speak?', 76.
19 I should acknowledge at this juncture that I did not actually visit this museum or see its featured exhibition. My interest in the exhibition arose from the discourses invoked to cover the exhibits and how the past was expropriated from an academic, archaeological, or historical discussion and into those well-worn grooves of systemic exclusion which I am trying to prove exist.
20 Kathleen Bickford Berzock, *Caravans of Gold, Fragments in Time: Art, Culture, and Exchange Across Medieval Saharan Africa* (Princeton, NJ: Princeton University Press, 2019), 26.
21 'George Smith', 11 March 2019. Comments taken from *The Sun*, 'The Golden King: Incredible Story of Mansa Musa', 10 March 2019, available online: https://www.thesun.co.uk/news/8603268/mansa-musa-richest-man-ever-crippled-economies/ (accessed 17 December 2020).

22 Derek Fewster, *Visions of Past Glory: Nationalism and the Construction of Early Finnish History* (Helsinki: Finnish Literature Society, 2006).
23 Stuart Hall, 'Whose Heritage?: Un-Settling "The Heritage," Re-Imagining the Post-Nation', *Third Text: Critical Perspectives on Contemporary Art and Culture* 49 (2000): 3–13.
24 Doug Jenness, 'Origins of the Myth of Race', in *Racism: Essential Readings*, ed. Ellis Cashmore and James Jennings (London; Thousand Oaks; New Delhi: SAGE Publications, 2001), 306.
25 Geraldine Heng, *The Invention of Race in the European Middle Ages* (Cambridge: Cambridge University Press, 2018), Chapter 1. See also Jonathan Hsy's introduction to *Antiracist Medievalisms: From 'Yellow Peril' to Black Lives Matter* (Amsterdam: Arc Humanities Press, 2021).
26 Heng, *The Invention of Race*, 3.
27 Eli Pariser, *The Filter Bubble: What The Internet Is Hiding From You* (Harmondsworth: Penguin UK, 2011).
28 Brian Winston, *Messages: Free Expression, Media and the West from Gutenberg to Google* (London: Routledge, 2006).
29 Henry Jenkins, *Convergence Culture: Where Old and New Media Collide* (New York: NYU Press, 2006).
30 Henry Jenkins, *Textual Poachers: Television Fans and Participatory Culture* (London: Routledge, 1992).
31 Axel Bruns and Joanne Jacobs, 'Introduction', in *Uses of Blogs*, ed. Axel Bruns and Joanne Jacobs (New York: Peter Lang, 2006), 6.
32 José Van Dijck, *The Culture of Connectivity: A Critical History of Social Media* (Oxford; New York: Oxford University Press, 2013), 4.
33 Bruns and Jacobs, 'Introduction', 5.
34 Clay Shirky, *Here Comes Everybody: The Power of Organizing Without Organizations* (New York; Toronto; London: Penguin Books, 2009).
35 Andrea Ceron, *Social Media and Political Accountability: Bridging the Gap between Citizens and Politicians* (London: Palgrave Macmillan, 2017), 5. The latest statistics (2021) give the internet access rate of 63 per cent of the world population, available online: https://www.itu.int/itu-d/reports/statistics/facts-figures-2021/ (accessed 16 March 2022).
36 James Curran, Natalie Fenton, and Des Freedman, *Misunderstanding the Internet* (Abingdon: Routledge, 2016), 139.
37 A. Ant Ozok and Panayiotis Zaphiris, 'Why People Use Social Networking Sites', *Online Communities and Social Computing: 5th International Conference, OCSC 2013, Held as Part of HCI International 2013, Las Vegas, NV, USA, July 21–26, 2013, Proceedings* (Berlin: Springer, 2009), 425.
38 Atsuyuki Morishima et al., 'Confirmatory Analysis on Influencing Factors When Mention Users on Twitter', *Web Technologies and Applications: APWeb 2016*

Workshops, WDMA, GAP, and SDMA, Suzhou, China, September 23–25, 2016, Proceedings (Cham: Springer, 2016), 112.
39 All data taken from Wikipedia's own, open access, user statistics, available online: https://en.wikipedia.org/wiki/Wikipedia:Statistics (accessed 17 December 2020).
40 Statistics on internet usage are, as suggested earlier, highly contested and always estimates based on sampling, pings, and the internet of things. The statistics used here are amalgamated from several sources, including HootSuite (https://wearesocial-net.s3.amazonaws.com/wp-content/uploads/2019/01/Screen-Shot-2019-01-30-at-12.02.22.png), statistica.com (https://www.statista.com/topics/1145/internet-usage-worldwide/), and then cross-referenced with reports from United Nations and International Telecommunications Union (e.g. https://news.un.org/en/story/2018/12/1027991). All sites last accessed 10 June 2020.

Chapter 1

1 Many thanks to Thomas L. Lowish for the present translation.
2 There are many survey works. See, for example, A. B. Rusanov, 'Medievalism Studies: kak izuchaetia "sovremennoe Srednevekov'e"?', *Vox medii aevi* 2, no. 5 (2020): 12–42, available online: http://voxmediiaevi.com/2019-2-rusanov (accessed 1 August 2020); A. I. Filyushkin, 'Chem porozhden novyi medievalism v Vostochnoi Evrope?', in *Mavrodinskie chteniia 2018: Materialy Vserossiiskoi nauchnoi konferentsii, posviashchennoi 110-letiiu so dniia rozhdeniia professora Vladimira Vasil'evicha Mavrodina*, ed. A. Iu. Dvornichenko (St Petersburg: Nestor-istoriia, 2018), 183–5.
3 D. V. Bodnarchuk, 'The Mobilized Middle Ages in Historical Memory', *Vestnik of Saint-Petersburg University, History* 64, no. 1 (2019): 159–76.
4 For ways in which the historiography has evaluated the many historical periods in pre-Petrine Rus, see, for instance, A. Iu. Dvornichenko, *Rossiiskaja istorija s drevneishick vremen do padeniia samoderzhaviia* (Moscow: Ves' Mir, 2010), 80–1, 262–3.
5 D. A. Sosnitskii, 'Istoricheskaia pamiat' o dopetrovskoi Rusi v Rossii vtoroi poloviny XIX–nachala XXI vv.' (PhD diss., St Petersburg State University, 2015).
6 E. A. Rostovtsev and D. A. Sosnitskii, 'Napravleniia issledovanii istoricheskoi pamiati v Rossii', *Vestnik SPbGU*, Seriia: Istoriia 2 (2014): 106–26.
7 See, for example, I. N. Danilevskii, *Drevniaia Rus' glazami sovremennikov i potomkov* (Moscow: Institut Vseobshchey istorii RAN, 1999); K. Iu. Erusalimskii, 'Poniatie "istoriia" v russkom istoriopisanii XVI veka', in *Obrazy proshlogo i kollektivnaia identichnost' v Evrope do nachala Novogo vremeni*, ed. L. P. Repina

(Moscow: Krug, 2003), 365–401; A. S. Usachev, 'Drevneishii period russkoi istorii v istoricheskoi pamiati Moskovskogo tsarstva', in *Istoriia i pamiat': Istoricheskaia kul'tura Evropy do nachala novogo vremeni*, ed. L. P. Repina (Moscow: Krug, 2006), 609–34.

8   D. E. Alimov and A. I. Filyushkin, eds., *'Mobilizovannoe srednevekov'e': medievalism i natsional'naia ideologiia v Tsentralno-Vostochnoi Evrope i na Balkanakh* (St Petersburg: SPbGU, 2020).

9   E. A. Rostovtsev, 'Srednevekov'e na karte pamiati rossiikogo obshestva v kontekste istoriografii memory studies', in *Mavrodinskie chteniia 2018: Materialy Vserossiiskoi nauchnoi konferentsii, posviashchennoi 110-letiiu co dnia rozhdeniia professora Vladimira Vasil'evicha Mavrodina*, ed. A. Iu. Dvornichenko (St Petersburg: Nestor-istoriia, 2018), 185–9.

10 See first of all texts by Dina Khapaeva and the reaction to them: D. Khapaeva, 'Neomedievalizm plus restalinizatsia vsei strany', *Neprikosnovennyi zapas* 1, no. 117 (2018): 173–86; D. Khapaeva, 'Neomedievalism as a Future Society: The Case of Russia', *The Year's Work in Medievalism* 32 (2017), https://sites.google.com/site/theyearsworkinmedievalism/all-issues/32-2017. Cf. R. Utz, 'Medievalism is a Global Phenomenon: Including Russia', *The Year's Work in Medievalism* 32 (2017); M. Wijermars, *Memory Politics in Contemporary Russia: Television, Cinema and the State* (London; New York: Routledge, 2019): 218.

11 Wijermars, *Memory Politics*.

12 Of these, we note the following projects: 'Strukturnye konflikty v istoricheskom soznanii rossiian kak potentsial'naia ugroza natsional'noi bezopasnosti: istoriko-sotsiologiceskii analiz', overseen by D. O. Tsypkin and A. Iu. Dvornichenko (St Petersburg, 2009); 'Rossiiskaia istoriografiia s drevneishikh vremen do 20-kh rr. XX veka: problemy periodizatsii, vsaimodeistvie nauchnykh paradigm i zakonomernosti razvitiia v obshestvenno-politicheskom kontekste', overseen by A. Iu Dvornichennko; '"Mobilizovannoe Srednevekov'e": obrashchenie k srednevekovym obrazam v diskursakh natsional'nogo i gosudarstvennogo sroitel'stva v Rossii i stranakh Tsentral'no-Vostochnoi Evropy i Balkan v Novoe i Noveishee vremia', overseen by A. I. Filyushkin; 'Obraz russkogo srednevekov'ia v SSSR: osobennosti gosudarstvennogo i sotsial'nogo zakaza', overseen by D. A. Sosnitskii; 'Rossiiskaia istoriia v zerkale massovogo istoricheskogo soznaniia (1991–2020)', overseen by E. A. Rostovtsev.

13 See, for instance, N. P. Ivanova, 'Tserkovnyi kalendar'-mesiatseslov kak istoricheskii istochnik', *Izvestiia Altaiskogo gosudarstvennoe universiteta* 3, no. 7 (1998): 22–6.

14 I. B. Mikhailova, 'Moskovskoe tsarstvo XVI v istoricheskoe pamiati russkogo naroda (po graviuram iz sobraniia D. A. Rovinskogo)', *Arkhivy i istoriia rossiiskoi gosudarstvennosti*, St Petersburg 1 (2011): 22–8.

15 O. Iu. Timonina, 'Dukhovnoe znachenie proobraza orla v narodnom iskusstve Drevnei Rusi', *Iskusstvo i kul'tura* 3 (2015): 78–84.

16 A. I. Filyushkin, 'Kogda i zachem stali stavit' pamiatniki istoricheskim personazham Drevnei Rusi?', *Drevniaia Rus': vo vremeni, v lichnostiakh, v ideiakh* 7 (2017): 382–97.
17 E. A. Rostovtsev and D. A. Sosnitskii, 'Srednekovye sobytiia i geroi v sovetskikh otryvnykh kalendariakh', *Noveishaia istoriia Rossii* 3 (2017): 163–81.
18 E. A. Rostovtsev and D. A. Sosnitskii, 'Russkoe srednevekov'e v kommercheskoi reklame: postanovka problemy i perspektivy issledovaniia (vtoraia polovina XIX-nachalo XXI vv.)', *Drevniaia Rus': vo vremeni, v lichnostiakh, v ideiakh* 7 (2017): 398–416.
19 E. A. Rostovtsev, 'Dopetrovskaia Rus' v zhanre internet-anekdota', *Istoricheskaia ekspertiza* 4 (2018): 173–84.
20 D. D. Konaneva, 'Srednevekov'e i otechestvennaia igroindustriia', *Istoricheskaia ekspertiza* 4 (2018): 163–72.
21 A. I. Filyushkin, 'Medievalism: pochemu nam segodnia nuzhny srednie veka?', *Istoricheskaia ekspertiza* 4 (2018): 153–64.
22 Iu. V. Shabarova, ed., *Obshchestvo vozrozhdeniia khudozhestvennoi Rusi i Fedorovskii gorodok Tsarskogo sela (sbornik dokumentov i materialov)* (St Petersburg: Obshchestvo russkoy traditsionnoy kul'tury, 2013).
23 See, for instance; E. V. Bykova and E. Iu. Mokerova, 'Representatsiia "istoricheskoi pamiati" v deiatel'nosti klubov rekonstruktsii srednekov'ia', in *Formirovanie grazhdanskoi ustoichivosti kak faktor protivodeistviia ideologii ekstremizma i terrorizma: Sbornik materialov Vserossiiskoi nauchno-prakticheskoi konferentsii* (Kazan: "Danis", 2017), 59–66.
24 M. Khal'bvaks [Maurice Halbwachs], *Sotsial'nye ramki pamiati*, ed. and trans. S. N. Zenkina (Moscow: Novoye izdatel'stvo, 2007).
25 Ia. Assman [Jan Assmann], *Kul'turnaia pamiat': Pismo, pamiat' o proshlom i politicheskaia identichnost v vyskokikh kul'turakh*, trans. M. M. Sokolskay (Moscow: Yasiki Slavyanskoi Kulturi, 2004).
26 See, L. P. Repina, *Kul'turnaia pamiat' i problem istoriopisaniia (istoriograficheskie zametki)* (Moscow: GU VSHE [SU HSE], 2003), 10–11.
27 Sosnitskii, 'Istoricheskaia pamiat' o dopetrovskoi Rusi', 7–9.
28 There are works that draw parallels from different positions. The most complete version is in the work of Russian émigrés (on this topic see: L. V. Pashchenko, 'Fenomen totalitarizma v traktovke predstavitelei russkogo zarubezh'ia', *Vestnik Murmanskogo gosudarstvennogo tekhnicheskogo universiteta* 11, no. 1 (2008): 89–93), and American historians and Sovietologists of the twentieth century (see, for instance, M. Fainsod, *How Russia is Ruled* (Cambridge, MA: Harvard University Press, 1963); B. N. Sumner, *Survey of Russian History* (London: Duckworth, 1947). See also V. A. Shutova, 'Evoliutsiia doktriny totalitarizma v sotsiologii SSHA v 1960–1970-kh vv.', in *Metodologicheskie problemy nauki*, ed. Yu. V. Petrov (Tomsk:

Izd-vo TGU, 1978), 135–42. Among later works, see, in particular, A. Ulam, *Bol'sheviki: Prichiny i posledstviia perevorota 1917 goda* (Moscow: Centerpolygraph, 2004); and G. G. Khazagerov, *Ritorika totalitarizma: stanovlenie, rastsvet, kollaps (sovetskii opyt)* (Rostov-on-Don: IuFU, 2012).

29 See, for instance, A. Iu. Dvornichenko, *Proshchanie s revoliutsiei* (Moscow: Ves' Mir, 2018).

30 See, for example, O. B. Leont'eva, *Istoricheskaia pamiat' i obrazy proshlogo v rossiiskoi kul'ture XIX–nachala XX vv* (Samara: OOO 'Kniga', 2011), 24–50.

31 For more on the method of analysis, see D. O. Tsypkin, M. A. Shibaev, N. I. Karbainov, A. P. Balachenkova, E. A. Rostovtsev, D. V. Solov'ev, A. M. Khokhlova, D. N. Shilov, A. V. Kincharova, S. V. Pavlov, E. V. Petrova, A. Iu. Rzheshevskaia, I. A. Rosugubu, I. V. Sidorchuk, D. A. Sosnitskii. 'Strukturnye konflikty v istoricheskom soznanii rossiian kak potentsial'naia ugroza natsional'noi bezopasnosti', overseen by D. O. Tsypkin and A. Iu. Dvornichenko (St Petersburg, 2009). This project is funded by Vekhi epokh; see also the website Memory Map of Contemporary Russian Society. Available online: https://historymap.spbu.ru/site/terminology (accessed 18 December 2020).

32 I. M. Savel'eva and A. V. Poletaev, *Znanie o proshlom: teoriia i istoriia*, vol. 1 (St Petersburg: Nauka, 2006), 421.

33 See Tsypkin et al., 'Strukturnye konflikty v istoricheskom soznanii rossiian kak potentsial'naia ugroza natsional'noi bezopasnosti'.

34 *Imia Rossii* (Russia-1, 2009), available online: http://www.nameofrussia.ru/ (accessed 30 January 2012).

35 Pyotr Stolypin ranked eighteenth to nineteenth place among the most important figures in Russian history in a 2011 poll conducted among students in St Petersburg. The poll was organized by the historical department of St Petersburg State University as part of a series of historical research projects. (The authors would like to thank I. P. Potekhina, *dotsent* at St Petersburg State Institute of Technology, for her help in organizing the survey).

36 Sosnitskii, 'Istoricheskaia pamiat' o dopetrovskoi Rusi', 200–1.

37 See, for instance, Savel'eva and Poletaev, *Znanie o proshlom*, 459.

38 Tables 1.3–5 are based on the author's previous study: E. A. Rostovtsev, 'The Immortal Host of Prince Igor', *Vestnik of Saint-Petersburg University, History* 65, no. 3 (2020): 883–903 and materials of the project 'Russian history in the mirror of mass historical consciousness (1991–2020)', headed by the author. See the project website at https://historymap.spbu.ru/.

39 See, among others, O. B. Leont'eva, 'Lichnost' Ivana Groznogo v istoricheskoi pamiati rossiiskogo obshchestva epokhi velikikh reform: nauchnoe znanie i khudozhestvennyi obraz', *Dialog co vremenem* (2007): 19–34; N. N. Mut'ia, *Ivan groznyi: istorizm i lichnost' pravitelia v otechestvennom iskusstve XIX–XX vv*

(St Petersburg: Aleteiia, 2010), 490; D. A Sosnitskii, 'Ivan Groznyi v istoricheskoi pamiati russkogo naroda (na materialakh khudozhestvennoi, publitsisticheskoi i uchebnoi liiteratury)', in *Lichnost' v istorii v epokhu novogo i noveishego vremeni (pamiati professora S. I. Voroshilova): Materialy mezhdunarodnoi nauchnoi konferentsii*, ed. V. A. Ushakov (St Petersburg: Izdatel'skiy dom Sankt-Peterburgskogo gosudarstvennogo universiteta, 2011), 471–4.

40 D. Brandenberger and K. M. F. Platt, 'Terribly Pragmatic: Rewriting the History of Ivan IV's Reign, 1937–1956', in *Epic Revisionism: Russian History and Literature as Stalinist Propaganda*, ed. D. Brandenberger and K. M. F. Platt (Madison: University of Wisconsin Press, 2006), 157–78. See also K. M. F. Platt, *Terror and Greatness: Ivan and Peter as Russian Myths* (Ithaca, NY: Cornell University Press, 2011); K. M. F. Platt, 'Allegory's Half-Life: The Specter of a Stalinist Ivan the Terrible in Russia Today', *Penn History Review* 17, no. 2 (2010): 9–24. S. M. Norris, *Blockbuster History in the New Russia: Movies, Memory, and Patriotism* (Bloomington: Indiana University Press, 2012); C. J. Halperin, 'Ivan the Terrible Returns to the Silver Screen: Pavel Lungin's Film Tsar', *Studies in Russian and Soviet Cinema* 7, no. 1 (2013): 61–72.

41 See, among others, I. N. Danilevskii, 'Ledovoe poboishche: smena obraza', *Otechestvennye zapiski* 5 (2004): 28–40; I. N. Danilevskii, 'Aleksandr Nevskii: Paradoksy istoricheskoi pamiati', in *Tsep' vremen: Problemy istoricheskogo soznaniia*, ed. L. P. Repina (Moscow: Institut Vseobshchey istorii RAN, 2005), 119–32; F. B. Shenk, *Aleksandr Nevskii v russkoi kul'turnoi pamiati: sviatoi, pravitel', natsional'nyi geroi (1263–2000)*, trans. E. Zemskovoi and M. Larinovich (Moscow: Novoe literaturnoe obozrenie, 2007); Iu. V. Krivosheev and R. A. Sokolov, *'Aleksdandr Nevskii': sozdanie kinoshedvra: Istoricheskoe issledovanie* (St Petersburg: Liki Rossii, 2012); R. A. Sokolov, 'Aleksandr Nevskii v otechestvennoi kul'ture i istoricheskoi pamiati' (PhD diss., SPGU, 2013).

42 See, among others, V. S. Belousov and E. S. Kuropatova, 'Velikii kniaz' Vladimir: Sovremennyi obraz i ego istoricheskie korni', *Iazyk i tekst* 2, no. 4 (2015): 55–64; T. A. Esina, 'Sakralizatsiia obraza politicheskogo lidera i natsional'naia konsolidatsiia rossiian: kniaz' Vladimir Sviatoi kak simvol gosudarstvennogo deiatelia i sovremennost'', *Izvestiia Tul'skogo gosudarstvennogo universiteta: Gumanitarnye nauki* 4-1 (2014): 128–40; D. A. Sosnitskii, 'Vladimir Sviatoi v istoricheskoi pamiati rossiiskogo obshchestva vtoroi poloviny XIX–nachala XXI veka (pa materialam narrativnykh istochnikov)', *Nauchno-tekhnicheskie vedomosti SPbGPU: Gumanitarnye i obshchestvennye nauki* 3, no. 203 (2014): 100–6.

43 E. A. Rostovtsev and D. A. Sosnitskii, 'Zabytyi zolotoi vek: Yaroslav Mudryi i Rus' Yaroslava – pereosmyleniia XIX–nachala XIX v.', *Rusin* 4, no. 4 (2016): 26–43.

44 C. J. Halperin, 'A Tatar Interpretation of the Battle of Kulikovo Field, 1380: Rustam Nabiev', *Nationalities Papers* 44, no. 1 (2016): 4–19. K. Parppei, *The Battle of*

Kulkovo Refought – "The First National Feat" (Leiden: Brill, 2017); A. E. Petrov, 'Evoliutsiia pamiati o Kulikovskoi bitve 1380g v epokhu stanovleniia Moskovskogo samoderzhaviia (rubezh XV–XVIvv.): K voprosu o momente transformatsii mesta pamiati', *Istoricheskie zapiski* 7, no. 125 (2004): 35–6; A. I. Filyushkin, 'Kulikovskii tsikl: opyt germenevticheskogo issledovaniia', in *Kulikovo pole: voprosy istoriko-kul'turnogo naslediia trudy nauchno-prakticheskoi konferentsii "Kulikovo pole – unikal'naia kul'turno-istoricheskaia i prirodnaia territoriia: Problemy izucheniia i sokhraneniia voenno-istoricheskogo i pripodnogo naslediia Tsentral'noi Rossi": Moskva – Tula, 25-27 oktiabria 1999g*, ed. A. N. Naumov (Tula: Tul'skii poligrafist, 2000), 172–86.

45 A. I. Filyushkin, 'Sotvorenie groznogo tsaria: zachem N. M. Karamzinu byl nuzhen 'tiran vsei Rusi'?', *Tetradi po konservatizmu* 4 (2016): 123–30.

46 See D. A. Sosnitskii, '"Poslednii geroi russkogo srednevekov'ia": Stepan Razin v massovom istoricheskom soznanii rossiiskogo obshchestva', in *Problemy i tendentsii razvitiia sotsiokul'turnogo prostranstva Rossii: istoriia i sovremennost': Materialy V mezhdunarodnoi nauchno-prakticheskoi konferentsii*, ed. T. I. Riabova (Bryansk: Federal'noye gosudarstvennoye byudzhetnoye obrazovatel'noye uchrezhdeniye vysshego obrazovaniya 'Bryanskiy gosudarstvennyy inzhenerno-tekhnologicheskiy universitet', 2018), 146–52.

47 See Filyushkin, 'Kogda i zachem stali stavit' pamiatniki', 394.

48 K. Iu. Erusalimskii, 'Zachem nuzhni pamiatniki Ivanu Groznomu?', *Istoricheskaia ekspertiza* 1 (2020): 48–73.

49 See A. A. Selin, 'Obraz Ryurika v sovremennom prostranstve Severo-Zapada Rossii', *Istoricheskaia ekspertiza* 4 (2016): 89–110.

50 E. A. Rostovtsev and D. A. Sosnitskii, 'Vladimir Sviatoi kak natsional'nyi geroi: voskreshenie obraza', *Dialog co vremenem* 4 (2019): 315.

51 Rostovtsev and Sosnitskii, 'Srednekovye sobytiia i geroi v sovetskikh otryvnykh kalendariakh', 48.

52 Filyushkin, 'Kogda i zachem stali stavit' pamiatniki'.

53 E. A. Rostovtsev and D. A. Sosnitskii, '"Kulikovskii plen": obraz Dmitriia Donskogo v natsional'noi istoricheskoi pamiati', *Quaestio Rossica* 5, no. 4 (2017): 1149–63.

54 For more detail, see E. A. Rostovtsev and D. A. Sosnitskii, 'Kniaz' Vladimir Velikii kak national'nyi geroi: sozdanie obraza', *Dialog so vremenem* 4 (2018): 150–64; Rostovtsev and Sosnitskii, 'Zabytyi zolotoi vek', 26–43.

55 'Poslanie Presidenta Federal'nomu Sobraniu', *Prezident Rossii*, available online: http://www.kremlin.ru/events/president/news/47173#sel=8:41:yaZ,8:65:CUc (accessed 17 April 2020).

56 'V den' narodnogo edinstvo v Moskve otkryt pamiatnik kniaziu Vladimiru', *Prezident Rossii*, available online: http://www.kremlin.ru/events/president/news

/53211#sel=11:1:7yf,11:36:iac (accessed 18 April 2020). More details can be found in Rostovtsev and Sosnitskii, 'Voskreshchenie obraza', 307–21. On Russian presidents' speeches and references to medieval history, see Parppei in this volume.

57 'Zakon Ukraini "Pro derzhavni nagorodi Urkaini"', *Verkhovna Rada Urkaini*, available online: http://zakon1.rada.gov.ua/laws/show/1549-14 (accessed 19 June 2016).

58 'Zakon o praznikakh i pamiatnykh datakh Yaroslavskoi oblasti', *Yaroslavskaia oblastnaia duma*, available online: http://www.duma.yar.ru/service/acts/z14088.html (accessed 19 June 2016).

59 'Ob universitete', *Natsional'nyi iuridicheskii universitet imeni Yaroslava Mudrogo*, available online: http://nlu.edu.ua/ru/%D0%BF%D1%80%D0%BE-%D1%83%D0%BD%D1%96%D0%B2%D0%B5%D1%80%D1%81%D0%B8%D1%82%D0%B5%D1%82/ (accessed 19 June 2016).

60 'Opredelenie Arhiereiskogo Sobora Russkoi Pravoslavnoi Tserkvi', *Ofitsial'nyi sait Moskovskogo Patriarchata*, available online: http://www.patriarchia.ru/db/text/4367765.html (accessed 19 June 2016).

61 For more details see Rostovtsev and Sosnitskii, 'Zabytyi zolotoi vek'.

62 O. I. Chapova, N. A. Artem'eva and L. V. Poshivalova, *Vse proizvedeniia shkol'noi programmy v kratkom islozhenii* (Moscow: Dom 21 vek, 2008), 3–4.

63 E. Soroka, 'Tam razvorachivalis sobytiia iz Slova o polku Igoreve: Shto v sebe tait novyi zapovednik DNP?' *Komsomol'skaia pravda v Donetske*, 5 February 2020, available online: https://www.donetsk.kp.ru/online/news/3756087/ (accessed 4 April 2020).

64 G. B. Benevich, 'Posziia gibridnoi voiny', *Novoe literaturnoe obozrenie* 3, no. 157 (2019): 226–38.

Chapter 2

1 Vladimir Putin, 'Soveshsanie s glavami regionov po bor'be s rasprostraneniem koronavirusa v Rossii', *Working Meetings and Conferences*, 8 April 2020, available online: http://kremlin.ru/events/president/news/63176 (accessed 28 May 2020). English translations of the quotes are provided by the Official internet resources of the president of Russia.

2 See e.g. Steve Gutterman, 'The Week in Russia: Putin, Pechenegs, And Pneumonia', *RadioFreeEurope*, 10 April 2020, available online: https://www.rferl.org/a/week-in-russia-putin-pechenegs-pneumonia/30546450.html (accessed 26 October 2020). See Evan Wallace's chapter in this volume on the Western audience's inability to interpret this and similar cases of Russian medievalism.

3 The events on 24 February 2022 made some of the notions in this chapter outdated. We now know that by launching a full-scale military invasion to Ukraine, President Putin proved wrong the somewhat optimistic assumptions that his primary aim was to maintain certain stability rather than profoundly challenge the existing international order. In hindsight, his plans became more evident already in summer 2021, when he wrote an article 'On the Historical Unity of Russians and Ukrainians', which took his imperialistic interpretations of history to a new level. Further, in his talks connected to the invasion Putin denied the right of Ukraine to exist as an independent nation, which puts his earlier references to history, too, into a revisionist context instead of a merely rhetorical one, especially the ones made on and after the annexation of Crimea in 2014.

4 Iu. M. Lotman and B. A. Uspenskij, 'The Role of Dual Models in the Dynamics of Russian Culture (Up to the End of the Eighteenth Century)', in *The Semiotics of Russian Culture*, ed. A. Shukman (Ann Arbor: Dept. of Slavic Languages and Literatures, University of Michigan, 1984), 3–35.

5 João Feres, 'Building a Typology of Forms of Misrecognition: Beyond the Republican-Hegelian Paradigm', *Contemporary Political Theory* 5 (2006): 259–77; Olli Löytty, 'Johdanto: Toiseuttamista ja tilakurittomuutta', in *Rajanylityksiä – tutkimusreittejä toiseuden tuolle puolen*, ed. Olli Löytty (Helsinki: Gaudeamus, 2005), 8–13.

6 Gail Lenhoff, 'The Construction of Russian History in *Stepennaia Kniga*', *Revue des études slaves* 76, no. 1 (2005): 31–50.

7 Kati Parppei, *The Battle of Kulikovo Refought – 'The First National Feat'* (Leiden: Brill, 2017), passim.

8 Parppei, *The Battle of Kulikovo Refought*, 101–38.

9 Jeffrey Brooks, *When Russia Learned to Read: Literacy and Popular Culture 1861–1917* (Evanston: Northwestern University Press, 2003), passim. Stephen Norris, *A War of Images: Russian Popular Prints, Wartime Culture, and National Identity 1812–1945* (DeKalb: Northern Illinois University Press, 2006), passim. See also E. A. Rostovtsev's chapter in this volume.

10 Kati Parppei, 'Enemy Images in the Russian National Narrative', in *Nexus of Patriotism and Militarism in Russia – A Quest for Internal Cohesion*, ed. Katri Pynnöniemi (Helsinki: Helsinki University Press, 2021), 23–47.

11 'Prezident: Uchebniki istorii dolzhny imet' edinuiu kontseptsiiu', *Rossiiskaia gazeta RGRU*, 25 April 2013, available online: https://rg.ru/2013/04/25/uchebnik-anons .html (accessed 28 May 2020); I. Pushkarev, 'Shkol'nikam rasskazhut pro 'uplyvshii Krym' i 'antirossiiskii front' – Chem novye uchebniki istorii otlichaiutsia ot starykh, Po punktam', *ZNAK*, 25 August 2016, available online: https://www.znak.com/2016 -08-25/chem_novye_uchebniki_istorii_otlichayutsya_ot_staryh_po_punktam (accessed 28 May 2020); Vladimir Putin, 'Zasedanie orgkomiteta "Pobeda"',

Commissions and Councils, 20 April 2017, available online: http://kremlin.ru/events/president/transcripts/54347 (accessed 28 May 2020); See also Igor Torbakov and Serhii Plokhy, *After Empire: Nationalist Imagination and Symbolic Politics in Russia and Eurasia in the Twentieth and Twenty-First Century* (La Vergne: Ibidem Press, 2018), 320–6. Keir Giles has noted that the contemporary state historiography in Russia has quasi-religious characteristics, which are reflected in the language used in the historical discourse; for instance, voices questioning the canonical version of history are sometimes called 'sacrilegious' or 'blasphemous', see Keir Giles, *Moscow Rules – What Drives Russia to Confront the West* (Washington: Brookings Institution Press, 2019), 105; see also 119–24.

12 I. Kurilla, S. Ivanov and A. Selin, '"Russia, My History": History as an Ideological Tool', *PONARS Eurasia*, 5 August 2018, available online: http://www.ponarseurasia.org/point-counter/russia-my-history-as-ideological-tool (accessed 28 May 2020).

13 For studies on presidential rhetoric and discourse in general, see, e.g. O. Drozdova and P. Robinson, 'A Study of Vladimir Putin's Rhetoric', *Europe-Asia Studies* 71, no. 5 (2019): 805–23; Veera Laine, 'New Generation of Victors: Narrating the Nation in Russian Presidential Discourse 2012–2019', *Demokratizatsiya: The Journal of Post-Soviet Democratization* 28, no. 4 (2020), 517–40. Besides speeches, Vladimir Putin has expressed his views on history also in articles he has written, see, e.g. Vladimir Putin, 'Rossiia: natsional'nyi vopros', *Nezavisimaia*, 23 January 2012, available online: http://www.ng.ru/politics/2012-01-23/1_national.html (accessed 31 May 2020).

14 Vladimir Putin, 'Poslanie federal'nomu sobraniiu Rossiiskoi federatsii', *Speeches and Transcripts*, 8 June 2000, available online: http://kremlin.ru/events/president/transcripts/21480 (accessed 28 May 2020).

15 About different connotations of patriotism and nationalism in Russia, see James Goode, 'Everyday Patriotism and Ethnicity in Today's Russia', in *Russia Before and After Crimea: Nationalism and Identity, 2010–17*, ed. Pål Kolstø and Helge Blakkisrud (Edinburgh: Edinburgh University Press, 2018), 258–81.

16 See, e.g. Patrick Geary, 'Writing the Nation: Historians and National Identities from the Nineteenth to the Twenty-First Centuries', in *The Middle Ages in the Modern World – Twenty-first Century Perspectives,* ed. Bettina Bildhauer and Chris Jones (Oxford: Oxford University Press, 2017), 73–80.

17 Drozdova and Robinson, 'A Study of Vladimir Putin's Rhetoric', 809.

18 Dmitrii Medvedev, 'Poslanie federal'nomu sobraniiu Rossiiskoi federatsii', *Speeches and Transcripts*, 5 November 2008, available online: http://kremlin.ru/events/president/transcripts/1968 (accessed 28 May 2020).

19 Medvedev, 'Poslanie federal'nomu sobraniiu Rossiiskoi federatsii', *Speeches and Transcripts*, 5 November 2008.

20 The exact nature of this turn, or whether there has been a turn at all, has been argued by researchers; see e.g. Matthew Blackburn, 'Mainstream Russian

Nationalism and the 'State-Civilization' Identity: Perspectives from Below', *Nationalities Papers* (2020), 3–5. Drozdova and Robinson, 'A Study of Vladimir Putin's Rhetoric'.

21 Vladimir Putin, 'Poslanie federal'nomu sobraniiu Rossiiskoi federatsii', *Speeches and Transcripts*, 12 December 2012, available online: http://kremlin.ru/events/president/transcripts/17118 (accessed 28 May 2020).

22 Putin, 'Poslanie federal'nomu sobraniiu Rossiiskoi federatsii', *Speeches and Transcripts*, 12 December 2012.

23 David Lowenthal, *The Past is a Foreign Country* (Cambridge: Cambridge University Press, 2011), 217–24. As noted above, the first sketches of a coherent history of the Muscovite power were made already in the sixteenth century.

24 Vladimir Putin, 'Poslanie federal'nomu sobraniiu Rossiiskoi federatsii', *Speeches and Transcripts*, 1 March 2018, available online: http://kremlin.ru/events/president/transcripts/56957 (accessed 29 May 2020).

25 Andrew B. R. Elliott, Introduction in this volume. See also *Medievalism, Politics and Mass Media: Appropriating the Middle Ages in the Twenty-First Century* (Woodbridge, Suffolk: D. S. Brewer, 2017), 22–3.

26 See e.g. Olga Malinova, 'Political Uses of the Great Patriotic War in Post-Soviet Russia from Yeltsin to Putin', in *War and Memory in Russia, Ukraine and Belarus*, ed. J. Fedor, M. Kangaspuro, J. Lassila and T. Zhurzhenko (Cham: Palgrave Macmillan, 2017), 45–6.

27 Putin, 'Poslanie federal'nomu sobraniiu Rossiiskoi federatsii', *Speeches and Transcripts*, 12 December 2012.

28 Putin, 'Poslanie federal'nomu sobraniiu Rossiiskoi federatsii', *Speeches and Transcripts*, 12 December 2012.

29 Gregory Carleton, *Russia – The Story of War* (Cambridge: The Belknap Press of Harvard University Press, 2017), 37–8. For analysis of presidential Victory Day speeches, see Malinova, 'Political Uses of the Great Patriotic War in Post-Soviet Russia', 58–64.

30 Vladimir Putin, 'Poslanie federal'nomu sobraniiu Rossiiskoi federatsii', *Speeches and Transcripts,* 25 April 2005, available online: http://kremlin.ru/events/president/transcripts/22931 (accessed 21 October 2020).

31 Malinova, 'Political Uses of the Great Patriotic War in Post-Soviet Russia'.

32 Putin, 'Poslanie federal'nomu sobraniiu Rossiiskoi federatsii', *Speeches and Transcripts,* 1 March 2018.

33 Vladimir Putin, 'Poslanie federal'nomu sobraniiu Rossiiskoi federatsii', *Speeches and Transcripts,* 1 December 2016, available online: http://kremlin.ru/events/president/transcripts/53379 (accessed 29 May 2020).

34 Putin, 'Poslanie federal'nomu sobraniiu Rossiiskoi federatsii', *Speeches and Transcripts*, 1 December 2016.

35 Vladimir Putin, 'Poslanie federal'nomu sobraniiu Rossiiskoi federatsii', *Speeches and Transcripts*, 16 May 2003, available online: http://kremlin.ru/events/president/transcripts/21998 (accessed 29 May 2020).
36 Putin, 'Poslanie federal'nomu sobraniiu Rossiiskoi federatsii', *Speeches and Transcripts*, 16 May 2003.
37 Putin, 'Poslanie federal'nomu sobraniiu Rossiiskoi federatsii', *Speeches and Transcripts*, 25 April 2005.
38 Putin, 'Poslanie federal'nomu sobraniiu Rossiiskoi federatsii', *Speeches and Transcripts*, 25 April 2005.
39 Vladimir Putin, 'Poslanie federal'nomu sobraniiu Rossiiskoi federatsii', *Speeches and Transcripts*, 26 April 2007, available online: http://kremlin.ru/events/president/transcripts/24203 (accessed 29 May 2020).
40 Medvedev, 'Poslanie federal'nomu sobraniiu Rossiiskoi federatsii', *Speeches and Transcripts*, 5 November 2008.
41 Putin, 'Poslanie federal'nomu sobraniiu Rossiiskoi federatsii', *Speeches and Transcripts*, 12 December 2012.
42 Pål Kolstø, 'The Ethnification of Russian Nationalism', in *The New Russian Nationalism: Imperialism, Ethnicity and Authoritarianism 2000–2015*, ed. Pål Kolstø and Helge Blakkisrud (Edinburgh: Edinburgh University Press, 2016), 18–45; Helge Blakkisrud, 'Blurring the Boundary Between Civic and Ethnic: The Kremlin's New Approach to National Identity under Putin's Third Term', in *The New Russian Nationalism*, 249–74.
43 See, e.g., Joep Leerssen, 'Nation and Ethnicity', in *The Contested Nation: Ethnicity, Class, Religion and Gender in National Histories,* ed. Stefan Berger and Chris Lorenz (Basingstoke: Palgrave Macmillan, 2008), 75–103.
44 Torbakov and Plokhy, *After Empire: Nationalist Imagination and Symbolic Politics*, 11–27.
45 Andreas Kappeler, *The Russian Empire: A Multiethnic History* (New York: Routledge, 2013), 370–92.
46 Matthew Schmidt, 'Is Putin Pursuing a Policy of Eurasianism?', *Demokratizatsiya: The Journal of Post-Soviet Democratization* 13, no. 1 (2005): 87–100.
47 Laine, 'New Generation of Victors', 522–9.
48 Vladimir Putin, 'Poslanie federal'nomu sobraniiu Rossiiskoi federatsii', *Speeches and Transcripts*, 3 December 2015, available online: kremlin.ru/events/president/transcripts/50864 (accessed 30 May 2020).
49 Putin, 'Poslanie federal'nomu sobraniiu Rossiiskoi federatsii', *Speeches and Transcripts*, 3 December 2015.
50 Vladimir Putin, 'Poslanie federal'nomu sobraniiu Rossiiskoi federatsii', *Speeches and Transcripts*, 4 December 2014, available online: http://kremlin.ru/events/president/transcripts/47173 (accessed 30 May 2020).

51 See e.g. Torbakov and Plokhy, *After Empire: Nationalist Imagination and Symbolic Politics*, 206–7. Carleton, *Russia – the Story of War*, 230–1; See also Rostovtsev's chapter in this volume.
52 Dina Khapaeva, 'Neomedievalism as a Future Society: The Case of Russia', *The Year's Work in Medievalism* 32 (2017). See also A. I. Filyushkin, '"Mobilisatsiia srednevekov'ia" kak instrument formirovaniia predstavlenii o slavianskom edistve', *Studia Slavica et Balcanica Petropolitana* 2, no. 22 (2017): 31.
53 Putin, 'Poslanie federal'nomu sobraniiu Rossiiskoi federatsii', *Speeches and Transcripts*, 4 December 2014.
54 Putin, 'Poslanie federal'nomu sobraniiu Rossiiskoi federatsii', *Speeches and Transcripts*, 3 December 2015.
55 Giles, *Moscow Rules – What Drives Russia to Confront the West*, 35–57.
56 N. A. Danilevskii, *Rossiia i Evropa: Vzgliad na kul'turnye i politicheskie otnosheniia slavianskogo mira k germane-romanskomu* (St Petersburg: Izdatel'stvo 'Glagol', 1995), 18–44.
57 Danilevskii, *Rossiia i Evropa*, 35–6.
58 Francis King, 'Making Virtual (Non)sense of the Past: Russian Nationalist Interpretations of Twentieth-century History on the Internet', in *Nationalist Myths and Modern Media: Cultural Identity in the Age of Globalisation*, ed. J. H. Brinks, S. Rock and E. Timms (London: I.B. Tauris, 2014), 227. On the relation of the slavophilism and nationalism, see e.g. Emil Pain, 'Contemporary Russian Nationalism in the Historical Struggle between 'Official Nationality' and 'Popular Sovereignty', in *Russia Before and After Crimea: Nationalism and Identity, 2010–17*, ed. Pål Kolstø and Helge Blakkisrud (Edinburgh: Edinburgh University Press, 2018), 23–49.
59 Vladimir Putin, 'Poslanie federal'nomu sobraniiu Rossiiskoi federatsii', *Speeches and Transcripts*, 12 December 2013, available online: http://kremlin.ru/events/president/transcripts/19825 (accessed 30 May 2020).
60 Putin, 'Poslanie federal'nomu sobraniiu Rossiiskoi federatsii', *Speeches and Transcripts*, 12 December 2013.
61 Putin, 'Poslanie federal'nomu sobraniiu Rossiiskoi federatsii', *Speeches and Transcripts*, 12 December 2013.
62 On the connotations of the concept of 'West' in Russia, see e.g. Marlene Laruelle, 'Russia as an Anti-Liberal European Civilisation', in *The New Russian Nationalism: Imperialism, Ethnicity and Authoritarianism 2000–2015*, ed. Pål Kolstø and Helge Blakkisrud (Edinburgh: Edinburgh University Press, 2016), 278–9.
63 Putin, 'Poslanie federal'nomu sobraniiu Rossiiskoi federatsii', *Speeches and Transcripts*, 1 December 2016.
64 Putin, 'Poslanie federal'nomu sobraniiu Rossiiskoi federatsii', *Speeches and Transcripts*, 1 March 2018.
65 Drozdova and Robinson, 'A Study of Vladimir Putin's Rhetoric', 816–18.

Chapter 3

1 Work on this essay was funded by the Emil Aaltonen Foundation's 'The Ancient Finnish Kings: A computational study of pseudohistorical medievalism and history politics in contemporary Finland and Russia (PSEUDOHISTORIA)' project funding and the European Union Horizon2020 research and innovation programme (Project no 810961) ERA Chair for Cultural Data Analytics CUDAN.
2 For a definition of pseudohistory, see Välimäki's Preface in this volume.
3 Johan Östling, David Larsson Heidenblad, Erling Sandmo, Anna Nilsson Hammar, and Kari H. Nordberg, 'The History of Knowledge and Circulation of Knowledge. An Introduction', in *Circulation of Knowledge: Explorations in the History of Knowledge*, ed. Johan Östling, Erling Sandmo, David Larsson Heidenblad, Anna Nilsson Hammar, and Kari H. Nordberg (Lund: Nordic Academic Press, 2018), 18; Maximilian Hösl, 'Semantics of the Internet: A Political History', *Internet Histories* 3, no. 3–4 (2019): 276–7.
4 O. V. Golovashina, "Liubiteli istorii' i istorija dlia liubitelei: predstavlenia o proshlym v sotsial'nykh setiakh', *Filosofskie traditsii i sovremennost'* 1, no. 5 (2014): 114–23; Ksenia Zharchinskaya, '"Mif i istoricheskaya pamiat": obrazy slavianskoi "traditsii" v sotsial'nykh setiakh', *Vestnik Tomskogo gosudarstvennogo universiteta. Istorija* 4, no. 30 (2014): 97–103.
5 Zharchinskaya, '"Mif i istoricheskaya pamiat"', 98.
6 E. A. Rostovtsev and D. A. Sosnitskii, 'Srednevekovye geroi i sobytija otechestvennoi istorii v setevyh resursah', *Istoricheskaia ekspertiza* 1 (2018): 54–5.
7 Vladimir Emel'ianenko, Aleksandr Vetoshko, and Irina Malashenko, 'Internet i mifologizatsija istoricheskogo soznanija (tsennostno-mirovozzrencheskii aspekt)', *Gramota* 2, no. 76 (2017): 100–4; Tat'iana Savel'eva, 'Mifotvorchestvo kak mediatekhnologija XXI veka', *Znak: problemnoe pole mediaobrazovanija* 2, no. 24 (2017): 87–91; M. P. Ajzenshtat, M. S. Bobkova, S. G. Mereminskii, and A. I. Sidorov, 'Istorija i mif: kto kogo?', *Lokus: Liudi, obshestvo, kul'tury, smysly* 4 (2017): 133–7; Darya Makovskaya, 'Istoricheskii mif i etnicheskii konflikt: teorija, metodologija, tekhnologija konstruirovanija', *Nauchnaya mysl' Kavkaza* 1, no. 77 (2014); Dmitrii Sergeev, 'Osnovnoe soderzhanie izobretennoi arkhaiki kak strategii preodolenija kul'turnogo krizisa', *Gumanitarnyi vektor, Pedagogika, psihologija* 1 (2010).
8 See for example Jade McGlynn, 'Engaging Young Russians in Military History', *ZOIS Spotlight*, 21 October, 2020, available online: https://en.zois-berlin.de/publications/zois-spotlight/engaging-young-russians-in-military-history/ (accessed 15 December 2020).
9 Evgenii Sukharinkov, 'Mifotvortsy psevdoistorii', *Istorija.rf website*, n.d., available online: https://histrf.ru/biblioteka/b/mifotvortsy-psievdoistorii (accessed 18 December 2020).

10 Rostovtsev and Sosnitskii, 'Srednevekovye geroi', 54–5; Mariëlle Wijermars, *Memory Politics in Contemporary Russia: Television, Cinema and the State* (London: Routledge, Taylor & Francis Group, 2019), 2, 4, 22.

11 Alexander Filyushkin, '"Mobilizatsija srednevekov'ja" kak poisk identichnosti: kakimi putjami Belorussia hochet uiti ot istoricheskogo nasledija Rossijskoi imperii i SSSR', *Quaestio Rossica* 5, no. 2 (2017): 569–90, 572–3; see also Parppei's and Rostovtsev's chapters in this volume.

12 Wijermars, *Memory Politics*, 2, passim; Suvi Kansikas, 'Menneisyys ulkopolitiikan välineenä: Venäjän muistilait ja historian politisoiminen', *Kosmopolis* 49, no. 3 (2019): 28–47, 29–32.

13 Rostovtsev and Sosnitskii, 'Srednevekovye geroi', 42; Andrew Hoskins, 'Digital Network Memory', in *Mediation, Remediation, and the Dynamics of Cultural Memory*, ed. Laura Basu and Paulus Bijl (Berlin: Walter de Gruyter, 2009), 91–106, 94.

14 Wijermars, *Memory Politics*, 3, 9, 223, 225.

15 Reima Välimäki, Olli Seuri, and Anna Ristilä, 'Pseudohistoriaa Suomen muinaisista kuningaskunnista – Ongelmallisen tiedon kierto laitaoikeiston mediaekosysteemissä', *niin & näin* 1 (2021): 118–35.

16 See Elliott's Introduction in this volume.

17 Olessia Koltsova, Sergei Koltcov, and Sergey Nikolenko, 'Communities of Co-Commenting in the Russian LiveJournal and Their Topical Coherence', *Internet Research* 26, no. 3 (2016): 710–32, 710–11; Albert-László Barabási and Réka Albert, 'Emergence of Scaling in Random Networks', *Science* 286, no. 5439 (1999): 509–12.

18 Jean-Pierre Eckmann and Elisha Moses, 'Curvature of Co-Links Uncovers Hidden Thematic Layers in the World Wide Web', *Proceedings of the National Academy of Sciences* 99, no. 9 (2002): 5825–9; Bálint György Kubik and Boróka Pápay, 'The Boundaries and External Connections of the Hyperlink Network of Hungarian Websites in Romania', *Intersections; Budapest* 3, no. 1 (2017): 76–95; Robert Ackland and Rachel Gibson, 'Hyperlinks and Networked Communication: A Comparative Study of Political Parties Online', *International Journal of Social Research Methodology* 16, no. 3 (2013): 231–44; Nuccio Ludovico, Marc Esteve Del Valle, and Franco Ruzzenenti, 'Mapping the Dutch Energy Transition Hyperlink Network', *Sustainability* 12, no. 18 (2020): 7629; Tianyu Ying, William C. Norman and Yongguang Zhou, 'Online Networking in the Tourism Industry: A Webometrics and Hyperlink Network Analysis', *Journal of Travel Research* 55, no. 1 (2016): 16–33; Ian Milligan, *History in the Age of Abundance?: How the Web Is Transforming Historical Research* (Montreal: McGill-Queen's Press – MQUP, 2019), 19, 45–6, 107.

19 Beloe Bratstvo, 'Another Look at the History of Rus' (Drugoi vzgliad na istoriju Rusi)', 8 November 2015, available online: https://beloe-bratstvo.ru/drugoj-vzglyad-na-istoriyu-rusi/ (accessed 16 December 2020); V. Karabanov, 'The Forbidden

History of Rus' (Zapretnaya istoriya Rusy)', *Agentstvo Russkoi Informatsii (ARI)*, 9 January 2013, available online: https://ari.ru/ari/2013/01/09/zapretnaya-istoriya-rusi (accessed 16 December 2020); Tainoe Info, 'The Unknown History of Ancient Rus' (Neizvestnaya istoriya drevnei Rusi)', 20 July 2015, available online: http://tainoe.info/neizvestnaya-istoriya-drevney-rusi.html (accessed 16 December 2020).
20 Yandex is the search engine used most widely in Russian language web searches.
21 The code used for scraping can be accessed here: https://github.com/aristila/PHist.
22 See, for example, Karabanov's profile page at the online library Rulit.me website https://www.rulit.me/author/karabanov-vladislav (accessed 14 January 2021).
23 Karabanov, 'The Forbidden History'. The author of the text is the Editor-in-Chief of the Agency of Russian Information (ARI) web portal and thus has clearly aimed the text as a publication. Therefore, it is grounded to publish the name of the author here.
24 Tainoe Info, 'The Unknown History'.
25 Tainoe Info, 'The Unknown History'.
26 Beloe Bratstvo, 'Another Look'.
27 Karabanov, 'The Forbidden History'; Beloe Bratstvo, 'Another Look'.
28 Beloe Bratstvo, 'Another Look'.
29 Jukka Korpela, *Itä-Euroopan historia keskiajalta 1700-luvulle* (Helsinki: Gaudeamus, 1999); Wijermars, *Memory Politics*.
30 Our network visualization shows a snapshot from autumn 2019, when the data were crawled. Since the World Wide Web is an interconnected and constantly changing organism, where parts die and degenerate soon, and new things and technologies are constantly born, this snapshot emphasizes the websites created in 2019 and shows those older websites that have been actively maintained.
31 Shawn Martin, W. Michael Brown, Richard Klavans, and Kevin W. Boyack, 'OpenOrd: An Open-Source Toolbox for Large Graph Layout', In *Visualization and Data Analysis 2011*, 7868:786806. Used specifications: Liquid% 25; Expansion% 25; Cooldown% 25; Crunch% 10; Simmer% 15; Edge Cut 0.8; Num Threads 11; Num Iterations 750; Fixed time 0.2; Random seed 3934011733980657700.
32 Urlik Brandes and Thomas Erlebach, 'Introduction', in *Network Analysis: Methodological Foundations*, ed. Ulrik Brandes and Thomas Erlebach (New York: Springer, 2005), 2; Urlik Brandes and Thomas Erlebach, 'Fundamentals', in *Network Analysis*, 8; Dirk Koschutzki, Katharina Anna Lehmann, Leon Peeters, Stefan Richter, Dagmar Tenfelde-Podehl, and Oliver Zlotowski, 'Centrality Indices', in *Network Analysis*, 17–18.
33 The in-degree specifications used: min 1; max 52,5.
34 The community detection was made with the Modularity algorithm in Gephi. Vincent D. Blondel, Jean-Loup Guillaume, Renaud Lambiotte, and Etienne Lefebvre, 'Fast Unfolding of Communities in Large Networks', *Journal of*

Statistical Mechanics: Theory and Experiment 10 (2008): P10008. Used parameters: Randomize: On; Use edge weights: On; Resolution: 5.0; Results: Modularity: 0,940; Modularity with resolution: 4,933. The algorithm detected altogether 212 separate communities in the network.

35 See the Beloe Bratstvo main page at https://beloe-bratstvo.ru/ (accessed 18 December 2020).
36 Ludovico et al., 'Mapping the Dutch', 3; Milligan, *History in the Age*, 139; Kubik and Pápay, 'The Boundaries', 91; Ying et al., 'Online Networking'; Ackland and Gibson, 'Hyperlinks', 231–3.
37 Milligan, *History in the Age*, 136.
38 The main website of ARI gained over 100,000, while Secret Info gained over 11,000 visitors in June–August 2020. SimilarWeb.com website analysis service, available online: https://www.similarweb.com/ (accessed 24 September 2020).
39 See the Agency of Russian Information website, available online: https://ari.ru/ (accessed 18 December 2020).
40 Zharchinskaya, '"Mif i istoricheskaya pamiat"', 101.
41 Beloe Bratstvo main page.
42 'Novoe Uchenie pridet iz Rossii, budet chistoi Rossija, budet Beloe Bratstvo v Rossii' translation from Russian to English by Oiva. Beloe Bratstvo main page.
43 Wijermars, *Memory Politics*, 88–9, 180.
44 Filyushkin, 'Mobilizatsija srednevekov'ja' kak poisk identichnosti', 575.
45 The Beloe Bratstvo gained over 7,000 visitors in June–August 2020. SimilarWeb.com.
46 Karabanov, 'The Forbidden History'; Beloe Bratstvo, 'Another Look'; see also Parppei in this volume.
47 Roger Griffin, *Fascism: Key Concepts in Political Theory* (Medford, MA: Polity Press, 2018), 72; Välimäki, Seuri, and Ristilä, 'Pseudohistoriaa Suomen muinaisista kuningaskunnista'.
48 Korpela, *Itä-Euroopan historia*; Oksana Drozdova and Paul Robinson, 'A Study of Vladimir Putin's Rhetoric', *Europe-Asia Studies* 71, no. 5 (2019): 805–23, 809. See also Parppei in this volume.
49 Wijermars, *Memory Politics*, 84.
50 Beloe Bratstvo, 'Another Look'.
51 Wijermars, *Memory Politics*, 6, 8.
52 'The Forbidden History' was established in January 2013, 'The Unknown History' on July 2015, and 'Another Look' in February 2014. Karabanov, 'Forbidden History'; Tainoe Info, 'Unknown History'; Beloe Bratstvo, 'Another Look'.
53 Barbara Törnquist Plewa, Tea Sindbæk Andersen, and Astrid Erll, 'Introduction: On Transcultural Memory and Reception', in *The Twentieth Century in European Memory: Transcultural Mediation and Reception*, ed. Barbara Törnquist Plewa and Tea Sindbæk Andersen (Leiden; Boston: Brill, 2017), 1–23, 11; Pertti Grönholm and

Heino Nyyssönen, 'Historian käyttö ennen ja nyt – faktana ja fiktiona', *Kosmopolis* 49, no. 3 (2019): 19.
54. Elliott in this volume.
55. Tainoe Info main page, available online: http://tainoe.info/ (accessed 18 December 2020).
56. Since some of the contents are closed VKontakte groups that require registration, we interpret this group as a semi-private sphere. Because providing the exact names and links of these websites would easily reveal the names of individuals active in these websites, we do not reveal them here.
57. Ackland and Gibson, 'Hyperlinks', 231–3; Ludovico et al., 'Mapping the Dutch', 3.
58. Kathy A. Mills, 'What are the Threats and Potentials of Big Data for Qualitative Research?' *Qualitative Research* 18, no. 6 (2018): 599.
59. Zharchinskaya, '"Mif i istoricheskaya pamiat"', 97, 101.
60. Beloe Bratstvo, 'The "Great" Jewish Revolution of 1917 ("Velikaya" Iudeiskaya Revolyutsija 1917 goda)', 13 November 2015, available online: https://beloe-bratstvo.ru/velikaya-iudejskaya-revolyuciya-1917-goda/ (accessed 21 September 2020); Beloe Bratstvo, 'Petr I – Not a Real Tsar (Petr Pervy: A tsar'-to ne Nastoyashchij)', 8 November 2015, available online: https://beloe-bratstvo.ru/petr-pervyj-a-car-to-ne-nastoyashhij/ (accessed 21 September 2020).

Chapter 4

1. Steve Gutterman, 'The Week in Russia: Putin, Pechenegs, And Pneumonia', *RadioFreeEurope/RadioLiberty*, 10 April 2020, available online: https://www.rferl.org/a/week-in-russia-putin-pechenegs-pneumonia/30546450.html (accessed 23 April 2020).
2. Jaroslaw Pelenski, 'The Origins of the Official Muscovite Claims to the "Kievan Inheritance"', *Harvard Ukrainian Studies* 1, no. 1 (1977): 29, 51–2.
3. Cf. Elliott in this volume.
4. Eugene Smelyansky, 'Enemies at the Gate: Political Medievalism, Russian Style', *The Public Medievalist*, 15 April 2021, available online: https://www.publicmedievalist.com/medievalism-russia-nevsky/ (accessed 16 May 2021).
5. Andrew B. R. Elliott, *Medievalism, Politics and Mass Media: Appropriating the Middle Ages in the Twenty-First Century* (Woodbridge, Suffolk: D. S. Brewer, 2017), 19.
6. Nikolay Shevchenko, 'Putin Compared Pechenegs and Polovtsy to the Coronavirus. But Who Are They?', *Russia Beyond*, 9 April 2020, available online: https://www.rbth.com/lifestyle/331992-putin-coronavirus-russia-pechenegs-polovtsy (accessed 7 May 2020).

7 On the contested legacy of the Kievan Rus', see Marvin L. Kalb, *Imperial Gamble: Putin, Ukraine, and the New Cold War* (Washington, DC: Brookings Institution Press, 2015), 19–36; Taras Kuzio, 'Nation Building, History Writing and Competition over the Legacy of Kyiv Rus in Ukraine', *Nationalities Papers* 33, no. 1 (2005): 29–58; Iryna Vushko, 'Historians at War: History, Politics and Memory in Ukraine', *Contemporary European History* 27, no. 1 (2018): 112–24.

8 Andrew B. R. Elliott, 'Internet Medievalism and the White Middle Ages', *History Compass* 16, no. 3 (2018): e12441.

9 Alexander Marrow, 'Invoking Medieval Invaders, Putin Rallies Russians against Coronavirus', *Yahoo! News*, 8 April 2020, available online: https://news.yahoo.com/putin-proposes-additional-coronavirus-relief-131856005.html (accessed 18 September 2020); 'Putin Vows to See off Pest like Past Hordes', *The Sunday Times*, sec. news, 9 April 2020, available online: https://www.thetimes.co.uk/article/putin-vows-to-see-off-pest-like-past-hordes-ttbqtknks (accessed 28 February 2021); Reuters Staff, 'Factbox: Quotes of Fear, Defiance and Hope as the Coronavirus Pandemic Spans the Globe', *Reuters*, 28 June 2020, available online: https://www.reuters.com/article/us-health-coronavirus-quotes-factbox-idUKKBN23Z04G (accessed 20 September 2020).

10 Henry Jenkins, Sam Ford, and Joshua Green, *Spreadable Media: Creating Value and Meaning in a Networked Culture* (New York: New York University Press, 2018), 6, 28–9.

11 Nicholas V. Riasanovsky and Mark D. Steinberg, *A History of Russia*, 7th edn (New York: Oxford University Press, 2005), 247.

12 Kate Starbird et al., 'Ecosystem or Echo-System? Exploring Content Sharing across Alternative Media Domains', in *Proceedings of the Twelfth International AAAI Conference on Web and Social Media*, 2018, 365.

13 Starbird et al., 'Ecosystem or Echo-System?', 366.

14 Starbird et al., 'Ecosystem or Echo-System?', 373.

15 Olessia Koltsova and Sergei Koltcov, 'Mapping the Public Agenda with Topic Modeling: The Case of the Russian Livejournal: The Case of the Russian LiveJournal (2011–2012)', *Policy & Internet* 5, no. 2 (2013): 208.

16 Miriam J. Metzger and Andrew J. Flanagin, 'Credibility and Trust of Information in Online Environments: The Use of Cognitive Heuristics', *Journal of Pragmatics* 59 (2013): 210.

17 Metzger and Flanagin, 'Credibility and Trust of Information in Online Environments', 211.

18 Smelyansky, 'Enemies at the Gate' at the *Public Medievalist* in fact comments on this case.

19 Jenkins, Ford, and Green, *Spreadable Media*, 60.

20 Jenkins, Ford, and Green, *Spreadable Media*, 132.

21 Janet Martin, *Medieval Russia: 980–1584*, 2nd edn (Cambridge: Cambridge University Press, 2007), 14; 'Oleg', Vikings Wiki, available online: https://vikings.fandom.com/wiki/Oleg (accessed 18 March 2021).

22 Nestor the Chronicler, *The Russian Primary Chronicle: Laurentian Text*, ed. Samuel H. Cross and Olgerd P. Sherbowitz-Wetzor (Cambridge, MA: Mediaeval Academy of America, 2012), 61–5.

23 The website referenced here claims to engage a historical question surrounding the show, that is how Oleg of Novgorod actually died. Instead, readers are presented with a veiled advertisement ridden website with next to no historically accurate information. Molli Mitchell, 'Vikings Season 6: How Did the Real Prince Oleg of Novgorod Die?', *Express.co.uk*, 10 October 2019, available online: https://www.express.co.uk/showbiz/tv-radio/1188336/Vikings-season-6-How-did-the-real-Prince-Oleg-die-Oleg-of-Novgorod-Rus-Vikings-myth (accessed 18 March 2021).

24 Konstantin Sheiko and Stephen Brown, *History as Therapy: Alternative History and Nationalist Imaginings in Russia, 1991–2014* (Stuttgart: Ibidem-Verlag, 2014), 71–3.

25 Sheiko and Brown, *History as Therapy*, 7, 120–2.

26 The author and the editor wish to thank Teemu Oivo for this observation.

27 Sheiko and Brown, *History as Therapy*, 71.

28 'New Chronology (Fomenko)', *Wikipedia*, available online: https://en.wikipedia.org/w/index.php?title=New_chronology_(Fomenko)&oldid=1009410069 (accessed 28 February 2021); 'Anatoly Fomenko', *Wikipedia*, available online: https://en.wikipedia.org/w/index.php?title=Anatoly_Fomenko&oldid=1000979024 (accessed 17 January 2021).

29 Desants, 'RYAZANSKIY DESANTNIK KRYAKUTNOY iz NEREKHTY', *Live Journal*, available online: https://desants.livejournal.com/202177.html (accessed 6 April 2021).

30 A. I. Sulakadzev, 'Yeshche ob odnoy rukopisi A. I. Sulakadzeva', in *Trudy Otdela drevnerusskoy literatury Instituta russkogo yazyka i literatury*, ed. A. I. Pokrovskaya (Leningrad: Institut russkoy literatury [Pushkinskiy Dom], 1958), T. XIV L.:634–7.

31 Desants, 'RYAZANSKIY DESANTNIK KRYAKUTNOY iz NEREKHTY'.

32 Metzger and Flanagin, 'Credibility and Trust of Information in Online Environments', 212–14.

33 The user that posted this comment has a private profile. In accordance with deontological coding strategies the author has opted to exclude their name and a direct link to their comment. Reddit User, 'Commentary on Ivar', *Reddit*, 'R/Vikingstv', 2020, available online: https://www.reddit.com/r/vikingstv/ (accessed 5 August 2020).

34 frayuk, '[History Spoiler] How Queen Elizabeth II Got Viking Blood. A Chart Showing the Blood Line between the Current Monarch and the Vikings', *Reddit*

Post, 'R/Vikingstv', 24 April 2015, www.reddit.com/r/vikingstv/comments/33r5g4/history_spoiler_how_queen_elizabeth_ii_got_viking/ (accessed 11 April 2021).
35. Jenkins, Ford, and Green, *Spreadable Media*, 133.
36. Christopher Paul and Miriam Matthews, 'The Russian "Firehose of False-Hood" Propaganda Model: Why It Might Work and Options to Counter It' (Santa Monica, CA: RAND Corporation, 2016), 1–2, available online: https://www.rand.org/pubs/perspectives/PE198.html (accessed 7 April 2020).
37. Paul and Matthews, 'The Russian "Firehose of False-Hood" Propaganda Model', 2.
38. Articles behind paywalls suffer immensely in their ability to be shared and thus spread. Anja Bechmann, 'Towards Cross-Platform Value Creation: Four Patterns of Circulation and Control', *Information, Communication & Society* 15, no. 6 (2012): 889; Although paywalls serve economic ends and means they come with reduced distribution and visibility. According to Myllylahti, at times 'newspapers might drop paywalls for major news events [so as to] gain the maximum number of page visits and readers', which can be in turn used to bolster distribution metrics. See Merja Myllylahti, 'Newspaper Paywalls – The Hype and the Reality: A Study of How Paid News Content Impacts on Media Corporation Revenues', *Digital Journalism* 2, no. 2 (2014): 190.
39. Linda A. Henkel and Mark E. Mattson, 'Reading is Believing: The Truth Effect and Source Credibility', *Consciousness and Cognition* 20, no. 4 (2011): 1706.

Chapter 5

1. 'Porwoon historiallinen juhla', trans. T. Ylimaunu, *Uusimaa* 96 (21 August 1899): 2.
2. Ulla-Maija Peltonen, 'Sisällissodan muistaminen', in *Sisällissodan Pikku Jättiläinen*, ed. P. Haapala and T. Hoppu (Helsinki: Werner Söderström Osakeyhtiö, 2009), 464–73. Timo Ylimaunu, 'Tornion taistelun muistomerkki', in *Toinen jalka haudassa: Juhlakirja Juhani Kostetille*, ed. Sanna Lipkin, Titta Kallio-Seppä, Annemari Tranberg, and Tiina Väre (Oulu: Oulun yliopisto, 2019), 28–37; Oula Seitsonen, Paul R. Mullins, and Timo Ylimaunu, 'Public Memory, National Heritage, and Memorialization of the 1918 Finnish Civil War', *World Archaeology*, 51, no. 5 (2019), 741–58.
3. Derek Fewster, *Visions of Past Glory: Nationalism and the Construction of Early Finnish History* (Helsinki: Finnish Literature Society, 2006).
4. Derek Fewster, '"Brave Step Out of the Night of Barrows": Regenerating the Heritage of Early Medieval Finland', in *The Uses of the Middle Ages in Modern European States*, ed. R. J. W. Evans and Guy P. Marchal (New York: Palgrave Macmillan, 2011), 45.

5 Fewster, *Visions of Past Glory*, 397.
6 Paul Connerton, *How Societies Remember* (Cambridge: Cambridge University Press, 1989); Reinhard Koselleck, 'War Memorials: Identity Formations of the Survivors', in *The Practice of conceptual history*, trans. Todd Presner (Stanford: Stanford University Press, 2002), 285–326; Siobhan Kattago, 'War Memorials and the Politics of Memory: The Soviet War Memorial in Tallinn', *Constellations* 16, no. 1 (2009): 150–66; Siobhan Kattago, 'Written in Stone: Monuments and Representation', in *The Ashgate Research Companion to Memory Studies* (Farnham, Surrey, UK: Routledge, 2014), 179–95; Ylimaunu, 'Tornion taistelun muistomerkki'; Seitsonen et al., 'Public Memory, National Heritage, and Memorialization of the 1918 Finnish Civil War'; Paul Mullins, *Revolting Things: An Archaeology of Shameful Histories and Repulsive Realities* (Gainesville: University Press of Florida, 2021).
7 For example, Kattago, 'War Memorials and the Politics of Memory'; Owen J. Dwyer and Derek H. Alderman, 'Memorial Landscapes: Analytic Questions and Metaphors', *Geojournal* 73 (2008): 165–78; Bill Niven, 'War Memorials at the Intersection of Politics, Culture and Memory', *Journal of War and Culture Studies* 1, no. 1 (2008): 39–45; Ylimaunu, 'Tornion taistelun muistomerkki'.
8 Dwyer and Alderman, 'Memorial Landscapes'; James A. Delle, 'A Tale of Two Tunnels: Memory, Archaeology, and the Underground Railroad', *Journal of Social Archaeology* 8, no. 1 (2008): 63–93; Mullins, *Revolting Things*.
9 John Carman and Marie Louise Stig Sørensen, 'Heritage Studies: An Outline', in *Heritage Studies: Methods and Approaches*, ed. Marie Louise Stig Sørensen and John Carman (London and New York: Routledge, 2009), 11–28.
10 Aleida Assmann, 'Memory, Individual and Collective', in *The Oxford Handbook of Contextual Political Analysis*, ed. Robert E. Goodin and Charles Tilley (Oxford: Oxford University Press 2006), 210–24.
11 Pierre Nora, 'From *Lieux de mémoire* to *Realms of Memory*', in *Realms of Memory: The Construction of the French Past*, under the direction of Pierre Nora (New York: Columbia University Press, 1996), xv–xxiv.
12 Andrew B. R. Elliott, *Medievalism, Politics and Mass Media: Appropriating the Middle Ages in the Twenty-first Century* (Woodbridge, Suffolk: D.S. Brewer, 2017), 6.
13 Timo Ylimaunu, Sami Lakomäki, Titta Kallio-Seppä, Paul R. Mullins, Risto Nurmi, and Markku Kuorilehto, 'Borderlands as Spaces: Creating Third Spaces and Fractured Landscapes in Medieval Northern Finland', *Journal of Social Archaeology* 14, no. 2 (2014): 244–67.
14 Vesa-Pekka Herva and Timo Ylimaunu, 'Folk Beliefs, Special Deposits, and Engagement with the Environment in Early Modern Northern Finland', *Journal of Anthropological Archaeology* 28, no. 2 (2009), 234–43; Vesa-Pekka Herva and Timo Ylimaunu, 'Coastal Cosmologies: Long-Term Perspectives on the Perception and Understanding of Dynamic Coastal Landscapes in the Northern Baltic Sea

Region', *Time and Mind: The Journal of Archaeology, Consciousness and Culture* 7, no. 2 (2014): 183–202; Ylimaunu et al., 'Borderlands as Spaces'; James Symonds, Timo Ylimaunu, Anna-Kaisa Salmi, Risto Nurmi, Titta Kallio-Seppä, Tiina Kuokkanen, Markku Kuorilehto, and Annemari Tranberg, 'Time, Seasonality, and Trade: Swedish/Finnish-Sami Interactions in Early Modern Lapland', *Historical Archaeology* 49, no. 3 (2015): 74–89; Timo Ylimaunu, Georg Haggrén, Risto Nurmi, and Paul R. Mullins, 'Medieval and Early Modern Marketplaces: Sites of Contacts, Trade and Religious Activities', in *Sacred Monuments and Practices in the Baltic Sea Region*, ed. Janne Harjula, Sonja Hukantaival, Visa Immonen, Anneli Randla, and Tanja Ratilainen (Newcastle upon Tyne: Cambridge Scholars Publishing, 2017), 262–82.

15 Seppo Suvanto, 'Keskiaika', in *Suomen historia* 2, ed. Eero Laaksonen and Erkki Pärssinen (Espoo: Weilin+Göös, 1985), 108.

16 Kalevi Paakki, *Vaasan patsaat ja muistomerkit – Vasas statyer och minnesmärken* (Vaasa: Vaasan kaupunki, 2008); Aimo Nyberg, 'Risti Korsholman valleilla, 19. kesäkuuta 1894', Vaasa ennen ja nyt – Vasa förr och nu, 18 June 2017, available online: http://vaasaenne njanyt.blogspot.com/2017/06/risti-korsholman-valleilla-19 -kesakuuta.html (accessed 10 April 2020).

17 'Laulu-ja soittojuhla Waasassa', *Wiipuri* 141 (22 June 1894): 1–2.

18 Paakki, *Vaasan patsaat ja muistomerkit*; Aimo Nyberg, 'Sundomin kylä 600 vuotta, 17. heinäkuuta 1977', Vaasa ennen ja nyt – Vasa förr och nu, 17 July 2017, available online: http://vaasaennenjanyt.blogspot.com/2017/07/sundomin-kyla-600-vuotta -17-heinakuuta.html (accessed 10 April 2020); Aimo Nyberg, 'Mussorin pitäjä 600 vuotta, 17. elokuuta 1958', Vaasa ennen ja nyt – Vasa förr och nu, 17 August 2020, available online: http://vaasaennenjanyt.blogspot.com/2017/08/mussorin -pitaja-600-vuotta-17-elokuuta.html (accessed 10 April 2020); Aimo Nyberg, 'NUIJASODAN 400-V MUISTOMERKKI', Vaasa ennen ja nyt – Vasa förr och nu, available online: http://vaasaennenjanyt.blogspot.com/search?q=nuijasot (accessed 15 April 2020).

19 'Nuijamiesten muistomerkkijuhlat Ilmajoella alkoivat tänään', *Vaasa* 152A (5 July 1924): 5–6.

20 'Santavuoren miesten muistojuhla', *Ilkka* 149 (4 July 1925): 3–4.

21 *Vaasa*, 'Nuijamiesten muistomerkkijuhlat', 5–6; *Ilkka*, 149, 'Santavuoren miesten muistojuhla', 3.

22 Cf. Nora, 'From *Lieux de mémoire* to *Realms of Memory*'.

23 Peltonen, 'Sisällissodan muistaminen', 464–73.

24 'Santavuoren miesten muistojuhla', *Ilkka* 150 (6 July 1925): 1–3.

25 'Linnukkapatsaan paljastamista todisti Limingassa 1500 henkinen yleisöjoukko', *Kaiku* 142 (26 June 1934): 1, 4; 'Linnukka-patsaan paljastusjuhlat', *Liitto* 142 (26 June 1934): 1, 4.

26 Cf. Nora, 'From *Lieux de mémoire* to *Realms of Memory*'.

27 *Kirjastovirma*, Pohjoispohjalaista kulttuuriperintöä, s.v. 'Hannu Krankan patsas', available online: http://www.kirjastovirma.fi/muistomerkit/liminka/07 (accessed 24 April 2020); *Kirjastovirma*, Pohjoispohjalaista kulttuuriperintöä, s.v. 'Hannu Krankka', available online: http://www.kirjastovirma.fi/henkilogalleria/Krankka _Hannu (accessed 30 April 2020); *Kansallisbiografia*, s.v., 'Kranck, Hans', available online: https://kansallisbiografia.fi/kansallisbiografia/henkilo/428 (accessed 30 April 2020).
28 'Hannu Krankan muisto Limingassa', *Uusi Aura* 3 (4 January 1934): 6.
29 Ylimaunu et al., 'Borderlands as Spaces'.
30 'Koko Ylikiiminki juhli viime sunnuntaina', *Kaleva* 223 (29 September 1936): 1–2; 'Vesaista ja hänen miehiään elähdytti vapauden rakkaus', *Kaiku* 223 (29 September 1936): 1, 4.
31 *Kaiku*, 'Vesaista ja hänen miehiään elähdytti vapauden rakkaus', 4.
32 'Juho Vesaisen muistomerkin', *Liitto* 41 (19 February 1935): 3; 'Pekka eikä Juho Vesainen', *Hakkapeliitta* 26 (18 June 1935): 803; 'Vesaisen muisto', *Pohjolan Vartio* 9 (1 September 1935): 216; 'Talonpoikaisjohtaja Vesaisen muistopatsashanke Iissä toteuttamisvaiheessa', *Kaiku* 200 (2 September 1939): 2; 'Juho Vesaisen patsas', *Uusi Suomi* 115 (30 April 1941): 1; 'Vesaisen patsashanke Iissä', *Aamulehti* 281 (17 October 1941): 4.
33 'Juho Vesaisen patsas paljastettu Iissä', *Uusi Suomi* 164 (21 June 1950): 9.
34 *Aamulehti*, 'Vesaisen patsashanke Iissä', 4.
35 *Uusi Suomi*, 'Juho Vesaisen patsas paljastettu Iissä', 9.
36 Jan Assmann, 'Communicative and Cultural Memory', in *Cultural Memory Studies: An International and Interdisciplinary Handbook*, ed. Astrid Erll and Ansgar Nünning (Berlin; New York: de Gruyter, 2008), 113.
37 Koselleck, 'War Memorials', 288; also Kattago, 'War Memorials and the Politics of Memory'; Kattago, 'Written in Stone', 185.
38 Fewster, 'Brave Step Out of the Night of Barrows', 49.
39 Ari Jääskeläinen, 'Kansallistava kansanrunous. Suomalaisuus ja folklore', in *Elävänä Euroopassa: Muuttuva suomalainen identiteetti*, ed. Pertti Alasuutari and Petri Ruuska (Tampere: Vastapaino, 1998), 54.
40 Fewster, *Visions of Past Glory*; Fewster, 'Brave Step Out of the Night of Barrows', 44.
41 Kattago, 'Written in Stone', 180.
42 Carl Jacob Gardberg, 'Porvoon kaupungin historia keskiajalla ja 1500-luvulla', in *Porvoon kaupungin historia I* (Porvoo: WSOY, 1996), 133.
43 'Festen för gamla Borgå', *Borgåbladet* 65 (23 August 1899): 2; *Uusimaa*, 'Porwoon historiallinen juhla'.
44 Merja Herranen and Olavi Hankimo, eds., *Natalia Linsénin ja John Granlundin Porvoo* (Helsinki: Siltala, 2014), 98–9.
45 Eva Ahl-Waris, *Historiebruk kring Nådendal och den kommemorativa anatomin av klostrets minnesplats* (Vadstena: Societas Sanctae Birgittae, 2010).

46 Tuomas Heikkilä, *Pyhän Henrikin legenda* (Helsinki: Suomalaisen Kirjallisuuden Seura, 2005).
47 Erkki Länsisyrjä, 'Legendan jälki maisemassa: Pyhän Henrikin tein historiaa ja tätä päivää' (MA diss., University of Turku, Turku, 2014), 20–31.
48 Cf. Nora, 'From *Lieux de mémoire* to *Realms of Memory*'.
49 Max Jakobsson, *Tilinpäätös* (Helsinki: Otava, 2003), 113–63; Ylimaunu, 'Tornion taistelun muistomerkki', 23–42.
50 Aapo Roselius, *Kiista, eheys, unohdus: Vapaussodan muistaminen suojeluskuntien ja veteraaniliikkeen toiminnassa 1918–1944*, Bidrag till kännedom av Finlands natur och folk 186 (Helsinki: Suomen Tiedeseura, 2010), 247.
51 Dwyer and Alderman, 'Memorial Landscapes', 165–78; also Assmann, 'Communicative and Cultural Memory', 215–16.
52 Anne Elizabeth Yentsch, *A Chesapeake family and their slaves: A Study in Historical Archaeology* (Cambridge: Cambridge University Press, 1994), 322.
53 Dwyer and Alderman, 'Memorial Landscapes'; Niven, 'War Memorials', 39–45.
54 Stuart Hall, *Identiteetti* (Tampere: Vastapaino, 2002).
55 Ylimaunu, 'Tornion taistelun muistomerkki'.
56 Timo Ylimaunu, 'Postimerkit ja identiteetti – kuva suomalaisesta yhteiskunnasta 1930-luvulta', *Tabellarius* 7 (2005): 95–100; cf. Hall, *Identiteetti*, 53–5. On masculine medievalism, see also Aali in this volume.
57 Kirsi Saarikangas, 'Puu, metsä ja luonto: Arkkitehtuuri suomalaisuuden rankentamisena ja rakentumisena', in *Suomi: Outo pohjoinen maa? Näkökulmia Euroopan äären historiaan ja kulttuuriin*, ed. T. M. S. Lehtonen (Jyväskylä: PS-Kustannus, 1999), 166–207; Riitta Nikula, 'Klassismi maailman sotien välisen ajan suomalaisessa arkkitehtuurissa', in *Kivettyneet ihanteet? Klassismin nousu maailmasotien välisessä Euroopassa*, ed. Marja Härmänmaa and Timo Vihavainen (Jyväskylä: Atena, 2000), 315–43; Timo Koho, 'Monikasvoinen arkkitehtuuri', in *Suomalaisten symbolit*, ed. Tero Halonen and Laura Aro (Jyväskylä: Atena, 2005), 72–7.
58 Saarikangas, 'Puu, metsä ja luonto'; Nikula, 'Klassismi maailman sotien välisen ajan suomalaisessa arkkitehtuurissa'; Koho, 'Monikasvoinen arkkitehtuuri'.
59 Karl C. Alvestad, 'The "Accurate" Deeds of Our Fathers: The "Authentic" Narrative of Early Norway', in *The Middle Ages in Modern Culture: History and Authenticity in Contemporary Medievalism*, ed. Karl C. Alvestad and Robert Houghton (London: Bloomsbury Academic, 2021), 15–27.
60 For example, news in 'Tervolan taistelun muistomerkki paljastettiin viime sunnuntaina', *Perä-Pohja* 148 (2 July 1929): 1, 3; 'Tornion taistelun muistomerkki', *Pohjolan Sanomat* 30 (8 February 1938): 1, 4.
61 Dwyer and Alderman, 'Memorial Landscapes'.
62 Ylimaunu, 'Tornion taistelun muistomerkki', 35.
63 Jens Brockmeier, 'Remembering and Forgetting: Narrative as Cultural Memory', *Culture & Psychology* 8, no. 1 (2002): 18.

64 Assmann, 'Communicative and Cultural Memory'.
65 Assmann, 'Memory, Individual and Collective', 210–24; Assmann, 'Communicative and Cultural Memory', 111–12; Connerton, *How Societies Remember*; Paul Connerton, *How Modernity Forgets* (New York: Cambridge University Press, 2009); Brockmeier, 'Remembering and Forgetting'.
66 Victor Buchli and Gavin Lucas, *Archaeologies of the Contemporary Past* (London: Routledge, 2001), 80–1; see Mullins, *Revolting Things*, 75–7.
67 A similar kind of erasing process took place in Tornio, where the Tornio battle memorial was modified in 1946. The memorial was unveiled in 1938 to commemorate a short battle where Finnish troops defeated Russian troops in early February 1918. The original memorial had the following inscription: 'At this site Finns triumphed over their archenemy at the dawn of liberty of the fatherland 6.2.1918.' However, the original inscription was changed to the inscription 'Tornio Battle 6.2.1918' by the order of the Finnish government in 1946. The Allied control commission, mainly Red Army officers, inspected several Finnish war memorials after the Second World War and they ordered some of them to be destroyed or changed. One of the memorials to be altered was the Tornio battle memorial, because it described Russians as archenemies. Finland had to build a new kind of political relationship with its former enemy in the post-Second World War period. Therefore, Russians and the Soviet Union had to be shown in a positive light by erasing the nationalistic past from some of the pre-Second World War period war memorials. See Mikko Oula, '*Suomi sitoutuu hajoittamaan…*' *Järjestöjen lakkauttaminen vuoden 1944 välirauhansopimuksen 21: artiklan perusteella*, Historiallisia tutkimuksia 205 (Helsinki: Suomen Historiallinen Seura, 1999), 180–8; Yrjö Alamäki, *Tornion muistomerkkiopas* (Tornio: Tornion kulttuuritoimisto, 2002), 35–6; Ylimaunu, 'Tornion taistelun muistomerkki'.
68 Dwyer and Alderman, 'Memorial Landscapes'; Niven, 'War Memorials'; Mullins, *Revolting Things*.
69 Karl. C. Alvestad, 'Middelalders helter og Norsk nasjonalisme før andre verdenskrig', *Slagmark* 79, no. 1 (2019): 77–95; Alvestad, 'The "Accurate" Deeds of Our Fathers'.
70 See Aali's chapter in this volume.
71 Assmann, 'Memory, Individual and Collective'.
72 Reinhart Koselleck, *Futures Past: On the Semantics of Historical Time* (New York: Columbia University Press, 2004), 257–8.
73 Brockmeier, 'Remembering and Forgetting', 19.

Chapter 6

1 Marit Åhlén, Tapani Tuovinen and Hans Myhrman, 'Ett runstensfragment från Hitis', *Muinaistutkija* 1 (1998): 18–20.

2 Janne Harjula, 'Runic Inscriptions on Stave Vessels in Turku: Materializations of Language, Education, Magic, and Domestic Religion', in *Objects, Environment, and Everyday Life in Medieval Europe*, ed. Ben Jervis, Lee G. Broderick, and Idoia Grau Sologestoa (Turnhout: Brepols, 2016), 213–34; Janne Harjula, 'For the Sake of Hair and Soul: Medieval Antler Comb with Runic Inscription from Turku', in *Tidens landskap: En vänbok till Anders Andrén*, ed. Cecilja Ljung, Anna Andreasson Sjögren, Ingrid Berg, Elin Engström, Ann-Mari Hållans Stenholm, Kristina Jonsson, Alison Klevnäs, Linda Qviström, and Torun Zachrisson (Lund: Nordic Academic Press, 2019), 246–8.
3 Heikki Oja, *Riimut: viestejä viikingeiltä* (Helsinki: Suomalaisen Kirjallisuuden Seura 2015), 84.
4 See discussion in Kendra Willson, 'A Putative Sámi Charm on a 12th c. Icelandic Spade: Runic Reception, Magic and Contacts', in *Finno-Ugric Folklore, Myth and Cultural Identity: Proceedings of the Fifth International Symposium on Finno-Ugric Languages, University of Groningen, June 7 9, 2011*, ed. Cornelius Hasselblatt and Adriaan van der Hoeven (Maastricht: Shaker, 2012), 267–81; Kendra Willson, 'Ahti on the Nydam Strapring: On the Possibility of Finnic Elements in Runic Inscriptions', in *Contacts and Networks in the Baltic Sea Region: Austmarr as a Northern Mare Nostrum, 500–1500 A.D.*, ed. Maths Bertell, Frog, and Kendra Willson (Amsterdam: Amsterdam University Press, 2019), 147–71.
5 Birgit Sawyer, 'Viking-Age Rune-Stones as a Crisis Symptom', *Norwegian Archaeological Journal* 24, no. 2 (1991): 97–112.
6 Kari Tarkiainen, *Sveriges österland: Från forntiden till Gustav Vasa*. Finlands svenska historia 1 (Helsingfors: Svenska litteratursällskapet i Finland / Stockholm: Bokförlaget Atlantis, 2008), 44–9.
7 Tarkiainen, *Sveriges österland*, 49.
8 Joonas Ahola and Frog, 'Approaching the Viking Age in Finland: An Introduction', in *Fibula, Fabula, Fact: The Viking Age in Finland*, ed. Joonas Ahola and Frog with Clive Tolley (Helsinki: Finnish Literature Society, 2014), 56.
9 Tarkiainen, *Sveriges österland*, 49–63.
10 Heikki Ojansuu, *Suomalaista paikannimitutkimusta 1: Tähänastisen tutkimuksen arvostelua*. Turun suomalaisen yliopistoseuran julkaisuja 41 (Helsinki: Otava, 1920), 261–74.
11 *Gesperrt* in original.
12 Ojansuu, *Suomalaista paikannimitutkimusta 1*, 262.
13 Ralf Saxén, 'Den svenska befolkningens ålder i Finland, belyst av ortnamn', *Finska fornminnesföreningens tidskrift* 21, no. 3 (1901): 1–46.
14 T. E. Karsten, 'Vieläkin rudbekkilaisuudesta paikannimitutkimuksessamme', *Uusi Suomi* 1, no. 146 (7 July 1919): 6–7, here 7.
15 Uppslagsverket Finland-webbutgåva, s.v. 'Karsten, (Tor)', Schildts förlags Ab, 2009–2012, SFV 2012-, available online: https://www.uppslagsverket.fi/sv/sok/view-103684-KarstenTor (accessed 14 July 2020).

16 Arnold Nordling, 'Varför tyckas inga runinskrifter ha utförts i Finland?', *Finsk tidskrift* 125 (1938): 35-43.
17 Nordling, 'Varför tyckas inga runstenar ha utförts i Finland', 42.
18 Oja, *Riimut*, 225-8.
19 Tuukka Talvio, *Coins and Coin Finds in Finland AD 800-1200* (Helsinki: Finnish Antiquarian Society, 2002); cf. Oja, *Riimut*, 226.
20 Matts Dreijer, 'De försvunna runstenarna i Kökar', *Åländsk odling* 6 (1945): 31-40.
21 Michelangelo Naddeo, *Germanico Runes: a Finnish Alphabet?* (s.l.: s.n., 2006).
22 Jukka Nieminen, *Vaiettu muinaisuus* (s.l.: Salakirjat, 2015), 193-9.
23 Gunnar Hård, 'Vörårunorna', *Oknytt* 3-4 (1983): 18.
24 J. P. Taavitsainen, 'Runinskriften vid Höjsal träsk i Vörå', *Horisont* 27, no. 3 (1980): 40.
25 Antti Lahelma, Jouko Pukkila and Tapani Rostedt, 'Fake or Not? Some Observations on Finds of Runic Inscriptions in South-Western Finland', in *Runes in Finland*, ed. Kendra Willson (forthcoming).
26 Jana Schulman, p.c.
27 David M. Krueger, *Myths of the Rune Stone. Viking Martyrs and the Birthplace of America* (Minneapolis: University of Minnesota Press, 2015).
28 Reider Thorbjorn Sherwin, *The Viking and the Red Man: The Old Norse Origin of the Algonquin Language* (New York & London: Funk & Wagnalls, 1940).
29 Verena Höfig, '"Re-Wild Yourself": Old Norse Myth and Radical White Nationalist Groups in Trump's America', in *Norse myths as Political Ideologies: Critical Studies of the Appropriation of Medieval Narratives*, ed. Nicolas Meylan and Lukas Rösli (Turnhout: Brepols, 2020), 209-31.
30 Merrill Kaplan, 'The State of Vinland', in *Norse myths as Political Ideologies: Critical Studies of the Appropriation of Medieval Narratives*, ed. Nicolas Meylan and Lukas Rösli (Turnhout: Brepols, 2020), 233-49.
31 Christopher Crocker, 'What We Talk about When We Talk about Vínland: History, Whiteness, Indigenous Erasure, and the Early Norse Presence in Newfoundland', *Canadian Journal of History/Annales canadiennes d'histoire* 55, no. 1-2 (2020): 91-122.
32 Henrik Williams, 'Arizona Runestone Carved in Phony Old Baltic', Uppsala University ms. 2015, available online: http://files.webb.uu.se/uploader/267/Mustang%20Mountain%20Stone%20-%20release.pdf (accessed 12 June 2021).
33 Wojciech Krawczuk, 'Runic Inscriptions in Poland: Do We Need an Inventory?' *Studia historyczne* 56, no. 3 (2013): 431.
34 Krzysztof Maciej Kowalski, 'The Fascination with Runes in Nineteenth- and Early Twentieth-Century Poland', in *Roman, Runes and Ogham. Medieval Inscriptions in the Insular World and on the Continent*, ed. John Higgitt, Katherine Forsyth, and David N. Parsons (Donington: Shaun Tyas, 2001), 147.
35 Tomasz Kosiński, *Runy słowiańskie* (Warszawa: Bellona, 2019), 16.

36 Winicjusz Kossakowski, *Polskie runy przemówiły* (Białystok: Wydano nakł. autora, 2008), 97–101.
37 Władysław Duczko, 'With Vikings or Without? Scandinavians in Early Medieval Poland. Approaching an Old Problem', in *Scandinavian Culture in Medieval Poland*, ed. Sławomir Moździoch, Błażej Stanisławski, and Przemysław Wiszewski (Wrocław: Institute of Archaeology and Ethnology of the Polish Academy of Sciences, 2013), 23.
38 Krawczuk, 'Runic Inscriptions in Poland', 434.
39 Tarkiainen, *Sveriges österland*, 36.
40 Victor Granö, 'De gåtfulla runorna i Vörå. I. Österbottens första viking. II. Mannen med metalldetektorn. III. I jakt på bevis', *Yle svenska*, 5 March 2017.
41 A. O. Freudenthal, 'Runinskriften å Tuukkala-spännet', *Finska vetenskaps-soc. förhandlingar* 35 (1893): 1–3.
42 Ralf Norrman, *Vörårunorna. Del 1. En bok om runinskrifterna i Höjsal och Härtull* (Jakobstad: Jakobstads tryckeri, 1983), 6–11.
43 Mirja Miettinen, 'Muistio ilmoitetun muinaisjäännöksen tarkastuksesta. Vöyri, Rejpelt, Båtholmen'. Report, Museovirasto, Helsinki, 28 November 1984; Joakim Donner, 'Bidrag till kännedomen om Vörårunornas ålder: exempel på ristningsteknik använd i runinskrifter och hällristingar', *Fennoscandia archaeologica* 111 (1986): 78.
44 Donner, 'Bidrag till kännedomen om Vörårunornas ålder', 78.
45 Granö, 'De gåtfulla runorna i Vörå'.
46 Aarne Europaeus, 'Etälä-Pohjanmaan asutuskysymyksiä', *Kalevalaseuran vuosikirja* 5 (1925): 144-89.
47 Donner, 'Bidrag till kännedomen om Vörårunornas ålder', 76–8.
48 Norrman, *Vörårunorna*.
49 Per Olof Sjöstrand, p.c.
50 Per Olof Sjöstrand, 'History Gone Wrong. Interpretations of the Transition from the Viking Age to the Medieval Period in Åland', in *The Viking Age in Åland. Insights into Identity and Remnants of Culture*, ed. Joonas Ahola, Frog, and Jenny Lucenius (Helsinki: Academia Scientiarum Fennica, 2014), 83–152.
51 Ella Kivikoski, 'Suomen varhaisin kristillisyys muinaistieteellisen aineiston valossa', in *Novella plantatio. Suomen kirkkohistoriallisen seuran juhlakirja Suomen kirkon juhlavuotena*. Suomen Kirkkohistoriallisen Seuran toimituksia 56 (Helsinki: [Suomen Kirkkohistoriallinen Seura], 1955): 34.
52 Jan-Henrik Fallgren, 'Some Thoughts about the Early Medieval Settlement on Åland, from a Western European Perspective', in *Re-Imagining Periphery. Archaeology and Text in Northern Europe from Iron Age to Viking and Early Medieval Periods*, ed. Charlotta Hillerdal and Kristen Ilves (Oxford & Philadelphia: Oxbow, 2020), 169–77.

53 Nils Edelman, 'Försök till en geologisk datering av en hällristning vid Kastelholm', *Åländsk odling* 29 (1968): 15–17; Ivar Lindquist, 'Nya rön om ett par runristningar', *Åländsk odling* 29 (1968): 23; Sjöstrand, 'History Gone Wrong', 84.
54 Torsten Edgren, 'Dreijer, Matts', *Biografiskt lexikon för Finland 3: Republiken A-L* (Helsingfors: Svenska Litteratursällskapet i Finland, 2011), 225.
55 Adam of Bremen, *History of the Archbishops of Hamburg-Bremen*, ed. and trans. Francis J. Tschan and Timothy Reuter (New York: Columbia University Press, 2005), 53.
56 Matts Dreijer, 'Landet Åland och Fornsveriges östgräns', *Åländsk odling* 11 (1950): 3–167.
57 For instance, Matts Dreijer, 'Det återfunna Birka', *Åländsk odling* 30 (1969): 3–35; Matts Dreijer, 'Åland och Bircaproblemet. Föredrag i Statens Historiska Museum i Stockholm den 21 mars 1974', *Åländsk odling* 35 (1974): 31–47.
58 Ivar Lindquist, 'Nya rön om ett par runristningar'; Ivar Lindquist, 'Ålands runinskrift, Sund-korset', *Åländsk odling* 30 (1969): 36–51.
59 Dreijer, 'De försvunna runstenarna i Kökar', 32–3.
60 Dreijer, 'De försvunna runstenarna i Kökar', 38.
61 Dreijer, 'De försvunna runstenarna i Kökar', 38.
62 Dreijer, 'De försvunna runstenarna i Kökar', 39.
63 Dreijer, 'De försvunna runstenarna i Kökar', 35.
64 Dreijer, 'De försvunna runstenarna i Kökar', 36–8.
65 Dreijer, 'De försvunna runstenarna i Kökar', 35.
66 Dreijer, 'De försvunna runstenarna i Kökar', 34.
67 Dreijer, 'De försvunna runstenarna i Kökar', 34.
68 Nieminen, *Vaiettu muinaisuus*.
69 Jukka Nieminen, *Muinaissuomalaisten kadonnut kuningaskunta* (s.l.: Kirjaparoni oy, 2010).
70 Nieminen, *Vaiettu muinaisuus*, 7.
71 Janne Ikäheimo and Wesa Perttola, 'Näennäisarkeologisia linjanvetoja Suomen muinaisuuteen', *Muinaistutkija* 4 (2010): 22–33; Inkeri Koskinen, *Villi Suomen historia: Välimeren Väinämöisestä Äijäkupittaan pyramideihin* (Helsinki: Kustannusosakeyhtiö Tammi, 2015), 132–8; Sirpa Aalto and Harri Hihnala, '"Saagat tuntevat Suomen kuninkaat" – pseudohistoriallisesta kirjoittelusta Suomen muinaisuudesta', *J@rgonia* 15, no. 29 (2017): 5.
72 Nieminen, *Vaiettu muinaisuus*, 193.
73 Nieminen, *Vaiettu muinaisuus*, 193–4.
74 Nieminen, *Vaiettu muinaisuus*, 194.
75 Janne Harjula, 'Alustavia ajatuksia Turun Tuomiokirkontorin tuohikirjeestä', *SKAS* 1–2 (2012): 3–21.
76 Nieminen, *Vaiettu muinaisuus*, 194.

77 Nieminen, *Vaiettu muinaisuus*, 199.
78 SSA 3: 277 s.v. 'tauti'.
79 Naddeo, *Germanico Runes*, 44–6
80 Erla Lund, 'Folksed och folktro i Malaks, Pörtom och Övermark', SLS 524, SLS arkiv (1931), 296–7.
81 Nieminen, *Vaiettu muinaisuus*, 6.
82 Nieminen, *Vaiettu muinaisuus*, 197.
83 Ove Berg, *Runsvenska, svenska, finska* (Gällivare: Skrivkammaren i Gällevare, 2003). Mentioned in Nimeminen, *Vaiettu muinaisuus*, 196.
84 'Muinaislöytö Pyhtäällä 1926', *Loviisan sanomat* 53 (23 July 1926): 2.
85 Nieminen, *Vaiettu muinaisuus*, 193–9.
86 Christfrid Ganander, *Nytt finskt lexikon*, ed. Liisa Nuutinen (Helsinki: Suomalaisen Kirjallisuuden Seura, 1997), 790 s.v. 'rijmut'.
87 Jussi Virratvuori, ed. *Kiveen hakattu historia. Sulo Strömberg – Kerimäen ja Puruveden alueen historiatiedon etsijä ja kerääjä* (Saarijärvi: Kustannusosakeyhtiö HAI, 2012), 134–5.
88 Johan Koren Wiberg, *Bomerker og innflyttere. Vedkommende Kontoret i Bergen*. Det Hanseatiske Museums Skrifter, Nr. 10 (Bergen: A.s John Griegs Boktrykkeri, 1935), 11–12, 29.
89 Göran Dahl, *Bomärken på Åland* (Mariehamn: Ålands folkminnesförbund, 1994), 9.
90 Georg W. Wallgren, *Boken om bomärken* (Helsingfors: Frenckellska tryckeri aktiebolaget, 1965), 17.
91 Elsa Aaltonen, *Kustavilaisia puumerkkejä* (Kustavi: E. Aaltonen, 1999), 5.
92 Paavo O. Ekko, *Puumerkit ja riimut menneisyyden avaimina* (Helsinki: Suomen Heraldinen Seura, 1984), 45–9, 74.
93 Nieminen, *Vaiettu muinaisuus*, 197.
94 Willson, 'A Putative Sámi Charm'; Willson, 'Ahti on the Nydam Strapring'.
95 Naddeo, *Germanico Runes*, 44–6.
96 Naddeo, *Germanico Runes*, 46.
97 Berg, *Runsvenska, svenska, finska*.
98 Berg, *Runsvenska, svenska, finska*, 2.
99 'Tutkijat lukevat suomea Ruotsin riimukivistä', Sveriges radio finska, 26 February 2004.
100 Nieminen, *Vaiettu muinaisuus*, 196.
101 SSA 2, 282, s.v. 'paasi'; SSA 3, 104, s.v. 'runo', SSA 3, 111, s.v. 'rustata'.
102 V. H. Juvelius, 'Faiskoksen diskoskiekko', *Suomalainen* 1, no. 1 (1913): 158–70.
103 'Suomalainen riimukirjoitustutkielma. Tri Valter Juvelius selittänyt riimukirjoituksen olevan muinaissuomea', *Karjala* 353 (30 December 1926): 8.
104 Aalto and Hihnala, 'Saagat tuntevat Suomen kuninkaat'.

Chapter 7

1 The earlier research on the theory of the Ancient Finnish Kings is quite scarce especially in English. A comprehensive study about the Finnish nation-building and uses of history since the eighteenth century is Derek Fewster's doctoral dissertation, *Visions of Past Glory: Nationalism and the Construction of Early Finnish History* (Helsinki: Finnish Literature Society, 2006). The dissertation closely examines the background of these theories circulating online and the way the nineteenth- and twentieth-century language disputes have affected the Swedish-speaking minority's role as the 'enemy'. See also, Derek Fewster, '"Braves Step out of the Night of the Barrows": Regenerating the Heritage of Early Medieval Finland', in *The Uses of the Middle Ages in Modern European States: History, Nationhood and the Search for Origins*, ed. R. J. W. Evans and Guy P. Marchal (London: Palgrave Macmillan, 2010), 31–51. Furthermore, an edited volume (edited by Joonas Ahola and Frog with Clive Tolley), *Fibula, Fabula, Fact. The Viking Age in Finland* (Helsinki: Finnish Literature Society, 2014) discusses extensively not only the actual research of the Viking Age but the myths related to the Finnish Viking Age. In Finnish, historians Sirpa Aalto and Harri Hihnala refute one by one the 'sources' on the Ancient Finnish Kings and demonstrate how the theories are based on a superficial reading of the medieval and early modern sources, see Sirpa Aalto and Harri Hihnala, 'Saagat tuntevat Suomen kuninkaat' – pseudohistoriallisesta kirjoittelusta Suomen muinaisuudesta', *J@rgonia* 15, no. 29 (2017): 1–30. Philosopher of science Inkeri Koskinen has published a fascinating study on Finnish historical conspiracy theories, where she discusses the theories of Ancient Finnish Kings as well: Inkeri Koskinen, *Villi Suomen historia: Välimeren Väinämöisestä Äijäkupittaan pyramideihin* ['Wild History of Finland: From the Mediterranean Väinämöinen to the Pyramids of Äijäkupittaa'] (Helsinki: Tammi, 2015); on political aspects of the Ancient Finnish Kings, see the recent article: Reima Välimäki and Heta Aali. 'The Ancient Finnish Kings and Their Swedish Archenemy: Nationalism, Conspiracy Theories, and Alt-Right Memes in Finnish Online Medievalism', *Studies in Medievalism* 31 (2022): 55–78.

2 See, for example, Johannes Messenius, *Suomen, Liivinmaan ja Kuurinmaan vaiheita sekä tuntemattoman tekijän Suomen kronikka*, trans. from Latin by Martti Linna, Jorma Lagerstedt, and Erkki Palmén (Helsinki: SKS, 1988). In this translation, there is a genealogical table for Fornjótr, the first king of the Ancient Kingdoms, made by Martti Linna. Messenius himself dates Fornjótr to seventh century BC. The genealogical table made by Linna is in fact the model for another, slightly altered genealogical map of 'Finnish Kings' that continues to circulate widely on the Finnish internet. In this more recent genealogical map, the first Finnish kings are named after *Kalevala*, thus linking the poetry directly to history. For example, on

the 'news media' site Nykysuomi, Sami Niemi has referenced the genealogical map as 'Martti Linna's research'. This 'news media' site has no current editor. See Sami Niemi, 'Suomen muinaiset kuninkaat saagojen mukaan', *Nykysuomi*, 17 September 2016, available online: https://www.nykysuomi.com/2016/09/17/suomen-muinaiset-kuninkaat-saagojen-mukaan/ (accessed 1 September 2020).
3 See Preface in this volume for a short overview of Finnish history.
4 The theory of the Ancient Finnish Kings is nearly a textbook example of a conspiracy theory as defined in *The Conspiracy Theory Handbook* by Stephan Lewandowsky and John Cook. For example, the Swedish and Swedish-speaking population are pictured with *nefarious intent* in concealing the Finnish Middle Ages. The theories are nearly *immune to evidence,* and those writing about the theories imagine themselves as *persecuted victims*. Stephan Lewandowsky and John Cook, *The Conspiracy Theory Handbook*, 2020.
5 The few women we have found writing or commenting on the topic include, for example, Helena Eronen, who wrote in her blog about the Swedish having distorted the medieval Finnish history. She does not directly support the theory of the Ancient Finnish Kings but shares many views of the theory – notably the role of the Swedish in covering up Finnish history, see Helena Eronen, 'Suomi on ruotsalainen?', *Uusi Suomi Puheenvuoro* [blog], 18 January 2013, available online: https://puheenvuoro.uusisuomi.fi/ohohupsis/130262-suomi-on-ruotsalainen/ (accessed 1 September 2020). Eronen is best known for working as an assistant for the right-wing party True Finn MP James Hirvisaari. Another, different type of author is Sirkka Mäki, who has published at least one book about the crusades to Finland. She does not seem to have any political motivations, only pseudohistorical theories. She has even invented a research centre for herself, 'The archaeological research centre of Vaasa', and she has entitled herself as researcher of prehistory. See Sirkka Mäki, 'Kyrö ja kirkko', *Ilkka-Pohjalainen*, 20 January 2010, available online: https://ilkkapohjalainen.fi/mielipide/yleisolta/kyro-ja-kirkko-1.972266 (accessed 1 September 2020). See also Sirkka Mäki, 'Böle-nimen käännös voisi olla uudiskylä', *Ilkka-Pohjalainen*, 25 August 2013, available online: https://ilkkapohjalainen.fi/mielipide/yleisolta/bole-nimen-kaannos-voisi-olla-uudiskyla-1.1450291 (accessed 1 September 2020). A third female author is Viola Heistonen, who has written a blog in which she claims all Russians are genetically Finnish and that there might have been a 'Great Finland' at some point in history: Viola Heistonen, 'Venäläiset ovat etnisiä suomalaisia!', *Uusi Suomi Puheenvuoro* [blog], 26 March 2013, available online: https://puheenvuoro.uusisuomi.fi/viovio/136349-venalaiset-ovat-etnisia-suomalaisia/ (accessed 1 September 2020).
6 'Suomen esikristillinen historia', *Hommaforum*, available online: https://hommaforum.org/index.php/topic,84732.0.html (accessed 26 May 2020).

7 'Uskooko kukaan Kvenlandiin ja siihen, että Suomessa olisi...', *Ylilauta*, available online: https://ylilauta.org/sekalainen/124116045 (accessed 26 May 2020).

8 Popular Finnish videos on the topic are the Myytinkertojat ('Myth tellers') YouTube videos that promote the theories of the Ancient Finnish Kings and have titles such as 'Olet suomalainen, olet harvinainen, olet Pohjolan valtias' [You are a Finn, you are rare, you are the leader of the North]. All commentators and supporters seem to be men. According to the comments, the video even increased their testosterone level. Thomas Wiren, 'Olet suomalainen, olet harvinainen, olet Pohjolan valtias', YouTube, 22 August 2019, available online: https://www.youtube.com/watch?v=GixpCJ9tYPQ&feature=youtu.be (accessed 1 September 2020). The video had 25,609 views as of 2 September 2020.

9 In addition to the various Wikipedia sites (which constitute by far the most popular source), for example, *The History Files* is regularly linked to Finnish discussion forums: 'Fenno-Scandinavia / Nordic Countries', *The History Files*, available online: https://www.historyfiles.co.uk/KingListsEurope/ScandinaviaFinland.htm#Kainu (accessed 1 September 2020). Another popular link is the *Survive the Jive* YouTube channel by Tom Rowsell. Especially his video 'Are Finns European?' (494,190 views as of 2 September 2020, published on 18 August 2017) has been shared multiple times. Rowsell has been strongly associated with far-right ideology and movements; see Joe Mulhall, 'Generation Identity UK Isolated and in Crisis', *HOPE Not Hate*, 29 July 2019.

10 The largest category of women's images are those of young, beautiful women, 'racially pure', and some nearly pornographic images. See, for example, 'Mitä tapahtui langalle suomen muinaiskuninkaista? Poistiko...', *Ylilauta*, available online: https://ylilauta.org/sekalainen/115520691 (accessed 27 May 2020), where there are images of young and beautiful women (three images) and the Minister of Justice, also a woman. The last image was to mock the government and especially the Swedish People's Party of Finland, from which the minister comes.

11 See, for example, commentators who refuse to believe there were no *kings* in Finland in the Middle Ages. 'Uskooko kukaan Kvenlandiin ja siihen, että Suomessa olisi...', *Ylilauta*, available online: https://ylilauta.org/sekalainen/124116045 (accessed 27 May 2020).

12 Toxic masculinity refers here to toxic practices, rigid gender roles and the 'endorsement of misogynistic and homophobic views'. See Mike C. Parent, Teresa D. Gobble and Aaron Rochlen, 'Social Media Behavior, Toxic Masculinity, and Depression', *Psychology of Men & Masculinities* 20, no. 3 (2019): 278.

13 The first one is the anonymous 'Suomen kuninkaat norjalais-islantilaisten saagojen mukaan', *iorbock.com*, 9 October 2007, available online: http://iorbock.com/ekirjasto/tuntematon/suomen-kuninkaat-saagojen-mukaan/ (accessed 1 September 2020). [The Finnish Kings according to the Norwegian-Danish Sagas]. The second one is Arto Pöllänen, 'Olivatko viikinkikuninkaat suomalaisia?', *Kaltio* no. 4 (2001), available

online: http://www.kaltio.fi/vanhat/index43ec.html?81 (accessed 1 September 2020) [Were the Viking Kings Finnish?]. The first, anonymous article also has an undated version from the 1990s that has been circulating online since at least 2002.
14 Matias Nurminen, 'Narrative Warfare: The "Careless" Reinterpretation of Literary Canon in Online Antifeminism', *Narrative Inquiry* 29, no. 2 (2019): 314. See also on the manosphere Debbie Ging, 'Alphas, Betas, and Incels: Theorizing the Masculinities of the Manosphere', *Men and Masculinities* 22, no. 4 (2019): 638–57. Also: Patrik Hermansson, David Lawrence, Joe Mulhall, and Simon Murdoch, *The International Alt-Right. Fascism for the 21st Century?* (London: Routledge, 2020), 163–80.
15 Ging, 'Alphas, Betas, and Incels', 640.
16 Eliisa Vainikka, 'Naisvihan tunneyhteisö – Anonyymisti esitettyä verkkovihaa Ylilaudan ihmissuhdekeskusteluissa', *Media & Viestintä* 42, no. 1 (2019): 1–25.
17 See, for example, the threads 'Uskooko kukaan Kvenlandiin ja siihen, että Suomessa olisi...', *Ylilauta*, available online: https://ylilauta.org/sekalainen/124116045 (accessed 27 May 2020) and 'Hesarilla damage controllit tulilla', *Ylilauta*, available online: https://ylilauta.org/sekalainen/115678586 (accessed 27 May 2020).
18 Nurminen, 'Narrative Warfare', 318.
19 Nurminen, 'Narrative Warfare', 325, 326.
20 Hermansson, *The International Alt-Right*, 174.
21 Ging, 'Alphas, Betas, and Incels', 642. Nurminen, 'Narrative Warfare', 317.
22 Mervi Pantti, Matti Nelimarkka, Kaarina Nikunen, and Gavan Titley, 'The Meanings of Racism: Public Discourses about Racism in Finnish News Media and Online Discussion Forums', *European Journal of Communication* 34, no. 5 (2019): 507–8.
23 'Euroopan juntein kansa', *Ylilauta*, available online: https://ylilauta.org/sekalainen/109333372 (accessed 27 May 2020).
24 '[. . .] oikeilta, alkuperäisiltä (euripidisilta arjalais-) suomalaisilta on varastettu jopa historia, kulttuurihistoria, esi-isiensä muinaisjäänteet, arvot, identiteetti ja oikeus omaan kulttuuriperintöönsä'. 'Baltian ja Suomen muinainen asutus geenitutkimuksen valossa', *Ylilauta*, available online: https://ylilauta.org/tiede/93452870 (accessed 27 May 2020).
25 'Nythän suomi on valkoisen pohjoisen viimeinen toivo, hurrien ja norskien ryhdyttyä aisuroimaan neekereitä, kuten meidänkin hurrit näyttävät tekevän'. 'Mitä tapahtui langalle suomen muinaiskuninkaista? Poistiko...', *Ylilauta*, available online: https://ylilauta.org/sekalainen/115520691 (accessed 27 May 2020).
26 Ging, 'Alphas, Betas, and Incels', 649.
27 For example, compared to a thread from 2013, the tone of the discussions is now much more fuelled by hatred and open misogyny and racism. 'Suomen muinainen kuningaskunta', *Ylilauta*, available online: https://ylilauta.org/tiede/19762800 (accessed 28 May 2020).

28 See Sinikivi.com by Jukka Nieminen and especially Jukka Nieminen, 'Pseudohistoriallisesta kirjoittelusta Suomen muinaisuudesta', *Sinikivi.com*, from 31 July 2018 to 17 May 2019, available online: https://www.sinikivi.com/keskustelu-sinikivi-com/pseudoilua/18422-pseudohistoriallisesta-kirjoittelusta-suomen-muinaisuudesta/ and Jukka Nieminen, 'Kainuun kuninkaat – totta vai tarua?', *Sinikivi.com*, 2020, available online: https://www.sinikivi.com/sinikiven-paakirjoitukset/298-kainuun-kuninkaat-totta-vai-tarua. Also, a blog by Arhi Kuittinen, 'Suomen muinaishistoria on Euroopan historia 100 linkkiä – NEWS Finnish ancient history archeology 2020 Finland bronze age – Arkeologia 10000 vuotta', *Finnsanity* [blog], 2016–2020, available online: https://finnsanity.blogspot.com/2016/06/suomen-muinaishistoria-on-euroopan.html (All sites accessed 28 May 2020).
29 Amy S. Kaufman, 'Muscular Medievalism', *The Year's Work in Medievalism* 31 (2016): 57.
30 Kaufman, 'Muscular Medievalism', 59.
31 Amy S. Kaufman, 'Purity', in *Medievalism: Key Critical Terms*, ed. Elizabeth Emery and Richard Utz (Cambridge: D. S. Brewer, 2014), 199–207.
32 Various genetic studies are discussed in nearly all sites related to the Ancient Finnish Kings even if they were not related to the Middle Ages or uniquely to the Finnish area. See, for example, the thread from 2019, 'Kertokaa faktoja Suomen historiasta. Siis faktoja, ei hur…', *Ylilauta*, available online: https://ylilauta.org/sekalainen/101432421 (accessed 29 May 2020). It is very typical that users share various genetic maps that are interpreted in any way they wish, often even without any source.
33 Ilona Pikkanen, 'The Dangers of "Too Easy a Life". Aarno Karimo's Historical Vignettes and the Post-Civil War Nation', in *Novels, Histories, Novel Nations. Historical Fiction and Cultural Memory in Finland and Estonia*, ed. Linda Kaljundi, Eneken Laanes, and Ilona Pikkanen (Helsinki: Finnish Literature Society, 2015), 171–3.
34 Ville Erkkilä, 'Jalmari Jaakkola – menneisyyden näkijä: historiankirjoituksen poliittisuudesta ja estetiikasta', *Historiallinen Aikakauskirja* 113, no. 4 (2015): 368–71.
35 Fewster, 'Braves Step Out', 48–9.
36 Nurminen, 'Narrative Warfare', 322 and passim.
37 See, for example, Sammy Nyman, 'Suomen salattu historia', *Uusi Suomi Vapaavuoro*, 3 March 2014, available online: https://vapaavuoro.uusisuomi.fi/sammynyman/162149-suomen-salattu-historia/ (accessed 1 September 2020). Nyman claims there were no raids because Finland ruled the neighbouring countries.
38 'Meikäläiselle sanottiin koulussa että suomalaiset olivat kirjaimellisesti paskaperseitä jotka keräili marjoja eikä hädin tuskin osannut puhua. Se että löytyy

miekka jossa kultaa ja erilaisia suomalaiseen mytologiaan liittyviä symboleita [...] on jo pelkästään itselleni iso asia ja tarkoittaa sitä että suomalainen kulttuuri oli jo erittäin asettunut asia paljon enne ruotsalaisia ja kristittyjä'. 'Hesarilla damage controllit tulilla', *Ylilauta*, available online: https://ylilauta.org/sekalainen /115678586 (accessed 28 June 2020).

39 'Miekka; huotra', *Finna.fi*, available online: https://www.finna.fi/Record/musketti .M012:KM11002:5?lng=en-gb/ (accessed 1 September 2020).

40 See, for example, a comment that reads next to the image of the Wikipedia page on the Ring-sword: 'Arkeologian valossa on päivänselvää, että Suomessa on ainakin merovingiajalla ollut kohtuullisen merkittävä valtakeskittymä, jolla oli kytköksiä Frankkien valtakuntaan, Ruotsin Vendel-kulttuuriin ja kentien Anglosaksien pikkukuningaskuntiin' ['In the light of archeology it is clear as day that there was a reasonably significant concentration of power in Finland during the Merovingian period that had connections to the Frankish empire, Sweden's Vendel culture and perhaps to Anglo-Saxon minor kingdoms']. 'Latinaa osaavat lukeeko tuossa tosiaan "Suomen muinainen . . ."', *Ylilauta*, available online: https://ylilauta.org/sekalainen /98560836 (accessed 28 June 2020).

41 Mikko Moilanen, *Marks of Fire, Value and Faith. Swords with Ferrous Inlays in Finland during the Late Iron Age (ca. 700–1200 AD)* (Turku: Suomen keskiajan arkeologian seura, 2015).

42 See especially two threads in Ylilauta: 'Uskooko kukaan Kvenlandiin ja siihen, että Suomessa olisi...', *Ylilauta*, available online: https://ylilauta.org/sekalainen /124116045 (accessed 28 June 2020) and 'Mitä tapahtui langalle suomen muinaiskuninkaista? Poistiko...', *Ylilauta*, available online: https://ylilauta.org/ sekalainen/115520691 (accessed 28 June 2020). There are many comments related to the swords, the anonymous map of the swords and references to Moilanen in both threads.

43 Mikko Moilanen, *Viikinkimiekat Suomessa* (Helsinki: SKS, 2018), 169–75.

44 See the thread started in 2013, 'Suomen muinainen kuningaskunta', *Ylilauta*, available online: https://ylilauta.org/tiede/19762800 (accessed 29 May 2020). The map was posted 21 January 2014.

45 Anne Stalsberg, 'The Vlfberht Sword Blades Reevaluated', *Zeitschrift für Archäologie des Mittelalters* 36 (2008): 89–118.

46 The swords are central to other sites related to the Ancient Finnish Kings as well. See, for example, Arhi Kuittinen, 'Viikinkiajan vääristely jatkuu museoviraston toimesta', *Finnsanity* [blog], 15 May 2015, available online: https://finnsanity .blogspot.com/2015/05/viikinkiajan-vaaristely-jatkuu.html (accessed 28 June 2020). The swords are also discussed in the Hommaforum thread starting from 2013. The tone is almost the same: how the 'official truth' would dismiss the swords but that the commentators know better than to indicate something glorious in the Finnish

past (especially by 'Kulttuurimono', 11.05.2015, 23:54:07.) In addition, the blogs by Sami Niemi, such as 'Suomen muinaiset kuninkaat saagojen mukaan', which use the sword findings as proof of the existence of Finnish Kings. Of the same author: 'Suomen muinainen kuningaskunta aikalaisten silmin, vanhoissa kronikoissa', *Nykysuomi*, 6 September 2016, available online: https://www.nykysuomi.com/2016/09/06/suomen-muinainen-kuningaskunta-aikalaisten-silmin-vanhoissa-kronikoissa/ (accessed 28 June 2020). This post does not refer to swords, but the main image is of a sword. See also, for example, the notorious right-wing populist counter-media *MV-Lehti*, who has published five articles about the Ancient Finnish Kings. One of them, from September 2018 (read 21,698 times), is a reproduction of Pöllänen's 2001 article that does not refer to swords. In the re-production, an image of the sword is added, see 'Olivatko viikinkikuninkaat suomalaisia?', *MV-Lehti*, 28 September 2018, available online: https://mvlehti.net/2018/09/28/olivatko-viikinkikuninkaat-suomalaisia/ (accessed 1 September 2020).

47 See, for example, the entire thread: 'Kyl me suomalaiset ollaan puhdasverisii kuninkaita poika', *Ylilauta*, available online: https://ylilauta.org/sekalainen/118808019 (accessed 28 June 2020) [Yeh, we were purebred kings, my boy], in which the Finnish men are simultaneously equated to Neanderthals and presented as better than everyone else.

48 See, for example, the thread: 'Harmi kun Suomi oli keskiajalla hiirenpaska toisin kuin Liet…', *Ylilauta*, available online: https://ylilauta.org/sekalainen/107546527 (accessed 28 June 2020), where there is even a map of the 'Finno-Ugric Master Race'.

49 'Miksi viikingit välttelivät Suomea?', *Ylilauta*, available online: https://ylilauta.org/sekalainen/108229725 (accessed 28 June 2020), especially comments no. 108238530, posted 30 September 2019, 9:13:00 PM, and no. 108239594, posted 30 September 2019, 9:21:26 PM. Original image by Elmer Boyd Smith. The image contains the caption: 'samaan aikaan hinttapuli Thor vaan tytyilee' ('And at the same time faggot Thor is being a sissy'), no. 108238530, posted 30 September 2019, 9:13:00 PM. Image is comment no. 108239594. Further information about the image of Thor dressed as a woman, see Linnea Hartsuyker, 'Queer Asgard Folk', *The Public Medievalist*, 7 March 2019, available online: https://www.publicmedievalist.com/queer-asgard/ (accessed 19 May 2021).

50 'Miksi viikingit välttelivät Suomea?', *Ylilauta*, available online: https://ylilauta.org/sekalainen/108229725 (accessed 30 June 2020), no. 108247430, posted on 30 September 2019, 10:45:42 PM. The same image was also posted in another thread, 'Suomalaiset muinaiskuninkaat. Mitä olet tehnyt tänään ede...', *Ylilauta*, available online: https://ylilauta.org/sekalainen/107429912 (accessed 30 June 2020), no. 107440092, on 18 September 2019, 5:40:53 pm.

51 See also about the Norse God Loki changing his biological sex: Amy S. Kaufman and Paul B. Sturtevant, *The Devil's Historians: How Modern Extremists Abuse the Medieval Past* (Toronto: University of Toronto Press, 2020), 123.
52 Posted on 6 May 2019. The thread has since been removed.
53 See the thread entitled 'Suomalaiset on cuck ja orjakansa se on historia todistanut', *Ylilauta*, available online: https://ylilauta.org/sekalainen/115097846 (accessed 30 June 2020) [Finland is cuck and slave nation history has proven it]. The thread was started on 8 January 2020.
54 Kaufman and Sturtevant, *The Devil's Historians*, 107.
55 Lauryn Mayer, 'Mythogyny: Popular Medievalism and Toxic Masculinity', *Studies in Medievalism* 29 (2019): 30.

Chapter 8

1 See Elliott in this volume.
2 SteamSpy, 'Crusader Kings II', no date, available online: https://steamspy.com/app/203770 (accessed 17 October 2020).
3 Adam Chapham, *Digital Games as History: How Videogames Represent the Past and Offer Access to Historical Practise* (London: Routledge, 2016), 110, 129, 232.
4 A. Martin Wainwright, *Virtual History: How Videogames Portray the Past* (London: Routledge, 2019), 77.
5 Sverre Bagge, *From Viking Stronghold to Christian Kingdom: State Formation in Norway, C. 900–1350* (Copenhagen: Museum Tusculanum Press, 2010), 108.
6 For a further analysis of the objective-setting in Grand Strategy Games see Robert Houghton, 'If You're Going to Be the King, You'd Better Damn Well Act Like the King: Setting Authentic Objectives to Support Learning in Grand Strategy Computer Games', in *The Middle Ages in Modern Culture: History and Authenticity in Contemporary Medievalism*, ed. Karl Alvestad and Robert Houghton (London: Bloomsbury Academic, 2021), 186–210.
7 The game map is a realistic world map, and the cultural and religious areas are fixed in each historical starting dates. The *Holy Fury* expansion, however, added the option of creating a shattered world, where the historical, cultural and religious data are mixed when the player chooses a random start, see 'Random World', *Crusader Kings II Wiki*, 21 April 2020, available online: https://ck2.paradoxwikis.com/Random_World (accessed 18 June 2020).
8 Cf. Jeremiah McCall, 'Video Games as Participatory Public History', in *A Companion to Public History*, ed. David M. Dean (Hoboken: Wiley Blackwell, 2018), 408.
9 In the version 3.3.3 the start dates and the names of the corresponding eras or historical situations are following: 1 January 769, Early Middle Ages; 1 January 867,

Viking Age; 7 August 936, The Iron Century; 15 September 1066, High Middle Ages; 26 December 1066, William the Conqueror; 1 April 1081, The Alexiad; 1 January 1187, The Third Crusade; 16 May 1204, The Latin Empire; 1 February 1220, Age of the Mongols; 1 May 1241, Rise of the Hansa; and 1 January 1337, Late Middle Ages. The game provides a short description of each era, and suggests interesting characters to be played by the player.

10 Simone Heidbrink, Tobias Knoll, and Jan Wysocki, 'Theorizing Religion on Digital Games – Perspectives and Approaches', in *Religion in Digital Games: Multiperspective & Interdisciplinary Approaches,* ed. Simone Heidbrink and Tobias Knoll / Online. *Heidelberg Journal of Religions on the Internet* 5 (2014): 5–50; Andrew B. R. Elliott and Matthew W. Kapell, 'Introduction: To Build a Past That Will "Stand the Test of Time" – Discovering Historical Facts, Assembling Historical Narratives', in *Playing with the Past: Digital Games and the Simulation of History,* ed. Matthew W. Kapell and Andrew B. R. Elliott (New York: Bloomsbury, 2013), 1–29.

11 See also Rebecca Mir and Trevor Owens, 'Modeling Indigenous Peoples: Unpacking Ideology in *Sid Meier's Colonization*', in *Playing with the Past: Digital Games and the Simulation of History,* ed. Matthew W. Kapell and Andrew B. R. Elliott (New York: Bloomsbury, 2013), 91–2.

12 Jeremiah McCall, 'Playing with the Past: History and Video Games (and Why it Might Matter)', *Journal of Geek Studies* 6, no. 1 (2019): 31–2.

13 Chapham, *Digital Games as History.*

14 Adam Chapham, 'Privileging Form Over Content: Analysing Historical Video Games', *Journal of Digital Humanities* 1, no. 2 (2012): 42.

15 Edward Said, *Orientalism* (1978, London: Penguin Books, 2008).

16 Stuart Hall, 'The West and the Rest: Discourse and Power', in *The Formations of Modernity,* ed. Stuart Hall and Bram Gieben (Cambridge: Polity Press, 1993), 275–320. In digital games, see Mir and Owens, 'Modeling Indigenous Peoples'; Manuel Alejandro Cruz Martinez, 'Playing with History's Otherness. A Framework for Exploring Historical Games', *DiGRA/FDG '16 – Proceedings of the 2016 Playing With History Workshop* 13, no. 3 (2016): 1–5.

17 E.g. Benson Saler, *Conceptualizing Religion: Immanent Anthropologists, Transcendent Natives, and Unbound Categories* (New York: Berghahn Books, 2000).

18 Suzanne Owen, 'The World Religions Paradigm. Time for a Change', *Arts and Humanities in Higher Education* 10, no. 3 (2011): 253–68.

19 Andrew B. R. Elliott, *Medievalism, Politics, and Mass Media: Appropriating the Middle-Ages in the Twenty-first Century* (Woodbridge, Suffolk: D. S. Brewer, 2017); Elliott in this volume.

20 'Clausewitz – Game Engine Written in C++', *MYCPLUS|com*, 29 March 2020, available online: https://www.mycplus.com/featured-articles/clausewitz-game-engine-cplusplus/ (accessed 18 June 2020); 'Scripting', *Crusader Kings II Wiki*, 29 May 2020, available online: https://ck2.paradoxwikis.com/Scripting (accessed 18 June 2020).

21 See Andreas Schwill, 'Cognitive Aspects of Object-Oriented Programming', *IFIP WG 3.1 Working Conference 'Integrating Information Technology into Education'*, 1994.
22 Although the *Crusader Kings II*'s historical accuracy is not at my focus here, in his analysis on the representations of the crusades in digital games, Robert Houghton has duly pointed out that the 'broad and open-ended nature of Grand Strategy Games' may lead to oversimplification. In other words, the game's open-endedness is the reason for the lack of historical particularity. Robert Houghton, 'Crusader Kings Too? (Mis)Representations of the Crusades in Strategy Games', in *Playing the Crusades*, ed. Robert Houghton (London: Routledge, 2021), 71–92, 73.
23 Jason Pitruzzello, 'Systematizing Culture in Medievalism. Geography, Dynasty, Culture, and Imperialism in *Crusader Kings: Deus Vult*', in *Digital Gaming Re-imagines the Middle Ages*, ed. David T. Kline (London: Routledge, 2014), 45.
24 *The Monks and Mystics* DLC allows the player to secretly profess another religion that he/she publicly claims to follow, 'Societies', *Crusader Kings II Wiki*, 23 May 2020, available online: https://ck2.paradoxwikis.com/Societies (accessed 18 June 2020).
25 'Culture', *Crusader Kings II Wiki*, 24 May 2020, available online: https://ck2.paradoxwikis.com/Culture (accessed 18 June 2020).
26 'Modding', *Crusader Kings II Wiki*, 6 May 2020, available online: https://ck2.paradoxwikis.com/Modding; Gareth Crabtree (accessed 18 June 2020); 'Modding as Digital Reenactment: A Case Study of the Battlefield Series', in *Playing with the Past: Digital Games and the Simulation of History*, ed. Matthew W. Kapell and Andrew B. R. Elliott (New York: Bloomsbury, 2013), 199–212; McCall, 'Video Games as Participatory Public History'.
27 'Portrait Modding', *Crusader Kings II Wiki*, 17 February 2020, available online: https://ck2.paradoxwikis.com/Portrait_modding (accessed 18 June 2020).
28 'Graphical DLC', *Crusader Kings II Wiki*, 22 January 2019, available online: https://ck2.paradoxwikis.com/Graphical_DLC (accessed 18 June 2020).
29 According to Sami Raninen and Anna Wessman, the historical Viking Age local social organization in Finland was looser, and there is no evidence of established local leadership or an early stage of state formation. Neither did Finnish or Sámi identity exist. There were signs of local feuding, but not necessarily large-scale warfare. See Sami Raninen and Anna Wessman, 'Finland as a Part of the "Viking World"', in *Fibula, Fabula, Fact: The Viking Age in Finland*, ed. Joonas Ahola and Frog, with Clive Tolley (Helsinki: Finnish Literature Society), 333.
30 Juho Vilho Itkonen, *Itkosten suku 1, Varhaisvaiheet vuoteen 1700* (Helsinki: Itkosten sukukunta, 1987), 36.
31 Chapham, *Digital Games as History*.
32 As of version 2.0, however, these limitations apply mostly to non-human controlled players.
33 'Kingdoms', *Crusader Kings II Wiki*, 26 April 2020, available online: https://ck2.paradoxwikis.com/Kingdoms (accessed 18 June 2020).

34 'Religious Head', *Crusader Kings II Wiki*, 30 May 2020, available online: https://ck2.paradoxwikis.com/Religious_head (accessed 18 June 2020); 'Religion', *Crusader Kings II Wiki*, 19 May 2020, available online: https://ck2.paradoxwikis.com/Religion (accessed 18 June 2020).
35 Owen, 'The World Religions Paradigm'.
36 Iiro Arola, '"Ni sit mä tajusin, et on muitakin kuin minä" – Suomenuskoisten sosiaalinen identiteetti' (MA diss., Faculty of Theology, University of Helsinki, 2010), 8; Mika Lassander, 'Pakanuus nykypäivän Suomessa', in *Monien uskontojen ja katsomusten Suomi*, ed. Ruth Illman, Kimmo Ketola, Riitta Latvio, and Jussi Sohlberg (Tampere: Kirkon Tutkimuskeskus, 2017), 207–9.
37 'Kysyttyä', *Taivaannaula*, 31 October 2015, available online: https://www.taivaannaula.org/yhdistys/kysyttya/ (accessed 18 June 2020).
38 Rasa Pranskevičiūtė, 'Contemporary Paganism in Lithuanian Context: Principal Beliefs and Practices of Romuva', in *Modern Pagan and Native Faith Movements in Central and Eastern Europe*, ed. Kaarina Aitamurto and Scott Simpson (London: Routedge, 2014), 78.
39 In the game's sequel, the *Crusader Kings III*, there are some changes in the naming: Romuva has become Visdilist, Slavic Paganism Slovianskan and Germanic paganism Ásatrú, while Suomenusko has remained.
40 'Suomenusko and Romuva', *Steamcommunity.com*, General Discussions, 19 October 2015, available online: https://steamcommunity.com/app/203770/discussions/0/483367798514314443/ (accessed 18 June 2020).
41 McCall, 'Video Games as Participatory Public History'.
42 Wainwright, *Virtual History*, 149.
43 Patrick J. Geary, 'European Ethnicities and European as an Ethnicity: Does Europe Have Too Much History?', in *The Making of Medieval History*, ed. G. A. Loud and Martial Staub (York: York Medieval Press, 2017), 66.
44 Elliott, *Medievalism, Politics, and Mass Media*, 136, 138.
45 McCall, 'Video Games as Participatory Public History'; McCall, 'Playing with the Past'.

Appendix 2

1 E. A. Rostovtsev, 'Dopetrovskaia Rus' v zhanre internet-anekdota', *Istoricheskaia ekspertiza* 4 (2018): 173–84; E. A. Rostovtsev and D. A. Sosnitskii, 'Srednevekovye geroi i sobytija otechestvennoi istorii v setevyh resursah', *Istoricheskaia ekspertiza* 1 (2018): 41–58; E. A. Rostovtsev, 'The Immortal Host of Prince Igor', *Vestnik of Saint-Petersburg University, History* 65, no. 3 (2020): 883–903.

Bibliography

Aalto, Sirpa, and Harri Hihnala. '"Saagat tuntevat Suomen kuninkaat" – pseudohistoriallisesta kirjoittelusta Suomen muinaisuudesta'. *J@rgonia* 15, no. 29 (2017): 1–30.

Aalto, Sirpa, and Veli-Pekka Lehtola. 'The Sami Representations Reflecting the Multi-Ethnic North of the Saga Literature'. *Journal of Northern Studies* 11, no. 2 (2017): 7–30.

Aaltonen, Elsa. *Kustavilaisia puumerkkejä*. Kustavi: E. Aaltonen, 1999.

Ackland, Robert, and Rachel Gibson. 'Hyperlinks and Networked Communication: A Comparative Study of Political Parties Online'. *International Journal of Social Research Methodology* 16, no. 3 (2013): 231–44.

Adam of Bremen. *History of the Archbishops of Hamburg-Bremen*, edited and translated by Francis J. Tschan and Timothy Reuter. New York: Columbia University Press, 2005.

Åhlén, Marit, Tapani Tuovinen, and Hans Myhrman. 'Ett runstensfragment från Hitis'. *Muinaistutkija* 1 (1998): 18–20.

Ahl-Waris, Eva. *Historiebruk kring Nådendal och den kommemorativa anatomin av klostrets minnesplats*. Vadstena: Societas Sanctae Birgittae, 2010.

Ahola, Joonas, and Frog. 'Approaching the Viking Age in Finland: An Introduction'. In *Fibula, Fabula, Fact: The Viking Age in Finland*, edited by Joonas Ahola and Frog with Clive Tolley, 21–84. Helsinki: Finnish Literature Society, 2014.

Ahola, Joonas, and Frog with Clive Tolley, eds. *Fibula, Fabula, Fact: The Viking Age in Finland*. Helsinki: Finnish Literature Society, 2014.

Ahtiainen, Pekka, and Jukka Tervonen. *Menneisyyden tutkijat ja metodien vartijat: matka suomalaiseen historiankirjoitukseen*. Helsinki: Suomen historiallinen seura, 1996.

Ajzenshtat, M. P., M. S. Bobkova, S. G. Mereminskii, and A. I. Sidorov. 'Istorija i mif: kto kogo?'. *Lokus: Liudi, obshestvo, kul'tury, smysly* 4 (2017): 133–7.

Alamäki, Yrjö. *Tornion muistomerkkiopas*. Tornio: Tornion kulttuuritoimisto, 2002.

Alimov, D. E., and A. I. Filyushkin, eds. *'Mobilizovannoe srednevekov'e': medievalism i natsional'naia ideologiia v Tsentral'no-Vostochnoi Evrope i na Balkanakh*. St Petersburg: SPbGU, 2020.

Allchin, Douglas. 'Pseudohistory and Pseudoscience'. *Science & Education* 13, no. 3 (2004): 179–95.

Alvestad, Karl C. 'Middelalders helter og Norsk nasjonalisme før andre verdenskrig'. *Slagmark* 79, no. 1 (2019): 77–95.

Alvestad, Karl C. 'The "Accurate" Deeds of Our Fathers: The "Authentic" Narrative of Early Norway'. In *The Middle Ages in Modern Culture: History and Authenticity in Contemporary Medievalism*, edited by Karl C. Alvestad and Robert Houghton, 15–27. London: Bloomsbury Academic 2021.

Arola, Iiro. '"Ni sit mä tajusin, et on muitakin kuin minä" – Suomenuskoisten sosiaalinen identiteetti'. MA diss., Faculty of Theology, University of Helsinki, 2010.

Assmann, Aleida. 'Memory, Individual and Collective'. In *The Oxford Handbook of Contextual Political Analysis*, edited by Robert E. Goodin and Charles Tilley, 210–24. Oxford: Oxford University Press, 2006.

Assmann, Ia. [Jan Assmann]. *Kul'turnaia pamiat'. Pis'mo, pamiat' o proshlom i politicheskaia identichnost v vyskokikh kul'turakh*, translated by M. M. Sokolskay. Moscow: Yazyki Slavianskoi Kul'turi, 2004.

Assmann, Jan. 'Communicative and Cultural Memory'. In *Cultural Memory Studies: An International and Interdisciplinary Handbook*, edited by Astrid Erll and Ansgar Nünning, 109–18. Berlin; New York: de Gruyter, 2008.

Bagge, Sverre. *From Viking Stronghold to Christian Kingdom: State Formation in Norway, C. 900–1350*. Copenhagen: Museum Tusculanum Press.

Barabási, Albert-László, and Réka Albert. 'Emergence of Scaling in Random Networks'. *Science* 286, no. 5439 (1999): 509–12.

Bechmann, Anja. 'Towards Cross-Platform Value Creation: Four Patterns of Circulation and Control'. *Information, Communication & Society* 15, no. 6 (2012): 888–908.

Belousov, V. S., and E. S. Kuropatova. 'Velikii kniaz' Vladimir: Sovremennyi obraz i ego istoricheskie korni'. *Iazyk i tekst* 2, no. 4 (2015): 55–64.

Benevich, G. B. 'Poeziia gibridnoi voiny'. *Novoe literaturnoe obozrenie* 3, no. 157 (2019): 226–38.

Berg, Ove. *Runsvenska, svenska, finska*. Gällivare: Skrivkammaren i Gällevare, 2003.

Berzins, Chris, and Patrick Cullen. 'Terrorism and Neo-medievalism'. *Civil Wars* 6, no. 2 (2003): 8–32

Berzock, Kathleen Bickford. *Caravans of Gold, Fragments in Time: Art, Culture, and Exchange Across Medieval Saharan Africa*. Princeton, NJ: Princeton University Press, 2019.

Blackburn, M. 'Mainstream Russian Nationalism and the 'State-Civilization' Identity: Perspectives from Below'. *Nationalities Papers* 49, no. 1 (2020): 1–19.

Blakkisrud, Helge. 'Blurring the Boundary between Civic and Ethnic: The Kremlin's New Approach to National Identity under Putin's Third Rerm'. In *The New Russian Nationalism: Imperialism, Ethnicity and Authoritarianism 2000–2015*, edited by Pål Kolstø and Helge Blakkisrud, 249–74. Edinburgh: Edinburg University Press, 2016.

Blondel, Vincent D., Jean-Loup Guillaume, Renaud Lambiotte, and Etienne Lefebvre. 'Fast Unfolding of Communities in Large Networks'. *Journal of Statistical Mechanics: Theory and Experiment* 2008, no. 10 (2008): P10008.

Bodnarchuk, D. V. 'The Mobilized Middle Ages in Historical Memory'. *Vestnik of Saint-Petersburg University, History* 64, no. 1 (2019): 159–76.

Bonacchi, Chiara, Mark Altaweel, and Marta Krzyzanska. 'The Heritage of Brexit: Roles of the Past in the Construction of Political Identities through Social Media'. *Journal of Social Archaeology* 18, no. 2 (2018): 174–92.

Brandenberger, D., and K. M. F. Platt. 'Terribly Pragmatic: Rewriting the History of Ivan IV's Reign, 1937–1956'. In *Epic Revisionism: Russian History and Literature as Stalinist Propaganda*, edited by D. Brandenberger and K. M. F. Platt, 157–78. Madison: University of Wisconsin Press, 2006.

Brandes, Urlik, and Thomas Erlebach. 'Fundamentals'. In *Network Analysis: Methodological Foundations*, edited by Ulrik Brandes and Thomas Erlebach, 7–15. New York: Springer, 2005.

Brandes, Urlik, and Thomas Erlebach. 'Introduction'. In *Network Analysis: Methodological Foundations*, edited by Ulrik Brandes and Thomas Erlebach, 1–6. New York: Springer, 2005.

Brockmeier, Jens. 'Remembering and Forgetting: Narrative as Cultural Memory'. *Culture & Psychology* 8, no. 1 (2002): 15–43.

Brooks, Jeffrey. *When Russia Learned to Read. Literacy and Popular Culture 1861–1917*. Evanston: Northwestern University Press, 2003.

Bruns, Axel, and Joanne Jacobs, eds. *Uses of Blogs*. New York: Peter Lang, 2006.

Buchli, Victor, and Gavin Lucas. *Archaeologies of the Contemporary Past*. London: Routledge, 2001.

Bykova E. V., and E. Iu. Mokerova. 'Representatsiia 'istoricheskoi pamiati' v deiatel'nosti klubov rekonstruktsii srednekov'ia'. In *Formirovanie grazhdanskoi ustoichivosti kak faktor protivodeistviia ideologii ekstremizma i terrorizma. Sbornik materialov Vserossiiskoi nauchno-prakticheskoi konferentsii*, 59–66. Kazan: "Danis", 2017.

Cashmore, Ellis, and James Jennings, eds. *Racism: Essential Readings*. London, Thousand Oaks, New Delhi: SAGE Publications, 2001.

Carleton, Gregory. *Russia – the Story of War*. Cambridge: The Belknap Press of Harvard University Press, 2017.

Carman, John and Marie Louise Stig Sørensen. 'Heritage Studies: An Outline'. In *Heritage Studies. Methods and Approaches*, edited by Marie Louise Stig Sørensen and John Carman, 11–28. London and New York: Routledge, 2009.

Ceron, Andrea. *Social Media and Political Accountability: Bridging the Gap between Citizens and Politicians*. New York: Springer, 2017.

Chapham, Adam. 'Privileging Form over Content: Analysing Historical Video Games'. *Journal of Digital Humanities* 1, no. 2 (2012): 42–3.

Chapham, Adam. *Digital Games as History. How Videogames Represent the Past and Offer Access to Historical Practise*. London: Routledge, 2016.

Chapova, O. I., N. A. Artem'eva and L. V. Poshivalova. *Vse proizvedeniia shkol'noi programmy v kratkom islozhenii*. Moscow: Dom 21 vek, 2008.

Connerton, Paul. *How Societies Remember*. Cambridge: Cambridge University Press, 1989.

Connerton, Paul. *How Modernity Forgets*. New York: Cambridge University Press, 2009.
Crabtree, Gareth. 'Modding as Digital Reenactment: A Case Study of the Battlefield Series'. In *Playing with the Past. Digital Games and the Simulation of History*, edited by Matthew W. Kapell and Andrew B. R. Elliott, 199–212. New York: Bloomsbury, 2013.
Crocker, Christopher. 'What We Talk about When We Talk about Vínland: History, Whiteness, Indigenous Erasure, and the Early Norse Presence in Newfoundland'. *Canadian Journal of History/Annales canadiennes d'histoire* 55, no. 1–2 (2020): 91–122.
Cruz, Martinez, and Manuel Alejandro. 'Playing with History's Otherness: A Framework for Exploring Historical Games'. *DiGRA/FDG '16 – Proceedings of the 2016 Playing With History Workshop* 13, no. 3 (2016): 1–5.
Curran, James, Natalie Fenton, and Des Freedman. *Misunderstanding the Internet*. London: Routledge, 2016.
Dahl, Göran. *Bomärken på Åland*. Mariehamn: Ålands folkminnesförbund, 1994.
Danilevskii, I. N. *Drevniaia Rus' glazami sovremennikov i potomkov*. Moscow: Aspect Press, 1999.
Danilevskii, I. N. 'Ledovoe poboishche: smena obraza'. *Otechestvennye zapiski* 5 (2004): 28–40.
Danilevskii, I. N. 'Aleksandr Nevskii: Paradoksy istoricheskoi pamiati'. In *Tsep' vremen: Problemy istoricheskogo soznaniia*, edited by L. P. Repina, 119–32. Moscow: Institut Vseobshchey istorii RAN, 2005.
Danilevskii, N. A. *Rossiia i Evropa. Vzgliad na kul'turnye i politicheskie otnosheniia slavianskogo mira k germane-romanskomu*. St Petersburg: Izdatel'stvo 'Glagol'', 1995.
D'Arcens, Louise, and Andrew Lynch, eds. *International Medievalism and Popular Culture*. Amherst, NY: Cambria Press, 2014.
Delle, James A. 'A Tale of Two Tunnels. Memory, Achaeology, and the Underground Railroad'. *Journal of Social Archaeology* 8, no. 1 (2008): 63–93.
Dijck, José Van. *The Culture of Connectivity: A Critical History of Social Media*. Oxford; New York: Oxford University Press, 2013.
Dinshaw, Carolyn. *How Soon Is Now? Medieval Texts, Amateur Readers, and the Queerness of Time*. Durham, NC: Duke University Press, 2012.
Donner, Joakim. 'Bidrag till kännedomen om Vörårunornas ålder: exempel på ristningsteknik använd i runinskrifter och hällristangar'. *Fennoscandia archaeologica* 111 (1986): 73–80.
Dreijer, Matts. 'De försvunna runstenarna i Kökar'. *Åländsk odling* 6 (1945): 31–40.
Dreijer, Matts. 'Landet Åland och Fornsveriges östgräns'. *Åländsk odling* 11 (1950): 3–167.
Dreijer, Matts. 'Det återfunna Birka'. *Åländsk odling* 30 (1969): 3–35.
Dreijer, Matts. 'Åland och Bircaproblemet: Föredrag i Statens Historiska Museum i Stockholm den 21 mars 1974'. *Åländsk odling* 35 (1974): 31–47.

Drozdova, O., and Robinson, P. 'A Study of Vladimir Putin's Rhetoric'. *Europe-Asia Studies* 71, no. 5 (2019): 805–23.

Duczko, Władysław. 'With Vikings or Without? Scandinavians in Early Medieval Poland: Approaching an Old Problem'. In *Scandinavian Culture in Medieval Poland*, edited by Sławomir Moździoch, Błażej Stanisławski, and Przemysław Wiszewski, 19–32. Wrocław: Institute of Archaeology and Ethnology of the Polish Academy of Sciences, 2013.

Dukes, Paul. *A History of Russia: Medieval, Modern, Contemporary*. 2nd edn. Basingstoke: Macmillan, 1990.

Dvornichenko, A. Iu. *Rossiiskaja istorija s drevneishikh vremen do padeniia samoderzhaviia*. Moscow: Ves' Mir, 2010.

Dvornichenko, A. Iu. *Proshchanie s revoliutsiei*. Moscow: Ves' Mir, 2018.

Dwyer, Owen J. and Derek H. Alderman. 'Memorial Landscapes: Analytic Questions and Metaphors'. *Geojournal* 73 (2008): 165–78.

Eckmann, Jean-Pierre, and Elisha Moses. 'Curvature of Co-Links Uncovers Hidden Thematic Layers in the World Wide Web'. *Proceedings of the National Academy of Sciences* 99, no. 9 (2002): 5825–9.

Edelman, Nils. 'Försök till en geologisk datering av en hällristning vid Kastelholm'. *Åländsk odling* 29 (1968): 15–17.

Edgren, Torsten. 'Dreijer, Matts'. *Biografiskt lexikon för Finland*. vol. 3: Republiken A-L, 224–7. Helsingfors: Svenska litteratursällskapet i Finland, 2011. http://www.blf.fi/artikel.php?id=9597

Ekko, Paavo O. *Puumerkit ja riimut menneisyyden avaimina*. Helsinki: Suomen Heraldinen Seura, 1984.

Elliott, Andrew B. R. *Medievalism, Politics and Mass Media: Appropriating the Middle Ages in the Twenty-First Century*. Woodbridge, Suffolk: D. S. Brewer, 2017.

Elliott, Andrew B. R. 'Internet Medievalism and the White Middle Ages'. *History Compass* 16, no. 3 (2018): e12441.

Elliott, Andrew B. R. 'Medievalism, Brexit, and the Myth of Nations'. *Studies in Medievalism* 29 (2020): 31–8.

Elliott, Andrew B. R., and Matthew W. Kapell. 'Introduction: To Build a Past That Will 'Stand the Test of Time' — Discovering Historical Facts, Assembling Historical Narratives'. In *Playing with the Past. Digital Games and the Simulation of History*, edited by Matthew W. Kapell and Andrew B. R. Elliott, 1–29. New York: Bloomsbury, 2013.

Emel'ianenko, Vladimir, Aleksandr Vetoshko, and Irina Malashenko. 'Internet i mifologizatsija istoricheskogo soznania (tsennostno-mirovozzrenicheskii aspekt)'. *Gramota* 2, no. 76 (2017): 100–4.

Erkkilä, Ville. 'Jalmari Jaakkola – menneisyyden näkijä: historiankirjoituksen poliittisuudesta ja estetiikasta'. *Historiallinen Aikakauskirja* 113, no. 4 (2015): 361–72.

Erusalimskii, K. Iu. 'Poniatie 'istoriia' v russkom istoriopisanii XVI veka'. In *Obrazy proshlogo i kollektivnaia identichnost' v Evrope do nachala Novogo vremeni*, edited by L. P. Repina, 365–401. Moscow: Krug, 2003.

Erusalimskii, K. Iu. 'Zachem nuzhni pamiatniki Ivanu Groznomu?'. *Istoricheskaia ekspertiza* 1 (2020): 48–73.

Esina, T. A. 'Sakralizatsiia obraza politicheskogo lidera i natsional'naia konsolidatsiia rossiian: kniaz' Vladimir Sviatoi kak simvol gosudarstvennogo deiatelia i sovremennost'. *Izvestiia Tul'skogo gosudarstvennogo universiteta. Gumanitarnye nauki* 4–1 (2014): 128–40.

Europeaus, Aarne. 'Etelä-Pohjanmaan asutuskysymyksiä'. *Kalevalaseuran vuosikirja* 5 (1925): 144–89.

Fallgren, Jan-Henrik. 'Some Thoughts about the Early Medieval Settlement on Åland, from a Western European Perspective'. In *Re-Imagining Periphery. Archaeology and Text in Northern Europe from Iron Age to Viking and Early Medieval Periods*, edited by Charlotta Hillerdal and Kristen Ilves, 169–77. Oxford & Philadelphia: Oxbow, 2020.

Fagan, Garrett G. 'Diagnosing Pseudoarchaeology'. In *Archaeological Fantasies: How Pseudoarchaeology Misrepresents the Past and Misleads the Public*, edited by Garrett G. Fagan, 23–46. London; New York: Routledge, 2006.

Fainsod, Merle. *How Russia is Ruled*. Cambridge, MA: Harvard University Press, 1963.

Feres, João. 'Building a Typology of Forms of Misrecognition: Beyond the Republican-Hegelian Paradigm'. *Contemporary Political Theory* 5 (2006): 259–77.

Fewster, Derek. *Visions of Past Glory: Nationalism and the Construction of Early Finnish History*. Helsinki: Finnish Literature Society, 2006.

Fewster, Derek. "Braves Step out of the Night of the Barrows': Regenerating the Heritage of Early Medieval Finland'. In *The Uses of the Middle Ages in Modern European States History: Nationhood and the Search for Origins*, edited by R. J. W. Evans and Guy P. Marchal, 31–51. London: Palgrave Macmillan, 2011.

Filyushkin, A. I. 'Kulikovskii tsikl: opyt germenevticheskogo issledovaniia'. In *Kulikovo pole: voprosy istoriko-kul'turnogo naslediia trudy nauchno-prakticheskoi konferentsii "Kulikovo pole – unikal'naia kul'turno-istoricheskaia i prirodnaia territoriia. Problemy izucheniia i sokhraneniia voenno-istoricheskogo i pripodnogo naslediia Tsentral'noi Rossi": Moskva – Tula, 25–27 oktiabria 1999g*, 172–86. Tula: Tul'skii poligrafist, 2000.

Filyushkin, A. I. 'Sotvorenie groznogo tsaria: zachem N. M. Karamzinu byl nuzhen "tiran vsei Rusi"?'. *Tetradi po konservatizmu* 4 (2016): 123–30.

Filyushkin, A. I. '"Kogda i zachem stali stavit" pamiatniki istoricheskim personazham Drevnei Rusi?'. *Drevniaia Rus': vo vremeni, v lichnostiakh, v ideiakh* 7 (2017): 382–97.

Filyushkin, A. I. '"Mobilisatsija srednevekov'ja" kak poisk identichnosti: kakimi putjami Belorussia hochet uiti ot istoricheskogo naslediia Rossijskoi imperii i SSSR'. *Quaestio Rossica* 5, no. 2 (2017): 569–90.

Filyushkin, A. I. '"Mobilisatsiia srednevekov'ia" kak instrument formirovaniia predstavlenii o slavianskom edistve'. *Studia Slavica et Balcanica Petropolitana* 2, no. 22 (2017): 22–39.

Filyushkin, A. I. 'Chem porozhden novyi medievalism v Vostochnoi Evrope?'. In *Mavrodinskie chteniia 2018. Materialy Vserossiiskoi nauchnoi konferentsii, posviashchennoi 110-letiiu so dniia rozhdeniia professora Vladimira Vasil'evicha Mavrodina*, edited by A. Iu. Dvornichenko, 183–5. St Petersburg: Nestor-istoriia, 2018.

Filyushkin, A. I. 'Medievalism: pochemu nam segodnia nuzhny srednie veka?'. *Istoricheskaia ekspertiza* 4 (2018): 153–64.

Filyushkin, A. I. '"To Remember Pskov": How the Medieval Republic was Stamped on the National Memory'. *Jahrbücher für Geschichte Osteuropas* 66, no. 4 (2018): 559–87.

Finke, Laurie A., and Martin B. Shichtman, eds. *Medieval Texts & Contemporary Readers*. Ithaca; London: Cornell University Press, 1987.

Freudenthal, Axel O. 'Runinskriften å Tuukkala-spännet'. *Finska vetenskaps-soc. förhandlingar* 35 (1893): 1–3.

Fritze, Ronald H. *Invented Knowledge: False History, Fake Science and Pseudo-Religions*. Chicago: Chicago University Press, 2009.

Ganander, Christfrid. *Nytt finskt lexikon*, edited by Liisa Nuutinen. Helsinki: Suomalaisen Kirjallisuuden Seura, 1997.

Ganim, John M. *Medievalism and Orientalism: Three Essays on Literature, Architecture and Cultural Identity*. London: Palgrave Macmillan, 2008.

Gardberg, Carl Jacob. 'Porvoon kaupungin historia keskiajalla ja 1500-luvulla'. In *Porvoon kaupungin historia I*. Porvoo: WSOY, 1996.

Geary, Patrick J. *The Myth of Nations: The Medieval Origins of Europe*. Princeton: Princeton University Press, 2003.

Geary, Patrick J. 'European Ethnicities and European as an Ethnicity: Does Europe Have Too Much History?'. In *The Making of Medieval History*, edited by G. A. Loud and Martial Staub, 57–69. York: York Medieval Press, 2017.

Geary, Patrick J. 'Writing the Nation: Historians and National Identities from the Nineteenth to the Twenty-First Centuries'. In *The Middle Ages in the Modern World – Twenty-first Century Perspectives*, edited by B. Bildhauer and C. Jones, 73–86. Oxford: Oxford University Press, 2017.

Giles, Keir. *Moscow Rules – What Drives Russia to Confront the West*, Washington: Brookings Institution Press, 2019.

Ging, Debbie. 'Alphas, Betas, and Incels: Theorizing the Masculinities of the Manosphere'. *Men and Masculinities* 22, no. 4 (2019): 638–57.

Golovashina, O. V. 'Liubiteli istorii' i istorija dlia liubitelei: predstavlenia o proshlym v sotsial'nykh setiakh'. *Filosofskie traditsii i sovremennost'* 1, no. 5 (2014): 114–23.

Goode, Erich, and D. Angus Vail. *Extreme Deviance*. Newbury Park, CA: Pine Forge Press, 2008.

Goode, J. Paul. 'Everyday Patriotism and Ethnicity in Today's Russia'. In *Russia Before and After Crimea: Nationalism and Identity, 2010–17*, edited by Pål Kolstø and Helge Blakkisrud, 258–81. Edinburgh: Edinburgh University Press, 2018.

Gorski, Bradley. 'The Battle for (Pre-)Modernity: Medieval Festivals in Contemporary Russia'. *The Russian Review* 78 (2016): 547–68.

Gray, Ann, Jan Campbell, Mark Erickson, Stuart Hanson, and Helen Wood, eds. *CCCS Selected Working Papers*. London and New York: Routledge, 2007.

Griffin, Roger. *Fascism. Key Concepts in Political Theory*. Medford, MA: Polity Press, 2018.

Grönholm, Pertti, and Heino Nyyssönen. 'Historian käyttö ennen ja nyt – faktana ja fiktiona'. *Kosmopolis* 49, no. 3 (2019): 7–27.

Hall, Stuart. 'The West and the Rest: Discourse and Power'. In *The Formations of Modernity*, edited by Stuart Hall and Bram Gieben, 275–320. Cambridge: Polity Press, 1993.

Hall, Stuart. 'Whose Heritage?: Un-Settling 'the Heritage,' Re-Imagining the Post-Nation'. *Third Text: Critical Perspectives on Contemporary Art and Culture* 49 (2000): 3–13.

Hall, Stuart. *Identiteetti*. Tampere: Vastapaino, 2002.

Halperin, Charles J. 'Ivan the Terrible Returns to the Silver Screen: Pavel Lungin's Film Tsar'. *Studies in Russian and Soviet Cinema* 7, no. 1 (2013): 61–72.

Halperin, Charles J. 'A Tatar Interpretation of the Battle of Kulikovo Field, 1380: Rustam Nabiev'. *Nationalities Papers* 44, no. 1 (2016): 4–19.

Hansson, Sven Ove. 'Defining Pseudoscience and Science'. In *Philosophy of Pseudoscience: Reconsidering the Demarcation Problem*, edited by Massimo Pigliucci and Maarten Boudry, 61–77. Chicago: University of Chicago Press, 2013.

Hansson, Sven Ove. 'Science and Pseudo-Science'. In *The Stanford Encyclopedia of Philosophy*, edited by Edward N. Zalta. Metaphysics Research Lab, Stanford University, 2017. https://plato.stanford.edu/archives/sum2017/entries/pseudo-science/ (Accessed 20 June 2021).

Hård, Gunnar. 'Vörårunorna'. *Oknytt* 3–4 (1983): 18–19.

Harjula, Janne. 'Alustavia ajatuksia Turun Tuomiokirkontorin tuohikirjeestä'. *SKAS* 1–2 (2012): 3–21.

Harjula, Janne. 'Runic Inscriptions on Stave Vessels in Turku: Materializations of Language, Education, Magic, and Domestic Religion'. In *Objects, Environment, and Everyday Life in Medieval Europe*, edited by Ben Jervis, Lee G. Broderick, and Idoia Grau Sologestoa, 213–34. Turnhout: Brepols, 2016.

Harjula, Janne. 'For the Sake of Hair and Soul. Medieval Antler Comb with Runic Inscription from Turku'. In *Tidens landskap. En vänbok till Anders Andrén*, edited by Cecilja Ljung, Anna Andreasson Sjögren, Ingrid Berg, Elin Engström, Ann-Mari Hållans Stenholm, Kristina Jonsson, Alison Klevnäs, Linda Qviström, and Torun Zachrisson, 246–8. Lund: Nordic Academic Press, 2019.

Hartsuyker, Linnea. 'Queer Asgard Folk'. *The Public Medievalist*. 7 March 2019. https://www.publicmedievalist.com/queer-asgard/ (Accessed 19 May 2021).

Hazell, Robert, and James Melton, eds. *Magna Carta and Its Modern Legacy*. Cambridge: Cambridge University Press, 2015.

Heidbrink, Simone, Tobias Knoll, and Jan Wysocki. 'Theorizing Religion on Digital Games – Perspectives and Approaches'. In *Religion in Digital Games: Multiperspective*

& Interdisciplinary Approaches, edited by Simone Heidbrink and Tobias Knoll / Online. *Heidelberg Journal of Religions on the Internet* 5 (2014): 5–50.

Heikkilä, Tuomas. *Pyhän Henrikin Legenda*. Helsinki: Suomalaisen Kirjallisuuden Seura, 2005.

Heng, Geraldine. *The Invention of Race in the European Middle Ages*. Cambridge: Cambridge University Press, 2018.

Henkel, Linda A., and Mark E. Mattson. 'Reading is Believing: The Truth Effect and Source Credibility'. *Consciousness and Cognition* 20, no. 4 (2011): 1705–21.

Hermansson, Patrik, David Lawrence, Joe Mulhall, and Simon Murdoch. *The International Alt-Right. Fascism for the 21st Century?* London: Routledge, 2020.

Herranen, Merja, and Olavi Hankimo, eds. *Natalia Linsénin ja John Granlundin Porvoo*. Helsinki: Siltala, 2014.

Herva, Vesa-Pekka, and Timo Ylimaunu. 'Folk Beliefs, Special Deposits, and Engagement with the Environment in Early Modern Northern Finland'. *Journal of Anthropological Archaeology* 28, no. 2 (2009): 234–43.

Herva, Vesa-Pekka, and Timo Ylimaunu. 'Coastal Cosmologies: Long-Term Perspectives on the Perception and Understanding of Dynamic Coastal Landscapes in the Northern Baltic Sea Region'. *Time and Mind: The Journal of Archaeology, Consciousness and Culture* 7, no. 2 (2014): 183–202.

Höfig, Verena. '"Re-Wild Yourself": Old Norse Myth and Radical White Nationalist Groups in Trump's America'. In *Norse Myths as Political Ideologies: Critical Studies of the Appropriation of Medieval Narratives*, edited by Nicolas Meylan and Lukas Rösli, 209–31. Turnhout: Brepols, 2020.

Horswell, Mike, and Akil N. Awan, eds. *The Crusades in the Modern World: Engaging the Crusades*, vol. 2. London: Routledge, 2019.

Hoskins, Andrew. 'Digital Network Memory'. In *Mediation, Remediation, and the Dynamics of Cultural Memory*, edited by Laura Basu and Paulus Bijl, 91–106. Berlin: Walter de Gruyter, 2009.

Hösl, Maximilian. 'Semantics of the Internet: A Political History'. *Internet Histories* 3, no. 3–4 (2019): 275–92.

Houghton, Robert. 'Crusader Kings too? (Mis)Representations of the Crusades in Strategy Games'. In *Playing the Crusades*, edited by Robert Houghton, 71–92. London: Routledge, 2021.

Houghton, Robert. 'If You're Going to Be the King, You'd Better Damn Well Act Like the King: Setting Authentic Objectives to Support Learning in Grand Strategy Computer Games'. In *The Middle Ages in Modern Culture: History and Authenticity in Contemporary Medievalism*, edited by Karl Alvestad and Robert Houghton, 186–210. London: Bloomsbury Academic, 2021.

Hsy, Jonathan. *Antiracist Medievalisms: From Yellow Peril to Black Lives Matter*. Amsterdam: Arc Humanities Press, 2021.

Huntuvuori, Hilda. *Erämaan nuotiolta Turun linnaan: kuvauksia keskiajalta*. Helsinki: Valistus, 1954.

Ikäheimo, Janne, and Wesa Perttola. 'Näennäisarkeologisia linjanvetoja Suomen muinaisuuteen'. *Muinaistutkija* 4 (2010): 22–33.

Isoaho, Mari. *The Image of Aleksandr Nevskiy in Medieval Russia: Warrior and Saint*. Leiden; Boston: Brill, 2006.

Itkonen, Juho Vilho. *Itkosten suku 1, Varhaisvaiheet vuoteen 1700*. Helsinki: Itkosten sukukunta, 1987.

Ivanova, N. P. '"Tserkovnyi kalendar"-mesiatseslov kak istoricheskii istochnik'. *Izvestiia Altaiskogo gosudarstvennoe universiteta* 3, no. 7 (1998): 22–6.

Jaakkola, Jalmari. *Suomen varhaiskeskiaika. Suomen historia 3*. Porvoo; Helsinki: WSOY, 1938.

Jääskeläinen, Ari. 'Kansallistava kansanrunous. Suomalaisuus ja folklore'. In *Elävänä Euroopassa. Muuttuva suomalainen identiteetti*, edited by Pertti Alasuutari and Petri Ruuska, 41–82. Tampere: Vastapaino, 1998.

Jakobsson, Max. *Tilinpäätös*. Helsinki: Otava, 2003.

Jenkins, Henry. *Textual Poachers: Television Fans and Participatory Culture*. London: Routledge, 1992.

Jenkins, Henry. *Convergence Culture: Where Old and New Media Collide*. New York: NYU Press, 2006.

Jenkins, Henry, Sam Ford, and Joshua Green. *Spreadable Media: Creating Value and Meaning in a Networked Culture*. Postmillennial Pop. New York: New York University Press, 2018.

Jenness, Doug. 'Origins of the Myth of Race'. In *Racism: Essential Readings*, edited by Ellis Cashmore and James Jennings, 304–10. London, Thousand Oaks, New Delhi: SAGE Publications, 2001.

Jussila, Osmo, Seppo Hentilä, and Jukka Nevakivi. *From Grand Duchy to Modern State: A Political History of Finland since 1809*, translated by David Arter and Eva-Kaisa Arter. London: Hurst, 1999.

Kalb, Marvin L. *Imperial Gamble: Putin, Ukraine, and the New Cold War*. Washington, DC: Brookings Institution Press, 2015.

Kansikas, Suvi. 'Menneisyys ulkopolitiikan välineenä: Venäjän muistilait ja historian politisoiminen'. *Kosmopolis* 49, no. 3 (2019): 28–47.

Kaplan, Jeffrey. *Encyclopedia of White Power: A Sourcebook on the Radical Racist Right*. London: Rowman & Littlefield, 2000.

Kaplan, Merrill. 'The State of Vinland'. In *Norse Myths as Political Ideologies: Critical Studies of the Appropriation of Medieval Narratives*, edited by Nicolas Meylan and Lukas Rösli, 233–49. Turnhout: Brepols, 2020.

Kappeler, Andreas. *The Russian Empire: A Multiethnic History*, New York: Routledge, 2013.

Katajala, Kimmo. 'Drawing Borders or Dividing Lands?: The Peace Treaty of 1323 between Sweden and Novgorod in a European Context'. *Scandinavian Journal of History* 37, no. 1 (2012): 23–48.

Kattago, Siobhan. 'War Memorials and the Politics of Memory: The Soviet War Memorial in Tallinn'. *Constellations* 16, no. 1 (2009): 150–66.

Kattago, Siobhan. 'Written in Stone: Monuments and Representation'. In *The Ashgate Research Companion to Memory Studies*, edited by Siobhan Kattago, 179–95. Farnham, Surrey, UK: Routledge, 2014.

Kaufman, Amy S. 'Medieval Unmoored'. *Studies in Medievalism: Defining Neomedievalism(s)* 19 (2010): 1–11.

Kaufman, Amy S. 'Purity'. In *Medievalism. Key Critical Terms*, edited by Elizabeth Emery and Richard Utz, 199–207. Cambridge: D. S. Brewer, 2014.

Kaufman, Amy S. 'Muscular Medievalism'. *This Year's Work in Medievalism* 31 (2016): 56–66.

Kaufman, Amy S. 'Dark Revivals: Medievalism and ISIS'. *The Public Medievalist*, 2014. http://www.publicmedievalist.com/dark-revivals-medievalism-isis/ (Accessed 27 October 2014).

Kaufman, Amy S., and Paul B. Sturtevant. *The Devil's Historians: How Modern Extremists Abuse the Medieval Past*. Toronto: University of Toronto Press, 2020.

Khapaeva, Dina. 'Neomedievalism as a Future Society: The Case of Russia'. *The Year's Work in Medievalism* 32 (2017). https://sites.google.com/site/theyearsworkinmedievalism/all-issues/32-2017

Khal'bvaks, M. [Maurice Halbwachs]. *Sotsial'nye ramki pamiati*, edited and translated by. S. N. Zenkina. Moscow: Novoye izdatel'stvo, 2007.

Khazagerov, G. G. *Ritorika totalitarizma: stanovlenie, rastsvet, kollaps (sovetskii opyt)*. Rostov-on-Don: IuFU, 2012.

King, Francis. 'Making Virtual (Non)sense of the Past: Russian Nationalist Interpretations of Twentieth-century History on the Internet'. In *Nationalist Myths and Modern Media: Cultural Identity in the Age of Globalisation*, edited by Jand Herman Brinks, Stella Rock, and Edward Timms, 215–28, London: I.B. Tauris, 2014.

Kingstone, Helen. *Victorian Narratives of the Recent Past: Memory, History, Fiction*. New York: Springer, 2017.

Kivikoski, Ella. 'Suomen varhaisin kristillisyys muinaistieteellisen aineiston valossa'. In *Novella plantatio. Suomen kirkkohistoriallisen seuran juhlakirja Suomen kirkon juhlavuotena*. Suomen Kirkkohistoriallisen Seuran toimituksia 56, 21–41. Helsinki: [Suomen Kirkkohistoriallinen Seura], 1955.

Kline, Daniel T. 'Participatory Medievalism, Role-Playing, and Digital Gaming'. In *The Cambridge Companion to Medievalism*, edited by Louise D'Arcens, 75–88. Cambridge: Cambridge University Press, 2016.

Koho, Timo. 'Monikasvoinen arkkitehtuuri'. In *Suomalaisten symbolit*, edited by Tero Halonen and Laura Aro, 72–7. Jyväskylä: Atena, 2005.

Kolstø, Pål. 'The Ethnification of Russian Nationalism'. In *The New Russian Nationalism: Imperialism, Ethnicity and Authoritarianism 2000–2015*, edited by Pål Kolstø and Helge Blakkisrud, 18–45, Edinburgh: Edinburgh University Press, 2016.

Koltsova, Olessia, and Sergei Koltcov. 'Mapping the Public Agenda with Topic Modeling: The Case of the Russian Livejournal: The Case of the Russian LiveJournal (2011–2012)'. *Policy & Internet* 5, no. 2 (2013): 207–27.

Koltsova, Olessia, Sergei Koltcov, and Sergey Nikolenko. 'Communities of Co-Commenting in the Russian LiveJournal and Their Topical Coherence'. *Internet Research* 26, no. 3 (2016): 710–32.

Konaneva, D. D. 'Srednevekov'e i otechestvennaia igroindustriia'. *Istoricheskaia ekspertiza*, no. 4 (2018): 163–72.

Korpela, Jukka. *Itä-Euroopan historia keskiajalta 1700-luvulle*. Helsinki: Gaudeamus, 1999.

Korpela, Jukka. 'Finland's Eastern Border after the Treaty of Nöteborg: An Ecclesiastical, Political or Cultural Border?' *Journal of Baltic Studies* 33, no. 4 (2002): 384–97.

Korpela, Jukka. 'Keskiaikainen itäraja läpi itäisen Fennoskandian metsävyöhykkeen – mikä se on!' *Historiallinen Aikakauskirja* 104, no. 4 (2006): 454–69.

Korpela, Jukka. '"The Russian Threat against Finland" in the Western Sources before the Peace of Noteborg (1323)'. *Scandinavian Journal of History* 22, no. 3 (1997): 161–72.

Korpela, Jukka. *The World of Ladoga: Society, Trade, Transformation and State Building in the Eastern Fennoscandian Boreal Forest Zone c. 1000 –1555*. Berlin: Lit, 2008.

Koschutzki, Dirk, Katharina Anna Lehmann, Leon Peeters, Stefan Richter, Dagmar Tenfelde-Podehl, and Oliver Zlotowski. 'Centrality Indices'. In *Network Analysis: Methodological Foundations*, edited by Ulrik Brandes and Thomas Erlebach, 16–61. New York: Springer, 2005.

Koselleck, Reinhard. 'War Memorials: Identity Formations of the Survivors'. In *The Practice of conceptual history*, translated by Todd Presner, 285–326. Stanford: Stanford University Press, 2002.

Koselleck, Reinhart. *Futures Past: On the Semantics of Historical Time*. New York: Columbia University Press, 2004.

Kosiński, Tomasz. *Runy słowiańskie*. Warszawa: Bellona, 2019.

Koskinen, Inkeri. *Villi Suomen historia: Välimeren Väinämöisestä Äijäkupittaan pyramideihin*. Helsinki: Kustannusosakeyhtiö Tammi, 2015.

Kossakowski, Winicjusz. *Polskie runy przemówiły*. Białystok: Wydano nakł. autora, 2008.

Kowalski, Krzysztof M. 'The Fascination with Runes in Nineteenth- and Early Twentieth-Century Poland'. In *Roman, Runes and Ogham. Medieval Inscriptions in the Insular World and on the Continent*, edited by John Higgitt, Kathryn Forsyth, and D. N. Parsons, 134–47. Donington: Shaun Tyas, 2001.

Krawczuk, Wojciech. 'Runic Inscriptions in Poland: Do We Need an Inventory?' *Studia historyczne* 56, no. 3 (2013): 431–5.

Krivosheev, Iu. V., and R. A. Sokolov. *'Aleksdandr Nevskii': sozdanie kinoshedvra. Istoricheskoe issledovanie*. St Petersburg: Liki Rossii, 2012.

Krueger, David M. *Myths of the Rune Stone. Viking Martyrs and the Birthplace of America*. Minneapolis: University of Minnesota Press, 2015.

Kubik, Bálint György, and Boróka Pápay. 'The Boundaries and External Connections of the Hyperlink Network of Hungarian Websites in Romania'. *Intersections; Budapest* 3, no. 1 (2017).

Kurilla, I., S. Ivanov, and A. Selin. "Russia, My History': History as an Ideological Tool'. *PONARS Eurasia*, 5 August 2018. http://www.ponarseurasia.org/point-counter/russia-my-history-as-ideological-tool (Accessed 28 May 2020).

Kuzio, Taras. 'Nation Building, History Writing and Competition over the Legacy of Kyiv Rus in Ukraine'. *Nationalities Papers* 33, no. 1 (2005): 29–58.

Lahelma, Antti, Jouko Pukkila, and Tapani Rostedt. 'Fake or Not? Some Observations on Finds of Runic Inscriptions in South-Western Finland'. In *Runes in Finland*, edited by Kendra Willson. Forthcoming.

Laine, Veera. 'New Generation of Victors: Narrating the Nation in Russian Presidential Discourse 2012–2019'. *Demokratizatsiya: The Journal of Post-Soviet Democratization* 28, no 4 (2020): 517–40.

Lakomäki, Sami, Sirpa Aalto, and Ritva Kylli. 'Näkymättömissä ja kuulumattomissa? Saamelaiset ja koloniaaliset arkistot'. *Historiallinen Aikakauskirja* 118, no. 4 (2020): 438–50.

Länsisyrjä, Erkki. 'Legendan jälki maisemassa. Pyhän Henrikin tein historiaa ja tätä päivää'. MA diss., University of Turku, Turku, 2014.

Laruelle, Marlene. 'Russia as an Anti-Liberal European Civilisation'. In *The New Russian Nationalism: Imperialism, Ethnicity and Authoritarianism 2000–2015*, edited by Pål Kolstø and Helge Blakkisrud, 275–97. Edinburgh: Edinburgh University Press, 2016.

Lassander, Mika. 'Pakanuus nykypäivän Suomessa'. In *Monien uskontojen ja katsomusten Suomi*, edited by Ruth Illman, Kimmo Ketola, Riitta Latvio, and Jussi Sohlberg, 202–12. Tampere: Kirkon Tutkimuskeskus, 2017.

Leerssen, Joep. 'Nation and Ethnicity'. In *The Contested Nation: Ethnicity, Class, Religion and Gender in National Histories*, edited by Stefan Berger and Chris Lorenz, 75–103. Basingstoke: Palgrave Macmillan, 2008.

Lenhoff, Gail. 'The Construction of Russian History in *Stepennaia Kniga*'. *Revue des études slaves* 76, no. 1 (2005): 31–50.

Leont'eva, O. B. 'Lichnost' Ivana Groznogo v istoricheskoi pamiati rossiiskogo obshchestva epokhi velikikh reform: nauchnoe znanie i khudozhestvennyi obraz'. *Dialog so vremenem* 18 (2007): 19–34.

Leont'eva, O. B. *Istoricheskaia pamiat' i obrazy proshlogo v rossiiskoi kul'ture XIX – nachala XX vv*. Samara: OOO 'Kniga', 2011.

Lewandowsky, Stephan, and John Cook. 'The Conspiracy Theory Handbook'. 2020. https://www.climatechangecommunication.org/conspiracy-theory-handbook/ (Accessed 18 May 2020).

Lind, John H. 'Early Russian-Swedish Rivalry: The Battle on the Neva in 1240 and Birger Magnussons' Second Crusade to Tavastia'. *Scandinavian Journal of History* 16, no. 4 (1991): 269–95.

Lind, John H. 'Nødeborgsfreden i Russisk Forskning'. In *Nöteborgsfreden och Finlands medeltida östgräns*, vol. 2, by Jarl Gallén and John H. Lind, 250–82. Helsingfors: Svenska litteratursällskapet i Finland, 1991.

Lindquist, Ivar. 'Nya rön om ett par runristningar'. *Åländsk odling* 29 (1968): 18–53.

Lindquist, Ivar. 'Ålands runinskrift, Sund-korset'. *Åländsk odling* 30 (1969): 36–51.

Lotman, Iu. M., and B. A. Uspenskij. 'The Role of Dual Models in the Dynamics of Russian Culture (Up to the End of the Eighteenth Century)'. In *The Semiotics of Russian Culture*, edited by A. Shukman, 3–35. Ann Arbor: Dept. of Slavic Languages and Literatures, University of Michigan, 1984.

Lowenthal, D. *The Past is a Foreign Country*. Cambridge: Cambridge University Press, 2011.

Löytty, Olli. 'Johdanto: Toiseuttamista ja tilakurittomuutta'. In *Rajanylityksiä – tutkimusreittejä toiseuden tuolle puolen*, edited by Olli Löytty, 7–24. Helsinki: Gaudeamus, 2005.

Ludovico, Nuccio, Marc Esteve Del Valle, and Franco Ruzzenenti. 'Mapping the Dutch Energy Transition Hyperlink Network'. *Sustainability* 12, no. 18 (2020): 7629.

Lund, Erla. 'Folksed och folktro i Malaks, Pörtom och Övermark'. SLS 524, SLS arkiv (1931).

McCall, Jeremiah. 'Video Games as Participatory Public History'. In *A Companion to Public History*, edited by David M. Dean, 405–15. Hoboken: Wiley Blackwell, 2018.

McCall, Jeremiah. 'Playing with the Past: History and Video Games (and Why it Might Matter)'. *Journal of Geek Studies* 6, no. 1 (2019): 29–48.

McGlynn, Jade. 'Engaging Young Russians in Military History'. *ZOIS Spotlight*, 21 October 2020. https://en.zois-berlin.de/publications/zois-spotlight/engaging-young-russians-in-military-history/ (Accessed 15 December 2020).

Mäkelä, Heidi Henriikka. 'The Desired Darkness of the Ancient: Kalevala-Metric Poetry, Medievalism, and Cultural Memory in the Books Niemi and Viiden meren kansa'. *Mirator* 21, no. 1 (2021): 22–49.

Makovskaya, Darya. 'Istoricheskii mif i etnicheskii konflikt: teorija, metodologija, tekhnologija konstruirovanija'. *Nauchnaya mysl' Kavkaza* 1 (2014): 77.

Malinova, Olga. 'Political Uses of the Great Patriotic War in Post-Soviet Russia from Yeltsin to Putin'. In *War and memory in Russia, Ukraine and Belarus*, edited by Julie Fedor, Markku Kangaspuro, Jussi Lassila, and Tatiana Zhurzhenko, 43–70. Cham: Palgrave Macmillan, 2017.

Marshall, David W. 'Neomedievalism, Identification, and the Haze of Medievalisms'. *Studies in Medievalism: Defining Neomedievalism(s) II* 20 (2011): 21–34.

Martin, Janet. *Medieval Russia: 980–1584*. 2nd edn. Cambridge Medieval Textbooks. Cambridge: Cambridge University Press, 2007.

Martin, Shawn, W. Michael Brown, Richard Klavans, and Kevin W. Boyack. 'OpenOrd: An Open-Source Toolbox for Large Graph Layout'. In *Visualization and Data Analysis 2011*, 7868:786806. International Society for Optics and Photonics, 2011.

Mayer, Lauryn. 'Mythogyny: Popular Medievalism and Toxic Masculinity'. *Studies in Medievalism* 29 (2019): 21–32.

Messenius, Johannes. *Suomen, Liivinmaan ja Kuurinmaan vaiheita sekä tuntemattoman tekijän Suomen kronikka*. Translated from Latin by Martti Linna, Jorma Lagerstedt, and Erkki Palmén. Helsinki: SKS, 1988.

Metzger, Miriam J., and Andrew J. Flanagin. 'Credibility and Trust of Information in Online Environments: The Use of Cognitive Heuristics'. *Journal of Pragmatics* 59 (2013): 210–20.

Mikhailova, I. B. 'Moskovskoe tsarstvo XVI v istorichesko pamiati russkogo naroda (po graviuram iz sobraniia D. A. Rovinskogo)'. *Arkhivy i istoriia rossiiskoi gosudarstvennosti*, St Petersburg 1 (2011): 22–8.

Milligan, Ian. *History in the Age of Abundance? How the Web Is Transforming Historical Research*. Montreal: McGill-Queen's Press - MQUP, 2019.

Mills, Kathy A. 'What Are the Threats and Potentials of Big Data for Qualitative Research?'. *Qualitative Research* 18, no. 6 (2018): 591–603.

Mir, Rebecca, and Trevor Owens. 'Modeling Indigenous Peoples: Unpacking Ideology in *Sid Meier's Colonization*'. in *Playing with the Past. Digital Games and the Simulation of History*, edited by Matthew W. Kapell and Andrew B. R. Elliott, 91–106. New York: Bloomsbury, 2013.

Moilanen, Mikko. *Marks of Fire, Value and Faith. Swords with Ferrous Inlays in Finland during the Late Iron Age (ca. 700–1200 AD)*. Turku: Suomen keskiajan arkeologian seura, 2015.

Moilanen, Mikko. *Viikinkimiekat Suomessa*. Helsinki: SKS, 2018.

Morishima, Atsuyuki, Rong Zhang, Wenjie Zhang, Lijun Chang, Tom Z. J. Fu, Kuien Liu et al. 'Confirmatory Analysis on Influencing Factors When Mention Users on Twitter'. *Web Technologies and Applications: APWeb 2016 Workshops, WDMA, GAP, and SDMA, Suzhou, China, September 23–25, 2016, Proceedings*. Cham: Springer, 2016.

Mulhall, Joe. 'Generation Identity UK Isolated and in Crisis'. *HOPE not hate*, 29 July 2019. https://www.hopenothate.org.uk/2019/07/29/generation-identity-uk-isolated-and-in-crisis/ (Accessed 1 September 2020).

Mullins, Paul. *Revolting Things: An Archaeology of Shameful Histories and Repulsive Realities*. Gainesville: University Press of Florida, 2021.

Mut'ia, N. N. *Ivan groznyi: istorizm i lichnost' pravitelia v otechestvennom iskusstve XIX–XX vv*. St Petersburg: Aleteiia, 2010.

Myllylahti, Merja. 'Newspaper Paywalls—the Hype and the Reality: A Study of How Paid News Content Impacts on Media Corporation Revenues'. *Digital Journalism* 2, no. 2 (2014): 179–94.

Naddeo, Michelangelo. *Germanico Runes: a Finnish Alphabet?* S.l.: s.n., 2006.

Nestor the Chronicler. *The Russian Primary Chronicle: Laurentian Text*, edited by Samuel H. Cross and Olgerd P. Sherbowitz-Wetzor. Cambridge, MA: Mediaeval Academy of America, 2012.

Nieminen, Jukka. *Muinaissuomalaisten kadonnut kuningaskunta*. S.l.: Kirjaparoni oy, 2010.

Nieminen, Jukka. *Vaiettu muinaisuus*. S.l.: Salakirjat, 2015.

Nikula, Riitta. 'Klassismi maailman sotien välisen ajan suomalaisessa arkkitehtuurissa'. In *Kivettyneet ihanteet? Klassismin nousu maailmasotien välisessä Euroopassa,* edited by Marja Härmänmaa and Timo Vihavainen, 315–43. Jyväskylä: Atena, 2000.

Niven, Bill. 'War Memorials at the Intersection of Politics, Culture and Memory'. *Journal of War and Culture Studies* 1, no. 1 (2008): 39–45.

Noppari, Elina, and Ilmari Hiltunen. 'Populistinen vastamedia eliittejä haastamassa'. In *Media & populismi: Työkaluja kriittiseen journalismiin*, edited by Mari K. Niemi and Topi Houni, 236–72. Tampere: Vastapaino, 2018.

Nora, Pierre. 'From *Lieux de mémoire* to *Realms of Memory*'. In *Realms of Memory: the Construction of the French Past*, under the direction of Pierre Nora, xv–xxiv. New York: Columbia University Press, 1996.

Nordling, Arnold. 'Varför tyckas inga runinskrifter ha utförts i Finland?' *Finsk tidskrift* 125 (1938): 35–43.

Norris, Stephen. M. *A War of Images. Russian Popular Prints, Wartime Culture, and National Identity 1812–1945*. DeKalb: Northern Illinois University Press, 2006.

Norris, Stephen. M. *Blockbuster History in the New Russia: Movies, Memory, and Patriotism*. Bloomington: Indiana University Press, 2012.

Norrman, Ralf. *Vörårunorna. Del 1. En bok om runinskrifterna i Höjsal och Härtull*. Jakobstad: Jakobstads tryckeri, 1983.

Nurminen, Matias. 'Narrative Warfare: The 'Careless' Reinterpretation of Literary Canon in Online Antifeminism'. *Narrative Inquiry* 29, no. 2 (2019): 313–32.

Oja, Heikki. *Riimut: viestejä viikingeiltä*. Helsinki: Suomalaisen Kirjallisuuden Seura, 2015.

Ojansuu, Heikki. *Suomalaista paikannimitutkimusta 1. Tähänastisen tutkimuksen arvostelua*. Turun suomalaisen yliopistoseuran julkaisuja 41. Helsinki: Otava, 1920.

Olesen, Jens E. 'The Swedish Expeditions ('Crusades') Towards Finland Reconsidered'. In *Church and Belief in the Middle Ages: Popes, Saints, and Crusaders*, edited by Kirsi Salonen and Sari Katajala-Peltomaa, 251–68. Amsterdam: Amsterdam University Press, 2016.

Östling, Johan, David Larsson Heidenblad, Erling Sandmo, Anna Nilsson Hammar, and Kari H. Nordberg. 'The History of Knowledge and Circulation of Knowledge. An Introduction'. In *Circulation of Knowledge: Explorations in the History of Knowledge*, edited by Johan Östling, Erling Sandmo, David Larsson Heidenblad, Anna Nilsson Hammar, and Kari H. Nordberg, 9–33. Lund: Nordic Academic Press, 2018.

Oula, Mikko. *"Suomi sitoutuu hajoittamaan…" Järjestöjen lakkauttaminen vuoden 1944 välirauhansopimuksen 21. artiklan perusteella*. Historiallisia tutkimuksia 205. Helsinki: Suomen Historialinen Seura, 1999.

Översti, Sanni, Kerttu Majander, Elina Salmela, Kati Salo, Laura Arppe, Stanislav Belskiy, Heli Etu-Sihvola, et al. 'Human Mitochondrial DNA Lineages in Iron-Age Fennoscandia Suggest Incipient Admixture and Eastern Introduction of Farming-Related Maternal Ancestry'. *Scientific Reports* 9, no. 1 (2019): 1–14.

Owen, Suzanne. 'The World Religions Paradigm: Time for a Change'. *Arts and Humanities in Higher Education* 10, no. 3 (2011): 253–68.

Ozok, Ant, and Panayiotis Zaphiris. 'Why People Use Social Networking Sites'. *Online Communities and Social Computing: 5th International Conference, OCSC 2013, Held as Part of HCI International 2013, Las Vegas, NV, USA, July 21–26, 2013, Proceedings*. Berlin: Springer, 2013.

Paakki, Kalevi. *Vaasan patsaat ja muistomerkit – Vasas statyer och minnesmärken*. Vaasa: Vaasan kaupunki, 2008.

Pain, Emil. 'Contemporary Russian nationalism in the Historical Struggle Between "Official Nationality" and "Popular Sovereignty"'. In *Russia Before and After Crimea: Nationalism and Identity, 2010–17*, edited by Pål Kolstø and Helge Blakkisrud, 23–49. Edinburgh: Edinburgh University Press, 2018.

Pantti, Mervi, Matti Nelimarkka, Kaarina Nikunen, and Gavan Titley. 'The Meanings of Racism: Public Discourses about Racism in Finnish News Media and Online Discussion Forums'. *European Journal of Communication* 34, no. 5 (2019): 503–19.

Parent, Mike C., Teresa D. Gobble, and Aaron Rochlen. 'Social Media Behavior, Toxic Masculinity, and Depression'. *Psychology of Men & Masculinities* 20, no. 3 (2019): 277–87.

Parppei, Kati. *The Battle of Kulikovo Refought – 'The First National Feat'*. Leiden: Brill, 2017.

Parppei, Kati. 'Enemy Images in the Russian National Narrative'. In *Nexus of Patriotism and Militarism in Russia – A Quest for Internal Cohesion*, edited by Katri Pynnöniemi, 23–47. Helsinki: Helsinki University Press, 2021.

Pariser, Eli. *The Filter Bubble: What the Internet Is Hiding from You*. Harmondsworth: Penguin UK, 2011.

Pashchenko, L. V. 'Fenomen totalitarizma v traktovke predstavitelei russkogo zarubezh'ia'. *Vestnik Murmanskogo gosudarstvennogo tekhnicheskogo universiteta* 11, no. 1 (2008): 89–93.

Paul, Christopher, and Miriam Matthews. *The Russian 'Firehose of False-Hood' Propaganda Model: Why It Might Work and Options to Counter It*. Santa Monica, CA: RAND Corporation, 2016. https://www.rand.org/pubs/perspectives/PE198.html (Accessed 6 April 2020).

Pelenski, Jaroslaw. 'The Origins of the Official Muscovite Claims to the "Kievan Inheritance"'. *Harvard Ukrainian Studies* 1, no. 1 (1977): 29–52.

Peltonen, Ulla-Maija. 'Sisällissodan muistaminen'. In *Sisällissodan Pikku Jättiläinen*, edited by P. Haapala and T. Hoppu, 464–73. Helsinki: Werner Söderström Osakeyhtiö, 2009.

Petrov, A. E. 'Evoliutsiia pamiati o Kulikovskoi bitve 1380g v epokhu stanovleniia Moskovskogo samoderzhaviia (rubezh XV–XVIvv.): K voprosu o momente transformatsii mesta pamiati'. *Istoricheskie zapiski* 7, no. 125 (2004): 35–56.

Pikkanen, Ilona. 'The Dangers of 'Too Easy a Life'. Aarno Karimo's Historical Vignettes and the Post-Civil War Nation'. In *Novels, Histories, Novel Nations. Historical Fiction and Cultural Memory in Finland and Estonia*, edited by Linda Kaljundi, Eneken Laanes, and Ilona Pikkanen, 159–81. Helsinki: Finnish Literature Society, 2015.

Pitruzzello, Jason. 'Systematizing Culture in Medievalism. Geography, Dynasty, Culture, and Imperialism in *Crusader Kings: Deus Vult*'. In *Digital Gaming Re-imagines the Middle Ages*, edited by David T. Kline, 43–53. London: Routledge, 2014.

Platt, Kevin M. F. 'Allegory's Half-Life: The Specter of a Stalinist Ivan the Terrible in Russia Today'. *Penn History Review* 17, no. 2 (2010): 9–24.

Platt, Kevin M. F. *Terror and Greatness: Ivan and Peter as Russian Myths*. Ithaca, NY: Cornell University Press, 2011.

Pranskevičiūtė, Rasa. 'Contemporary Paganism in Lithuanian Context: Principal Beliefs and Practices of Romuva'. In *Modern Pagan and Native Faith Movements in Central and Eastern Europe*, edited by Kaarina Aitamurto and Scott Simpson, 77–93. London: Routedge, 2014.

Raninen, Sami, and Anna Wessman. 'Finland as a Part of the "Viking World"'. In *Fibula, Fabula, Fact. The Viking Age in Finland*, edited by Joonas Ahola and Frog, with Clive Tolley, 327–46. Helsinki: Finnish Literature Society, 2014.

Rees-Mogg, Jacob. *The Victorians: Twelve Titans Who Forged Britain*. London: Random House, 2019.

Repina, L. P. *Kul'turnaia pamiat' i problem istoriopisaniia (istoriograficheskie zametki)*. Moscow: GU VSHE [SU HSE], 2003.

Riasanovsky, Nicholas V., and Mark D. Steinberg. *A History of Russia*. 7th edn. New York: Oxford University Press, 2005.

Roselius, Aapo. *Kiista, eheys, unohdus. Vapaussodan muistaminen suojeluskuntien ja veteraaniliikkeen toiminnassa 1918–1944*. Helsinki: Suomen Tiedeseura, 2010.

Rostovtsev, E. A. 'Dopetrovskaia Rus' v zhanre internet-anekdota'. *Istoricheskaia ekspertiza* 4 (2018): 173–84.

Rostovtsev, E. A. 'Srednevekov'e na karte pamiati rossiikogo obshchestva v kontekste istoriografii memory studies'. In *Mavrodinskie chteniia 2018. Materialy Vserossiiskoi nauchnoi konferentsii, posviashchennoi 110-letiiu so dnia rozhdeniia professora Vladimira Vasil'evicha Mavrodina*, edited by. A. Iu. Dvornichenko, 185–9. St Petersburg: Nestor-istoriia, 2018.

Rostovtsev, E. A. 'The Immortal Host of Prince Igor'. *Vestnik of Saint-Petersburg University, History* 65, no. 3 (2020): 883–903.

Rostovtsev, E. A., and D. A. Sosnitskii. 'Napravleniia issledovanii istoricheskoi pamiati v Rossii'. *Vestnik SPbGU*, Seriia: Istoriia, 2 (2014): 106–26.

Rostovtsev, E. A., and D. A. Sosnitskii. 'Zabytyi zolotoi vek: Yaroslav Mudryi i Rus' Yaroslava – pereosmyleniia XIX – nachala XIX v'. *Rusin* 4, no. 4 (2016): 26–43.

Rostovtsev, E. A., and D. A. Sosnitskii. "Kulikovskii plen': obraz Dmitriia Donskogo v natsional'noi istoricheskoi pamiati'. *Quaestio Rossica* 5, no. 4 (2017): 1149–63.

Rostovtsev, E. A., and D. A. Sosnitskii. 'Russkoe srednevekov'e v kommercheskoi reklame: postanovka problemy i perspektivy issledovaniia (vtoraia polovina XIX-nachalo XXI vv.)'. *Drevniaia Rus': vo vremeni, v lichnostiakh, v ideiakh* 7 (2017): 398–416.

Rostovtsev, E. A., and D. A. Sosnitskii. 'Srednekovye sobytiia i geroi v sovetskikh otryvnykh kalendariakh'. *Noveishaia istoriia Rossii* 3 (2017): 163–81.

Rostovtsev, E. A., and D. A. Sosnitskii. 'Srednevekovye geroi i sobytiia otechestvennoi istorii v setevykh resursakh'. *Istoricheskaia ekspertiza* 1 (2018): 41–58.

Rostovtsev, E. A., and D. A. Sosnitskii. 'Kniaz' Vladimir Velikii kak national'nyi geroi: sozdanie obraza'. *Dialog so vremenem* 4, no. 65 (2018): 150–64.

Rostovtsev, E. A., and D. A. Sosnitskii. 'Vladimir Sviatoi kak natsional'nyi geroi: voskreshenie obraza'. *Dialog so vremenem* 4, no. 69 (2019): 307–21.

Rusanov, A. B. 'Medievalism Studies: kak izuchaetsia "sovremennoe Srednevekov"e?'. *Vox medii aevi* 2, no. 5: 12–42. http://voxmediiaevi.com/2019-2-rusanov (Accessed 1 August 2020).

Saarikangas, Kirsi. 'Puu, metsä ja luonto. Arkkitehtuuri suomalaisuuden rankentamisena ja rakentumisena'. In *Suomi: Outo pohjoinen maa? Näkökulmia Euroopan äären historiaan ja kulttuuriin*, edited by Tuomas M. S. Lehtonen, 166–207. Jyväskylä: PS-Kustannus, 1999.

Said, Edward W. *Orientalism*. 1978. Reprint, London: Penguin Books, 2008.

Saler, Benson. *Conceptualizing Religion: Immanent Anthropologists, Transcendent Natives, and Unbound Categories*. New York: Berghahn Books, 2000.

Sarviaho, Samu. 'Ikuinen rauha: vuoden 1323 Pähkinäsaaren rauha suomalaisessa historiantutkimuksessa ja historiakulttuurissa 1800- ja 1900-luvuilla'. PhD diss., Oulun yliopisto, Oulu, 2017.

Savel'eva, I. M., and A. V. Poletaev. *Znanie o proshlom: teoriia i istoriia*, vol. 1. St Petersburg: Nauka, 2006.

Savel'eva, Tat'iana. 'Mifotvorchestvo kak mediatekhnologija XXI veka'. *Znak: problemnoe pole mediaobrazovanija* 2, no. 24 (2017): 87–91.

Sawyer, Birgit. 'Viking-Age Rune-Stones as a Crisis Symptom'. *Norwegian Archaeological Journal* 24, no. 2 (1991): 97–112.

Saxén, Ralf. 'Den svenska befolkningens ålder i Finland, belyst av ortnamn'. *Finska fornminnesföreningens tidskrift* 21, no. 3 (1901): 1–46.

Schenk, Frithjof Benjamin. *Aleksandr Nevskij: Heiliger, Fürst, Nationalheld: eine Erinnerungsfigur im russischen kulturellen Gedächtnis (1263–2000)*. Köln: Böhlau, 2004.

Schmidt, Matthew. 'Is Putin Pursuing a Policy of Eurasianism?'. *Demokratizatsiya: The Journal of Post-Soviet Democratization* 13, no. 1 (2005): 87–100.

Schwill, Andreas. 'Cognitive Aspects of Object-Oriented Programming'. *IFIP WG 3.1 Working Conference "Integrating Information Technology into Education"*, 1994.

Seitsonen, Oula, Paul R. Mullins and Timo Ylimaunu. 'Public Memory, National Heritage, and Memorialization of the 1918 Finnish Civil War'. *World Archaeology* 51, no. 5 (2019): 741–758. https://www.tandfonline.com/doi/full/10.1080/00438243.2020.1724821 (Accessed 10 May 2020).

Selart, Anti. *Livonia, Rus' and the Baltic Crusades in the Thirteenth Century*. Leiden; Boston: Brill, 2015.

Selin, A. A. 'Obraz Ryurika v sovremennom prostranstve Severo-Zapada Rossii'. *Istoricheskaia ekspertiza* 4 (2016): 89–110.

Sergeev, Dmitrii. 'Osnovnoe soderzhanie izobretennoi arkhaiki kak strategii preodolenija kul'turnogo krizisa'. *Gumanitarnyi vektor* 1 (2010): 188–92.

Shabarova, Iu. V., ed. *Obshchestvo vozrozhdeniia khudozhestvennoi Rusi i Fedorovskii gorodok Tsarskogo sela (sbornik dokumentov i materialov)*. St Petersburg: Obshchestvo russkoy traditsionnoy kul'tury, 2013.

Sheiko, Konstantin, and Stephen Brown. *History as Therapy: Alternative History and Nationalist Imaginings in Russia, 1991–2014*. Stuttgart: Ibidem-Verlag, 2014.

Shenk, F. B. *Aleksandr Nevskii v russkoi kul'turnoi pamiati: sviatoi, pravitel', natsional'nyi geroi (1263–2000)*, translated by E. Zemskovoi and M. Larinovich. Moscow: Novoe literaturnoe obozrenie, 2007.

Sherwin, Reider Thorbjorn. *The Viking and the Red Man: The Old Norse Origin of the Algonquin Language*. New York & London: Funk & Wagnalls, 1940.

Shirky, Clay. *Here Comes Everybody: The Power of Organizing Without Organizations*. New York, NY; Toronto; London: Penguin Books, 2009.

Shutova, V. A. 'Evoliutsiia doktriny totalitarizma v sotsiologii SSHA v 1960–1970-kh vv'. In *Metodologicheskie problemy nauki*, edited by Yu.V. Petrov, 135–42. Tomsk: Izd-vo TGU, 1978.

Sjöstrand, Per Olof. 'History Gone Wrong. Interpretations of the Transition from the Viking Age to the Medieval Period in Åland'. In *The Viking Age in Åland. Insights into Identity and Remnants of Culture*, edited by Joonas Ahola, Frog, and Jenny Lucenius, 83–152. Helsinki: Academia Scientiarum Fennica, 2014.

Smelyansky, Eugene. 'Enemies at the Gate: Political Medievalism, Russian Style'. *The Public Medievalist*, 15 April 2021. https://www.publicmedievalist.com/medievalism-russia-nevsky/ (Accessed 16 May 2020).

Sokolov, R. A. 'Aleksandr Nevskii v otechestvennoi kul'ture i istoricheskoi pamiati'. PhD diss., St Petersburg State University (SPGU), 2013.

Sosnitskii, D. A. 'Ivan Groznyi v istoricheskoi pamiati russkogo naroda (na materialakh khudozhestvennoi, publitsisticheskoi i uchebnoi literatury)'. In *Lichnost' v istorii v epokhu novogo i noveishego vremeni (pamiati professora S. I. Voroshilova). Materialy mezhdunarodnoi nauchnoi konferentsii*, edited by V. A. Ushakov, 471–4. St Petersburg: Izdatel'skiy dom Sankt-Peterburgskogo gosudarstvennogo universiteta, 2011.

Sosnitskii, D. A. 'Vladimir Sviatoi v istoricheskoi pamiati rossiiskogo obshchestva vtoroi poloviny XIX – nachala XXI veka (po materialam narrativnykh istochnikov)'. *Nauchno-tekhnicheskie vedomosti SPbGPU. Gumanitarnye i obshchestvennye nauki* 3, no. 203 (2014): 100–6.

Sosnitskii, D. A. 'Istoricheskaia pamiat' o dopetrovskoi Rusi v Rossii vtoroi poloviny XIX—nachala XXI vv'. PhD diss., St Petersburg State University (SPGU), 2015.

Sosnitskii, D. A. "Poslednii geroi russkogo srednevekov'ia': Stepan Razin v massovom istoricheskom soznanii rossiiskogo obshchestva'. In *Problemy i tendentsii razvitiia sotsiokul'turnogo prostranstva Rossii: istoriia i sovremennost'*. *Materialy V mezhdunarodnoi nauchno-prakticheskoi konferentsii*, edited by. T. I. Riabova, 146–52. Bryansk: Federal'noye gosudarstvennoe byudzhetnoye obrazovatel'noe uchrezhdeniye vysshego obrazovaniya 'Bryanskiy gosudarstvennyi inzhenerno-tekhnologicheskiy universitet', 2018.

Spivak, Gayatri Chakravorty. 'Can the Subaltern Speak?' In *Marxism and the Interpretation of Culture*, edited by Cary Nelson and Lawrence Grossberg, 66–111. Urbana: University of Illinois Press, 1988.

SSA. *Suomen sanojen alkuperä. Etymologinen sanakirja*. 3 vols. Helsinki: Suomalaisen Kirjallisuuden Seura / Kotimaisten kielten tutkimuskeskus, 1992–2000.

Stalsberg, Anne. 'The Vlfberht Sword Blades Reevaluated'. *Zeitschrift für Archäologie des Mittelalters* 36 (2008): 89–118.

Starbird, Kate, Ahmer Arif, Tom Wilson, Katherine Van Koevering, Katya Yefimova, and Daniel Scarnecchia. 'Ecosystem or Echo-System? Exploring Content Sharing across Alternative Media Domains'. In *Proceedings of the Twelfth International AAAI Conference on Web and Social Media*, 365–74, 2018.

Sulakadzev, A. I. 'Yeshche ob odnoy rukopisi A. I. Sulakadzeva'. In *Trudy Otdela drevnerusskoy literatury Instituta russkogo yazyka i literatury*, edited by A. I. Pokrovskaya, T. XIV L, 634–7. Leningrad: Institut russkoy literatury (Pushkinskiy Dom), 1958.

Sumner, B. H. *Survey of Russian History*. London: Duckworth, 1947.

Suvanto, Seppo. 'Keskiaika'. In *Suomen historia 2*, edited by Eero Laaksonen and Erkki Pärssinen, 8–225. Espoo: Weilin+Göös, 1985.

Symonds, James, Timo Ylimaunu, Anna-Kaisa Salmi, Risto Nurmi, Titta Kallio-Seppä, Tiina Kuokkanen, Markku Kuorilehto, and Annemari Tranberg. 'Time, Seasonality, and Trade: Swedish/Finnish-Sami Interactions in Early Modern Lapland'. *Historical Archaeology* 49, no. 3 (2015): 74–89.

Taavitsainen, J. P. 'Runinskriften vid Höjsal trask i Vörä'. *Horisont* 27, no. 3 (1980): 37–40.

Talvio, Tuukka. *Coins and Coin Finds in Finland AD 800–1200*. Helsinki: Finnish Antiquarian Society, 2002.

Tarkiainen, Kari. *Sveriges österland. Från forntiden till Gustav Vasa*. Finlands svenska historia 1. Helsingfors: Svenska litteratursällskapet i Finland / Stockholm: Bokförlaget Atlantis, 2008.

Timonina, O. Iu. 'Dukhovnoe znachenie proobraza orla v narodnom iskusstve Drevnei Rusi'. *Iskusstvo i kul'tura* 3 (2015): 78–84.

Torbakov, I., and S. Plokhy. *After Empire: Nationalist Imagination and Symbolic Politics in Russia and Eurasia in the Twentieth and Twenty-First Century*. La Vergne: Ibidem Press, 2018.

Törnquist Plewa, Barbara, Tea Sindbæk Andersen, and Astrid Erll. 'Introduction: On Transcultural Memory and Reception'. In *The Twentieth Century in European Memory: Transcultural Mediation and Reception*, edited by Barbara Törnquist

Plewa and Tea Sindbæk Andersen, 1–23. European Studies 34. Leiden; Boston: Brill, 2017.

Ulam, A. *Bol'sheviki. Prichiny i posledstviia perevorota 1917 goda*, translated by L. A. Igorevsky. Moscow: Centerpolygraph, 2004.

Usachev, A. S. 'Drevneishii period russkoi istorii v istoricheskoi pamiati Moskovskogo tsarstva'. In *Istoriia i pamiat'. Istoricheskaia kul'tura Evropy do nachala novogo vremeni*, edited by L. P. Repina, 609–34. Moscow: Krug, 2006.

Utz, Richard. 'Medievalism is a Global Phenomenon: Including Russia'. *The Year's Work in Medievalism* 32 (2017). https://sites.google.com/site/theyearsworkinmedievalism/all-issues/32-2017.

Vainikka, Eliisa. 'Naisvihan tunneyhteisö – Anonyymisti esitettyä verkkovihaa Ylilaudan ihmissuhdekeskusteluissa'. *Media & Viestintä* 42, no. 1 (2019): 1–25.

Välimäki, Reima. '"Uusi Turku tupineen". Hilda Huntuvuoren (1887–1968) historialliset romaanit ja kuva varhaiskeskiajan Turusta'. In *Turun tuomiokirkon suojissa: pohjoinen hiippakuntakeskus keskiajan ja uuden ajan alun Euroopassa*, edited by Marika Räsänen, Reima Välimäki, and Marjo Kaartinen, 215–40. Turku: Turun historiallinen yhdistys, 2012.

Välimäki, Reima, and Heta Aali. 'The Ancient Finnish Kings and Their Swedish Archenemy: Nationalism, Conspiracy Theories, and Alt-Right Memes in Finnish Online Medievalism'. *Studies in Medievalism* 31 (2022): 55–78.

Välimäki, Reima, Olli Seuri, and Anna Ristilä. 'Pseudohistoriaa Suomen muinaisista kuningaskunnista – Ongelmallisen tiedon kierto laitaoikeiston mediaekosysteemissä'. *niin & näin* 1 (2021): 118–35.

Valkeapää, Leena. 'Historiakulttuurinen keskiaika: tiedon ja mielikuvituksen liitto'. In *Ilmaisun murroksia vuosituhannen vaihteen suomalaisessa kulttuurissa*, edited by Yrjö Heinonen, Leena Kirstinä, and Urpo Kovala, 245–62. Helsinki: Suomalaisen Kirjallisuuden Seura, 2005.

Valkeapää, Leena. 'Käyttökelpoinen keskiaika: historiakulttuuria nykypäivän Ulvilassa ja Raumalla'. *Alue ja ympäristö* 35, no. 2 (2006): 79–91.

Virratvuori, Jussi, ed. *Kiveen hakattu historia. Sulo Strömberg – Kerimäen ja Puruveden alueen historitiedon etsijä ja kerääjä*. Saarijärvi: Kustannusosakeyhtiö HAI, 2012.

Vushko, Iryna. 'Historians at War: History, Politics and Memory in Ukraine'. *Contemporary European History* 27, no. 1 (2018): 112–24.

Wainwright, A. Martin. *Virtual History. How Videogames Portray the Past*. London: Routledge, 2019.

Wallgren, Georg W. *Boken om bomärken*. Helsingfors: Frenckellska tryckeri aktiebolaget, 1965.

Wertsch, James V. *Voices of Collective Remembering*. Cambridge: Cambridge University Press, 2002.

Wiberg, Johan Koren. *Bomerker og innflyttere. Vedkommende Kontoret i Bergen*. Det Hanseatiske Museums Skrifter, no. 10. Bergen: A.s John Griegs Boktrykkeri, 1935.

Wijermars, Mariëlle. *Memory Politics in Contemporary Russia: Television, Cinema and the State*. Studies in Contemporary Russia. London: Routledge, Taylor & Francis Group, 2019.

Williams, Henrik. 'Arizona Runestone Carved in Phony Old Baltic', Uppsala University ms. 2015. s.d. http://files.webb.uu.se/uploader/267/Mustang%20Mountain%20Stone%20-%20release.pdf

Willson, Kendra. 'A Putative Sámi Charm on a 12th c. Icelandic Spade: Runic Reception, Magic and Contacts'. In *Finno-Ugric Folklore, Myth and Cultural Identity. Proceedings of the Fifth International Symposium on Finno-Ugric Languages, University of Groningen, June 7 9, 2011*, edited by Cornelius Hasselblatt and Adriaan van der Hoeven, 267–81. Maastricht: Shaker, 2012.

Willson, Kendra. 'Ahti on the Nydam Strapring. On the Possibility of Finnic Elements in Runic Inscriptions'. In *Contacts and Networks in the Baltic Sea Region: Austmarr as a Northern Mare Nostrum, 500–1500 A.D.*, edited by Maths Bertell, Frog, and Kendra Willson, 147–71. Amsterdam: Amsterdam University Press, 2019.

Winston, Brian. *Messages: Free Expression, Media and the West from Gutenberg to Google*. London: Routledge, 2006.

Winston, Brian. *Misunderstanding Media*. London: Routledge & Kegan Paul, 1986.

Wollenberg, Daniel. 'The New Knighthood: Terrorism and the Medieval'. *Postmedieval: A Journal of Medieval Cultural Studies* 5, no. 1 (2014): 21–33.

Wollenberg, Daniel. 'Defending the West: Cultural Racism and Pan-Europeanism on the Far-Right'. *Postmedieval: A Journal of Medieval Cultural Studies* 5, no. 3 (2014): 308–19.

Wollenberg, Daniel. *Medieval Imagery in Today's Politics*. Kalamazoo: Arc Humanities Press, 2018.

Yentsch, Anne Elizabeth. *A Chesapeake Family and Their Slaves. A Study in Historical Archaeology*, Cambridge: Cambridge University Press, 1994.

Ying, Tianyu, William C. Norman, and Yongguang Zhou. 'Online Networking in the Tourism Industry: A Webometrics and Hyperlink Network Analysis'. *Journal of Travel Research* 55, no. 1 (2016): 16–33.

Ylimaunu, Timo. 'Postimerkit ja identiteetti — kuva suomalaisesta yhteiskunnasta 1930-luvulta'. *Tabellarius* 7 (2005): 95–100.

Ylimaunu, Timo. 'Tornion taistelun muistomerkki'. In *Toinen jalka haudassa: Juhlakirja Juhani Kostetille*, edited by Sanna Lipkin, Titta Kallio-Seppä, Annemari Tranberg, and Tiina Väre, 28–37. Oulu: Oulun yliopisto, 2019.

Ylimaunu, Timo, Georg Haggrén, Risto Nurmi, and Paul R. Mullins. 'Medieval and Early Modern marketplaces: Sites of Contacts, Trade and Religious activies'. In *Sacred Monuments and Practices in the Baltic Sea Region*, edited by Janne Harjula, Sonja Hukantaival, Visa Immonen, Anneli Randla, and Tanja Ratilainen, 262–82. Newcasle upon Tyne: Cambridge Scholars Publishing, 2017.

Ylimaunu, Timo, Sami Lakomäki, Titta Kallio-Seppä, Paul R. Mullins, Risto Nurmi and Markku Kuorilehto. 'Borderlands as Spaces: Creating Third Spaces and Fractured Landscapes in Medieval Northern Finland'. *Journal of Social Archaeology* 14, no. 2 (2014): 244–67.

Zharchinskaya, Ksenia. "Mif i istoricheskaya pamiat': obrazy slavianskoi 'traditsii' v sotsial'nykh setiakh". *Vestnik Tomskogo gosudarstvennogo universiteta. Istorija* 4, no. 30 (2014): 97–103.

Index

accuracy 8, 14, 82, 207
Adam of Bremen 113
Africa
  medieval 10–13, 17, 18
  North 52, 138
Agency of Russian (russkoi) Information, ARI 66
Åland 105, 111–15, 143
Aleksey Mikhailovich, Tsar of Russia 29
Alexander II of Russia 28
Alexander Nevsky, prince of Novgorod xv, 7, 22, 26, 28–31, 34
alt-right, *see* far-right
anachronism xvii, 141
Ancient Finnish Kings xix, 10, 115, 125–35
Anderson, Amos 96–7
Anglo-Saxon 80, 138, 142
antifeminism xiv, 129
antiquarianism xviii, 107
anti-Semitism 128
anti-Zionism 69
archaeology 11, 24, 93, 103, 105, 106, 108–12, 115, 133
architecture 12, 91
Ásatrú 148
al-Assad, Bashar 76
authenticity 9, 14, 74, 108
authority 2–4, 8, 9, 12–14, 19, 59, 76, 77, 82, 83, 108, 109, 132, 146
autocracy 25

Bat Ye'or (Gisèle Littman) 5
Belarus xiv, 48, 67
Bezos, Jeff 11, 12
Bible 12, 62
Birka 111–13
Block Museum of Chicago 10
Board of Antiquities (Finland) 110, 116
Bolshevism 25
Breitbart News Network 5
Breivik, Anders Behring 4, 5, 18

Brexit 6, 7
Brigittines 96
British Empire 7
Buchanan, Pat *Suicide of a Superpower* 5
Buddhism 140, 147
Bulgaria 61
burghers 21
Byzantium xvi, 105

Cameron, David 8
Canada 4
Catherine II, Russian Empress 28, 75
Catholicism 147
Celts 61, 69
Centre for Contemporary Cultural Studies (CCCS) 1
Chechnya 45
China 10
chivalry 135
Christchurch, New Zealand 4, 5
Christianity xix, 5, 28, 31, 35, 40, 49–51, 78, 102, 104, 105, 131–3, 139, 140, 145–8, 150
cinema 26, 27, 31, 42
Club War 89–91, 98
collective memory 24, 37, 87, 100, 102
computer games, *see* digital games
conspiracy theories xxi, 70, 71, 109, 115, 116, 126, 127, 199
contrafactual history 137, 138, 144, 148, 150
coronavirus, *see* Covid-19
counterjihad 5, 151
Covid-19 7, 39, 73
Crimea 8, 35, 48–51, 54, 175
Crusader Kings II, (digital game) 137–51
crusades xiii, xv, 105, 151
cultural appropriation 2, 11, 13, 14
Cultural Marxism 12
cultural memory xii–xiv, xx, 22–5, 27, 36, 37, 101
cultural studies 1

Dalarna   105
Danilevskii, N. A.   51
de jure   144, 145, 148, 149
Diet of Porvoo in   1809   96
digital games   23, 26, 34, 38, 137–51
digital media   14, 73–7
Disraeli, Benjamin   6
Dmitry Donskoy, fourteenth-century prince of Moscow   28–30, 34
Donetsk People's Republic   37
Dostoevsky, Fyodor   27, 28
Dreijer, Matts   105, 111–15, 118
Druids   61

Earth Chronicles   64
Edelfelt, Albert   96
Elizabeth II, Queen of England   80
England (medieval)   7, 8, 141
Estonia   112, 120, 122, 143, 146
ethnicity   47, 48, 67
ethnocentric nationalism   81
European Union   8
extreme Orthodox   67
extremist right-wing, *see* far right

Facebook   4, 65, 128
fake news   12, 59
far-right   xiii, xix, 4, 5, 19, 58, 78, 107, 129, 134
fascism   40, 67
February Manifesto   85
February Revolution   45
feminism   129
Fenno-Ugrians   xiv, 140, 143, 148
feudalism   21, 25, 145, 147, 149
Finlandization   99
Finland Proper   96
Finnish Civil War (1918)   90, 112
Finnish Continuation War (1941–4)   x, 85
Finnsanity   130
First World War   44, 104
Fjordman (Peder Are Nøstvold Jensen)   5
Fomenko, Anatoly   78, 79, 81
France   4
Franks   133, 142
Freyja   134

Game of Thrones (TV series)   130
Gates, Bill   11
Gazprom   41

Geller, Pamela   5
gender   99, 127, 128, 200
genetics   xvi, xvii, 61, 62, 130, 131, 143
Global North   17
Godunov, Boris   29
Goths   61, 62, 65, 66
Great Britain   6, 7, 9, 61, 62, 104
Great Patriotic War   44
Great Replacement (theory)   5
Greenland   104
Green League, Finland   130

Hall, Stuart   1
Halonen, Pekka   135
Hannu Krankka   91, 94
Hamnodius, Gabriel Olai   113
Henry, Bishop of Finland   96
   memorial for   97, 99
heresy   146, 147
Hinduism   140, 147
Hirst, Michael   78
historical fiction   26
historical memory   22–9
historical revisionism   6, 9, 18
historiography   xiii, xv–xvii, 8, 23, 25, 26, 31, 37, 86, 126, 128, 131, 149
history culture   57, 58, 60
history of memory   21
history parks, *see* theme parks
Hitis stone   103
Hommaforum   115, 127, 128, 130, 134
homophobia   129
human rights   26
Huns   62
Huntuvuori, Hilda   x

Iberia   145
iconography   150
Igor Svyatoslavich, prince   29
imperialism   8, 9
incel   5, 129, 134
Instagram   32
Iron Age   xix, 130, 131
Islam   4, 5, 10, 40, 46, 51, 139, 140, 145–8, 150, 151
Islamic State, IS   76
Islamists   46
Islamophobia   151
Ivan III of Russia   27
Ivan the Terrible   xiv, 22, 28–31, 67

Jaakko Ilkka 90, 99
Jaakkola, Jalmari xv, 131
Jerusalem 51
Jews 70, 128, 130
jihad 146, 147, 149, 151
Jöns Budde 96
Joseph II of Austria, Emperor 75
Judaism 51, 140

Kalevala xviii, 86, 91, 98, 126, 134, 135
Kallio, Kalervo 92
Karabanov, Vladislav 61
Karelia 88, 91, 144, 148
Karelianism 91
Karimo, Aarno x, 131
Kastelholm 112
Kensington runestone 107
Kiev x, 35, 36, 80
Kirill, Patriarch 68
knight 21
Kökar 113, 114
Korsholma fortress 89
Köyliö 89, 95-7, 99
Kremlin 35, 50
Kulikovo Field, the battle of (1380) 28

Lalli 96, 97, 99
Lammy, David, MP 9, 10
Lapland 143
Latin 104, 117, 142
Lay of the Host of Igor 36, 37
Left Alliance, Finland 130
Lenin, Vladimir 28
liberalism 25
lieux de mémoires 87
linguistics 61, 105, 106, 111, 120, 123
Linnukka memorial 3, 13, 90, 91, 94, 95, 99
LiveInternet 64
local history 95, 97, 100, 102
London 9, 11, 61
Lord of the Rings (Film series 2001-3) 132
ludonarratives 138, 144, 145, 150

Magna Carta 8
Magnus Eriksson, king of Sweden xvi, 95
Magnus Tavast, bishop 96
Mali 10, 17, 18

manosphere 10, 127-9, 132
Mansā Musā Keita, emperor of Mali 10, 11, 18
masculinity 91, 125, 127, 128, 130, 132, 134-6, 200
mass media 1, 2, 24, 27, 32, 58, 74
material culture 98
Matrix (Film 1999) 129
Mecca 10, 145
medieval fairs xxii, 101
medievalism
  amateur 3
  banal xi, 2, 9, 43, 46, 54, 74, 76
  digital 14, 141
  exclusionary 9
  global xi, xii
  meta- xi, xii, 1, 3, 4, 6-9, 11-14, 18, 19, 69, 74, 78, 98-100, 102, 133, 137
  militant x, 94, 99, 131
  muscular 130, 132
  neo- 11, 22, 50
  participatory xi, xxii, 2-4, 6, 8, 10, 12, 14, 17-19
  political 1, 2, 5
  secondary 2, 12
  teleological 13
  white, eurocentric 9
Medvedev, Dmitrii 41, 42, 47
memes 127, 130, 134
memorials 31, 34, 44, 85-91, 93-102
memory culture 85, 87, 98, 99, 102
memory politics 22, 23, 25, 30, 31, 34, 35, 37, 58
Mendeleev, Dmitri 28
Messenius, Johannes 126
Metzger, Tom 5
Middle East 138
misinformation 58
misogyny 5, 129, 135
Mongols 25, 29, 61, 62, 67
Monroe, Marilyn 69
Moscow xvi, xvii, xxii, 35, 36, 40, 45, 50, 54, 68, 79
Muslims, *see* Islam

Naantali 89, 95-7, 99, 101
Napoleonic wars xviii, 51, 69
nationalism x, xii-xiv, xix, 5, 43, 81, 87, 95, 126
national memory 22, 24, 27-30, 34, 36

national romanticism, *see* romantic nationalism
Nazism   49
neo-Nazis   5
neopaganism   57, 67, 71, 137, 148
network analysis   60, 63
Neva, Battle of the (1240)   xv–xvii, 28
New Chronology   78, 79
Nicholas II, tsar   85
Nieminen, Jukka   105, 115–20, 122
Norsemen   104, 108, 142
    culture   107, 143, 148
    gods   134
    mythology   134, 135
Northern Caucasus   45, 46
Norway   4, 17, 100, 101, 125, 130, 133, 143
Nöteborg, Treaty of (1323)   xv–xvii
Novgorod   xiv–xvii, xx, 35, 36, 62, 78, 105

October Revolution (1917)   45, 59
Old Hate (1570–95)   91
Old Norse   106, 107, 118, 121, 122
Oleg the Wise of Novgorod   78–80
Oppression, period of the (1899–1917)   99
Oprichnina, 1565–72   22, 29
orientalism   12, 13
Orthodox Church   xiv, 32, 34, 36, 61, 62, 65, 67, 146
Ostrobothnia   86–91, 94, 95, 97, 99–102, 106, 108–11, 116, 118
Oulu   88, 90, 91
Our Island Story (Book 1905)   8

paganism   40, 62, 78, 133, 139, 140, 146–50
patriotism   28, 41–5, 53, 54, 58, 59, 66, 69, 71, 90–2, 94, 95, 97, 99, 100, 102, 123
Pechenegs   14, 39, 73, 74
Peel, Robert, sir   6
Persian   143
Peter I, the Great   28
philology   109, 149
pilgrimage   11, 97, 145, 147
Poland   75, 103, 108
Polish-Lithuanian Commonwealth   69

Polovtsy   14, 39, 73, 74
Porvoo   85, 89, 95–7
Potemkin, Grigory   75
Potemkin Village   17, 75–7, 81
Primary Chronicle   78
Prince Igor's Host   36
programming   137, 141, 150
propaganda   xix, 26, 35–7, 41, 53, 68, 81, 82, 98, 108
pseudohistory   xii, xiii, xix, xxi, 5, 57, 58, 69, 119
pseudoscience xxi, 116
public history   8, 19
purity   131
Pushkin, Alexander   27, 28
Putin, Vladimir   7, 14, 25, 31, 35, 39, 41–54, 68, 73–6

race   13, 14
racism   xiv, xix, 9, 13, 128, 129, 133–5
Reconquista   145
Reddit   78, 80, 81
re-enactment   23
Rees-Mogg, Jacob, *The Victorians*   6–8, 14, 18
Reformation   103
restalinization   22
right-wing ideologies, *see* far right
Rodnovere   148
romanticism   86, 91
romantic nationalism   xiii, xvi, xviii, 43, 48, 126
Romuva   146–8
Runeberg, J. L.   96
runestones   7, 103–23
Rurik   31, 62
Rus'
    ancient   xiv, 27, 36, 37, 61, 66
    Kievan   31, 39, 73–5, 78, 80, 82
    Muscovite   21, 29, 32, 40
    pre-petrine   xiv, 21, 22, 25, 28–31, 34, 37
Russian Academy of Sciences   78
Russian literature   27, 79
Russian Military-Historical Society   58
Russia Today (RT)   82
Russification   xviii, 85, 94, 106
Russo-Georgian war (2008)   47
Russo-Turkish War (1877–8)   51

St Erik, legend of   96
St Petersburg   xv, 35, 96
Saints Peter and Fevronia   32
St Volodymyr, *see* Vladimir I
Sámi   xvii, xxii, 88, 143
    language   104, 121
Sauvo   107
Saxons   146
Scandinavia   17, 103–5, 107–13,
    115, 118, 121–3, 125, 133, 144,
    148
Second World War   xi, xiv, xx, 59,
    66, 85, 102
Sevastopol   49, 51
sexism   129
sexuality   127, 133–5
Shia   146
Sinikivi   130
Slavic swastika   66
Slavs   50, 61, 69, 108, 140
Slovensk   62
social media   xiv, 4, 5, 15–18, 24, 32,
    39, 57, 65, 66, 81, 82, 128
social memory   21
Society for the Rebirth of Fine Arts of
    Ancient Rus'   23
Soldiers of Odin   xiii, 134
Solomon, King   12
Solzhenitsyn, Aleksandr   27, 43
Somalia   135
Soviet Union   x, xi, xiv, xx, 44–6, 48,
    58, 59, 69, 82, 93, 97
Spencer, Richard   5
Stalin, Joseph   28, 59
Stalinism   31
Stanislaw Poniatowski, king   75
Stepan Razin   28–31
Stolypin, Pyotr   27, 28
Stormfront   5
study of religion   140
Sulakadzev, A. I.   79, 81
Sunni   146, 147
Suvorov, Alexander   27, 28
Sweden   xiv, xv–xix, 85, 86, 91, 101–3,
    105, 109, 111, 112, 121, 125, 126,
    133–5, 145
Swedish historiography   126
Swedish People's Party of Finland
    126

Swedish-speaking Finns   xviii, xix, 104,
    105, 109, 115, 120, 126, 128–30,
    134, 135
sword   80, 92, 94, 127, 132–3, 136, 139
Syria   48, 76

Tarrant, Brenton Harrison   5, 14, 18
Tatar-Mongol rule   29, 61, 62, 67
Tatars   62
Tavastia   xv, 144
teleology   144, 150
terrorism   4, 5, 18, 19, 45, 48
theme parks   40, 41, 50, 55
Thor   134
Timbuktu   11
Tolkien, J. R. R.   132
Tolstoy, Leo   27
Torgils Knutsson   94
totalitarianism   25, 31
transphobia   129
Trump, Donald   11
Turkey   48
Turku   90, 101, 103, 117, 119
Twitter   16, 17, 65, 128

UFO-believing   57
Ukraine   xii, xiv, xix, 4–6, 48, 50, 51, 68,
    104, 114
United Kingdom   4
United Nations   18
United States   4, 11
Unni, archbishop   113

Väinämöinen   134
Valdemar II, king   114
Vallgren, Ville   94
vassals   138, 146
Vedic religion   69
Vesainen, Pekka (or Juho)   13, 91–5,
    98–100
Viborg   94
Victoriana   7
Victory Day   44
videogames, *see* digital games
Vikings   xvii, xix, 80, 103–12, 114,
    115, 132, 134, 135, 144, *see also*
    Norsemen
Vikings (TV show)   78, 80, 81
Vínland   107

VKontakte 32, 65, 69, 70
Vladimir I, saint xiv, 8, 28–32, 34, 35, 49, 50
Vladimir the Great, *see* Vladimir I
Vörå (Vöyri) 106–16
Vyborg xvi

Web 2.0 4, 14–16, 18, 19, 73
White Brotherhood (Beloe Bratstvo) 65–8, 70
White Extinction theory 5

white nationalist groups, *see* far right
white supremacism, *see* far right
Wikipedia 17, 26, 32, 64, 79, 80, 132, 144
Winter War (1939–40) 85, 99
world religion paradigm 147

Yandex 60
Yaroslav the Wise 29, 30, 34–6
Yeltsin, Boris 35
Ylilauta 115, 127–30, 132–4
YouTube 4, 61, 128

www.ingramcontent.com/pod-product-compliance
Lightning Source LLC
Chambersburg PA
CBHW071820300426
44116CB00009B/1377